NO MISSION IMPOSSIBLE

Memoirs of a General in War and Insurgency

NO MISSION IMPOSSIBLE

Memoirs of a General in War and Insurgency

Lt Gen JBS Yadava (Retd)
PVSM, AVSM, VrC, VSM

PENTAGON PRESS LLP

First published in 2025 by
PENTAGON PRESS LLP
206, Peacock Lane, Shahpur Jat
New Delhi-110049, India
Contact: 011-26490600

Printed at Aegean Offset Printers, Greater Noida

ISBN 978-81-980002-4-8 (HB)

www.pentagonpress.in

Dedicated to
The Indian Army
and
11 Gorkha Rifles

यत्राहं विजयस्तत्र

in Memory of
my parents
Maj JNS YADAVA
(Aug 1916 - Mar 1988)
&
Smt GYANDEVI
(Dec 1916-Apr 2012)

Contents

Preface

No Mission Impossible is my firsthand experience of war and insurgencies. It was rather a unique experience and not everyone gets to see and feel death and destruction at so close quarters as I have, while protecting innocent lives, their property and culture and ensuring hope and a better future for them. It is also my journey through various cantonments, military stations and field areas. I was motivated to write this book by Lt. Col. Dina Nath, a veteran of the Second World War, Brig. N.S. Tanwar and many others who had been associated with me. Both my children, Akshay and Kanupriya, and wife, Neera, also goaded me to pen the story of my life. Major Probal Das Gupta from my battalion who is a famous writer himself needs special mention as he not only helped me finish this book but also guided me from time to time. All of them felt that I should share the rich experience that I had gathered in various wars, operational situations and during my other assignments with future generations.

The period from 1947 to 2005 had been very eventful for the country. The horror of Partition, the 1947 Kashmir conflict, humiliating defeat of the Indian Army in 1962, the inconclusive war of 1965, liberation of Bangladesh, turmoil in Punjab and J&K, the Kargil war and, finally, Operation Parakram or the war that went wrong were part of my life. I was either a witness or a participant to all these events of historic importance that shaped our destiny. I have tried to reconstruct or recapitulate some of the actions of this period so that we create a better history for the future.

During my service, I had the opportunity to serve with some of the finest officers and Generals including FT Dias, Vinod Sehgal, Vijay Oberoi, S.K. Sharma, Gen. B.C. Joshi and V.P. Malik who shaped my destiny and gave me the space and flexibility for creative military thinking.

I have dwelt on my lineage—the Bhattis, Yadavas and Ahirs—and their evolution so that we do not forget our cultural roots in the middle of modernity. The colonial hangover existed in cantonments post-independence and life was easy and good. The officers really lorded it during that period. I have tried to capture the images of this period as accurately as possible. The NDA and IMA are the finest training institutions but they have become factories that produce officers who are operationally the best but not military leaders who are thinkers and strategists. I have also tried to bring out the absence of strategic thinking in our leadership in the early years after independence. The strategic brilliance in the liberation of Bangladesh during the 1971 war was lost due to poor diplomacy. The chapter on intervening years captures the laissez-faire environment that prevailed after the1971 war. Anti-militancy in Punjab was again a brilliant success mainly due to political will and correct execution of policy by all instruments of the state after a long period of flawed policies and decisions. The anti-terror operations in J&K, Operation Vijay, followed by Operation Parakram have been dealt with in detail to bring out the tactical and operational successes and strategic atrophy that had set in and the dithering and lack of political will in the national leadership of that time. The state continues to suffer even now. Army HQ is a monolithic and over-staffed like all other departments of the government where jobs are halved or quartered among incumbents. A lot can however be achieved with ingenuity instead of the slow pace that prevails in its corridors. For me, life after retirement was as exciting and purposeful as it was during service. I was fortunate to serve in the public and corporate sectors and as a bureaucrat in the State of Haryana.

Finally, I thank all my friends and colleagues who have helped me with inputs and data and, in many cases, with their opinions.

Lt Gen JBS Yadava (Retd)
PVSM, AVSM, VrC, VSM

Chapter One

Ancestry and Early Life

I was born in a peasant family in a village called Achina, in the erstwhile state of Jind, now in Haryana. My birth was of great significance as a male child born to my parents after ten years on 28 February 1945. Our ancestry is traced back to Raja Bhupat Singh,[1] a Bhatti Rajput, who established the kingdom of Bhatner, the present-day Hanuman Garh in 288 AD. Bhatner attained great historical status as it lay on the route of invasion from Central Asia to India. It was a constant irritant in the path of Islamic invaders. Bhiroo Singh[2] was the last Bhatti Hindu ruler of Bhatner, who capitulated to the Chigat Khans of Hissar Subah on orders by the Sultan of Delhi around 1450 AD and converted to Islam.

Bhatner changed hands between the Bhattis, Bhutti Khans (Muslims) and the Rathors of Bikaner from time to time between the 13th and 17th centuries. Raja Soorat Singh Rathore of Bikaner wrested the fort permanently in 1805 AD, from Bahadur Khan Bhutti, and named it Hanuman Garh. Hindu Bhattis reside in Rajasthan, Haryana, and Delhi and UP while the Muslims reside in Sind and Southern Punjab of Pakistan. Hindu Bhattis were known for their courage and chivalry in battle. They are hardy and frugal by nature. However the Muslim Bhuttis,[3] on conversion, drifted away and there was a total metamorphosis in them. They lost much of their moral values, civility, and reputation for courage retaining only the merit of being dexterous thieves and bandits. They divested themselves of noble moral attributes and tolerance. Instead they imbibed ignorance, bigotry and the ferocity of Islam. They became cruel, intolerant, cowardly, and inhospitable. They were called beasts or sons of the devil by Hindu Bhattis.

Once the clan expanded, they dispersed to various parts of Rajasthan. Raja Lamb Raj, an ancestor of ours, was one of them who established Lambana in 463 AD in the district of Amber. It is worth mentioning here that Raja Jait Singh married Jeeva Kanwar, a princess from Pattan, located near Kot Putli in Rajasthan. Pattan[4] was a very influential and important kingdom at that period and its sway extended up to Delhi. Rani Jeeva Kanwar attained 'Sati' on the demise of her husband in 651 AD. Since then, she is worshiped by the entire clan as our ruling deity. A shrine in her honour exists in our village revered as "Dadi Shilah" or "Dadi Sati". Her blessings are invoked by everyone on important occasions and in distress. All marriages and births are sanctified at the shrine.

As time passed, there were further migrations either due to increase in population, socio-economic reasons, wars, or feuds between tribes and members of the clan. The Bhattis had started visiting the area of Rewari since long in search of pastures. One of our ancestors, Kumbha Ram, moved east past Rewari with his family and founded Kumrodha[5] in 824 AD in Kanina Tehsil (Rewari). The clan flourished in this area for two centuries and coexisted with the Abhirs and Shahrawat Jats. Both the Bhattis and Abhirs are Yaduvanshis and part of the 36 royal races of Rajasthan[6] as per the bard, Chund and Colonel Tod. Abhir has been corrupted to Ahir or Aheer, who mostly reside in Rajasthan, Haryana, Gujarat, UP, Central India, and other parts of the country. In 1056 AD a serious feud took place between the Bhattis and the Shahrawat Jats at Kumrodha which resulted in substantial destruction of the Bhattis forcing yet another migration. The ruins of their settlement and the Samadhi of "Dadi Shilaha" also exist there and is worshipped by the Jat inhabitants.

After their destruction, a small group consisting of two brothers, Bhimsen and Ramchander, with their families landed in an area called Dhul Bhari, near Morwala village on the Charkhi Dadri-Delhi road. While they were resting in their encampment, the entourage of the local Rajput Rani was attacked by bandits. Bhimsen and Ramchander, along with their family members, joined the Rani's escorts in defeating the outlaws and rescuing her. Pleased with their bravery and help, she adopted the family and granted them a large tract of land in a place called Ranila in Rohtak Division.

Bhimsen and Ramchander founded a new settlement in the vicinity of Ranila with the consent of the Rani, their godmother and named it Achina.[7] Ramchander died a bachelor. Our village is thus a progeny of one man—Bhimsen. The descendents of Bhimsen settled down to farming in their newly-granted land measuring approximately 1,800 hectares. The village was located on a raised sand dune near two depressions that were the only source of water called *jhor* and *jheel.* Geo-physically, the area is part of southern Rajasthan which is semi desert, arid and dry consisting of sand dunes and flat stretches of sand for miles. Climatically, the area experienced long spells of hot and dry summers dominated by sandstorms followed by a short season of scanty rain in July-August. Then, severe winters followed from November to February. The water was brackish and unfit for consumption or irrigation. Famines were quite common. People depended on the water collected in the *jhor, tals* or one or two deep wells for drinking and cooking. One of the two sweet water wells in the village was dug by my great–grandfather, Mansa Ram.

A large part of the area was covered with forests called *banis*. The flora consisted of *jaal, janti, kikar, neem, peepal, sisham*, and *kair. Peel,* a variety of wild berry was the only fruit that the *jaal* trees bore during the rainy season. Extensive fauna in the form of hyenas, wolves, wild boar, foxes, jackals, jungle cats, black bucks, chinkaras, neelgais, and hares existed till 1960.The area abounded in peacocks, black partridges, hawks, eagles and vultures. However, with the pressure of the population there are no more *banis* or wildlife except neelgais, hares, and partridges. A fox or jackal may be sighted occasionally.

The village was full of domesticated animals like buffalos, cows, oxen, camels, and horses. Jawar, bajra, barley, and chana were the only crops that were cultivated. The prosperity and status of a family was measured by land and cattle holdings. The residents seem to have led a peaceful life for several years. It is not known as to when we merged with the Ahirs but it can be assumed that when Kumbha Ram founded Kumrodha, his family would have inter-married with the Ahirs and merged with them while retaining their Bhatti identity. It was common practice then to move up or down the social ladder by such alliances. So it seems that by migrating far away from dominant Bhatti areas he had no choice but to merge with the Ahirs, basically through marriage alliances or accepting their patronage/ protection, as was done by those Bhattis who had merged with the Jats, Gujjars and Sikhs.

Occupation was yet another factor that decided caste. Here it appears that my ancestors took to farming as their main occupation like the Jats, Gujjars and resident Ahirs. Kumbha Ram must have been assimilated easily as both the Bhattis and Ahirs were Yaduvanshis. Even in their new-found home at Achina, my ancestors flourished, though they were a single family amongst a sea of Tanwar and Panwar Rajputs and Phogat and Sangwan Jats; and later the Rangar Muslims. As the family roots deepened and it expanded to a cognizable size, our family Brahmins from Kumrodha joined in 1332 AD. Other ancillary communities like banias, khatis, sunars, lohars, kumhars, nais, telis, chamars, churas and dhanaks were also added. There were one or two Dum families (Muslims) whose job was to skin dead animals and bury them, and beating drums, singing and dancing during festivities. They migrated to Pakistan in 1947. All the ancillary castes were settled in specified pockets and live in great harmony like a family even today.

My village is only 80 km from Delhi and it can be presumed that from the mid-12th century to 1857 we must have been ruled by Muslim nawabs from Jajjar, Rohtak or Dadri. The area was also under the control of George Thomas,[8] an Irish mercenary and self-proclaimed rajah from 1797 to 1802. He operated from a mud fort near Jajjar and named it George Garh—the present Jahajgarh. The last Muslim nawab of Dadri, Bahadur Jung, was hanged by the British along with those of Jajjar, Narnaul and Balabgarh for the Mutiny in 1857. Since the Sikh rulers of Patiala, Jind, and Nabha had actively helped the British quell the mutiny, they were rewarded[9] with the captured territory. Patiala got the pargana of Narnaul worth Rs. 2,00,000 a year, Nabha got Bawal worth Rs. 1,06,007 and Jind got Dadri worth Rs. 1,24,000. We were now under the Sikh rule since 1858.

Since my ancestors had identified themselves with the Ahirs/Yadavs, it becomes necessary to describe them in detail at this stage. Our area is called Ahirwal where the majority population is Ahirs. They are agriculturists by profession and soldiering is their passion. They were considered accomplished farmers. They also made excellent soldiers and were part of Mughal, Maratha and British armies. The Ahirs were included in the list of martial races by the British for their soldierly attributes.[10] They were basically recruited in Russel's Infantry (19 Hyderabad Regiment), presently the Kumaon Regiment, Artillery and the Services. A small number found their way into the Cavalry including the Viceroy's Bodyguard. Nearly 19,546 Ahirs[11] were enrolled during the First World War and fought in almost all theatres. Similarly, more than 20,000 Ahirs were recruited for the Second World War. Rao Balbir Singh, the Rao of Rewari, was granted the rank of captain for his contribution to the war effort. His successor, Rao Birendra Singh, was also a captain during the war. He was the Chief Minister of Haryana and a senior cabinet minister at the centre later. At the time of Independence, 11 and 13 Kumaon, 8 and 22 Field Regiments and 26 Air Defence Artillery Regiment were pure Ahir.

Unlike the other tribes and clans of India, the Ahirs are not region-based but are found in all parts of India. Thus, there are many theories about their origin.[12] Many authorities believe that the Ahirs were part of pastoral tribes that migrated from central Asia/Europe before the Huns or Jats. Since the people of Yadava/Ahir origin are settled in various parts of the country, they have adopted the local customs and languages of those regions. Thus the Yadavs/Jadavs of Maharashtra and those in Haryana, Rajasthan and UP are alike people of these states. The ballads of Alla-Udal in Malwa and the bravery of Yadavs of Dev Nagri against Allah udin Khilji are legendary.

Though the Yadavs/Ahirs[13] are spread over all parts of India, we will now concern ourselves with those in Haryana, as my ancestors had established their roots here. Ahirs are industrious, patient, orderly, hardy and simple of habit. An Ahir does not make an immediate impression but his qualities, character and bravery make a lasting impact. Lt. Gen. Sir George MacMunn describes them as men of stamina and great daring. They are muscular, hardworking, rather stupid yeoman farmers. In Gen. Thimayya's biography also they have been described as hardy, frugal and with great stamina. They could travel long distances on foot and endure privation with minimum sustenance. A typical Ahir, like the Rajputs or

Jats, is of long limb, wiry, with dark eyes and hair. His complexion may vary from light wheat to dark brown. They have strong family ties and lead frugal lives. Till recently, they lived in joint families, were vegetarians and eschewed alcoholic drinks. But with the change in socio-economic conditions, education and exposure to the outside world, all this is changing rapidly. There are many sub-castes and *gotras* among the Ahirs. My *gotra* is Lamba.[14] It is a very prominent and influential *gotra* and is listed in almost all the old British books and documents that describe the Ahirs of Haryana. Over a period, people of my *gotra* have settled down in 22 villages including Rewari, Gurgaon, Delhi and Meerut districts.

The Ahirs follow the same customs as the Rajputs and Jats in births, marriages and deaths. They are exogamous and do not marry within their *gotras* and close relations. Usually they go for early arranged marriages. Like most Hindu castes and tribes, the dowry system is prevalent and *gauna* is practiced in which the couple is allowed to consummate their marriage after a suitable interval.

Widow remarriage is permitted for both economic reasons and keeping family ties intact. Levirate is encouraged wherein the widow marries the younger brother or cousin of the deceased. Ahir women are hardy, robust and well-built. They observe purdah. Besides their household chores, they work alongside their men folk in the fields. They dress differently from the Jats, wearing red and yellow striped skirts with a red or yellow shawl. They also wear blue *lehangas*. They wear the same jewellery as others. The men wear white shirts, dhotis and a saffa.

In the social ladder, the Ahirs are grouped with Jats, Gujjars and Rors, and in some places, with Rajputs. They inter-dine and smoke together but do not inter-marry. They eat *kachhi* and *pakki* with Brahmins and Vaisyas but the latter do not eat *kachhi* from them. Ahirs, both Hindu and Muslim, are also called Ghosi around Delhi. Some Ahir *gotras* follow the system of hereditary choudhary. Ahirs celebrate all Hindu festivals but Teej during the monsoons is their favourite in Haryana and Rajasthan. Like all peasant communities their music is simple with minimum instruments. Ragni is their favourite form of song and dance.

I spent my early childhood in the village. We lived in a *haveli* as a joint family. Life there revolved around mainly farming and associated activities. Our village had grown from one family to almost 300 families and four *panas* by the time I was born. The chowk (village square) was a prominent place where people gathered in the evenings for a smoke, sharing news, resolving disputes or just gossiping. The day started with *arti* in the temple. Immediately after that grinding of flour in hand mills, milking of cattle and churning of buttermilk by the women followed. Men went to their fields or the grain market in a convoy of bullock carts. The ladies would fetch water from the wells and then carried food to the men in the fields.

Our village was privileged as the Raja of Jind had established a primary school in 1920, where I started my schooling. He held his durbar and disposed off appeals and petitions from "Dorthy" a rest house/hunting lodge near Dadri railway station. Kabaddi, wrestling, and horse and camel races were popular forms of entertainment. Hockey, football, volleyball and basketball were played in the school and most of the boys would be on the sports ground in the mornings and evenings to practice and improve their eligibility for the army. We sat on mats and read aloud or recited lesson/tables. Older boys left school as soon as they were selected for the army or due to domestic compulsions. Some went to complete their matriculation at Ahir High School in Rewari. No one had gone to college then except for Capt. Ganeshi Lal, whose father was a tehsildar in Jind. He was the first commissioned officer from our village.

My grandfather, Chelu Ram, had retired as a havildar from the army. He was a strict disciplinarian and quick of temper. He had become a money lender after retirement and was quite rich. But he was a miser who hoarded all his wealth in brass pitchers and buried them under ground in the bedroom. He lost most of it when a village midwife, at the time of my cousin's delivery dug it out on the sly. Similarly, one night the entire loan vouchers (*bahi-khata*) were stolen from his room and he could not recover most of the loans.

My father was born in 1916 and named Jai Narain Singh. His mother Smt. Siria of Jhall village in Rewari district was of extraordinary beauty but died when he was a child. Consequently, he was brought up by his aunts.

He was very intelligent, handsome, fair, well built and athletic. He had an estranged relationship with his stepmother. He was married in his teens. In contrast, my mother, Gyan Devi, was short, brown and of average looks. She belonged to a wealthy and influential family of village Akodha, also in Jind state. Her father, Nand Ram, was addressed as Borhaji in deference to his status and wealth. They lived in a fort like building called the Kachahri where he adjudicated justice. After finishing his primary education, my father qualified for a scholarship and was enrolled in Ahir High School Rewari from where he completed his matriculation.

As he was good both in studies and sports, a recruiting team from 19 Hyderabad Regiment selected him as a clerk that commenced his career in the army. He was posted to 2/19 Hyderabad in 1936 after training at their Centre in Agra and allotted Army No. 12441-B. The battalion was then deployed in the North-West Frontier. During the Second World War, he moved with the battalion to Palel-Imphal sector under 23 Infantry Division in May 1942 against the Japanese advance. The battalion suffered heavily in enemy action as well as due to epidemics. Malaria and dysentery had crippled the battalion. It was withdrawn and sent to Agra for refitting, recuperation and training. During the retreat, my father also suffered a bout of severe dysentery and was given up as dead. But he survived miraculously.

In 1942, he was promoted a Viceroy Commissioned Officer as IO-40564 and appointed Head Clerk. His battalion fought the Japanese in the Battle of Tiddim Road and later evicted them from Kohima and Imphal. They were at Bombay for rest and recuperation at the time of the unconditional surrender by the Japanese. They were now ordered to sail to Port Dickson, Malaya, for clearing it of the enemy. The battalion was sent to Batavia (Djakarta) to round up the Japanese who had continued to fight even after the surrender. The battalion suffered a number of casualties in the ensuing operations and my father was 'Mentioned in Despatches'.

The battalion returned to India from Indonesia in 1946 when the reorganization was underway. Its nomenclature was changed from 19 Hyderabad Regiment to Kumaon Regiment as the composition of troops had changed predominantly to Kumaonis with 25 per cent Ahirs.

2/19 Hyderabad became 2 Kumaon. Simultaneously, 13 Kumaon,[15] a battalion camposed of only Ahirs was raised at Kanpur in August 1948 out of 2/19 Hyderabad. My father was part of this new raising and granted temporary commission in the battalion.

During the turbulence of Partition, life in rural areas was as badly affected as in urban population centres. There was uncontrolled and wanton looting, arson and killing of Muslims. Organized teams went on forays in all the Muslim villages and the entire area of Rohtak, Mahendragarh and Jajjar were 'cleansed'. After peace was restored sometime in 1950, my father was posted to the Corps of Military Police Centre, Faizabad. That was the first time we joined him as a family. It was our first experience to travel in a train and the ride in the lift at the Old Delhi Railway Station was a novelty. Since it was our first outing from the village, it was an entirely new experience and cultural transformation. We shed our rustic manners and language remarkably fast and adopted the new way of life under supervision of a pandit ji and an English tutor employed by my father. Once our initial training was over, we were admitted to St. Mary's Convent School, where the Irish Nuns and Brothers laid our educational foundation.

We lived in bungalow number 9 on the now Mahatma Gandhi Road. It was a trademark British colonial type of building. It was a mix of British, and Mughal architecture with vernacular features. British colonnades and cornices mixed with Indian-style arches and the special design of the vaulted ceiling gave it a pleasing façade. The Indian Army officers, on independence had inherited all the privileges enjoyed by British officers. The bungalow was spread over 3 to 4 acres of land. It had a huge beautifully laid-out lawn, flower beds and a well in one corner. There were residential quarters for the servants and ancillary staff in the rear. There was a stable/shelter for horses and cattle. The bungalow was full of mango, guava, and jamun trees. The bungalow was razed and an officer's mess has been constructed in its place now.

Faizabad was founded by Nawab Saadat Ali Khan in 1722[16] when he was appointed the Governor of Awadh by Emperor Muhammad Shah. He led the Mughal forces against Nadir Shah in 1737, but failed to stop the invader and the massacre that followed at Delhi. He committed suicide in remorse. After his death, his nephew and son-in-law, Abdul Mansur Khan, known as Safdar Jung succeeded him in 1739. However it was under Shuja-ud-Daula, who came to power in 1754 that Faizabad flourished, gained fame and became an important commercial centre. The Nawab led the Mughal army in the third battle of Panipat and Battle of Buxar in 1764. Even though, he lost both the battles he remained an important functionary in the Mughal court. Many landmark buildings such as Moti Mahal and Bahu Begum Maqbara were constructed during his reign. Sheesh Mahal, in the area of the ASC depot, was constructed for his son. Lord Warren Hastings stayed in this palace during his impeachment. The fourth Nawab, Asaf-ud-Daula shifted the capital to Lucknow due to estrangement with his mother, the Bahu-Begum who ran a parallel court. The decline of Faizabad commenced thereafter.

A British cantonment was raised here in 1858 after the mutiny. It was well laid out with separate residential areas for officers, and British and Indian troops. Sadar Bazaar, Lal Kurti and Top Khana Bazaar met the administrative requirements. St Andrews Church is a notable landmark constructed in 1860. The Victoria Memorial or town hall where the Cantonment Board Office is now located is also a historic building of the British era. St. Mary's Church and School catered to the spiritual and educational requirements. Social life in the cantonment revolved around the Faizabad Club located at 83 Park Road on the river front. It was a beautiful building constructed in British Mughal style. We children attended many a memorable Christmas and New Year parties in this club.

Only a few officers owned cars or motorbikes. Most used cycles to commute. Tongas, ekkas or rickshaws were used by families as conveyance. Normal peace-time activities dominated the official routine that included visits, inspections and parades. Shikar, boating, annual sports and tattoos were the other social events that stand out in my memory. The officers would go for shikar early in the morning. They would mount elephants to shoot tigers, leopards, wild boar, deer and fowl. Ladies and children would join them later for lunch when the shoot was over. The officers and ladies participated in fancy dress or river dance parties on amphibians. My mother invariably won the fancy dress in her traditional attire and jewellery. We children enjoyed elephant rides, family boating on the Ghagar River or cycling on the circular road hugging the river. Baskets of quails and partridges would be roasted by cooks for parties hosted by my father.

Lt. Col. Brijpal Singh of the Rajput Regiment replaced Lt. Col. Mohan Lal as the commandant in 1953. He belonged to Bapora village very close to ours. Gen. V.K. Singh, who became the COAS was his cousin. My father was his close friend and my mother a companion of Mrs. Brijpal Singh who was a very religious and a devout Hindu. She would walk to Guptar Ghat on every festival or religious day with my mother to bathe and pray, with all of us in tow. In 1953, my grandfather died of cancer in spite of the best treatment at Patna Medical College. We travelled to our village for his last rites that were quite elaborate. Soon after our return, my father was posted to 1 Armed Division Provost Unit at Jallandhar.

We reached Jallandhar in early 1954. Our residence was on Puran Singh Road near the military hospital that is now the Army School of Nursing. It was a big colonial house. Jallandhar cantonment[17] was established immediately after the First Anglo-Sikh War by John Lawrence in 1847. Brig. H.M. Wheeler with two infantry battalions and two artillery companies, who had accompanied Lawrence, camped in an area that is now the Cantonment. Jallandhar is located on the GT road and its strategic importance was not lost on the British who developed it as a transit base for troops deployed in Punjab and the NWFP. One brigade of the Lahore Division was always located here. Gen. R. Dyer,[18] who was responsible for the Jallianwala massacre commanded this brigade from 1917 to 1919. Even though he was indicted in an enquiry by Lord Hunter and told to resign, he was not remorseful and continued to justify his action. Rudyard Kipling raised a sum of 30,000 pounds for his rehabilitation. His residence in Jallandhar cantonment is now an officer's mess.

King George's School to prepare wards of Indian soldiers for the British army was established in 1924. Presently, the Corps Headquarters is located in this building and the school has moved out to Chail. The Jallandhar Club was established in 1909 to cater for the social activities of the British. Company Bagh was created in 1922; St. Luke's Church and St. Mary's Cathedral Church are the other landmarks of the British era. Jallandhar developed into an important town and educational hub during British time and a number of important personalities hailed from here, notably K.L. Saigal, Ch. Muhammad Ali, PM of Pakistan, Gen. Zia-ul-Haq, President of Pakistan, Lala Amarnath, the cricketer, Sardar Swaran Singh, Defence Minister, and Balbir Singh and Udham Singh, Olympic hockey players.

Sikh peasants dominated the countryside, while the town was full of refugees from Pakistan, both Hindus and Sikhs. People had overcome the initial effects and horrendous experiences of Partition and were busy rebuilding their lives. The climate of Jallandhar was subtropical with very hot summers and cold winters. The rainy season was short but intense. We were admitted to ND Victor High School. It had been established by Lala Narain Dass in 1889 and became ND Victor to commemorate the visit of Prince Albert Victor in 1900. Most of the students were from Sadar Bazaar or nearby villages. The medium of instruction was Hindi and Punjabi. It was a quantum change for us and I found it difficult to adjust to the environment. Our classes were held in the open. The teachers were abusive and physical punishment, especially caning and slapping, was common for small infringements. Most teachers wore baggy shalwars and kula turbans. Whatever we had imbibed in the convent at Faizabad was undone within a short time.

However after a year's ordeal, we were admitted in the newly established Garrison School which is now Central School No 1. Most of the students were wards of military personnel. In 1955, there were rumours of retrenchment in the army. Fearing that he would be released, my father purchased a high powered diesel engine from Phagwara and set up a flour and oil mill in the village as an alternate occupation. It was transported from the railway station to our village part by part in bullock carts as roads did not exist then. It brought great business and a lot of income for the family. Within a year the investments were recovered and unimaginable profits made. But due to the greed and mismanagement by my uncle who was the manager, the venture was doomed in next three years.

My father was now posted to 5/11 Gorkha Rifles as Quartermaster. We joined him in mid-1956 at Bolarum that was part of the Secunderabad

Cantonment.[19] After Asaf Jah II, the second Nizam, was defeated by the British, he allowed British troops to replace the French as part of the treaty signed in 1798. The first settlement was in a village called Ulwal, north-east of Hussain Sagar that Sikander Jah, the third Nizam renamed Secunderabad in 1803 and a cantonment was established there in 1806. It was under British control. English was the official language and no customs duties were levied on imports. Therefore, the city grew quickly with a number of markets such as the Regimental Bazaar, James Street and other smaller markets.

The business was mostly managed by Parsis and Anglo Indians. The railway station came up in 1874 and became an important junction connecting Delhi, Bombay, Madras and Calcutta. The cantonment grew mainly around the villages of Bolarum, Trimulgerry, and Hakimpet with All Saints Church and Military Prison Trimulgery as the main landmarks. The Secunderabad Club was a country house of Salar Jung[20] that he had gifted to the British in 1878. The Rashtrapati Nilayam was a hunting lodge of the Nizam, constructed in 1860. It was later converted into country house of the British Resident and on Independence; it became a retreat for the President of India.

We were once again allotted a sprawling bungalow on Stewart Road. I was admitted to St. Mary's High School that was part of a cluster of four convent schools—St. Anne's and St. Francis for girls and St. Patrick's and Mary's for boys. I commuted to school by bus and local train. The standard of education was far superior to that in Jallandhar. I had to struggle hard to cope with the syllabus. Our Principal, Father Fernandez, was a tall Goan who rose to become a bishop. The School of Electric and Mechanical Engineering is also located at Bolarum. We witnessed the legendary Milkha and Makhan Singh participate in army athletics meets at Secunderabad. At that time none of us imagined they would create history for the country in the Asian and Olympic Games.

After about a year, my father's battalion was relocated near Golconda Fort. We took up our residence in Mansab Tank in a house that belonged to an officer of the Nizam's army. The unit was located on Lancer Road that was on the route to Golconda Fort. We could now visit the city of

Hyderabad as also other historic places around in buses or cycles. My favourite places were the Salar Jung Museum, King's Kothi, Falaknama Palace, Char Minar, the Zoo, the Hussain Sagar Bund Road and, of course, the fort and the tombs of Kutab Shahi rulers. I could walk around these historic places for hours and marvel at their architecture. Banjara Hills was an exclusive area for the wealthy. Jagirdar College, Begumpet, was established by Nizam Usman Ali in 1923 exclusively for sons of nawabs, talukdars and aristocrats on the lines of Mayo College, Ajmer. It was renamed Hyderabad Public School in 1951.

In 1958, my father was posted to 1 Armoured Division Provost Unit again, now at Jhansi. While the family moved to Jhansi, I stayed back to finish my secondary school. My younger brother, Joginder, was also left behind with me. Father Fernandez had now become the Rector of the prestigious St. Patrick's Anglo-European High School. This school, unlike St. Mary's, was meant only for Europeans and Anglo Indians as the name suggested. They opened it to high status Indians when most of the Europeans and Anglo Indians had left India by 1954 or so. They also provided free education and lodging to orphans of Europeans or Anglo Indians. Father Fernandez allowed me to be a resident of the school while I was on the rolls of St. Mary's.

I was now living among sons of wealthy talukdars, rich businessmen, and Anglo Indians. Danziel Francis, son of a retired RIAF corporal and Habib Ansari, son of a talukdar were my good friends. Habib was intelligent, philosophical, and gentle unlike the other Muslim boys who were uncouth. The administrator, ward master and physical training masters were all British/Anglo Indian sergeants who had stayed back in India. They were dedicated and meticulous in their duties. The dormitory was well laid out with separate partitions for senior and junior students. We had a common dining hall. Father Fernandez presided over the meals. After dinner, he would invite us to his parlour for an informal chat. We were allowed to go out only with our guardians. I generally accompanied Habib and his father whenever he visited him. We would shop around the clock tower and end up in the best restaurant for a lavish dinner of biryani and kebabs. After my Board exams in March 1959, I joined the family at Jhansi.

Jhansi is famous because of Rani Lakshmibai[21] who became a legendary leader during the uprising of 1857 against the British. The fort was constructed by Bir Singh, a Chandela king of Orcha and was originally known as Balwant Nagar but acquired the colloquial name of Jhansi subsequently. It passed into the hands of the Marathas in 1742 and was governed by one of their regents till it eventually became independent fiefdom in 1802 under the Maratha chieftain, Ram Chander Rao Newalkar. His brother, Gangadhar Rao, succeeded him and later married Manikarnika, Rani Lakshmibai, in 1842.

Jhansi was annexed by the British after the death of Raja Gangadhar Rao in 1854,[22] but Rani Lakshmi Bai continued to rule from 1854 to 1858 as a regent for her adopted son, Damodar Rao. During the uprising, the Rani fought the British forces commanded by Sir Hugh Rose at Jhansi, Kalpi and finally at Gwalior where she died on 17 June 1858 in a combat with the 8 Hussars.[23] The British developed it into a big cantonment to control the central Indian princely states and the lines of communication that passed through this area. It became a railway hub in 1880 with a large Anglo Indian community as employees. Jhansi also became an important transit and training area during the Second World War due to the vast forests around it. The fort, palace of Rani Lakshmibai, Lakshmi temple and the cenotaph of Raja Gangadhar are historical places worth visiting.

We stayed for a while in Jhansi Hotel, which was part of the cantonment. Jhansi Hotel is a historic place. It was constructed by Captain John Harold Abbott, a Scot whose parents, William Lumesden Abbott and Margret was posted at Sitapur in a Highlander regiment in1857. He was seriously wounded by the rebels but managed to escape to Lucknow and survived the 87 days siege there. He was evacuated to Scotland for convalescence where his son, John Harold Abbott, was born in 1863. He returned to India in 1866 and died at Gwalior in 1880 leaving the responsibility to 17 years-old Harold to look after his mother and six siblings. Harold moved out of Gwalior and settled down at Jhansi on plot nos. 37 and 38 in the cantonment with his meagre savings. He built a hotel on one of the plots in 1905. The business flourished and he became a big supplier and contractor to the British army during the First World War. He helped in recruiting 500 Anglo Indians during the war and was awarded an OBE for his effort. We lived in one of the large cottages of the hotel till a house was allotted to my father. The hotel is presently run by his descendents. We moved into a bungalow behind the MES yard.

I joined the Government Intermediate College as a science student. It is located in the Mission Compound area on Gwalior road. The college was established in 1921 and had an excellent building and educational infrastructure and faculty. While I was aspiring to qualify for engineering, my destiny took me to a different field altogether. John Vimal Abraham, a good friend and class fellow joined the NDA in our second year. He motivated us to follow him. Luckily, I passed both the written and the SSB without any hassle. I stayed in a dharamshala near New Delhi Railway Station and went to Harcourt Butler High School on Reading Road for the written exam during our summer break. I appeared for the SSB at Allahabad in September 1960. When I received the joining letter for the NDA, all my friends and father's colleagues convinced me to join the army against a long wait to become an engineer. I was also excited to venture out in a new field.

The dice was cast and I boarded a first class compartment in the Punjab Mail bound for Bombay/Poona. Along with me were some other cadets from Delhi and Central India. We were loaded into trucks at Poona station and transported to Khadakvasla, 17 km SW of Pune. It was to be my home for the next three years.

Pune is located in the centre of the SW Indian Peninsular Plateau. It rose to prominence during Shivaji Maharaj's revolt against the Sultan of Bijapur and the Mughals. The Maratha confederate under the Peshwas[24] emerged as a great power in India on the heels of the Mughal decline. Pune became their capital from where they ruled India till 1820. After their defeats in a series of battles between 1804 and 1820 by the British, Pune became the military HQ of the British Southern Command. The Indian Army took over this HQ on independence. Operations against the Nizam of Hyderabad, the Nawab of Junagarh in 1948; and against the Portuguese in Goa were conducted from here in 1961.

I was awestruck by the seer magnificence of the NDA and its beauty and size, the layout and vastness of its campus, the architecture and grandeur of its buildings. The NDA started as the joint services wing of the IMA on 1 January 1949 at Clement Town. Khadakvasla was chosen as the permanent location of the NDA on the recommendation of a military committee headed by Field Marshal Claude Auchinleck, the C-in-C of the Indian Army. It was constructed with funds donated by the Government of Sudan and various states of the Union of India. Khadakvasla is surrounded by hills and forests on three sides and the Mulla River and the lake formed by the dam on the fourth. The campus is spread over 8,000 acres of forest and green lush land. The city of Pune is beyond the lake.

The Sudan block is the HQ and heart of the Academy from where all the activities are controlled and supervised. It is the most impressive of all the buildings with a grand appearance, and built of asphalt and granite. The Humanities classes are conducted in this block. Then we have the Science block now named Manoj Pandey block, an alumnus of the Academy and officer of my regiment who was awarded a PVC during the Kargil War. I was the chief guest at its naming ceremony as Colonel of the Regiment. This block is imposing, has excellent laboratories and modern class rooms. The cadets' mess was fully automated to cater for 1,500 cadets. It is aesthetically furnished and decorated for formal banquets. The gymnasium, drill square, equestrian and training areas, playing fields, aerodrome and Peacock Naval Bay—all are very imaginatively laid out, equipped with the latest gadgets and have a conducive ambience.

The Academy was inaugurated on 7 December 1954 and the first passing out parade was conducted on 1 January 1955. A lot has been written about the NDA and its activities by many officers before me so I will confine myself to the experiences that were unique to me. I was greatly impressed by the staff and the cadets who received us. They were the very embodiment of smartness and efficiency. Our commandant was Rear Admiral B.A. Samson, an eloquent speaker with an impressive personality, effective and popular. He was followed by Air Vice Marshal K.L. Sondhi and then came Maj. Gen. R. Bakshi, MC, a gunner. I was allotted to 29 division of Kilo Squadron with 4221 as my cadet number. We were 23 freshers from 4207 to 4230 who became part of the squadron.

The Academy was organized in three battalions in serial number and 10 Squadrons in alphabetical order. Three squadrons were added later. The State of Assam had donated Rs. 5 lakh for the construction of the Kilo squadron building. We were approximately 120 cadets in a squadron with an overall strength of 1,200 cadets in the Academy. Our squadron commander was Maj. P.C. Khanna (Arty) and divisional commanders were Lt. K.N. Dabash (IN), Capt. Gilani, 8 Fd Regt and Flt. Lt. Conquest (IAF). In hindsight, I feel the squadron commander played no role at all in our development and the divisional commanders routinely watched us perform PT and drill. They reviewed our performance once in a term. During our golden jubilee function we were allowed to see our dossiers as they had been declassified by then.

I was disappointed to note how sketchy and perfunctorily they had been written. There was no mention of strong or weak traits, no counselling notes and all of us had been graded similarly. The year was divided into spring and autumn terms. Although I had lived in cantonments, I was not prepared for a regimented life and was distraught with what I experienced. We were put under the care of Corporal H.S. Boparai, a fourth-term Sikh cadet with a smart and impressive military bearing. He was a hard taskmaster, perfectionist, very efficient but considerate, fair and caring like an elder brother. He acted both as our guide and philosopher for the next six months. While we went about the routine activities and curriculum, ragging took centrestage—all in the name of training, imbibing military ethos, discipline, obedience to orders and mental and physical toughness. We were running, rolling, jumping on our haunches, leapfrogging or crawling most of the free time, particularly after diner till midnight.

We would be wet with sweat and grime or water and undergoing all this in the bathrooms, corridors or hard gravel of the parade ground. We were not spared even during our meal times in the mess. At times, it was inhuman, degrading, sadistic and perverse. In hindsight, it did more harm than good to us. It broke our spirit, destroyed individuality, made us submissive; hurt our pride and dignity, affected efficiency and creativity. While it produced group cohesiveness, camaraderie and raised our threshold and tolerance for privation, it also dehumanized us to an extent. We had been transformed into walking, talking robots.

The weak had no place in this Academy and left soon after arrival. I hated this so called conditioning but bore it stoically. Our cabins were very comfortable and tastefully furnished with teak furniture. The view of the hills from my window was beautiful. It gave me great solace watching them when I was forlorn and homesick. We had to keep them neat, tidy and arranged all the time as a cabin inspection could be ordered any time. Reveille, lights out and the four muster parades were followed very rigidly on working days. The silence of the study period was my best friend. I wish it was longer. The ragging reduced by midterm. We were now more focused on our academics and physical training. I was graded well in academics and placed in class 2. I was a quick learner and passed my mandatory drill and PT tests before the term ended.

Novices' boxing competition was yet another important event that I cannot forget. I was no boxer. Yet we all had to participate in it. During the competition I was pitted against Amrik Singh Hansrao, a well built and sturdy fellow cadet from Punjab. He was very aggressive and charged into me like a bull. He applied brute force to knock me out as early as possible. However, I gave him blow for blow and exhausted him by quick footwork and straight punches. Even though I was bleeding profusely I refused to throw in the towel despite medical advice. I lost narrowly but was declared the best loser. I got a standing ovation from the spectators and was made a hero by my squadron at the dinner muster for my stubbornness and never say die attitude. I enjoyed the hobby periods that were held on Wednesdays. I learnt aero modelling and later excelled in riding and shooting through club activities. I was in the show jumping and trick riding teams and won the silver spoon in the shooting competition.

We attended Camp "Greenhorn" in the second term. The aim of this camp was to teach us tent and bivouac pitching, map reading, day and night navigation by map and compass, trench digging and sentry duty. Basically, it was an introduction to military life and judge/develop leadership qualities. I was selected one of the leaders and we stood first in the competition. Workshop was another activity that I liked and excelled in. We learnt foundry work, carpentry, blacksmithy, welding and machine tooling. After passing our compulsory Hindi test, I was allotted Chinese as a foreign language. I regret to confess that I did not take interest in it and managed to pass only the elementary exam. In hindsight, it was a terrible error. This language would have improved my merit and been very useful to me later in service.

During our second term, Goa was captured by the Indian defence forces on 19 December 1961[25] and there was a sense of great jubilation among all of us. Of all the midterm excursions, my visit to Mahabaleshwar, a hill station near Pune, and Goa immediately after its liberation in 1962 was most memorable. We also enjoyed trekking up to the legendary Singhgarh fort overlooking the Academy and a great source of motivation and inspiration. We all looked forward to Wednesdays as it was movie day and we saw some of the best war movies in the auditorium-cum-theatre. It is an imposing and beautiful building with a capacity for about 2,000 people and equipped with the latest gadgets and acoustics. We also saw great performances by renowned artists like Uday Shankar and his dance troupe and famous Prithvi Theatre artists under the legendary Raj Kapoor. Indian and foreign artists also gave some enthralling musical performances.

While most of my colleagues went on liberty out passes on weekends, I enjoyed spending my spare time in the library that is co-located with the auditorium. Not only is the ambience good, it is a repository of knowledge with more than 100,000 books on all subjects. Discipline in the Academy was good; baring an odd black sheep, all the others walked the straight line. A few cadets smoked at night or drank beer—all as part of their macho image or the sheer adventure of growing up. Only once in our three years were three cadets punished for visiting a place of ill repute. A promulgation parade was held and the cadets were disgraced publically and withdrawn in the presence of the battalion.

I passed all my PT, swimming and riding tests by the third term. I am grateful to Subedar Balbir Singh, MC, Kumaon Regiment, and Hav. Fauza Singh, APTC, for PT and Subedar Chotu Ram of PBG and Hav. Varender Singh for equestrian training. Camp "Rover" was held in the fourth term. It was an advance version of "Greenhorn" with almost the same subjects and objectives. Once again I was selected as one of the leaders and this time we stood second. I continued to do well in academics and at the end of the fourth term allotted to the science stream. However I declined on the advice of my seniors and instead opted for Humanities with English Honours and Economics. The 1962 Indo-China war[26] brought sadness to all of us. Brigadier Hoshiar Singh, IOM, IDSM, Croix de Guerre, our Deputy Commandant, who was a distinguished Second World War hero, was selected to command 62 Infantry Brigade at Sela against the Chinese. We gave him a rousing farewell. Unfortunately, his brigade was annihilated and he was killed in battle. This created an atmosphere of gloom and brought anguish and disappointment in all the cadets. Service subjects were introduced in our fifth term and the Air Force and naval cadets were separated from us for subjects specific to them. Gliding and sailing were part of their training while we learnt weapons training, field craft and battle drill. I am thankful to Hav. Hari Singh, Jat Regiment, for imparting these basic skills to me. In the wake of the 1962 military disaster, our training was made more practical and tougher. Military history and military geography were also introduced which were rather interesting and absorbing. I had done well so far. I had been good in studies and outdoors. I never attended extra classes or coaching, failed or recalled for any retest. I was never awarded extra drills for any lapse. I was therefore happy with my performance but disappointed when it was not recognized. Less meritorious cadets were favoured and I remained a plain cadet to the surprise of my squadron mates.

The Academy is a cradle of leadership, an iconic institution with the hallmark of excellence. It is a unique institution where cadets from even foreign countries trained with us. I am proud to be a product of this great institution for shaping my character, teaching me the highest standards of moral values, and giving me a life with a purpose to serve the people and country selflessly. However, I felt that entry level at high school and passing out at 12th class level was low. Fortunately, it has been now rectified. Even though we had excellent faculty under Mr. Vyas, the Principal, I felt that the syllabus was not in keeping with future requirements.

The Military subjects took back stage and we were introduced to Military History and Geography rather late. Geopolitics, international relations, armament technology, and laws of armed conflict were not covered. The over centralized curriculum and emphasis on instant obedience to command curbed our ability of questioning, reasoning and analysis was lost in the process. The training did not encourage or stimulate intellectual growth. Ends justifying the means, survival of the fittest, beg, borrow, or steal, never volunteer, and never own up are part of the in-house training imparted to the cadets by their seniors and passed down from one course to the other. Stealing, usurping and extortion by seniors become a chain reaction and impinge on integrity, honesty and truthfulness that are vital qualities in a leader. Two of the three commandants and half the military or civil instructors failed to be our role models. The junior staff was however excellent.

It is said in private that a NDA cadet never grows up, and I tend to believe it. Many of the cadets, after passing out, remain intellectually stagnated. The Academy has not produced outstanding strategists, thinkers or military philosophers who can be counted among the best internationally. Yes, we have produced the finest young leaders who are fearless, lead from the front and are good at operational art. They have brought glory to the nation. The last term ended with Camp "Torna". It was tough and involved forced marches with full packs, jungle survival, and sighting of defences at section level besides a bayonet competition. We stood last as no one was motivated at that stage to work hard. All had gone well so far for me when suddenly I fell afoul of my drill instructor, Subedar Chuna Ram, MVC, an excellent instructor from the Rajputana Rifles.

Chuna Ram was an embodiment of a perfect soldier except that he was abusive and foul mouthed at times. I objected to his abusive language and indecent gestures at cadets while drilling us for the passing out parade. This infuriated him and he took it as a challenge to his authority. I was charged for disobedience, misbehaviour and indiscipline. When asked to state my defence by the Squadron Commander, I told him the truth. The enquiry upheld my version and the charges were dropped. Chuna Ram remained antagonistic towards me thereafter. However at the time of my departure, he apologized and shook hands with me. My moral courage had won him over. Each term ended with a farewell to the passing out cadets at squadron level. I was surprised by the popularity and high esteem bestowed on me by the juniors. At the Academy level, there would be a PT display, horse show, dramatics, academy award dinner and the final parade. The passing out parades were generally reviewed by eminent personalities as it was a grand event. Our passing out parade on 4 December 1963 was reviewed by Mr. Y.B. Chavan, who was now the Raksha Mantri. The quarterdeck was manned by cadets of 30th course while we marched passed saluting in slow march to the tune of Auld Lang Syne. The fly past by the IAF did the last honour for us. I was now a confidant, self-reliant, audacious and mature man, looking to the future determined to carve out a niche for myself.

We took the Military Special for our last journey back home. During the journey, I had enough time to reflect on the time that had gone past. I concluded that the NDA was actually a factory that produced officers for the Indian Defence Forces somewhat like the novel written by Hans Hellmut Kirst in 1962. The SSBs selected the raw material (cadets) through a battery of tests that had similar specifications. Then, this raw material, in the form of cadets, was trained by a uniform set of rules, syllabi, and activities under a constantly strict environment. The product was similar in thinking and behaviour. The majority of the cadets would endorse the German or Japanese samurai philosophy, Aryan superiority or the martial race theory with no place for any other ideology.

In the din of 1962, my father was posted to 11 GRRC at Clement Town, Dehra Dun, as the administration officer. The Doon Valley had been ceded to the British by the Gorkhas under the treaty of Sugauli in 1816. The valley is enclosed by the higher Himalayas to the north, the Shivallik hills and Doiwalla forest in the south, the Yamuna River in the west and the Ganga River in the east. The British established a cantonment at Dehradun. The FRI and Railway Training Institute were located at Prem Nagar.

The Indian Military Academy[27] was established in 1932 in the Railway Training Institute campus. The first batch passed out in 1934. R.C. Clement, an Italian, founded Clement Town in 1932. Later, in 1941, a cantonment was established at Clement Town[28] during the Second World War to intern Italian and German prisoners. After independence, on 1

January 1949, the JSW was established in the same POW barracks. 11 GRRC occupied them when they moved out to Khadakvasla in 1954. We lived in a temporary house on Dakota Road. A Second World War Dakota plane had been placed there as a monument. Every winter, the Centre would organize a shikar event in the Lachiwala/Doiwala Shivalik forest blocks. These blocks were earmarked for various clubs to hunt wild animals by the forest department. While I was waiting to join the IMA in January 1964, I was invited to join one of these hunts by the Centre Commandant, Colonel R.D. Hira. The recruits were used as beaters when the hunt started at first light. All went well till 0800 hrs and by then we had shot a few deer, jungle fowls and a wild boar. It was almost time to call off the shoot when suddenly a leopard appeared in front of us, disturbed by the noise and din of the beaters. The unexpected confrontation between the bewildered animal and the hunters caused utter confusion and panic in both. No one was prepared except me with my loaded gun. I fired at the animal and wounded it in the paw when he was preparing to break the cordon. The wounded leopard turned ferocious and crouched to leap at me when I fired my second shot that killed him on the spot. I became an instant hero as had this not happened many of us, including the Commandant and his son, could have been mauled by the animal. The leopard skin is displayed in the Officers Mess as a trophy.

Due to the Indo-China war, the training at IMA had been truncated to six months instead of a year. The 34th Regular Course to which we belonged had already passed out in December 1963. We, the remnants, were grouped with the EC 10 course. The Academy had been divided into three parts to cater for additional intakes. The first batch was in the old Collins and Kingsley blocks with good accommodation and infrastructure, the second batch was in the Forest Research Institution and the third batch was in the Prisoners-of-War-barracks in Clement Town. Maj. Gen. S.C. Pandit, VrC, 4 GR, was the commandant. We joined the Academy in February as part of G Battalion, 19 Company, and 52 Platoon at FRI. I was allotted GC 7072 as my Academy number and made commander of the technical graduates platoon. We had some very bright engineers in the platoon.

I enjoyed working with the techies, as they were called. They did very well in all activities. Our training revolved around field craft and battle drill, weapons training, night training, physical toughness, firing, map reading and platoon tactics. The one year curriculum was encapsulated in six months. We had no rest during either the day or the night and scurried from one class to another or from one training area to another. This technical batch and EC officers did very well in the army as well subsequently. Capt. Kamal Mohan Chadha, Engrs, Capt. Satnam Jit Singh, Engrs, and Capt. R.K. Pandit, Sigs, rose to become secretary, ambassador and DG Police, respectively. Many others also did equally well. My platoon commander was Capt. K.C. Singh of the Dogra Regiment and company commander was Maj. Mangat, Mahar Regiment, initially and later, Maj. Rastogi, Para Engineers. Our battalion commander was Lt. Col. S. Mann Singh, Para Artillery. Capt. K.C. Singh liked me immensely. He had fought the 1962 war with China and had been a prisoner of war. He was practical, tough and a hard taskmaster. It was difficult to meet his standards but I was his favourite cadet due to my sincerity and hard work.

After midterm, we moved into the new campus in the tea garden area, in temporary barracks. The summers were exceptionally hot and the monsoons humid. The Doon Valley was not a pleasant place as we had imagined it to be. Camp Chindit was held in July in the hot barren rocky hills overlooking the Tons River valley and contiguous to the Mussoorie Range called 'Clouds End'. The exercise was based on a platoon in defence in mountainous terrain. It was tough work digging trenches among rocks and living on scanty rations and water. The days were hot and nights windy and cold. The last part of the exercise was to race back to the Academy in complete battle kit with all the platoon weapons.

I played for the Academy hockey team and participated in a squash tournament as well. During the midterm break, we visited Mussoorie which was a pristine hill station. The intense training gave us great experience and knowledge about military life. The aim was to make us bold and competent junior military leaders and that I think was achieved by the end of our six months training. Both the officer and JCO/NCO instructors were fully involved in our training. We however remained ignorant about the art of warfare as subjects like military history, geo-strategy, case studies of various battles, biographies of military leaders, and international relations were not covered in the syllabus. Military law and administration were also not taught. There was no time for hobbies, library or cultural events.

In the final week of our stay, like in the NDA, I got into trouble in the IMA also. This time, it was for violation of Academy orders. Our training was over and we were now practicing for the passing out parade. At that time 'Sangam' a blockbuster movie by Raj Kapoor, was playing in the cinema hall near the Clock Tower. Due to our busy schedule, there was no possibility to see it except the late night show for which we were not allowed out passes. Some of us decided to bunk from the Academy for the second show at 10 PM. Ashok Nagpal, R.K. Singh, S. Bhargav, V. Kochar and R.K. Pandit and I decided to take the risk. We slipped out of the Academy dressed as civilians. The guard did not suspect anything unusual and allowed us to pass. We saw the movie tucked away in a dark corner. On our return, all went fine till we were about to enter the Academy when we were recognized by the Adjutant, HH, Major Bhawani Singh of Jaipur, who was returning from the town with his fiancée, Princess Padmini Devi of Sirmoor.

We were ordered to report to him the next morning. I was charged-sheeted for violating Academy Orders, being improperly dressed and misconduct. It was a fit case for relegation. I truthfully accepted my fault when arraigned in the orderly room. The Adjutant, after reviewing my excellent performance and positive feedback from the company commander, decided to drop the charges against me with a stern warning. I had been recommended by Capt. K.C. Singh to join the Dogra Regiment but to my surprise I was allotted 11 GR. I learnt subsequently that the change was arranged by Colonel R.D. Hira, who had been greatly impressed by me during the leopard shoot. We passed out on 2 August 1964 under the monsoon clouds and a drizzle to the tune of Auld Lang Syne in the shadow of Chetwood Hall. We took the oath to the Constitution in our respective messes and became commissioned officers. I was allotted IC 16095 P as my commission number and received my parchment from the President of India accordingly. I spent 20 days of break with my parents at Clement

Town and boarded the train to Binaguri in West Bengal where my unit was located.

I travelled to Binaguri via Barauni, Kathiar and Siliguri on a metre gauge train. The countryside was lush green due to the monsoons but all along the route poverty and underdevelopment was glaringly visible. Binaguri was a wayside small station primarily serving the defence forces then. It was famous for its tea gardens and the forest stretching for miles up to the foothills. Herds of elephants were often seen in vicinity of settlements that fell along their migratory routes. Bengal Tigers, bears and wild boar were found in abundance. Pythons were encountered lying across roads and jungle lanes. Leopards were spotted frequently in tea gardens that preyed on domestic animals. The monsoons was at its peak when I arrived at Binaguri.

Incessant rain lashed our bamboo huts flooding the entire area. The rains were followed by severe winters. The summers were humid and miserably hot. Binaguri station housed the entire 20 Mountain Division that was part of 33 Corps. 5/11 GR,[29] the Battalion I joined, was raised on 8 May 1948 out of Gorkha troops of 7 and 10 GR. The unit was located in a compact area with offices, quarterguard, administrative area and living huts in one cluster. The playgrounds and training area were on the periphery. The officers' quarters and mess were located a walking distance from the unit in a separate cluster. There was no electricity and we worked in the light of kerosene or battery lamps at night. Our rooms were furnished with camp furniture. Water was supplied by trucks once a day. A rudimentary toilet system existed with dry sanitation.

My interview by the commanding officer, Lt. Col. K.N. Bhalla, was very short and crisp. All that he said was to work hard. He had been commissioned during the war. He was a tall, handsome bachelor, anglicized in accent and conduct. He was very polished, sophisticated and reticent. The battalion had been withdrawn for rest and training to Binaguri after a rigorous and strenuous tenure at Chola-Changu in Sikkim against the Chinese. Due to the sudden expansion of the army, the officer structure had been disturbed. The service gap was more than 12 to 15 years. The majority of the officers were emergency commissioned with less than two year service. We were all dressed in battle fatigues while training and walking outs on other occasions. Col. Bhalla followed a very rigid routine with strict timings. Wednesdays were movie days at Planters Club[30] where officers could be found socializing with the planters or flirting with their wives. During weekends, officers socialized among themselves ending with heavy drinking or playing cricket, tennis and squash with the planters. Some officers were allowed to visit Darjeeling or Kalimpong at the pleasure of the commanding officer.

All of us attended training cadres under experienced JCOs and NCOs who repeated the syllabus that we had undergone in the IMA. We graduated from one squad post to another till posted to a specialist platoon. Day and night firing, night marches and field firing were compulsory. We also joined various cadres at the brigade/divisional level on direction of artillery fire, infantry-tank cooperation, signal communication, administration-related subjects and so on. Games and sports with troops were compulsory in the evenings. Pay collection from banks and monthly pay parade was a major event when we physically disbursed pay to our men. Over payments/ shortages resulted in the disbursing officer being penalised. A lot of importance was given to inter-battalion championships in sports and we spent substantial resources and time on them. We won the command football trophy but failed miserably in all the other events.

Major Sushil Kumar replaced Major G.S. Harika as the second-in-command. He was a very energetic and professionally highly qualified officer. He was a graduate from the Staff College and had been Assistant Military Attaché at the High Commission of India in London. The environment in the battalion changed dramatically with his arrival. Battalion collective training under his supervision was operationally oriented and practical. I was sent on commando course at Infantry School, Mhow, at short notice. It was considered a very tough course and not many officers qualified. Lt. Col. T.S. Oberoi, Maj. M.K. Lahiri, and captains A.S. Chadha and Rathode were my instructors who had been trained in the USA. Our syllabus was based on the American Rangers' course. We were trained to operate behind enemy lines, collect intelligence and destroy vital enemy installations. I did well and my CO was extremely happy with my performance though I had missed the top grading by a whisker. I had done them proud.

NOTES

1. Old records held with Pt. Kishan Singh, village Bichoon, district Jaipur, known as Jaggas.
2. *Annals and Antiquities of Rajasthan,* by James Tod, vol. 2, p. 165.
3. *Annals and Antiquities of Rajasthan* by James Tod, vol. 2, pp. 256-257.
4. *Rajasthan Through the Ages* by R.K. Gupta and S.R. Bakshi, pp. 244-250.
   Annals and Antiquities of Rajasthan by James Tod, vol. 1, pp. 208, 596.
   Rajputana Gazeteer by J. Digges, p. 140.
5. Verified on ground by the author. The village and remnants of abandoned settlement exist.
6. *Annals and Antiquities of Rajasthan* by James Tod, vol. 1, p. 69.
7. Records held by Pt Kishan Singh Jagga.
8. *Memoirs of George Thomas* by William Franklin.
9. *Modern Haryana* by K.C. Yadav, p. 114.
10. *Martial Races of India* by Lt. Gen. Sir George MacMunn, pp. 237, 383.
11. *The Indian Army* by Stephen P. Cohen, p. 69.
12. *Tribes & Castes of NW Provinces* by W. Crookes, BA, vol. 1, pp. 49-71 and vol. 3, p. 6.
13. *Glossary of Tribes & Castes of the Punjab & NW Frontier Provinces,* Census Report by Denzil Ibretson RCSI and E.D. MacLagan, GSI, and compiled by H.A. Rose, vol. 2, pp. 4-7.
14. *Handbooks for Indian Army, Rajputana Classes Jats, Gujjars and Ahirs* by B.L. Cole and R.C. Christie, p. 124; *Jats, Gujjars & Ahirs* by Major Bingley, p. 45.
15. *History of Kumaon Regiment* by K.C. Praval.
16. *History of Awadh* by Hameed Akhtar Siddiqui.
17. 'Old and Beautiful Cantonment', *The Tribune,* 5 June 2017; *Hand book of Punjab, Western Raputana, Kashmir, Sindh* by John Murray, p. 176, sec. 2.
18. *Butcher of Amritsar* by Niggel Collett.
19. *The Lashkar* by Narendra Luther.
20. *The Princes of India* by Sir William Barton, chapter on Hyderabad.
21. *The Rani of Jhansi* by Rainer Jerosch.
22. *Under Doctrine of Lapse* by Lord Dalhousie; Lebra Chapman, chapter 2; Kaye's and Malleson's *History.*
23. *The Rani of Jhansi* by Rainer Jerosch, ch. 1.
24. *The Marathas 1600-1818* by Gordon Stewart.
25. *Indian Army After Independence* by Maj. K.C. Praval, p. 214; 'Obituaries' by Lt. Gen. K.P. Candeth, *The Independent* 19 July 2003.
26. *India's China War* by Neville Maxwell, p. 24; *The Himalayan Blunder* by Brig. John Dalvi; *India-China war 50 Years later,* articles published in *The Tribune,* October 2012.
27. *History of Indian Military Academy* by Brig. M.P. Singh; *Valour & Wisdom: Genesis and Growth of The Indian Military Academy* by B.P.N. Sinha; *A Soldiers Life in War and Peace* by A.S. Naravane, pp. 9-14.
28. *TKS Tales* by Air Commodore T.K. Sen.
29. *Path to Glory* by Lt. Col. Gautam Sharma.
30. *Recollections of a Tea Planter* by W.M. Fraser; *Through my Looking Glass* by Partha Chatterjee.

Chapter Two

1965—A War of Lost Opportunities

By April 1965, relations between India and Pakistan had deteriorated substantially that resulted in the war of that year. In 1962, India had been squarely defeated by China. Our politico-military weaknesses had been exposed. Pakistan, at that time, did not take advantage of the situation by opening a second front in the West as both the USA and the USSR did not want the war to escalate. In retrospect, Pakistan thought that it had missed a great opportunity to annex Kashmir. Due to the weak military, political, and economic conditions prevailing in India then, Pakistan was emboldened and the hawkish foreign minister of Pakistan, Z.A. Bhutto, goaded President Field Marshal Ayub Khan to seize the opportunity before it was too late. Sheikh Abdullah was released from prison by Mr. Nehru on 8 April 1964 so that he could once again join mainstream politics and integrate J&K fully with the rest of India.

He was allowed to visit Pakistan in May 1964. There he made statements to India's discomfort. The situation in J&K, instead of improving, nosedived. In the meantime, Mr. Nehru passed away and substantial talks to solve the Kashmir issue could not be held between India and Pakistan. The world saw India under Mr. Shastri as a weak and fragile country that would not be able to hold on for long as both internal and economic conditions were worrisome. Mr. Shastri[1] was a diminutive person with an average personality. He was from a humble and conservative background. This was in stark contrast to the aristocratic, suave, anglicized Nehru. He was a butt of jokes in India and many doubted his capabilities to run the country. In December, when the Government extended certain provisions of the Constitution to J&K that were not part of Article 370, the hardliners, including Sheikh Abdullah, Mirza Afzal Beg and Pakistan criticized them vehemently. Between February and April 1965, Sheikh Abdullah and Mirza Afzal Beg were allowed to visit foreign countries including London, Saudi Arabia and Algiers. They criticized the Indian Government and its J&K policy on foreign soil that embarrassed the government.

They even met Mr. Chou-en-Lai, the Chinese PM, and accepted his invitation to visit China. During this period, the situation in the Kashmir Valley was getting restive on the instigation of the hardliners. Mr. Z.A. Bhutto, who was both foreign minister and a close confidant of the President,[2] was to a great extent responsible for the bad Indo-Pak relations. He was rabidly anti India even though he was born of a Hindu mother, Lakhi Bai, who converted to Islam and became Khursheed Begum and his father, Shah Nawaz Bhutto,[3] was the prime minister of Junagarh at the time of independence.

The leadership of Pakistan at that time thought that India did not enjoy the confidence of the people of the Kashmir Valley and so it could be easily defeated to achieve the unfinished agenda of 1947. The connivance of Sheikh Abdullah cannot be ruled out. From 9 to 21 April 1965, skirmishes took place in the Rann of Kutch[4] where India did not fare well. This convinced Pakistan further that India could be defeated. The arrest of Sheikh Abdullah resulted in a volatile situation in the Valley. Pakistan took advantage of these negative sentiments.

As a consequence of the events in the Rann of Kutch, both the Western and Eastern Commands were mobilized against Pakistan in early April 1965. We were deployed on the East Pakistan border. Our task was to infiltrate into enemy territory and disrupt its communications and command structure in support operations by 165 Mountain Brigade. We lived hidden and camouflaged under bamboo groves during the day time. Movement was strictly restricted. At night the tents and bivouacs came up but not a light flickered. We sweated in the hot and humid climate during the day in our assembly area waiting for orders to cross the border. Water, food and essential supplies were received during the night. The area was infested with poisonous snakes. We found them coiled up in the cool of our snake trenches every morning. Mosquitoes and leeches also played hell with us during the night. Each day of deployment was a curse due to the intense heat, humidity, snakes and the mosquitoes.

Our ordeal was over with the signing of the disengagement agreement on 30 June 1965 between the two countries that was facilitated by British Prime Minister Mr. Harold Wilson. We moved back to barracks. Soon thereafter, Lt. Colonel K.N. Bhalla was posted out and Major Sushil Kumar became the officiating CO on 8 July. The battalion received orders to move to Ambala in August. As I had passed my retention and regimental language exam and had completed one year, I was granted annual leave.

Even though disengagement between the armies of India and Pakistan had taken place in July, the threat from Pakistan had not completely receded. Army HQ and Western Command were apprehensive of their intentions and continued to plan for operations in case of an aggression. Army HQ had directed the command to plan for an offensive through a corridor formed by the Jammu-Sialkot road and Basantar Nala towards Chiwanda. Initially, only 6 Mountain Division and 2 Armoured Brigade, less a regiment, were available for this task but by July, 1 Corps with 1 Armoured Division, 6 Mountain Division, the newly-raised 14 Infantry Division and 26 Infantry Division were made available for this offensive. The plans had been finalized by July-August.

The task of 1 Corps was to establish a bridgehead in the Pagowal-Phillora area and thereafter breakout towards the Marala-Ravi link canal and secure the Dhallewali-Wuhulam-Daska-Mandhali line. 11 Corps, commanded by Lt. Gen. J.S. Dhillon, a brilliant and bold commander, was to not only defend Punjab but capture all territory up to the Ichogil Canal from Ranian in the north to its junction with Dipalpur canal in the south. 4 Mountain Division was to launch an offensive along the Khem Karan-Kasur axis. 7 Infantry Division was to advance along Bhikiwind-Kalra and capture Burki. 15 Infantry Division was to advance along the GT Road axis and capture area up to the Ichogil Canal. Simultaneously, it had to eliminate the Dera Baba Nanak bridgehead and capture the rail bridge intact.

Pakistan's offensive in Punjab from Kasur towards Amritsar, Jandiala Guru and Beas Bridge with their 1 Armoured Division had also been factored into the plans. Tension between India and Pakistan started brewing from August. By 5 August, massive infiltration[5] by Pakistan had been detected in J&K. The entire ceasefire line was live with both sides firing at each other. Border intrusions from the Pakistan side commenced with vigour. Acts of sabotage in the Valley had increased. Encounters with the infiltrators took place on a daily basis. The aim of Pakistan was to create mayhem and armed insurrection in the Valley so that they could annex the entire state. India took rapid counter-measures. Our forces captured Haji Pir Pass on 28 August and some other important places in Pakistan-Occupied Kashmir to seal the infiltrators. By the end of August, when the infiltration failed to achieve its objective and they were in retreat, Pakistan launched an offensive to capture Akhnoor on the Chenab River. This was a bold and audacious plan.

While all this was going on in August/September, my battalion, 5/11 GR, was on the move to Ambala without any notion that it would soon plunge into the war. I met the battalion at Saharanpur railway station in the evening of 4 September, where lunch had been organized by 11 GRRC. It was to be a lavish reception. Even though tension had been brewing between India and Pakistan since August and some bitter actions had already been fought in J&K, no one talked of the impending war even in passing. The conversation was over the wonderful days ahead in Ambala. Since the battalion had arrived late, lunch had been converted to dinner. Half way through the reception, an urgent message was received through the station master to clear the platform as soon as possible to make way for other red hot military special trains passing through Saharanpur. The dinner was hastily concluded and the battalion moved out immediately.

War with Pakistan had been declared on 4 September and all of us who were on leave were asked to join our units forthwith through an announcement on All India Radio on 5 Sep. I left to join my unit on 6 September 1965 from Clement Town, Dehradun. I was asked to report to the transit camp at Jammu for further despatch. When Pakistan's endeavour to capture the Srinagar Valley under 'Operation Gibraltar' was petering out, they launched Operation 'Grand Slam' and opened the Chhamb front on 1 September. Jaurian, across the Manawar Tawi, fell on 5 September and they nearly captured the Akhnoor bridge. In order to relieve the pressure on Chhamb-Jaurian, the Indian Army was mobilized on 1 September and opened the Lahore front on 6 September.

By the time 5/11 GR reached Ambala on 5 September, 4 Mountain Division, the formation that it was to join, had already left for operations in the Khemkaran sector. After collecting their arms, ammunition and equipment, the unit travelled during the night of 6/7 September in civilian trucks and reported to 6 Mountain Division. By 7 September, they were launched for operations. Now the battalion was asked to join 19 Infantry Brigade of 26 Infantry Division at Jammu. I had travelled from Dehradun in a train that was full of officers and troops who had been recalled from leave. En-route between Ambala and Pathankot, we saw a number of dog fights between aircraft of the IAF and the PAF. These dog fights were thrilling and spectacular and ended with the enemy aircraft turning tail and heading for Pakistan. Rumours were rife that Pakistan had infiltrated paratroopers in civil dress to sabotage our lines of communications to J&K, particularly the Sutlej and Beas bridges and the Madhopur barrage over vital road communications.

We saw a number of volunteers as part of the civil defence organization patrolling the railway tracks and searching the sugarcane fields to hunt down these saboteurs. They were armed with swords, private firearms and staves. They took their duties seriously. We also saw a large number of enthusiastic ladies and children on the railway platforms offering food, fruits, milk and water to the soldiers as a token of their love and affection for those moving to the front. We were overwhelmed by these simple acts. I reported to the transit camp at Pathankot near the railway station in the evening of 7 September. It was overflowing with officers and men due to the mobilization. I could get a bed with great difficulty. The night was uneasy with the air-raid sirens blaring frequently. Pathankot airfield was supporting operations in Chhamb-Jaurian and had been very active and continuously attacked by the PAF with some success initially. The firing by anti-aircraft guns filled the sky with tracers and exploding shells throughout the night. I had not seen such live fire earlier from so close a range. It produced a lot of excitement and confidence in us.

In the morning, I was allotted a seat in a convoy of 3-ton vehicles to Jammu. We crossed the Ravi River on the pontoon bridge. In every truck, transistors were relaying news about the fighting with patriotic songs between the news bulletins. Pakistan's thrust in the Akhnoor sector had been checked. We had counter-attacked Pakistan in Khem Karan–Kasur, Kalra-Burki, Lahore and Gurdaspur sectors. We had surprised Pakistan and our troops were on the East bank of the Ichogil Canal. Our troops had contacted Burki, and were threatening Lahore. After crossing the Ravi River, our troops fell back and blew up the Dera Baba Nanak rail-road bridge in panic. Thus, there were a mixed feeling of jubilation and disappointment among us.

The road to Jammu was one-way. Our convoy negotiated the causeways with great difficulty as bridges did not exist on it then. I was advised by officers travelling with me to disembark at Kaluchak, where HQ 1 Corps was located in order to join my unit quickly instead of reporting to transit camp Jammu. I met Major F.T. Dias from my battalion who was GSO2 (OPS) at Kaluchak for help. Though tired after a long day in the operations room hidden in a grove, he greeted me with a smile. The Corps HQ had been raised on 1 April 1965 under Lt. Gen. P.O. Dunn, 3 GR. He was to retire shortly but an extension had been granted and he was promoted over Major General Rajinder Singh GOC 1 Armoured Division. Although an officer of high professional repute, he proved to be inadequate for the tasks given to his Corps.

The HQ had been mobilized on 1 September from Mathura and launched into operations on 6 September. It was not an easy task for a newly-raised Corps HQ to undertake offensive operations against a well-prepared enemy at such short notice. The Corps had concentrated and was ready for offensive by 7 Sep. Except for 1 Armoured Division, all the other divisions had been raised recently and had to be concentrated post-haste from various cantonments. It was planned for 6 Mountain Division to establish a bridgehead in the Charwa and Maharajke areas by first light 8 September. 26 Infantry Division with 162 and 168 brigades was to protect the flank of 1 Corps and threaten Sialkot by capturing Unche Wains, Niwe Wains and Anula, and Bajraggarhi, respectively, by 8 September.

All the objectives were secured as per plan. 1 Armoured Division broke out of the bridgehead at 0400 hrs on 8 September. It made good progress till early morning but thereafter the offensive slowed down and they were nowhere near their objective by last light. Major Dias organized my transportation to 26 Infantry Division HQ at Kharian near Ranbir Singhpura on the Jammu-Sialkot road in a 1-ton dak vehicle. I reached there around 1700 hrs and the scene was chaotic. No one could tell me where my battalion was and how I could reach them. Suddenly, enemy aircraft appeared out of the blue and started strafing the HQ and all of us ducked for cover. After the all-clear siren, whistles were sounded and we were once again in chaos. We saw our troops thrashing some soldiers dressed in khaki, presuming them to be Pakistani saboteurs. Their fingers had been broken and their nails pulled out during interrogation. Their lips were swollen and bleeding. They were writhing in pain and wailing. Without heeding to their pleas that they were Indians, they had been mercilessly beaten blue and black by the crowd and soldiers surrounding them.

Subsequently it was revealed that they were jawans from the Madhya Pradesh Armed Police who had been deputed to work with the PAP for internal guard duties. They were apprehended by an army patrol by mistake when searching the area near the Division HQ perimeter for suspected saboteurs. While all this was happening I went to the operations branch to get help to reach my battalion. Pakistani aircraft appeared again and we dived for cover. In the din, one of the officers advised me to stand near the traffic control post and hop in any vehicle that was going to Suchetgarh to reach my battalion. The enemy aircraft appeared again and this time they dropped bombs on the bridge. Fortunately, they fell away causing no damage. To my good luck, I managed a lift in a truck that was heading for 5/11 GR. It was now dark and I was happy to leave the chaos behind.

I reached my battalion base past last light when the stand-to had just finished. I learnt that the troops had been issued ammunition for the first time. One of the non-combatant riflemen, waiter Ramjanam, out of curiosity, had pressed the trigger of a loaded medium machine gun, killing and injuring some persons standing around. Captain Naresh Bhasin, the Quarter Master, disposed off a serious case of death by negligence with just a warning to the culprit on the spot. This was bizarre but from Captain Bhasin's perspective, action against the defaulter had been taken and the ends of justice had been met as the offence was not intentional. Curiously, no one questioned his action or judgment. To enable me to join my men immediately, he put me in a field echelon truck that was carrying food for my company.

After three days of continuous journey, I finally joined 6 Platoon Bravo Company under Major B.S. Negi at 2200 hrs on 8 September, starving and fully exhausted. That day was also when the historic battle of Asal Uttar[6] commenced between our 4 Infantry Division and 1 Armoured Division of Pakistan. The 4 Mountain Division, after launching an offensive on 6 September fell back when Pakistani forces retaliated with tanks and massive artillery. They took up defensive positions around Asal Uttar to protect the flank of 11 Corps against any major offensive by Pakistan on 7 September. The formation was in a very critical situation then. The battle was fought from 8 to 10 September. 4 Mountain Division along with 2 Independent Armoured brigade was able to defeat the Pakistani forces decisively by skilful use of natural and artificial obstacles and intelligent deployment of tanks, troops and reserves. The leadership that had cracked up in the face of enemy pressure on 6 Sep rallied, reorganized and gave an excellent account under very severe battle conditions. Much of the credit for this rally by the Indian forces goes to the Corps and Army Commanders who, with their determined and resolute leadership, held the front intact. However, many battalion and brigade commanders were sacked for their cowardly and incompetent actions between 6 and 8 September, including the GOC.

We were deployed at Mahute, north of Ranbir Singhpura. 26 Infantry Division had both an offensive role towards Sialkot as well as a defensive role to protect Jammu. While the rest of the Corps went in on an offensive through the Shakargarh Bulge for Philora and Chiwanda, 26 Infantry Division was to threaten Sialkot from Suchetgarh and also protect the flank of 1 Armoured Division from the Sialkot side. Our task was to defend Jammu from the north between Suchetgarh and the Jammu Tawi River. We dug trenches in rice fields that were half filled with water due to a high water table. The days and nights were hot and humid like Bengal. There was no dearth of swarms of mosquitoes, fleas and snakes here also. Life was tough and very uncomfortable.

During the nights we often witnessed dog fights between enemy and our aircraft over our area. They also dropped 1000-lb bombs that damaged the road. The sky lit up with tracer fire, reminiscent of Diwali fireworks. We were repeatedly subjected to strafing by enemy aircraft during day. During one of the strafing and enemy shelling on our positions, some of our men at Chakroi including a senior JCO abandoned their positions out of fear and took shelter in unoccupied houses. Even the CO and his rover group were separated in the confusion. They were later rounded up and dismissed from service for cowardice. The border was guarded by the Punjab Armed Police, who on the outbreak of hostilities, vacated the posts and fell back on Ranbir Singh Pura along with the civilian population. On 9 September, 2/Lt. B.K. Bopanna, Y.K. Khanna and I was tasked to reconnoitre the area of Karotana, Khatmaria and 32 r, on the border, and find out if the enemy had made any intrusions.

Since it was my first patrol in a war zone, we made very elaborate preparations and moved out as per our pamphlet on patrolling and ambush. Very soon we were tired doing all the drills of crossing tracks, small drains and other minor obstacles that had been taught to us in the Academy. Our initial apprehensions and fear were behind us after an hour or so of these tedious and tiresome drills. We moved more rapidly and confidently up to very close to the post on the border. The last few hundred yards were however very torturous and slow, as the Punjab Police inspector who was our guide and had been the post commander before abandoning it, cautioned us every now and then to be careful and alert. Every shadow appeared to be an enemy in waiting. Every sound or crackling of a twig produced a surge of tension. The time to cover just 500 metres looked like eternity.

Finally, we reached the Karotana post and found it unoccupied. It was outside the village surrounded by a crescent-shaped water body on one side and tall *sarkandas* on the other with a clear field of fire. We found it undisturbed. All the beds were neatly made; uniforms and clothes were hanging neatly in the living area. The stores and cook house were untouched. Although we were drenched in sweat, we were happy to have succeeded in our task. I occupied the post the next night to restore the sanctity of our border, while B Company occupied 32 r on 11 September. Signallers under Lt. J.M. Talwar laid a line to Battalion HQ. We were now in communication with them both on wireless set 31 and by magneto telephone.

Next day, we reconnoitred the areas of Gugh, Dhure, Malane and Nandpur—all small villages opposite us two km inside Pakistan and found them vacated. I was admonished for venturing into enemy territory without orders. Had we occupied this area and gone up to the bund the operational situation would have accrued dramatic results. HQ 162 Infantry Brigade was operating along the Suchetgarh-Sialkot axis and in the proccss had captured two small villages of Unche and Niche Wains, two km inside Pakistan that were advance positions held by a company each of Pakistan's 19 Punjab and 13 FF. It was an insignificant territorial gain. The enemy first tier of defence was about 3,000 metres from the border and the main defences a further 2,000 metres in.

Our troops made feeble attempts to contact the enemy's first tier of defences. Similarly, 104 Infantry Brigade of the Pakistan Army made half-hearted attempts to evict us and capture Suchetgarh. One of the squadron of 18 Cavalry Regiment made forays up to Ura Bridge, in the suburbs of Sialkot. Pakistan was very sensitive to any move towards Sialkot and reacted with tanks and intense artillery shelling. Since our post was on the flank of this engagement, we were bombarded heavily. We could see enemy tanks and infantry formed up to attack us around 1730 hrs on 12 September. Except for a 3.5-inch rocket launcher, we had no other anti-tank weapon, should they attack our post. If they succeeded in capturing my post, they could easily roll back 162 Infantry Brigade from the flank and get behind Suchetgarh.

When I reported this development to the Commanding Officer, he ordered me to hold the post till the last man and last round and promptly organized a massive barrage of medium gun fire ahead of my post. We had not seen such a massive volume of artillery fire so close to our defended locality before. The earth shook and there was dust, smoke and the smell of gunpowder everywhere. Due to this effective artillery fire, the enemy tanks retreated without assaulting us. We were now more confident than ever that no one could evict us from our defences. However, one tank continued to be in the vicinity of our post. It neither moved towards us nor retreated like the rest. This kept us on tenterhooks throughout the night. Fearing that the enemy may rally and assault us any time, we continued to be in stand-to throughout the night with artillery fire on call.

At first light we were curious to know why this tank had not made any move. We approached it stealthily, taking advantage of the tall *sarkanda* grass with Molotov cocktails to attack it, if necessary. We reached undetected and found it abandoned. In order to evade the intense artillery fire the previous evening, this tank had got stuck in a blind well and the crew abandoned it in panic without switching off the engine or disabling it. The tank engine continued to run while aground. This tank was in running condition when recovered by 26 Infantry Division after the war and is displayed in the HQ as a war trophy. We were subjected to intense enemy air burst artillery and mortar fire every day. This was nerve-racking as we got very little warning to jump into our trenches to escape death or injury. However, we got used to this nuisance and lived with it throughout the war.

On 14 or 15 September, when the battle for Chiwanda was being fought by 1 Corps, Major Sushil Kumar visited us. We took him across the border to show him the abandoned Pakistani tank. Just as he was leaving, the Pakistanis brought down heavy artillery fire on our post. One of their tanks fired a direct shell at our observation post, demolishing the 20-feet high brick structure completely. The sentry survived the hit miraculously and was pulled out of the debris smiling. Sometime around 13 September, it was realized that the enemy had intruded into our territory in an area called Badulia in front of 32 r. Immediate restoration of the situation was ordered. Patrols from D and B companies at 32 r made attempts to evict them on successive nights of 14 and 15 September but failed. Finally, it was decided to launch a strong raid on the enemy post before an attack if necessary.

I was ordered to carry out this task on 16 September. I moved from Karotana in the afternoon and was provided 17 men from B Company. Most of these boys had been out patrolling this area for the past two days. They were fatigued and apprehensive. However, after a little rest and with scanty information, we set out for our task at 2300 hrs. The post was not more than 2,000 yards from our location. We moved very stealthily and were able to reach within 100 yards of it undetected and ready to assault by 0030 hrs. I, along with the assault group, crawled and reached within 10 yards of the enemy bunker and could see the sentry clearly through the loop hole. He was half-inclined with his back towards us talking to someone in the bunker. I asked rifleman Shyam Bahadur Rai to crawl and lob a grenade into the bunker before assaulting it. However, he fumbled and his grenade, instead of falling in the bunker, struck the edge and bounced off.

His buddy threw the grenade without pulling out the pin in sheer panic. The enemy was alerted and opened with automatic fire. The whole post came alive and opened with all the weapons they had. They were supported by heavy fire from the Chaprar Bund in depth. The assault party made a bold attempt to charge but in face of the intense and accurate fire, could not reach the objective and melted into the tall *sarkanda*. Tracers and bullets from automatic weapons grazed past me. Mortar fire opened up from the bund and they exploded all around us. Our post at 32 r also opened up with mortar and MMG fire. We were now sandwiched in the crossfire from both sides. We had no choice but to abandon. The entire party ran helter skelter in panic in all directions. However, in spite of the resultant chaos, all of us were able to meet at the rendezvous.

By 0300 hrs, everyone had been accounted for except for Shyam Bahadur. Although we had failed in our task, we had badly rattled the Pakistanis. They reinforced the post making it even more difficult for us to capture it. Shyam Bahadur was declared missing believed killed in action. He was 'Mentioned in Despatches' for his bravery. After the war, he was repatriated as a prisoner of war. During the debriefing, he told me that once the enemy opened up, he ran away from the enemy fire in panic and lost direction. When he could not find the rendezvous and was exhausted, he hid in the *sarkandas*. He was confused and disoriented and continued to run away from the firing. Finally, when he reached a post that he presumed was ours, he found himself surrounded by Pakistani soldiers and was captured. He was brutally tortured but not killed. He was guilty of executing the task clumsily and its failure. He had acted cowardly and did not deserve any award as the true circumstances were now known. He requested that he be discharged as he was unable to face his companions and serve with honour and dignity. In spite of my counselling, he was adamant and proceeded on discharge.

Between 14 and 16 September, a number of officers visited my post for reconnaissance, including Brigadier R.D. Hira, Commander 52 Infantry Brigade, Lt. Col. R.H. Beginia, Commanding Officer 10 Mahar and Lt. Col. Menon, Commanding Officer 1 Madras. 52 Infantry brigade[7] had been placed under 26 Infantry Division to attack Sialkot from the north. This would have resulted in the enemy pulling out troops from the Chiwanda sector and facilitated the operations of 1 Armoured Division which were progressing very slowly in the face of the enemy's 6 Armoured Division and 15 Division. I briefed them about the terrain and assured them that there was no enemy up to the Sialkot-Chaprar Bund road. On 17 September, 5/11 GR was placed under command of 52 Infantry Brigade. It was to provide a firm base to the brigade by occupying the villages of Nandpur, Malane, and Dhure by 18 September. I returned to my company and occupied Nandpur by 0300 hrs on 18 September as there was no enemy there. Similarly, C Company under Major T.R. Prashar occupied Malane and Dhure. D Company under Sub. C.B. Limbu remained at 32 r. Battalion HQ and A Company under Captain M.S. Negi occupied Chanduchak village.

The objective of 1 Madras was Tilakpur and that of 10 Mahar was Muhadipur, to cut off Sialkot from the north and exploit up to Khanpur. In the subsequent phase, operations would be developed towards Sialkot or Chaprar. The H Hour for the attack was 2330 hrs, 18 September. I marked the forming up place and secured the entire area for the attacking troops of 10 Mahar. The attacks by 1 Madras and 10 Mahar were successful and the enemy was surprised. The troops were on their objectives and even reached Khanpur unopposed. By first light of 19 September the area from

Mile 8 Road to Sialkot-Chaprar-Tilakpur-Muhadipur-Chhani was in our hands.

However the enemy reacted violently. Its 104 Infantry Brigade launched counter-attacks with 14 and 9 Baluch and 20 Lancers on 19 September. They penetrated our forward positions and reached the battalion HQ of 10 Mahar. Capt. Harjit Singh, their IO, died fighting and some of their troops after bitter fighting fell back on our positions. The situation was stabilized and the enemy evicted after a hard fight. Some of the jawans who had been wounded in battle fell back in our positions. They were in a terrible condition. One of the jawans had a severed arm that was dangling from the elbow and another had his left eye gouged due to shell shrapnel. One of them was hit in the head and died in my arms. B and C companies collected 60 to 70 such wounded persons or who had abandoned their positions due shell shock. We were prepared to reinforce or counter-attack the enemy should he succeed against 52 Infantry Brigade. We evacuated all the wounded persons after first aid and despatched those fit to their battalions. The Pakistanis counter-attacked again on the nights of 20/21 and 22/23 September without any success. A Company was moved to Ghug as an immediate reinforcement and the Battalion HQ also located itself at Karotana to exercise better command and control. Throughout the period from 19 to 23 September, all our positions were shelled by the Pakistanis with great intensity and accuracy and without any predictability.

We were unable to move and remained confined to our trenches and bunkers. When the situation in front of 52 Infantry Brigade stabilized, 5/11 GR was tasked to capture Palaura Nikka but the ceasefire was announced in the afternoon of 22 September effective from 0300 hrs of 23 September. The attack was called off to our disappointment. Both sides indulged in massive artillery firing before the ceasefire with the result that one JCO and 2 OR were killed and one officer and 5 OR including 2/Lt. P.K. Ghosh were wounded on 23 September.

The operations of 1 Corps came to an end on the night of 23 September. Much could have been achieved by this force consisting of one armoured division and three infantry divisions. The initiative was with us and we had achieved complete surprise when the operations were launched. As per General Harbaksh Singh our performance was deplorable and the Corps failed to achieve its objectives. The approach to battle was sluggish and complacent. It is said that the Corps Commander had virtually no control over GOC 1 Armoured Division who fought his own battle. The division was very cautious and lost many fleeting opportunities that would have unhinged the enemy and brought glory to us. Coordination between 1 Armoured Division, 6 Mountain and 14 Infantry Division during the battle of Chiwanda-Zaffarwal was missing. In this Corps battle, the Corps Commander did not play an effective and forceful role and the rot permeated to the lower echelons of command as well. Leadership, both at the higher level and battalion and brigade levels was dismal. The commanders were not bold and enterprising. They failed to lead from the front with the result they did not have a grip over the fast-changing situation in a fluid environment.

26 Infantry Division was a well trained and old formation that had been in the operational area since 1948. It showed no enterprise and was content to capture a few villages two to three km into enemy territory. The GOC, Major General M.L. Thapan was a very cautious and conventional commander whose contribution to the operations of 1 Corps was negligible. With the force available to him, he could have easily threatened and invested Sialkot on his own to speed up the operations of 1 Corps. His division virtually sat through the war. The operations of 52 Mountain Brigade were the only silver lining. The operations of 1 Corps were a classic study in command failure and poor execution. With poor leadership at all levels, disaster in most battles was inevitable. The outcome of the campaign was disappointing.

The next day, we moved out to lay claim to as much area as possible and to hold it physically. On 24 or 25 September, a JCO of the Pakistan army along with two jawans appeared in front of our Company with a white flag. He was very smart and immaculately dressed in khaki uniform. Major B.S. Negi and I met him about 300 mtrs ahead of our sentry post. He congratulated us on our success and mentioned that the raid on their post was remarkable and that they were shaken by the daring act of the raiding party. His company was deployed in front of us. Since the ceasefire had been ordered, he was duty bound not to violate it and requested us to do the same. He was a Second World War veteran and recollected his association with Indian Army officers of his regiment. After mutual assurances of goodwill, the meeting was over. 52 Infantry Brigade was withdrawn after declaration of the ceasefire and we were reverted to 19 Infantry Brigade. We consolidated our positions and laid extensive mine fields.

One night, we were awakened by two successive explosions. We suspected that the enemy was breaching the minefields and were put on alert. However, in the morning, we found that one of our patrols had strayed into the mine field and two fatalities had been caused by M 16 jumping mines. It was a tedious and herculean task to retrieve these casualties by the sappers who took considerable time to prod a two-foot wide and 100 yards long safe lane to pull the bodies out. We settled down to normal routine and our supply chain was restored. However there was no shortage of food as the villagers had left ample supply of flour, lentils, ghee and livestock. In November, I moved to the Battalion HQ as Intelligence Officer.

On 10 January 1966, the Tashkent Declaration was announced. As per the agreement, both countries were to vacate territory that had been occupied between 5 August 1965 and the ceasefire. This was to be completed by 25 February 1966. We were extremely saddened to learn about the death of Mr. Lal Bahadur Shastri[8] on 11 January at Tashkent where he had gone to sign the agreement with FM Ayub Khan. Our admiration of Mr. Lal Bahadur Shastri had gone up many notches during his bold conduct of the war. This diminutive person took bold decisions that surprised both his countrymen as well as the Pakistanis. He had coined the slogan 'Jai Jawan–Jai Kisan' in honour of soldiers and farmers who had sacrificed the most during those difficult days. India was facing a food crisis at that time and he declared that all Indians must forgo at least one meal a week to save food. We fasted every Tuesday under Major Sushil Kumar to confirm our solidarity with the cause. Some time in winter, Mr. Sunil Dutt, the famous actor, and his gorgeous and equally famous wife, Nargis Dutt, came to Jammu and performed a musical programme for the jawans in KC Theatre. It was a great performance by his team and we appreciated it very much.

From November to March till we finally moved back to our peace locations, a lot of reconnaissance was carried out for defensive and offensive operations. I accompanied the commanding officer to every corner of the division area of responsibility. I got to meet the Corps Commander, Lt. General P.O. Dunn and the legendary Major General Rajinder Singh 'Sparrow' who was the hero of the battle of Zoji La in 1948 and was now commanding 1 Armoured Division. All these commanders carried a great aura but unfortunately their achievements in the 1965 war were low. Except for some minor successes, it was a catalogue of lost opportunities. We made plans to defend Jammu along every possible approach from Pakistan.

In January, Major H.S. Mamik joined us as the second-in-command after completing his Staff College. It was my task to familiarize him with the battalion defended area. By now both sides were in eyeball to eyeball contact at most places. During a visit to our forward locations, Major Mamik, while scanning the enemy area through his binoculars, brought them down abruptly and started abusing the Pakistanis in Punjabi. He wanted to move away from the vantage point immediately. The Pakistani soldiers were resting, playing cards and cleaning their weapons when I had pointed out the landmarks to him. I was intrigued as to what had upset Major Mamik that made him lose his cool so suddenly. I scanned the post again through my binoculars and found that the entire post had lined up with their front trouser flap open and were making obscene gestures at him. It was in bad taste and not keeping with the high standards of the Pakistan army. Major Mamik was difficult to please. The battalion staff was a harried lot and were victims of his wrath on flimsy grounds. He was totally in contrast to Major Sushil Kumar who was a great team leader whereas Major Manik was just a bully.

We received orders to vacate enemy territory by the midnight of 24 February and occupy defences on our side of the border. The Battalion HQ moved to Bidipur and later to Baspur. I was tasked to supervise the withdrawal of B Company. I found that hordes of civilians had descended upon the Pakistani villages under our occupation and looted them wantonly. They carried away every article that they could lay their hands on including hay cutting machines, sugarcane crushers, beds, doors and windows, utensils and even quilts. They cut off the trees and carried away the wood. All the cattle were also carted away. The entire area was laid waste like in a scorched earth policy. These people refused to listen to orders and retorted that the Pakistanis were doing the same in areas under their occupation so they were paying them back.

Lt. Gen. Harbaksh Singh, the Army Commander, visited us. He was pleased with our performance even though we had played a minor role in the war. The battalion constructed a memorial at Karotana in remembrance of the men who had died in the war. Finally, in the first week of April, we returned to Damana. We marched the whole night in field service order wading through the cold waters of the Jammu Tawi River and its various channels. Thus ended the 1965 war.

Both sides made big claims at the end of war but it had ended in a stalemate with a marginal advantage for India. Whatever leverage that we had was given away at Tashkent. We had ample time to plan and judge Pakistani intentions after Kutch and infiltration in J&K and yet we failed miserably to appreciate the unfolding events. We were surprised in Chhamb and had our Air Force not been employed, the strategic Akhnoor bridge would have been lost. Our Air Force and Navy were not given enough warning to be ready. As a consequence, we lost a large number of aircraft on the ground and our Navy did not come into play at all.

Our politico-military objectives were not clear. Even if they were, we did not show adequate vigour to achieve them. Our initial gains in Punjab and J&K were not followed up and we simply recoiled under pressure retaining a narrow strip of land across the border. The loss of Chhamb and Jaurian was a big setback. 1 Corps had its own problems as a newly-raised formation. Gains made by 1 Corps were due to fluke or chance and military ingenuity hardly played any part in it. Similarly, 26 Infantry Division was timid and cautious. The road to Sialkot was open and yet it showed no enterprice or inclination to attack till 52 Infantry Brigade was loaned to it in the dying moments of the war. 19 Infantry Brigade virtually remained out of the war. They could have secured the area up to Tilakpur and Muhadipur on their own. The war has been rightly called 'A War of Missed Opportunities.'

Map 1: 5/11 Gorkha Rifles, Indo-Pak War, 1965

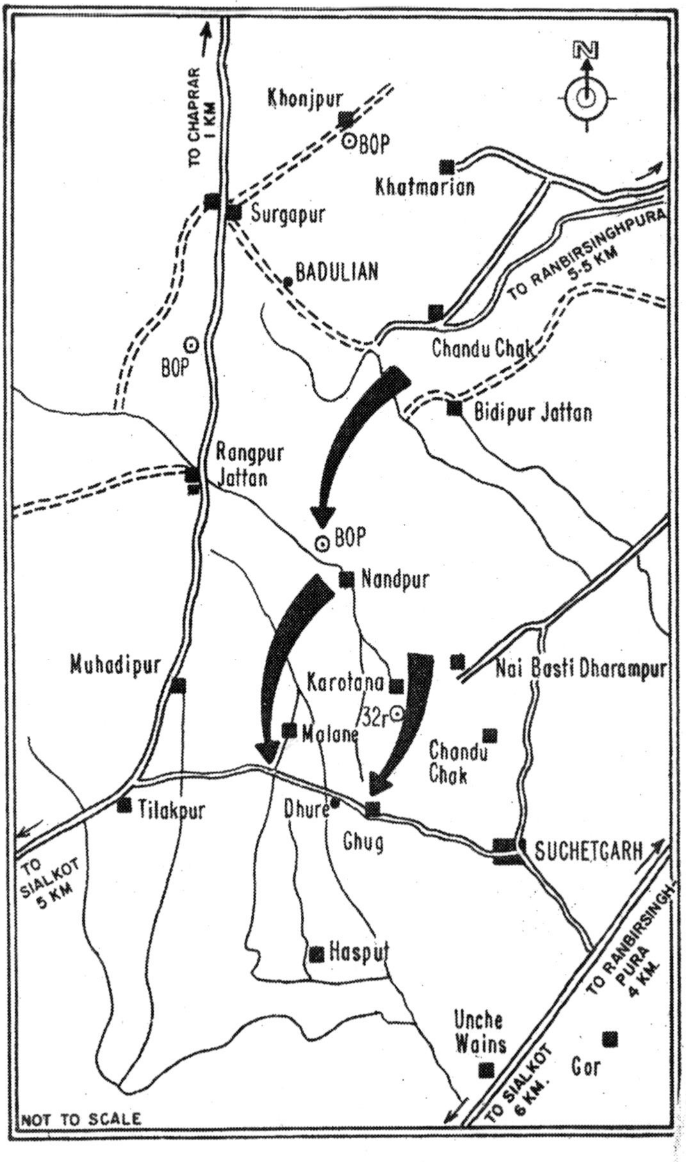

Map 2: Sialkot Sector, 1965

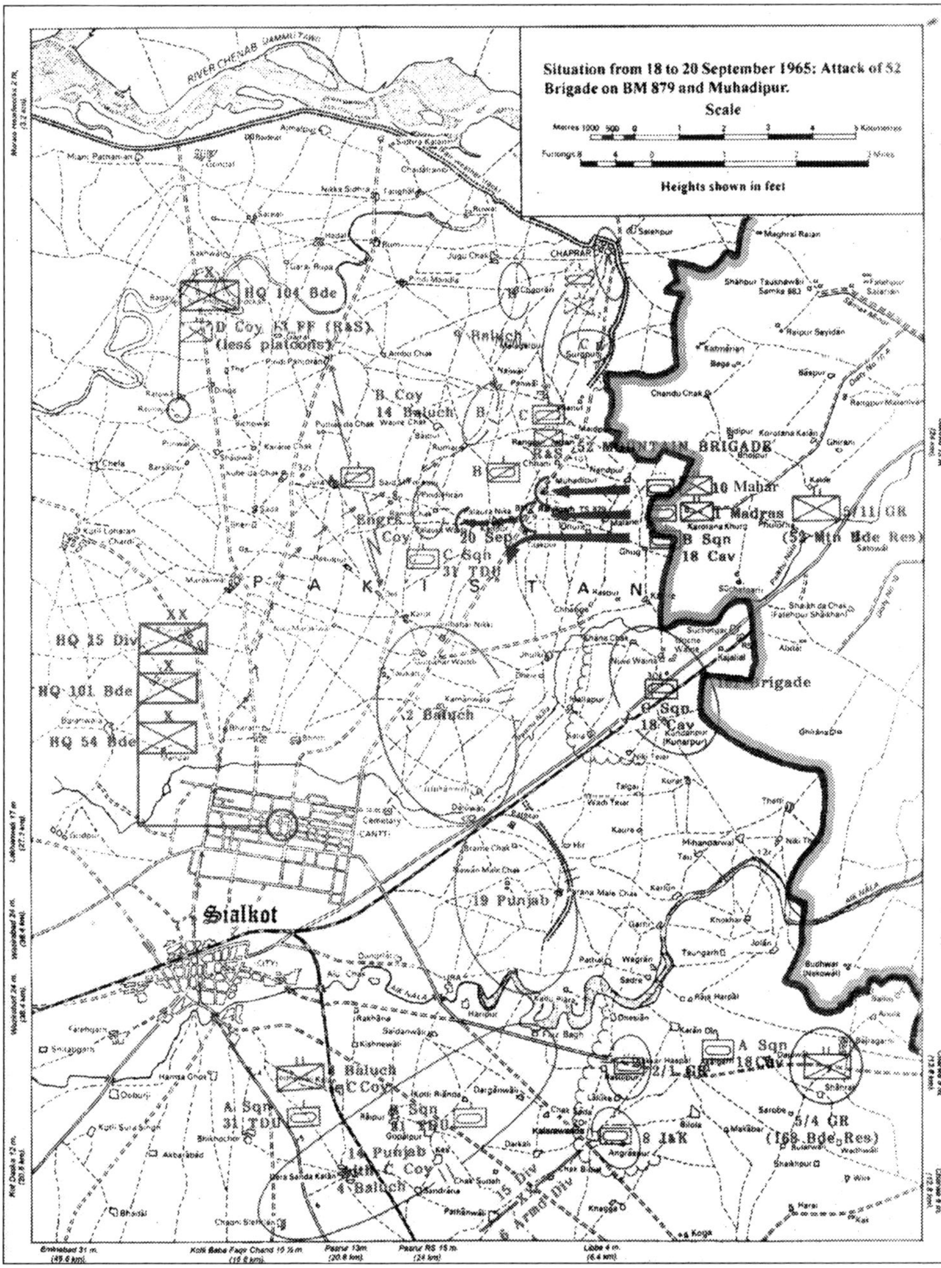

After the withdrawal from the border, the battalion settled down to peace station routine at Damana, a cantonment on the Jammu-Akhnoor road. The Ranbir canal flowed on the east and the Chenab River on the north. It made a beautiful sight. I was detailed for platoon weapons course at Infantry School, Mhow, in the summer of 1966. Mhow[9] was established as a cantonment by the British in 1818 after Sir John Malcolm defeated the Holkar to control the activities of all the rulers of Malwa plateau. An officers training academy was set up there during the World War II. The Infantry and Signal Schools were the premier training centres bubbling with activities. The climate was moderate and healthy throughout the year. We got ample opportunities to visit historic places like Indore, the capital of the Holkar state and now an important commercial town. We also visited Mandu fort that had been the capital of the Rajputs, Muslim kings and later the Mughals. The famous courtesan, Roopmati, and the warrior, Ala Udal belonged to this place. Maheshwar, the earlier capital of the Holkars, Ujjain the famous holy town and Dhar were also nearby. I did very well on the course and secured an 'A' grading.

By the time I returned to the battalion, it had been reverted to 7 Infantry Brigade of 4 Mountain Division and replaced 1/9 GR at Nahan, capital of Sirmoor state, now part of Himachal Pradesh. Nahan[10] is a small hill station and ideal place for rest and training. We occupied the British-era barracks that were quite comfortable. By that time, most of the families had also joined and many bachelors got married. Our training was orientated to mountain warfare as our operational role was to fight the Chinese now. The study of Chinese military organizations, weapons and equipment and tactics was compulsory during all discussions and model exercises.

I was sent on Infantry Signals course to Mhow in the winter. The School, now MCTE, is located in the old British barracks in a compact and well laid out area near the Bircha Lake, popular for picnics, angling and sailing. The Signals course was semi technical and very interesting. We learnt planning and execution of radio and line communications besides cipher and Morse code. We had to attain a high degree of proficiency, accuracy and speed in both encoding, decoding and Morse. I did extremely well on the course and this time scored an instructor's grading.

By the time I returned to the battalion, we were asked to move to Dharamshala,[11] an old British cantonment and a hill station in the Dholadhar mountains. The British established the cantonment in 1849 and in 1860 it became the home of 1 GR. The Depot Bazaar, Pensioner's Lines, Tirah Lines and Bharatpur Lines are all related to 1 GR. By now I was appointed the adjutant of the battalion. Although Dharamshala was a peace station, life was very busy with both peace and operational activities. Major General H.C. Rai, a World War II veteran who had seen service in the European theatre was General Officer Commanding. Since the performance of the Division in 1962 and 1965 wars had been dismal, he was determined to reclaim its past glory.

Thus, we spent a major part of our time preparing for quick mobilization. We practiced deep outflanking movements against the enemy in exercises and marched over razor-thin ridges in the Dhola Dhar ranges overlooking Mandi and Joginder Nagar at heights above 7,000 to 8,000 feet. Lt. Col. Sushil Kumar and the entire battalion were complimented by Lt. Gen. Harbaksh Singh, the Army Commander, for these professional achievements. During one of these exercises Major N. Bhasin, the vanguard commander, fell 200 feet in a gorge. He suffered severe head injuries and had to be evacuated on a stretcher the whole night by the men which was a test by itself in real casualty evacuation. He remained in a coma for over 20 days.

Next year, once again, we marched more than 40 km in the night, outflanking the enemy and staged a coup de main by capturing intact a bridge on the Ravi River at Chamba under Lt. Col. L.S. Rawat. We were once again singled out for appreciation during the summing up by the Army Commander. Our tenure in Dharamshala was indeed very eventful, besides heavy doses of training. Gen. Kumarmangalam, the COAS and Lt. Gen. P.S. Bhagat, VC, visited the battalion. Dharamshala had many places in and around for sightseeing and hiking such as Kangra, Yol, Palampur, Alhilal, Mandi, Jogindernagar, Dalhousie and Kulu-Manali. The Nawab of Bahawalpur liked the Kangra valley and built a palace at Alhilal. It was later purchased by Maharaja Hari Singh for queen Tara Devi and named Tara Niwas. Our officers' mess and most of the officers' residences were of British vintage. They had a beautiful view of the snow-clad mountains and valleys. The bungalow of Chief Justice Mehar Chand Mahajan who had been the prime minister of Maharaja Hari Singh and later Chief Justice of India was a beautiful building. It overlooked a valley with a mountain brook.

I had the privilege of being invited by him along with Lt. Col. Sushil Kumar for tea at his residence. The other bungalow that needs to be mentioned belonged to a famous British painter, Alfred W. Hallet who stayed in Dharamshala after independence. He purchased this church property and renovated Carlton Cottage, the residence of a British major built in 1840, to rent out to tourists for additional income. He was tucked in a remote hill top of Dharamkot and lived in the lap of nature. The British cemetery in the church of St. John was yet another place worth mentioning. It had a very serene and peaceful environment. Here were buried the soldiers of the East India Company and their wives and children. The most prominent and elegant grave there was the memorial of the Governor-General and Viceroy, Sir James Bruce, the 8th Earl of Elgin, who died of exhaustion while travelling from Shimla to Sialkot on 20 November 1863. The church bell, beautifully cast and crafted weighing about one ton of brass, now rests on two stone pillars.

Then there was the Tibetan monastery at Macleodganj, the home of the Dalai Lama and offices of his government- in-exile since 1959. Macleodganj is now a mini-Tibet and many foreigners visit it in search of peace and spirituality. Our tenure at Dharamshala came to an end and we moved to Darbuk in Ladakh in summer of 1968 in 60 trucks. After halts at Chaki Bank, Ramban and Srinagar, we finally reached Sonamarg to acclimatize for seven days. Sonamarg is a beautiful meadow with green pastures and snow-clad mountains all around. Our routine was mandated as per the training manual. Every day, the altitude of training increased till we were able to work effortlessly above 12,000 feet. In this process we visited Amarnath cave via Baltal. The full-size ice Shivling was in an undisturbed state in the cave in its original shape and form.

Besides the religious mythology connected with the Shivling, it is basically an ice formation due to dripping of water in the limestone cave.

The ice thus formed is shaped like a Shivling by the winds that swirl around it. It was discovered hundreds of years ago and is venerated by Hindu sadhus; it is now a famous pilgrimage centre. The one-day trek was long and difficult but extremely enjoyable through scenic country and clean water streams flowing along. The flora and fauna was at its prime. We saw beautiful flowers, rabbits, mountain goats and marmots along the way. After seven days we embarked on our journey again. Our first halt across the Zoji La Pass was at Drass. It was very windy and immediately to the north of the pass there was no greenery.

The Ladakh region had started. It was stark barren with rocky peaks and valleys. The climb and descent was laborious for the vehicles due to the harsh terrain and lack of oxygen. Temperatures there are as low as minus 40 degrees in winter. The next day, we made it to Kargil, first along the Suru River and then along the Indus. On the third day, we were in Leh. We reached Darbuk, our destination, after following a strict acclimatization regime again for seven days at Leh. The road to Darbuk via Karu and over Changla was quite torturous. The convoy negotiated the slopes and acute curves with great difficulty and it was no mean feat on part of the drivers.

We replaced 1/9 GR and became part of 114 Infantry Brigade. The Tangtse valley is above 12,000 feet. The mountains are generally 17,000 to 20,000 feet high and most passes are above 14,000 feet. There is scanty rain but plenty of snow during winter. Winters last from October to March when temperatures dip below minus 15 degrees. Summers are mild when some agricultural activities take place. Since the plateau is above the tree line in the rain shadow area, only a few trees like willow, peaches and apples grow in the valleys. Snow leopards, ibex, mountain goats and some rodents live on the mountains. Double-hump camels are found in the Nubra and Syok valleys. The wild ass is found in the plains of Kiari and Chusul. The yak is the domestic all-purpose animal. Ponies and mules are also found in small numbers. The apso and Tibetan mastiff are famous dog breeds. 114 Mountain Brigade had fought valiantly under Brig T.N. Raina against the Chinese at Chusul and Rezangla. Much has already been written about Ladakh and the Indo-China War of 1962. I will give my impressions as I perceived the events then. Topographically, Ladakh is enclosed by the

Karakoram Range, the Hindu Kush, the Zanskar, Greater Himalayas and the Tibetan plateau. The people are of Indo-Aryan and Tibetan descent. Baltistan, Upper Indus Valley, Zanskar, Lahaul-Spiti, Ngari, Rudok, Guge and Aksai Chin are part of Ladakh. The Ladakh plateau is a unique high-altitude desert. The general height of the valleys is 10,000 to 12,000 feet. The strategic importance of Ladakh lies in the ancient trade routes that cross through it and the immense minerals hidden under the mountains.

Historically, Ladakh was a Buddhist country ruled by independent kings till the thirteenth century. Islam penetrated through Baltistan. Ladakh always looked for spiritual guidance from Tibet when besieged by Muslim invaders while the Namgyal rulers ensured its independence. In 1834, Zorawar Singh the Dogra general of Maharaja Ranjit Singh, annexed Ladakh for the Sikh empire. The Namgyal ruling family became a principality of Stok which is nominally held by them even today. After the Anglo-Sikh wars, the control of Ladakh passed into the hands of the Dogras till 26 October 1947. The British had defined the boundaries between Ladakh and Tibet that India inherited in 1947. Tribal invaders had occupied areas of Kargil and Leh in 1947 and had to be evicted by Indian forces. Because of its strategic importance, the British connived with Pakistan who occupied Baltistan in 1947 with the help of the British agent and officers with Gilgit Scouts.

In 1949, China closed the border between Nubra and Xinjang and in 1954 it occupied Aksai Chin. The administrative division of Ladakh was formed after independence. Ladakh by now had 39 per cent Buddhist, 12 per cent Hindu and 46 per cent Muslim population. India did not take any action militarily or diplomatically when the Chinese occupied Aksai Chin. Our farthest post was at Chusul and our patrols went only up to Lanak pass. Although we claimed Aksai Chin, we never ventured into this territory nor did we explicitly tell the Chinese that it was Indian territory till 1958.[12] In 1956, the Chinese commenced construction of a road through Aksai Chin and we took no action.

By the time the Chinese presence became public it was late. India tried to show its presence by patrolling the area with two J&K Militia battalions that were located in Ladakh. 1/8 GR joined them in the summer of 1961 and 5 Jat in June 1962. They were grouped under 114 Mountain Brigade when the Forward Policy[13] was adopted from October/November 1961. At the time of the war, 5 Jat was located in Chip Chap and Galwan, 1/8 GR was in the Pangong-Spangur lakes Gap and 13 Kumaon was at Chusul. Initially, the Jats and Gorkhas were deployed in small pockets as part of the forward policy. Subsequently, the Gorkhas and Kumaonis were deployed in properly defended areas to protect Chusul, the vital ground. When talks between the two countries failed to resolve the dispute, a brief war was fought in October-November 1962. Although China was able to push back the Indians to the line of their claim, the Gorkhas and Kumaonis fought well. 3 Mountain Division was raised and deployed in Ladakh post 1962 to stop further incursions by the Chinese. From these events we can only conclude that India virtually gifted away Aksai Chin to China, a territory that was under us since 1834.

After Leh had been secured by October 1948, we did not take possession of the area up to the border and allowed the Chinese to occupy it without protest till it was too late. Leh was not connected even by a road till 1960. J&K militias and an odd infantry battalion were located at and around Leh without adequate logistic support. By the time we reached there in August 1968, the situation was stable. The 114 Mountain Brigade was defending the Lukung and Chusul axes. The 70 Mountain Brigade was defending the Kiari axis and 163 Mountain Brigade at Karu was in depth as reserve. Our main task was to patrol up to the Line of Actual Control and link up with ITBP outposts.

We had located one company each at Lokung and Chusul as advance positions in the event of war. Dorbuk-Tangtse was a formidable defensive complex and it could not have been defeated easily as long as it was well stocked and the troops fought with determination. Bypassing it was not easy, capturing it was difficult. Our defences were strong and well stocked to fight for more than three months. We were supplied by road during summer and air during winter. We had plenty of water. The medical facilities were adequate. The battalion was concentrated at the base and could occupy its defences within four hours. Our highest position was called 'one less' because the height of this mountain top was one foot less than 20,000 feet. It was difficult to live at that height without oxygen but live we did to fight and defeat the Chinese. The other positions were equally difficult at 14,000 to 17,000 feet and above.

The initial two days were difficult but then we got acclimatized and were comfortable. Our stay at Tangtse after the first six months was uneventful. Besides patrolling to Hot Springs, Chang Chenmo River and link up patrols to Karakoram Pass, the Shyok and Nubra River valleys, we practiced our deployment drills every year. The view of Pangongso was simply breathtaking. Tso-Muriri was another enchanting place. There were many hot water geysers in this area that sprouted water to a considerable height. The mountains, valleys, lakes and rivers presented different panoramas in each season. It was a beautiful white, crimson or yellow shade of snow on the mountain tops in winter. Lakes and rivers were sheets of blue ice over which even our vehicles could move. Ice hockey was a popular sport during winter. The spring brought greenery in the valleys and some mountain slopes were covered with wild flowers. The lakes were host to thousands of migratory birds. Summers were pleasant. Autumn was stark barren—all brown like a moon, very dull and boring.

The locals lived in small villages around our camps. They were very gentle, friendly, hardworking, religious and honest people. We provided them employment as porters. They also acted as our guides and provided us mules and yaks for transportation. The womenfolk were very sturdy and were always dressed traditionally. There were no schools or hospitals except in Leh. The Ladakhis made excellent soldiers. They had fought bravely against the Pakistanis in 1947 and 1965. They were great assets in 1962 against the Chinese. Our brigade commander was Brigadier Chaju Ram, a veteran of the 1965 war. He was a good administrator and strict disciplinarian. He was replaced by Brigadier H.C. Dutta, 8 GR, a great professional. He broke the invincibility myth of the Chinese by practically proving to us that they could be easily defeated. The brigade organized tactical exercises without troops on likely battle options. Battle and terrain studies were also carried out. We practiced pre-emptive offensive operations, spoiling attacks, and operations behind enemy lines of communications, aggressive defence operations and counter-attacks. Brig. Dutta brought life into the operational environment and taught us manoeuvre operations in high altitudes.

Thereafter the orientation of the entire division changed from defensive to offensive defence and attack operations. We stayed mostly inside dugouts during winter when the temperatures were below minus 30 during the night and minus 10 during the day. The Tangtse-Darbuk stream froze completely and we had to melt ice for cooking and bathing. The oil stoves were our best friends. The winter also gave us ample time to study. I prepared for my Part B exam that I passed easily. During the winter, predators like snow leopards would descend to prey on local dogs, sheep or baby yaks. Our meat on the hoof was normally air-dropped once a week by Russian-built AN 12 aircraft from the supply depot at Chandigarh. These sheep were kept in pens. We found every morning that one or two had died with wounds around their throats. The injuries indicated presence of a leopard in the vicinity.

Nb. Sub. Man Bahadur, a hunter, was given the task of tracing the predator. Snow leopards are an endangered animal and shooting them was prohibited unless declared a man eater or in self-defence. Our efforts to trap it had failed as it continued to avoid the traps and got away with its kill every time. Man Bahadur took a few days to track it after studying its pattern. It was found basking in the early morning sun on a rock and it was a sudden and unexpected confrontation. Man Bahadur did not take any chances and shot the leopard. The skin adorns our officers' mess. When I had completed about one year in Ladakh, the GOC, Major General P. Choudhary, got me posted to the division headquarters as the GSO3 Operations. I was quite happy with my posting after five years of regimental duty.

The Division HQ was located at Leh. The Indus River flowed to the west with Hemis Gompha on top of the hill. The airport was about five km away. The residential area was in the shadow of a mountain and the offices were about two km away in a bowl surrounded by hills that could not be easily attacked by air. Over the past five years, many facilities had come up to reduce the hardships of living. A sports stadium had been constructed where most competitions were held. There was a cinema hall where movies were screened regularly for all ranks. Entertainment troupes also staged shows in this hall. The supply depot met our bakery and confectionary requirements. The MH was air conditioned and a fully functional all-specialist hospital. We had two transit camps that were well furnished and equipped for prolonged halts due to bad weather, road blocks or irregular traffic. There was heavy road and air traffic between June and November when winter stocking, induction and de-induction of units took place. Almost every item had to be transported from the hinterland as Ladakh had no resources at all. Besides all food, fuel and war-like stores, complete building, engineering, electrical and communications material had to be brought in convoys. Electricity was produced by diesel generators for hospitals and essential requirements. We depended on kerosene lamps for lighting and heating.

The division HQ had efficient staff who worked diligently. Lt. Col. Wakankar, an artillery officer, was the GSO 1 and Major D.V. Kalra, AOC, the GSO2 as my superiors. Maj. Kalra was a brilliant staff officer. I learnt a lot under his tutelage and he laid the foundation of my staff work. I not only monitored the day-to-day operational activities of the division frontage but also managed the operations room. I accompanied the GOC on all operational visits and thus was most knowledgeable about the terrain and the operational matters in the division. After the visit of Lt. Gen. Sartaj Singh, Corps Commander, sometime in late 1970, the operational orientation changed to offensive operations. Every brigade was exercised in offensive operations by the division HQ. This not only improved our operational capabilities but also broke many myths related to Chinese capabilities. Major H.S. Choudhary, our DAQMG, was another outstanding officer. He was an air observation officer and very talented. After the back-breaking working days I would accompany him for trout fishing in the Indus or for photography in the hills and developing them in the dark room as a hobby.

Only IAF planes operated at Leh, Thoise, Chusul and Fukche airfields. Foreigners and civilians were not allowed to visit. It had remained a non-family station since 1948. The division undertook a mountaineering expedition to Phunangma, a virgin peak in the Sasir Kangri complex of the Eastern Karakorams as part of adventure training. Major P.R.C. Naidu, 2/4 GR, was the leader and I his deputy. We landed at Thoise in a C-119 Packet aircraft that was fitted with a booster engine. It was a marvel that this vintage aircraft could still fly. All the parts rattled and it appeared that they were coming apart when it crossed the Khardungla Pass. Capt F.J. Bahadur, 2/4 GR, along with four others was able to scale the peak. Trekking through the Nubra and Syok valleys was an exhilarating experience.[14]

Maj. Gen. S.C. Malhotra, Guards, replaced Gen. P. Choudhary. The relations between India and Pakistan had deteriorated due to hijacking and destruction of an Indian airlines plane from Srinagar to Lahore on 30 January 1971. Gen. Malhotra visited all the brigades to review their operational plans in anticipation. I visited Pratap Pur sector, especially Turtuk, along with the General Officer to review their plans. Pratap Pur sector was defended by four companies of Ladakh Scouts. This was the most dormant sector at that time but during the 1971 war, it was the only sector that made news as India made some modest territorial gains. The capture of Turtuk opened the avenues to Siachen Glacier and Skardu. This task was accomplished by Major Rinchin of the Ladakh Scouts. However we could have made substantial gains if the operations had been launched from Sirchip with a bigger force. I had completed about two and a half years in high altitude by March 1971. I was posted back to my battalion that was located at Jaurian under Lt. Col. F.T. Dias.

Chhamb-Jaurian is strategically very important for both India and Pakistan. Pakistan had tried to capture this area since 1947. In 1965, they nearly succeeded had the IAF not been employed. We were part of 191 Infantry Brigade of 10 Infantry Division. The other battalions were 5 Sikh at Dewa, ahead of Manawar Tawi, 5 Assam and 4/1 GR. Our defences were based on the Kalit-Troti-Dhon-Chak Ridge. We practiced countless counter-attacks on Mandiala heights and other important features should the enemy penetrate our forward defences. The main emphasis was on defensive battle; an offensive in Pakistan was never discussed. No one thought of posing a threat to Pakistan's sensitive hinterland. This thought process was eventually enunciated by Major General Jaswant Singh, the

GOC to the COAS, in October/November 1971 during a review of the operational readiness.

It was a bold and brilliant plan that was accepted reluctantly by his superiors who did not help him execute it smoothly. If launched, it would have accrued great strategic advantage. Even when the offensive by 23 Pakistan infantry division had been blunted by 09/10 December and the enemy had thinned out considerably to reinforce the Shakargarh sector, the offensive was not launched to evict and reclaim the lost areas. That is a strategic disadvantage even today.

The situation in the subcontinent had changed dramatically after rebellion in East Pakistan had broken out on March 25/26. In the end of June 1971, four Pakistan Army Bengali officers defected and surrendered to our post near the international border. These four officers were Captain Mohiuddin Jehangir, Captain Anam, Captain Salahuddin and Captain Shahriar Rashid Khan. On interrogation, they revealed that after the crackdown in East Pakistan they had decided to quit and join the liberation struggle. They got together in Green Café at Sialkot on a Sunday and told their superiors that they were going on a picnic. They travelled in a taxi short of Marala HW. Then they walked towards the border and hid in the tall grass for the day. At dark, they changed into Pakistani Ranger uniform and slipped through the border to India undetected. They swam across the Manwar Tawi and surrendered to a post of my battalion. These officers were despatched to New Delhi immediately. Later, they joined the Mukti Bahini and fought bravely for the liberation of the country. By July we had received our orders to move to Trivandrum and handed over to 10 Garhwal Rifles. However, we were diverted to join 20 Mountain Division in the Eastern Theatre. Speculations of a war were rife and in that eventuality, we were sorry to leave Chhamb-Jaurian where we had trained for such a contingency. Some of the bloodiest and fiercest battles of the 1971 war in the western sector[15] were fought there.

Map 3: Battle of Chamb: Deployment of 191 Infantry Brigade, 3 Dec 1971

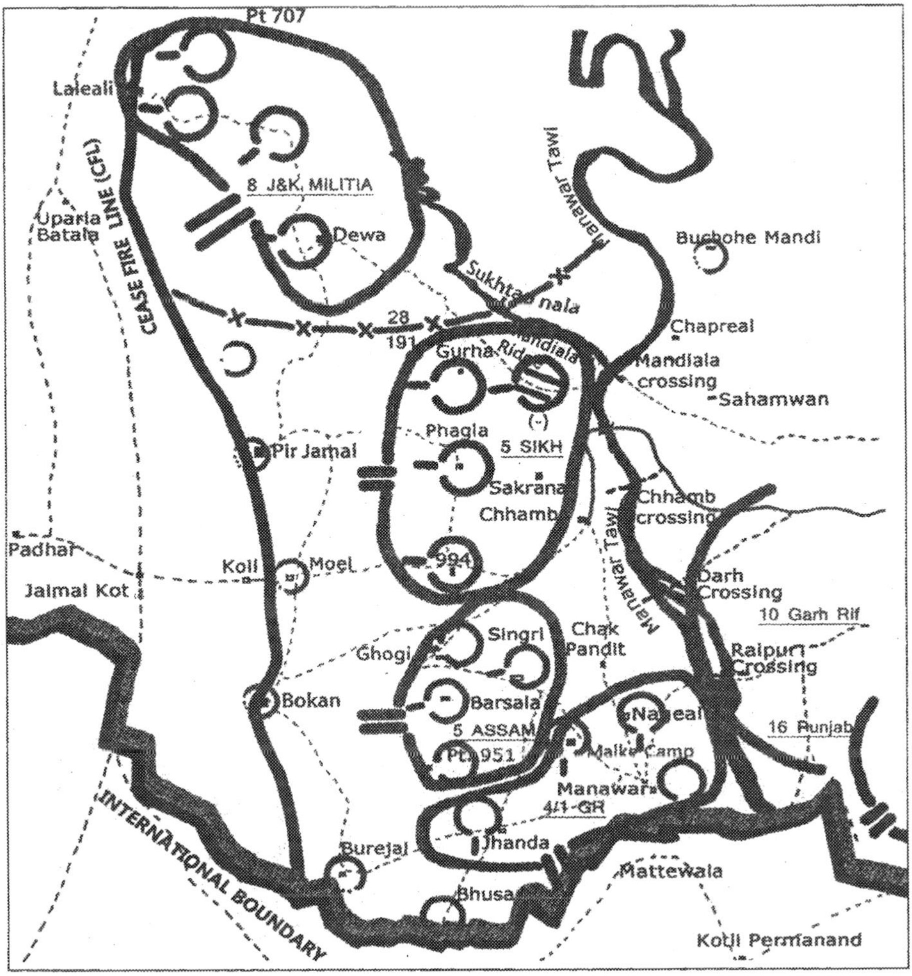

Map 4: Battle of Chamb: Pakistan offence, 4 Dec 1971

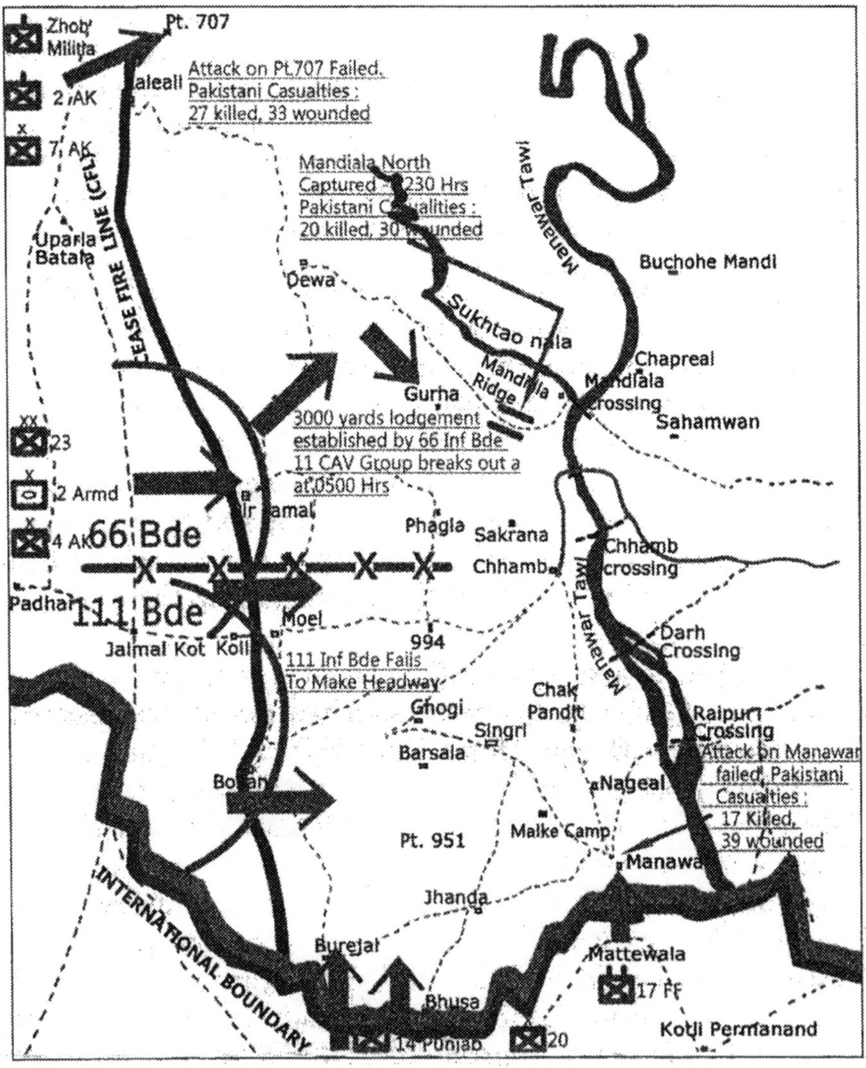

Map 5: Battle of Chamb, 10 Dec 1971

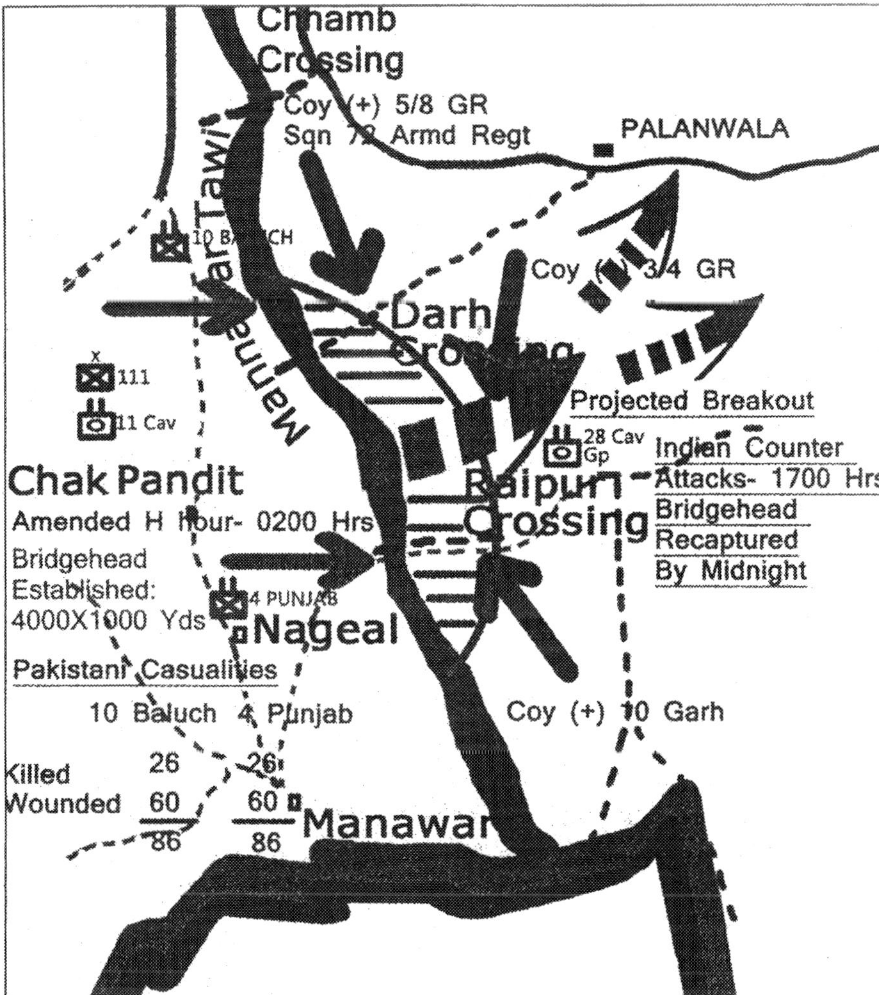

NOTES

1. *Lal Bahadur Shastri* by C.P. Srivastav. Biography of Mr. Shastri.
2. *The Pakistan Army War* 1965 by Major General Shaukat Riza, p. 20.
3. Web site on the Bhuttos .
4. *The Pakistan Army 1965 War* By Major General Shaukat Riza, Ch. 3, pp. 77-102.
5. *The War Despatches* by Lt. Gen. Harbaksh Singh, p. 25; *Missed Opportunities* by Maj. Gen. Lachhman Singh, pp. 127-132; *Lal Bahadur Shastri* by C.P. Srivastav.
6. *War Despatches* by Lt. Gen. Harbaksh Singh, p. 103, 159-62.
7. *War Despatches* by Lt. Gen. Harbaksh Singh, p. 157; *The Pakistan Army war 1965* by Maj. Gen. Shaukat Riza, p. 178.
8. Read *Lal Bahadur Shastri* by C.P. Srivastav for details of negotiations and death of Mr. Shastri.
9. *The Last Post at Mhow* by Arthur Hawkey - Glimpse in a British cantonment in India and *From A Sepoy to Subedar* by Sita Ram Pandey - Life of an Indian soldier in the service of the Bengal Native Infantry.
10. The state of Sirmoor was founded by a Bhati Prince, Raja Rasaloo from Jaisalmer, in 1095. Nahan became the capital in 1621. The Rajas of Nahan helped Guru Gobind Singh to fortify Paota Sahib against the Mughals. The Gorkhas occupied Nahan briefly. The state was restored to the king by the British. The rulers of Sirmoor helped the British in the Anglo-Sikh and Anglo-Afghan wars. *Tarik-i-Riyasat Sirmaur* by Kanwar Ranzor Singh.
11. Dharamshala was part of Kangra State ruled by the Katoch family. Under the treaty of Jawalamukhi in 1810, Maharaja Ranjit Singh annexed much of its territory reducing the status of the ruler to a mere jagirdar.
12. *India's China War* by Neville Maxwell, pp. 95, 159.
13. *India's China War* by Neville Maxwell, p. 204.
14. Detailed account published in *Sainik Samachar* 20 December 1970; *The Gorkha 1970-71*, p. 122; *The Owl 1977-78*, p. 72.
15. *Battleground Chhamb* by Major General A.J.S. Sandhu, chapters 3, 7 & 8.

Chapter 3

The War for Liberation of Bangladesh

Many important events had taken place in the subcontinent by the end of August 1971, creating a war-like situation when we reached Kishanganj. A devastating cyclone in November and elections in East Pakistan in December 1970,[1] the hijacking of an Indian plane on 30 January 1971,[2] the crackdown in East Pakistan on 25/26 March 1971,[3] and a revolt by Bengalis and the mass exodus of refugees to India were among them. The chasm between the two wings of Pakistan was unbridgeable and the alienation of Bengalis was complete. Yahya Khan, the president, Vice Admiral S.M. Ahsan, the Governor of East Pakistan, and Sahabzada Yakub Khan,[4] MLA and Commander, Eastern Command, had handled the situation most insensitively. Mujib-ur-Rehman was denied the post of PM after the Larkana conspiracy[5] that was hatched by Bhutto in January 1971. Unrest by the Awami League led to 'Operation Search Light' under Lt. Gen. Tikka Khan[6] to teach them a lesson.

Mass-scale wanton killings and massacre of Bengali students, intellectuals and innocent population; rape of Bengali women, destruction of property, pillage and looting took place. When Niazi took over as Eastern Army Commander from Tikka Khan, the atrocities committed by the forces multiplied manifold. An influx of more than ten million refugees from East Pakistan to India took place. During the initial stage of the revolt, the entire country, except for the cantonments, was under the control of the rebels. A Government of Bangladesh-in-exile had been established on Indian territory.

India was in a precarious situation and great dilemma. These events could not be ignored in the strategic context. The Bengali population of

East Pakistan looked to India for help in their existential crisis. This humanitarian crisis posed security and immense financial burdens on India. The West and the Islamic world that were heavily tilted towards Pakistan were not ready to recognize this tragedy and refused to help India or the hapless Bengalis. India was friendless and the USSR was the only country that stood by it in this hour of crisis. The Indo-USSR defence agreement signed in August 1971 gave us some confidence and comfort.

Our military special train was given top priority and we travelled from Chakki Bank to Kishanganj nonstop. I, as the officer in charge, military special, rode in the driver's cabin to ensure that we reached our destination on time. We billeted near Kishanganj with the rest of the brigade and immediately got down to train in offensive operations in riverine terrain. Emphasis was given to infantry-tank cooperation, bunker bursting, fighting in built-up areas, waterman-ship training, and night operations. The monsoon was at its peak during this period and we were always drenched and wet. The humidity, mosquitoes, leeches, and snakes made life miserable. However this did not affect our training or morale. While the concentration of the Indian forces was progressing steadily, we went through numerous discussions and reconnaissance trips to the border to finalize our plans. Here, it is important to recapitulate some of the other events that had taken place between April and September 1971. Lt. Gen. A.A.K. Niazi had replaced Tikka Khan in April 1971. By this time, the strength of the Pakistan Army rose from one to four divisions. Gen. Niazi launched operations and applied brute force to regain control and by the end of May, he had driven the rebels out of their strongholds. Niazi had carried out his operations in four phases. He sealed the routes of infiltration and ex-filtration in phase 1 and opened up all essential river, road, and rail communications in phase 2. Coastal areas were cleared of the Mukti Bahini in phase 3 and all rebel resistance defeated in phase 4.

During these operations, the conduct of the Pakistan Army was horrific, depraved, and ruthless. They crossed all limits of humanity and violations of human rights.[7] The Hindu population suffered the maximum. Young people were tied with ropes in groups, painted with a number on their backs, and then made to scramble towards the border while the Pakistanis fired at them as targets. None of them reached the border. Army units would cordon a village or town and then bombard it. Most of the fleeing men and women would be mowed down with automatic fire and those unable to escape would be burnt inside their houses by the fire caused by the bombardment. The town would then be looted. The loot was shared between the officers and men. Most of it such as cars, electronic goods, and gold was transported to West Pakistan. Raping of young women was carried out on a competitive basis in the name of Islam. Young women were kept in camps as sex slaves.

Some of these acts were so heinous and barbaric that a few god-fearing JCOs and NCOs deserted their units rather than be part of these sinful activities. These horrendous actions however failed to break the spirit of Bengali nationalism. They put up a valiant resistance and retreated to Indian territory to continue with the struggle for independence. The main reasons for the failure of the rebels were inadequate leadership, lack of higher organization, coordination, and proper planning. They also lacked artillery and heavy arms. They adopted inappropriate tactics and their logistics was weak. The rebels used conventional tactics when operations were launched against them. They were easily defeated by the Pakistan army. Major Zia-ur-Rahman,[8] Khalid Musharraf,[9] Saifullah, Usman and Jalil emerged as the main rebel leaders.

Indo-Pak relations had been strained ever since Pakistan had invaded Kashmir in 1947 and particularly after the 1965 war. India had accommodated all concerns of that country to its own detriment including the Indus Water Treaty so that the two could live in peace. Yet they availed every opportunity to interfere in India's internal affairs and fomented trouble in one state or the other, including Nagaland and Mizo Hills. There was thus a strong feeling among every Indian to teach Pakistan a lesson by taking advantage of the revolt in East Bengal. Indian strategic thinkers including Mr. K. Subramaniam felt the dismemberment of Pakistan would be in our favour. The circumstances were now opportune to achieve this. The Indian Border Security Force had provided some limited support to the rebels in the initial stages but it was not enough to sustain the freedom movement. The suddenness of events had caught India by surprise and the

Indian Army was not prepared for active involvement at that stage. Senior Ministers including Mr, Jagjivan Ram, the Defence Minister, and Y.B. Chavan, the Finance Minister, wanted immediate involvement and urged Mrs. Indira Gandhi to take action. General S.H.F.J. Manekshaw, the COAS, was however against any hasty action that did not guarantee a total victory. He was able to prevail upon the PM. His reasons were:

The thrust of Indian war plans was mainly directed against West Pakistan and China. Plans against East Pakistan were limited in scope. New force levels and logistics had to be created for a major operation against four divisions that Pakistan had concentrated there by then. It would be difficult to operate during the monsoons in Bengal. Shortages in men, equipment, and ammunition needed to be made up to fight Pakistan on both fronts. A minimum of 8 to 9 divisions were required to fight in East Pakistan while the rest of the army, navy and air force had to be mobilized to fight against West Pakistan and China. These divisions had to be concentrated and trained for war. He could not guarantee success under the present state of preparedness based on the experience of the past three wars. The threat from China, an ally of Pakistan, had to be factored in. The best time to fight Pakistan was in winter when threat from China would be easy to handle. War with another country required international acceptance. Such a situation did not exist. Most countries still called the unrest an internal affair of Pakistan; and under such conditions India had no convincing reason to invade East Pakistan. Thus, the international opinion and strategic environment was not in favour of India.

The PM accepted the advice. Though the economic burden of 10 million refugees estimated at Rs. 525 crore a year was unbearable, still India hoped that the problem would be solved politically and decided to wait for the time being. However, it was decided to prepare for a war in a comprehensive and coordinated manner if it had to be fought. It should be at the time and place of our choosing.

The Mukti Bahini

It was also decided to train and equip the freedom fighters or Mukti Bahini for war against East Pakistan. The Eastern Command was given the task to organize, equip, train, coordinate and supervise the operations of the Mukti Bahini on 15 May without getting directly involved in the actual operations. Major General O.S. Kalkat, and later, Major General Majumdar were to oversee the operations and coordinate with the Government of Bangladesh-in-exile. The entire area was divided into A to E sectors with a brigadier in charge of each. These sectors established training camps close to the border. Able-bodied men from refugee camps were trained and equipped as freedom fighters. Colonel M.A.G. Usmani was appointed as the commander in chief. Eleven sectors were created by the Mukti Bahini, each commanded by a sector commander who had been an officer in the Pakistan Army. Besides the sectors, five battalions of the East Bengal Regiment that had defected, the personnel of East Pakistan Rifles and the police were grouped under K, S, and Z forces.

K Force under Lt. Col. Khalid Musharraf operated against Chittagong, S Force under Lt. Col. K.M. Saifiullah operated opposite Sylhet and Z force under Lt. Col. Zia-ur-Rahman operated opposite Mymensingh. The battalions were provided one battery each of 105 mm field guns beside all other weapons and radio communications by the Indian Army. Students composed the largest number of freedom fighters who were deeply committed and provided leadership to the movement. They contributed the maximum to the freedom struggle. Peasants were the foot soldiers as they were familiar with the terrain, could merge with the population, endure hardship and were not afraid to face the enemy. The operations of the freedom fighters can be divided into four phases. The revolt and retreat into India from 25 March to June in phase 1; reorganization and training in camps in India from July to September in phase 2; conduct of sabotage, guerrilla warfare, special ops and intelligence collection from October to 3 December in phase 3; and finally, conduct of joint operations with the Indian Army from 4 December till the liberation in phase 4.

It was aimed to train at least 20,000 freedom fighters a month in each camp so that by October one million of them were available. Amongst those who were trained at our camps was Sheikh Kamal, son of Sheikh Mujibur Rehman. Brigadier Shahbeg Singh, responsible for Sectors 1, 2, and 3 and K Force and Brigadier Uban who trained the special force contributed substantially to the success of the Mukti Bahini. They caused substantial damage, destruction and mayhem in the Chittagong area and other parts. The Indian Navy set up a special secret camp for naval operations called "Operation Jackpot". Activities in ports, river transportation and sea traffic around the ports virtually came to a halt due to their operations. The Indian RAW also set up a secret force under Sheikh Fazlul Huq Moni, a confidant of Sheikh Mujibur Rehman. They were highly motivated but politically aligned to the Awami League. The intelligentsia, writers, journalists and personnel of East Pakistan radio stations who had fled to India also actively supported the war. They operated the Swadhin Bangla Betar Kendra from Mujibnagar near Calcutta. A 50-KW transmitter was provided by India to them. They played a vital role in waging psychological war and sustaining the morale of the Mukti Bahini and the Bangladeshis.

5/11 GR was also associated with the operations of the freedom fighters. Capt. Kamei Gaigunglung and Capt. T.C. Bhagwati with 15 to 20 men were deputed to train and operate with them. Sector 6 located opposite Rangpur and Dinajpur and Sector 7 opposite Rajshahi and Naogaon were in our area and they operated from a lodgement inside East Pakistan opposite Malda. Capt. Jahangir Mohiuddin, who had surrendered to us in Chhamb sector in May, was in charge here and we were happy to meet him again. He died while leading a daring assault on the Pakistan army position at Nawabganj on 13 December 1971 and was posthumously awarded "Bir Srestho", the highest award for bravery.

Among the others who had surrendered to us, Capt. Salahuddin was a staff officer in the HQ and retired as a colonel, while Capt. Khairul Anam operated with sector 4 and Capt. Sultan Shahriar Rashid Khan with sector 6. Both retired as Lt. Col. The Mukti Bahini had performed very well. They tied down a substantial number of Pakistani troops on lines of communication duties and created the fear of the unknown in them. They also disabled power supply, and damaged the Chittagong oil refinery and railway network. The Pakistan army also created the East Pakistan civil armed force and the razakars to counter the Mukti Bahini. Their task was to guard bridges, railway lines, and installations and reinforce police and border posts. Most of them were Biharis and loyal to Pakistan. Two other forces called Al Badr and Al Shams were also created from among members of Jamaat-e-Islami, a rabidly fundamentalist set up and Bengali traitors. They were controlled by Major General Rao Farman Ali, the advisor to the governor. Their task was to assassinate intellectuals, collaborators and designated targets and terrorize the Bengalis to weaken the freedom movement. They also carried out sabotage and internal disturbances in border areas.

By October, India was convinced that war was inevitable. The PM made a final attempt to convince the world community to resolve the problem. She undertook a three-week tour of the USA, France, West Germany, Britain and Australia from 23 October onwards. The world community however failed to respond. Therefore, the formations were ordered to move to their concentration areas. My battalion moved to Malda, while I stayed back and was given the responsibility to protect the Kishanganj corridor. Our vital rail and road communications to Assam and the North-East passed through this narrow corridor. Kishanganj was a Muslim-majority area. It was very fertile but under-developed and impoverished. Since I was in charge of the security of this area, I included the deputy collector and superintendent of police in the operations. I held a very tight control over the area with constant patrolling, flag marches and random checks.

The Pakistanis managed to explode a bomb in the local cinema hall in the heart of the city that killed several people. I had left the cinema hall only a few minutes before the explosion. Their attempts to sabotage rail and road communications were however foiled. Because of massive poverty, Kishanganj was also notorious for human and animal trafficking between India and East Pakistan. The local weekly *haat* not only traded agricultural produce but also girls as young as 12 and women. These girls and women were exhibited in open thatched huts for as little as Rs. 2. Such poverty, human degradation and depravity were a shame. Venereal diseases and other infections was rampart because of the cheap and open sex trade. This market also harboured many spies and saboteurs so it was imperative to keep it under strict surveillance. In spite of my strict vigil, three jawans became victims to carnal temptation. They were discharged from service by me for violation of orders. During this period, I visited the border and 71 Mountain Brigade. They were responsible for the defence of the Siliguri corridor and were deployed opposite Pachagarh and Thakurgaon. Cross-border firing with Pakistan had commenced. Later, towards November, they widened the corridor by capturing these two places. This gave us a fair idea of the defence works and strong fortified localities that the Pakistanis had created. I met a number of Mukti Bahini personnel returning to their bases after carrying out operations. They looked cheerful and confident. As November neared, the firing became more frequent and intense.

From May to October, feverish activities were taking place for the build-up for war. Deficiencies of weapons, equipment and manpower were made up in our battalion. All weapons, vehicles, communications and other equipment were repaired, tested and fired before the war. The logistics areas were created. Bridging and river crossing equipment was dumped in the concentration areas. All ammunition and supply depots were replenished. Hundreds of convoys and trains carrying stores passed through the Kishanganj corridor that I was guarding.

Area of Operations

East Pakistan was surrounded by India on three sides and the Bay of Bengal in the south. Three major rivers flow and divide the country in four distinct sectors. These rivers are so wide that it is difficult to see their far banks during the monsoon.

The North-Western sector is formed by the Ganga in the west and Brahmaputra, locally called Jamuna, in the east. It includes the areas of Dinajpur, Rangpur, Rajshahi, Pabna and Bogra. It is connected with the South-Western sector by Hardinge Bridge at Pabna and to the Northern sector by a ferry at Gaibanda and Sirajganj. 33 Corps (20 Mountain Division) was to operate in this sector.

The South-Western sector lies west of the Ganga or Padma and includes the area of Jessore, Khulna, Faridpur and Kushtia. 2 Corps (4 and 9 Mountain Division) was to operate in this sector.

The Nnorthern sector lies between the Jamuna and Meghna and

includes the areas of Dacca, Tangail and Mymensingh. 101 Area (95 Mountain Brigade) was responsible for this sector.

The Eastern sector lay east of the Meghna and consists of Sylhet, Comilla and Chittagong. 4 Corps (8, 23 and 57 Mountain Division) was to operate in this sector.

We were part of the North-Western sector that was strategically important to both India and Pakistan. Pakistan could interdict the Kishanganj-Siliguri corridor and the Farakka Barrage. They could also link up with China in Chumbi Valley separated by only 20 km, should they collude with Pakistan. India could easily sever the neck at Hilli and either roll down south or jump across the Jamuna and head for Dacca. The terrain was flat and fit for cross-country movement by track vehicles except during the monsoon. Wheeled vehicles could only move along the tracks but they could not sustain heavy traffic. Besides the Jamuna and Teesta rivers, there were numerous rivulets such as the Deepa, Atrai, Karatoya and Mahananda that ran north–south and created a water system that drained into the Jamuna. While small nalas could be forded during the winter, the main rivers required bridging to cross. Karatoya River was the main obstacle that ran almost parallel to the Rangpur-Bogra highway crossing it at Gobindganj and then again north of Bogra near Mahasthan. Another branch of this river was the Ichamati that also ran a somewhat similar course.

The road communication on the Indian side was good. We could move up to our concentration areas in vehicles. The road network on the Pakistani side was poor. There was only one all-weather north-south highway connecting Dinajpur-Rangpur-Bogra-Bera and then the ferry over the Jamuna to Dacca. A tarmac road also connected Nawabgang-Rajshahi-Ishurdi-Pabna to Bera. Tracks that were important to us were Phulbari-Nawabganj-Pirganj/Goraghat; Hilli-Jaipurhat-Naogaon; Jaipurhat-Khetlal-Bogra; and Bogra-Khetlal-Goraghat. A broad gauge railway line connected Hardinge Bridge, Ishurdi, Naogaon, and Hilli to Parvatipur. A metre-gauge line also connected Dianjpur, Rangpur, Gaibanda, Bogra, Naogaon, Nator, Rajshahi, and Nawabganj, Pabna and Sirajganj. Airports existed at Lalmanirhat and Ishurdi and airstrips at Thakugaon, Saidpur, Rangpur,

Bogra and Rajshahi. Biharis who had migrated from India formed the majority population. They were opposed to the Bengalis in their war of independence. It was apparent that the North-Western sector favoured the defender and was important to Pakistan.

Enemy Forces and Plans

East Pakistan was defended by 14 Infantry Division consisting of four brigades up to March 1971. The strength of the Pakistan army was increased to four divisions by the end of March after induction of 9, 16 and 39 infantry divisions. Thirty-five infantry battalions, seven wings of para military forces and 5,000 policemen were brought from West Pakistan. East Pakistan Civil Armed Force, mujahids and razakars were also created. There were six regiments of artillery and some independent mortar and field batteries. One regiment of Chaffee tanks, two independent squadrons of Chaffee tanks and some PT 76 tanks formed their armoured force. The Pakistan air force operated from Dacca with 20 to 25, F-86 (Sabre jet) and a flight of helicopters. The navy consisted of four gunboats and a number of river craft fitted with guns, operating in the coastal and inland waters. Chittagong was the main base. They were deployed as follows:

- 14 Infantry Division was at Bhairab Bazaar and responsible for the NE sector.
- 39 Infantry Division was located at Chandpur and responsible for the SE sector.
- 9 Infantry Division was located at Jessore and was responsible for the SW sector.
- 16 Infantry Division was located at Nator responsible for the NW sector.

All these divisions were well trained and equipped except for their tank regiments, part artillery brigades and engineering equipment that could not fetch up. They were stocked for 30 days of rations, stores, equipment, spares, and ammunition.

16 Infantry Division in the NW sector was commanded by Major General Nazar Hussain Shah a devout Muslim from Chakwal and a "Pir".

He was very well qualified and experienced with previous postings in Turkey, the USA and Bangkok. However, he was huge and bulky in size and easy going. His personality and actions did not inspire his command. His HQ was located at Nator.

The North-Western sector was distinctly divided into three sub sectors. The Northern sub-sector comprised the important towns of Dinajpur, Saidpur and Rangpur. It ran close to the Siliguri corridor and holding it was necessary to tie down Indian forces as also to coordinate operations with China if they decided to assist Pakistan. It was held by 23 Infantry Brigade under Brigadier Shafi. He had occupied Dinajpur, Saidpur and Rangpur[10] with one battalion each. Two squadrons of 29 Cavalry and 48 Field Regiment was in support of this Brigade.

The Central sub-sector consisted of the waistline from Hilli to Goraghat, Palasbari and Gaibanda. The north-south communications in this sub sector were good. A ferry at Gaibanda over the Jamuna connected it with Dacca. Holding it was important to avoid India, severing the waistline and defeating them piecemeal thereafter. 205 Infantry Brigade commanded by Brigadier Tajummul Hussain Malik was responsible for this sector. Accordingly, 13 FF was deployed at Jaipurhat, 4 FF at Hilli and 8 FF at Bhaduria and Goraghat. 80 Field Regiment was in support of the brigade. 32 Baluch and two troops, 29 Cav ex 34 Infantry Brigade was allotted to 205 Infantry Brigade and deployed hurriedly at Gaibanda and subsequently at Palasbari, Govindganj and Mahasthan, when the Indian Army penetrated the defences and turned the flank to Bogra.

The Southern Sub-sector consisted of the important communication centres of Rajshahi, Nator, and Pabna. This sub-sector was connected to Jessore and Khulna over the Hardinge Bridge and to Dacca by ferry at Sirajgang. The shortest approach from India emanated from Malda. It was necessary to hold it strongly for India could hit the underbelly with ease. 34 Infantry Brigade commanded by Brigadier Naeem was responsible for its defence. Accordingly, Nawabganj, Rajshahi, Naogaon, Nator and Pabna were developed as defended areas. One squadron of 29 Cavalry was in Pabna in support. These brigades were widely separated and not mutually supporting each other. Reinforcing them was not possible. The division was also allotted 18,000 East Pakistan Civil Armed Force personnel including the Industrial Security Force and Razakars. They were holding 60,000 to 70,000, point 303 rifles with them.

Each battalion was stocked in rations, fuel, ammunition and other ordnance stores for a period of 30 days. A central reserve of these items was kept at the brigade logistic area. This was based on the presumption that the operations would not last for more than 30 days and they would be able to restrict the Indian Army to the periphery of the main towns when the war ended. Punjabi Musalmans, Pathans and Baluchis formed the backbone of the army; they had been classified as martial races by the British. Post Partition, they were led to believe that Hindus were infidels and cowards who could be defeated easily. The false sense of superiority and a foolhardy notion of invincibility were misplaced, forgetting that almost all of them were descendants of Hindu converts with the same traits. The frenzy created by their religion gave them some short of cohesion and a sense of martyrdom that sustained them in battle. Once the initial frenzy was over, they collapsed quickly. This was evident throughout the war. Except for a few instances, they did not put up lasting or dogged resistance. They utilized their resources innovatively, especially the artillery but there was no flexibility or requisite reaction to the changing battle situation. They were paralyzed into inaction once they were outflanked or cut off. While the men were sturdy and fought well, the officers were comfort-loving. The life of abundance and absolute power had corrupted them morally and professionally.

As a concept, the Pakistan army believed that the defence of East Pakistan[11] lay in West Pakistan. The war with India would be decided on the western front while East Pakistan would only hold out and tie down Indian forces opposing them. The war fighting by Lt. Gen. Niazi was based on this philosophy and till the end he banked on a Pakistan victory in the west or intervention by the Chinese and the USA to save East Pakistan. Niazi had three options to fight the Indian Army. In option one; he could deploy his forces based on the massive river obstacles in a compact area to defend all the approaches to Dacca and leave much of the territory undefended. This was not acceptable as the Mukti Bahini and Indian forces would then occupy large tracts of land and declare an independent Bangladesh. The second option was to adopt a forward posture and hold the border strongly. In this option there was little depth and no reserves. It would result in attrition and gradual destruction of his force. The third option was to adopt the forward posture with additional troops in depth as reserves. Eight to nine additional battalions, armour and artillery were required this to be effective.

The Army HQ approved the third option and promised to provide additional resources. However Gen. Niazi did not get the promised reinforcements and he eventually fought the war deployed in a forward posture. His concept of defence envisaged defence based on different layers that would augment each other to cause unacceptable attrition on the attacking forces. He thus ordered his forces to create strong outposts as far forward as possible covering all the axes and delay the attackers as much as possible. The second line of defence was based on strong points located 8 to 10 km in depth in small towns. The third line of defence was based on main towns in depth. This line of defence was also designated as a no penetration line and troops were not allowed to withdraw from there. He also ordered that no forward position would be vacated unless a unit defending it had suffered 75 per cent casualties. With this term of reference, units were not withdrawn to the second or third line of defence in time when they had been bypassed. Niazi was convinced through intelligence reports and perhaps Indian deception plans that India was unlikely to resort to an all-out war and would be content to nibble away some territory for the rebel cause. This reinforced their conviction that the forward posture was the best option.

Planning for War

As soon as the events in Bangladesh were triggered in March 1971, the planning for a war at both Indian Army HQ and HQ Eastern Command started. The plans would have gone through many changes given the evolving nature of strategic environment. It can be presumed that initially, India would have had limited objectives to carve out a few enclaves on East Pakistan territory for rehabilitation of the refugees and setting up of an independent government of Bangladesh. As the magnitude of the problem increased and Pakistan adopted an uncompromising policy, it was evident that India's involvement might have to be deeper than imagined. It also became evident that nothing less than an independent Bangladesh would satisfy the Bengalis. Any half measures would only create more problems for India in the future. Both Army HQ and Eastern Command had prepared tentative plans by May. Army HQ issued an operational directive to Eastern Command in July that was discussed in early August at Calcutta. From these, it is clear that Dacca was the final objective and the centre of gravity in the calculations of the Army HQ and Eastern Command.

Plans were made at HQ 33 Corps and 20 Mountain Division based on this directive. It was obvious that some troops would be required to keep the Pakistan brigade in the northern sector tied down while the major force would try to cut the waistline. The town of Hilli would have to be captured at some stage to open the Goraghat-Gaibanda/Jaipurhat-Bogra axes. Development of operations towards Bogra and Rajshahi were important to link up with the South-Western sector. From the narrative in the book "*The Indian Sword Strikes in East Pakistan*" by Maj. Gen. Lachhman Singh, it appears that he was not happy with the initial tasking and method of execution of the plan given to him. They were to contact Dinajpur from the north and the main divisional thrust was to be developed along the Hilli-Gaibanda axis with the option to capture Rangpur or Bogra.

However, Army HQ suggested an improved plan[12] under which three thrust lines were to be developed. One brigade was to operate along the Thakurgaon-Atrai axis to secure the Siliguri corridor. A second was to move along the Phulbari-Nawabganj-Palasbari axis to protect the northern flank of the main divisional thrust with flexibility to reduce Rangpur or Bogra as the opportunity arose. The main divisional thrust was to be developed along the Hilli-Jaipurhat-Bogra and the Balurghat-Panitola-Naogaon-Bogra axes. They felt that these two mutually supporting thrusts would divide the enemy to his piecemeal destruction. This would also influence the operations in the South-Western sector. The division was allotted 3 Independent Armoured Brigade with two regiments less a squadron and a full engineer brigade. Most of the time we were conjecturing based on sand model discussions or reconnaissance of the border areas that took us from the Pachagarh salient to Malda.

It was quite natural for us to discuss the events in East Pakistan, performance of the Mukti Bahini, deployment and strength of the enemy as also the personalities of commanders conducting the war. All of us had full faith in Sam Manekshaw and his ability to lead us to victory. However our views about Lt. Gen. Jagjit Singh Aurora, the army commander and Lt. Gen. M.L. Thapan, the corps commander were not assuring. Relations between the two were far from normal. Aurora had climbed the promotion ladder because of his mild nature, pliability and good connections. He could not stand up to his superiors and protect his command.[13] Thapan, on the other hand, was very conventional, rigid, lacked imagination and enterprise. Maj. Gen. Lachhman Singh, GOC, was an artillery officer with considerable war and staff experience but handicapped due to the sandwich affect of the corps and the army commanders. He could not exploit his genius due to the adverse working relationship of his two superiors. He was energetic, innovative and intelligent but his impact as a commander was not fully transmitted. As the war progressed he showed great flexibility, boldness and seized fleeting opportunities to finish the tasks allotted to him in time. Brigadier Lakhpat Singh, our commander, was replaced by Brigadier B. Joginder Singh sometime in early November due to professional reasons. Joginder Singh gave us full freedom to execute the tasks allotted. He was not a meddler. He was bold, decisive, and flexible and led from the front.

Maj. Gen. Lachhman Singh had to struggle hard to get the resources and to formulate the plan as he would be expected to execute it. After numerous discussions, the Eastern Command relented to allot 71 Mountain Brigade to the division as an additional force. The final plan was war gamed in October and approved by the army commander. Under this plan:

- Dinajpur was to be captured from the south by troops of 340 Brigade while 71 Brigade was to advance to Thakurgaon and contact Dinajpur from the north.
- 66 Mountain Brigade was to secure Phulbari and Charkai and then advance to capture Palasbari with the brigade (202 Brigade) advancing from Hilli.

- 202 Mountain Brigade was to advance north of Hilli to capture Palasbari in conjunction with the brigade (66 Brigade) advancing from Charkai.
- 165 Mountain Brigade was to establish a firm base in the Balurghat Bulge.

After capture of Palasbari, capture Gaibanda and thereafter either capture Rangpur or Bogra.

The relative strength between us and the enemy was marginally in our favour and not overwhelming as the Pakistanis claimed. In infantry it was 5:3; armour 2:1; artillery 4:2 and engineers 3:1. The task achieved by 20 Mountain Division with this force level against an experienced and entrenched enemy is commendable. Senior commanders in the Indian Army do not give any flexibility to a subordinate to plan and execute a task as per his genius. They thrust a plan on a commander and then leave him to execute it where they have no accountability.

As per the plan, the division was mobilized in the first week of November and we moved in our concentration area at Malda as part of 340 Independent Infantry Brigade. We visited 71 and 165 Mountain Brigades to carry out reconnaissance of Thakurgaon, Dinajpur, Phulbari and Charkai. We also visited our side of Hilli and 202 Mountain Brigade. We were able to see some of the Pakistani defences and fortifications that were visible. We gathered from the troops deployed in the firm base that the fortifications were very strong and it would not be easy to capture them. The approaches were covered with fire and any direct assault would be preposterous and fraught with heavy casualties. The bunkers were layered and inter-connected with communication trenches. Ponds, marshes and groves formed natural obstacles. Mines were laid extensively. Defence works were camouflaged cleverly. The area was littered with alternate defensive positions to cover all possible approaches and to absorb reinforcements. We were informed that direct hits on these bunkers by 106 mm RCL guns, tanks and artillery guns had little effect.

Escalation Leading to War

After facilitating Henry Kissinger's clandestine visit to China in July 1971 and another by Bhutto in November 1971 to China, the Pakistanis were confident of US and Chinese help during any military conflict with India. They were not ready for any amicable solution to the existing refugee crisis. The deployment of Pakistan forces both in the east and the west had been completed by mid-October. India had also exhausted all diplomatic and political means by then. It was quite clear to Indian strategic planners that the best window of opportunity for any military action by them was open only for a limited period from November to January. If this was not utilized for resolution of the crisis, then it was lost forever. Therefore, from October onwards the Mukti Bahini commenced their raids and nibbling actions in East Pakistan to carve out as many free enclaves as possible. The rebel activities progressively increased to the interior. Attacks on police stations, centres of the authorities and assassination of collaborators instilled a sense of insecurity in the enemy.

Yahya Khan warned that if Indian troops crossed the border in East Pakistan, it would be considered an act of war. As events moved to a climax, the Pakistani troops spread out on the border to pursue the rebels and violated it in some cases. The actions of the Mukti Bahini gradually engulfed the entire border. Operations by the Pakistan Army against them forced them to fire artillery inside Indian territory on their bases that resulted in retaliation by us. The BSF and the Army also started assisting the Mukti Bahini where ever required. Thus, by November, the time had come to put in place the final plan into action. Preliminary operations as described below were planned at five places with the aim of testing our plans against the enemy.

Battle of Dhalai

The first action was at Dhalai tea garden some 2,000 yards north of the border town of Kamalpur in Tripura. The enemy border post had become a nuisance as it subjected Indian positions continuously to mortar and artillery fire. The task of eliminating it was given to the Mukti Bahini. Their attack failed as the post had been reinforced the previous night. The complex consisted of a border outpost, twin huts, factory area and Patrakhala. 61 Mountain Brigade was given the task of clearing the border outpost. 2 Jat attacked on the night of 28/29 October. The initial operation was successful but the main attack was day lighted and not pressed home with vigour. The second attempt also failed. By 30 October, the enemy reinforced the complex with three companies ex 28 FF and elements of commando battalion. 2 Jat was tasked to capture this position at all costs. In the attack on 30/31 October, the battalion was able to capture Coolie Lines by first light but failed to progress further. At this juncture, Brigadier S.D.S. Yadava, commander, was wounded by enemy MMG fire. On the night of 31 Oct/1 Nov, 7 Rajputana Rifles was tasked to capture the remainder complex but the battalion was able to capture only the border outpost. The commanding officer was wounded and the artillery OP was killed by enemy shelling causing confusion and delay in the progress of operations. But order was restored quickly and the battalion captured the factory area soon thereafter. The twin huts area was vacated by the enemy on 2 November. 14 Guards cleared the enemy by 3 November. Poor planning, faulty execution and timid and weak leadership were the main cause of failures.

Battle of Bayra

"Operation AXE" was launched in the SW sector by 9 Infantry Division in Bayra Bulge, at a point where the Kabak River demarcates the boundary. Our troops crossed the river, intruded 1,000 yards into East Pakistan and established two strong points. The enemy reacted swiftly but the counter attacks were defeated. On the night of 17/18 November, a heavy assault bridge was put across the river and 14 Punjab with a squadron of PT-76 tanks ex 45 Cavalry were inducted. On 21 November, the enemy attacked 14 Punjab with a battalion supported by a squadron of tanks from the north and another battalion to cut them off from the west. The tank action was short and swift in the misty morning and the enemy lost eight tanks. The assaulting battalions withdrew after suffering casualties. A second assault was launched on 22 November. In this action three enemy tanks were destroyed and three were abandoned. The assault failed in which the commanding officer of the Pakistani battalion was killed. In the air battle that followed in support of this operation, the Pakistanis lost three Sabre aircraft to our Gnats. The air battle was fought on Indian territory and the Pakistani pilots were made prisoners of war. This was a major victory for the Indians and made headlines internationally.

Battle of Hilli

The action to capture Hilli in the NW sector also made great headlines due to severity of the fight between two equally strong opponents. Hilli guards the waistline. One half is located in India and the other in Pakistan. The railway line passes through the village. It was held very strongly by 4 FF Battalion. Its capture would have opened the way to cut the waistline. 8 Guards was tasked to capture it. They were allotted 63 CAV less one squadron and 10 fire units. The operation was to be completed in three phases. While the first phase commenced on 22 November and was successfully completed, the second phase ran into difficulty. The enemy counter attacked on positions captured by us and we suffered heavy casualties. Four officers, two JCOs and 61 ORs were killed and three officers, two JCOs and 85 ORs were wounded. All subsequent attempts by the battalion were stalled in the face of stiff opposition. Armour also could not succeed due to boggy ground, marsh land and ponds. The enemy reinforced the area with additional troops making the task even harder. The operation was halted on 24 November. In this botched-up operation, Indians made many mistakes at great cost. In hindsight, the brigade and battalion commanders were solely responsible for bad planning and the fiasco. Hilli was eventually captured on 12 December.

Battle of Belonia Bulge

This operation was conducted in the SE sector by 23 Infantry Division. Belonia Bulge is 15 miles long and 7 miles across. It juts out from Fenny towards Tripura. It was defended by one regular and one para military battalion. 23 Infantry Division was tasked to clear the Bulge up to Fenny. The division launched the operation on 23 November. The enemy defences were contacted by one battalion aided by the Mukti Bahini while 83 and

181 Infantry brigades cut off the defenders from all directions. The enemy was unnerved when they found themselves encircled and cut off from all sides. They abandoned the defences leaving behind large quantities of arms, ammunition and equipment. A sizeable number of Pakistanis were made prisoners but a major portion of the force managed to escape before the noose was effective.

The Battle of Akhaura

This area also lies in the SE sector opposite Tripura. Akhaura is a railhead near the border. It was held by two regular and two razakar companies. To its south, at Gangasagar, two more companies were deployed. The defenders were supported by field artillery and a troop of tanks. A brigade operation was launched to secure a launch pad for further operations by 57 Mountain Division. On the night of 1 December, 10 Bihar launched a feint from the north of Akhaura while the main attack went from the south. By 0700 hrs the battalion fought its way to the objective and occupied the outskirts of the town. 18 Rajput, the follow-up battalion made steady progress on 2 December. 4 Guards was tasked to block the enemy from behind and capture the remaining objective from the west. They captured the depth positions in face of resistance by Razakar companies. Their attempt to capture the second bridge on Akhaura-Brahmanbaria could not succeed as it was held strongly by the enemy. PT-76 tanks could not support the operation due to marshes and water obstacles. The enemy vacated the position on 3 December when the war broke out.

The preliminary operations taught us some very valuable lessons. The Indian Army was not short on valour at the unit and sub unit levels. The troops and officers were highly motivated and fought with dogged determination. The pattern of enemy fortifications, their clever use of water bodies and other natural obstacles in conjunction with mine fields and cleverly-sited automatic weapons brought home the importance of detailed reconnaissance to avoid such obstacles. It was also apparent that the orthodox concept of reduction of a strong point was fruitless. It was costly both in terms of casualties and time. The answer lay in containing and then by-passing them. Penetrating through the gaps and hitting the soft underbelly of depth defences was the best way to unhinge the enemy.

These provocative operations forced the enemy to react violently, resulting in repeated counter attacks and reinforcement of forward areas at the cost of heavy casualties and dispersal of forces. The enemy foolishly lost 13 tanks, three F-86s and a number of soldiers at Bayra. But it also convinced them that the forward policy of defence would stall the Indian Army in its tracks at the border itself. After the action at Boyra, the Pakistan President appealed to the UN to stop India attacking East Pakistan and its grave consequences. They were, of course, refuted by us. Gen. Yahya Khan also told a Chinese delegation at that time that in the next ten days, he might be fighting a war and may not be at Pindi. This proved prophetic as while the battle of Akhaura was raging on 2 December, Mrs. Indira Gandhi said India would not be pressurized from doing what was in its national interest. We are strong enough to stand on our own legs. Pakistan declared an all-out war on India on 3 December at 1730 hrs.

The War

Towards the end of November, I had joined the battalion at Malda. We visited Hilli and 71 Mountain Brigade that had secured Pachagarh Salient and Thakurgaon by then to absorb the lessons learnt firsthand.

Operations up to Pirganj

The declaration of war on 3 December was announced on radio when we had assembled in the mess for dinner. We were immediately mobilized to support 5 Garhwal Rifles at Debkhanda village. 71 Mountain Brigade commenced operations against Dinajpur from the north with 4 Madras from 340 (I) Brigade contacting it from the south when the war commenced. 66 Mountain Brigade was ordered to advance to Phulchari-Charkai through the gap between Dinajpur and Hilli. 202 Mountain Brigade was ordered to move north of Hilli and link up with 66 Mountain Brigade at Charkai. In the process, 5 Garhwal Rifles, that was to move north of Hilli via Debkhnada-Dangapara, got embroiled in a fight with the enemy at Debkhanda.

We marched whole night and reached the outskirts of Debkhanda by first light and dug in. The Garhwalis attacked their objectives on the forenoon of 4 December. They suffered heavy casualties. Two officers, one JCO and 10 jawans were killed and three officers, three JCOs and 46 jawans including their commanding officer were wounded. Once again, we paid heavily for attacking a fortified village conventionally. We were also subjected to intense mortar fire frequently as our movement and assembly had been detected by the enemy. In one of these mortar attacks, we were surprised and the bombs came raining on us. While we dived in the trenches and piled on top of each other, Rifleman Ishwar Singh Thapa and one more jawan reacted late and were fatally wounded. They were the first battle casualties in the battalion.

By 5 December, it was realized that 202 Mountain Brigade had failed to make any progress towards Charkai from the north due to heavy enemy resistance at Debkhanda and Dangapara that seemed to have been reinforced. The firm base brigade was ordered to take over the situation and 202 Mountain Brigade asked to disengage and move to Charkai via Balurghat and Patiram. The brigade failed to disengage and could not move out in the given time, so this order was rescinded. However 5/11 GR, 69 Armoured Regiment, 100 Field Regiment and 13 Engineer Regiment were ordered to disengage and move to Charkai on the night of 5 December. Accordingly, I joined the battalion while 5 Garhwal Rifles continued to fight at Debkhanda. By 6 December, 66 Infantry Brigade was able to secure Phulbari and the crossings over the Karatoya River but lost the momentum of the advance. We walked the whole night along the deck board track constructed by the engineers to Bejai-Phulbari and from there along the railway line to Charkai. The track from Phulbari to Charkai was not fit for traffic and that delayed operations towards Pirganj and Gaibanda. 13 Engineer Regiment blasted the existing railway line and converted it in a gravel class 40 track. We marched from Charkai to Nawabganj and took up defences at Parmanandpur crossing by 1600 hrs on 6 December after clearing it. At 2200 hrs, on 6 December, orders were received to concentrate at Kanchdaha crossing on the Karatoya River on 7 December when relieved by 17 Kumaon. The build-up of 340 (I) Infantry Brigade was complete by last light of 6 December. We were to be ready to move to Pirganj at short notice either mounted on tanks or on foot. It was very cold at night and our field echelon vehicles did not fetch up, so we lived on rice and chicken found in the abandoned village. We slept on heaps of rice straw to keep the cold out. By the morning of 7 December, the crossings over Karatoya River were ready and necessary force had been concentrated for further operations. We received orders to move after breakfast.

I handed over my position to Major B.S. Negi who was commanding "C" Company, 17 Kumaon. He had been my company commander in 1965. By coincidence, we were together again fighting another war but from different battalions. His battalion was to capture Bhaduria and link up at Ghoraghat to open the axis of advance to Bogra. On 7 December this position was held by only one company, by the next day, the enemy reinforced it with a company each of 8 Baluch and 13 FF making the task difficult. Finally, the position was captured on 11 December after suffering many casualties.

The division now launched 340(I) Infantry Brigade to advance and capture Pirganj as soon as possible with 2/5 GR and 5/11 GR while 66 Mountain Brigade would consolidate. 2/5 GR moved, mounted on PT-76 tanks, while 5/11 GR force marched. 6 Guards and 5 Garhwal Rifles, grouped with the brigade, were to follow. "A" and "D" companies were ordered to establish a road block at Laldighi Bazaar while the rest of the battalion was to secure Kumedpur. The aim was to cut off the national highway and prevent enemy reinforcements from Rangpur to Pirganj. While the tanks rumbled off, we treaded along the dusty track. I was leading the advance of 5/11 GR. We made rapid progress. We saw the GOC at the starting point conferring with some of his commanders sitting on a camp stool while tanks, guns and we marched past him. It was an inspiring site. The leading elements of the mounted force cut off the road north of Pirganj by 1630 hrs.

At 1645 hrs, the mounted column reported that an enemy jeep convoy approaching from Rangpur had been ambushed by them. They did not investigate it further as their primary task was to clear and capture Pirganj. However, two enemy soldiers were captured by them later and it was then learnt that the convoy belonged to Major General Nazar Hussain, the GOC

16 Division, who was returning to his HQ from Rangpur after a conference. A further search of the area led to the abandoned jeep of the GOC and recovery of marked maps. We were ordered to speed up our move and reach Pirganj before the enemy could react. We trotted nonstop and reached Pirganj crossing by midnight covering a distance of 39 km in 12 hours. By 0100 hrs, "A" and "D" companies under me and Major Abjeet Singh Mamik had established ourselves at Priganj/Laldigi Bazaar crossing when a counter attack by the enemy, supported by tanks, was launched to evict us. There was intense firing for about 30 minutes from both sides. We fired 57 mm recoilless rifles on the enemy tanks under the flares of 2-in mortars. The tanks with us also joined in. The enemy did not close in and withdrew after realizing that it was beyond their capability to remove the road block.

During the night, 5/11 GR consolidated itself at the Cross Road while 2/5 GR did so at Pirganj. After the war, it was revealed that the GOC of Pakistan 16 Infantry Division had held a conference of the commanders 23 and 205 Infantry Brigade at Rangpur on 7 December where they felt that Indian troops were unlikely to penetrate up to Pirganj for some time as they were still embroiled in the Hilli and Badhuria complexes. However, they were surprised when the ambush took place. Still the gravity of the situation did not down on them and they felt it was a raiding force as the axis of advance could not sustain a main thrust. After the ambush, some of the escapees informed the garrison at Rangpur of the encounter who feared that the GOC had been killed. However, the GOC, with a few men, hid in the bushes till it was dark and then escaped on foot towards Rangpur. He was later retrieved by the counter attack force consisting of two companies and a troop of tanks half way to Rangpur.

While the Commander 205 Infantry Brigade was able to join his brigade by first light 8 December, the GOC was flown out in a helicopter on 9 December. Brigadier Tajjamul had skirted the Pirganj road block from the east and had met the CO 32 Baluch at Gaibanda whom he ordered to remove the road block as soon as possible. After this, he proceeded via Palasbari to join his HQ. The commanding officer of 32 Baluch, Lt. Col. Raza Sultan Mahmud reacted with alacrity without reconnaissance or adequate information. He attacked a well entrenched 2/5 GR at Pirganj in the morning of 8 December. The counter attack failed and he, along with seven men was killed. In the morning of 8 December, a military jeep tried to rush the road block. However, we blasted it to smithereens. The body parts of enemy dead were strewn all over the area. After this no one dared to approach us. The whole of 8 December was spent in consolidating at Laldighi Bazaar crossing against enemy reaction. But this did not happen as it seemed the enemy command and control had been paralyzed. He however reinforced Bhaduria and Goraghat with two companies each and withdrew 32 Baluch from Gaibanda to Govindganj to block our advance.

Advance up to Govindganj

On 8 December when our build up at Pirganj was strong enough for further operations, the divisional plan envisaged that 202 Mountain Brigade would capture Hilli and link up with 66 Mountain Brigade at Goraghat for operations towards Bogra. 66 Mountain Brigade was to capture Bhaduria and then advance to Goraghat to link up with 340(I) Infantry Brigade; and 340(I) Infantry Brigade to capture Govindganj and advance to Bogra. 340(I) Infantry Brigade left 2/5 GR and 5 Garhwal Rifles to hold the defences at Pirganj while the rest of the brigade commenced advancing towards Govindganj on 9 December. 69 Armoured Regiment led the advance with 6 Guards mounted on tanks. By 1100 hrs, Palasbari was captured. The column was diverted to Gaibanda to intercept the enemy withdrawing from Rangpur to Bogra. This information turned out to be wrong. Gaibanda was captured without resistance. The civil administration welcomed the liberating force and handed them the key of the town in a grand ceremony. The force in their enthusiasm destroyed the jetty, a strategic error that was regretted later when there was a need to reinforce the Northern Sector for the race to liberate Dacca. 5/11 GR was relieved by 5 Garhwal Rifles at 0900 hrs on 9 December and was asked to concentrate at Palasbari by 1300 hrs. The battalion was now tasked to capture Ghoraghat if possible otherwise establish a firm base on the east bank of the Karatoya River.

Our advance commenced at 1340 hrs on 9 December with "D" Company mounted on tanks of 69 Armoured Regiment and rest of the battalion in vehicles. The enemy was contacted just before last light. It was estimated that two companies had dug in on both the banks of the river. Since the enemy was in fortified defence, "D" Company was asked to establish a firm base and extensive patrolling was carried out during the night. It was confirmed by the morning of 10 December that both the east and west banks were held by two platoons each. Area embankment was also held. One MMG each was located at Monglishpur, River bend and the ferry. The defences were mined and the Karatoya was not fordable. Based on this information, it was decided to clear the East Bank immediately. I was ordered to advance with a troop of tanks along a dusty track along Kayarpar-Birkhandi-Phulbari and capture Chak Malik up to the road junction by 0900 hrs in phase one. I was able to reach my objective in the face of light opposition that withdrew to the road junction after offering feeble resistance. "D" Company was to capture the road junction in phase two from the Southeast. They formed up at Hussainpur and came under very heavy and effective MMG and anti-tank fire from the road junction and the west bank while attacking the objective.

An immediate air strike was called which was directed by the FAC who was with me at that time. The bombs and rockets came down with devastating effect and the enemy was completely neutralized. This air strike was also witnessed by the GOC and the commander who were in my vicinity. The medium artillery also pounded enemy positions. The ground shook and trembled with each salvo. The enemy could not withstand the fire and withdrew from the road junction which was occupied by "D" company by midday. Phase three was launched with "C" Company under Major Naresh Bhasin to capture Monglishpur via Jhapur from the east. "C" Company formed up in Jhapur and attacked Monglishpur at 1400 hrs. When the enemy found itself under attack by another company, it abandoned Monglishpur and withdrew. They brought down heavy MMG fire from the west bank on the attacking troops. Major Bhasin who was leading the attack was severely wounded. The objective was finally under our control by last light. We consolidated on the objective during the night and carried out intensive patrolling to capture the west bank. Three other ranks were killed and one officer and three other ranks were wounded during this operation. The air strike and artillery had played a vital role in this attack. At 0800 hrs, the battalion was asked to concentrate at Palasbari leaving "D" Company to hold the east bank till relieved by 2/5 GR for advance to Govindganj. Since the east bank was fully secured and part of west bank was already under our control the enemy could not interfere with our operations towards Bogra, it was thus decided that 66 Mountain Brigade would reduce it after the capture of Bhaduria. Therefore 5/11 GR was ordered to disengage and advance to Govindganj on the morning of 11 December that had become more important than capturing Ghoraghat.

Battle of Govindganj

The advance by 6 Guards from Palasbari encountered strong enemy opposition at Govindganj. The enemy defences were based on the south bank of the Karatoya River and was held by 32 Baluch that had withdrawn from Gaibanda on 8 December. The bridge over the river had been demolished. The T-55 tanks of 63 Cavalry that were leading the advance were hit by anti-tank mines while probing gaps in the defences. They came under effective tank and RCL fire from coordinated defences. The GOC 20 Mountain Division had expected both 66 and 202 Mountain brigades to capture their objectives and advance to Govindganj by 10 December. Their move would have avoided crossing the Karatoya River that was holding up the advance of 340 (I) Infantry Brigade. But this did not happen as Bhaduria was captured on 11 December and Hilli capitulated on 12 December. A hasty assault on the enemy by 6 Guards was fraught with heavy casualties with no guarantee of success. A deliberate river crossing operation would be time consuming, allowing the enemy to reinforce Bogra with troops withdrawing from Hilli and Bhaduria. Therefore it was decided to out flank Govindganj from the east by a mechanized column and attack it from the southeast—a most unexpected direction.

A task force consisting of 5/11 GR and 69 Armoured Regiment was formed with 64 Mountain Regiment, 44 Medium Gun Battery, 115 Light Gun Battery and 52 Engineer Regiment in support. The enemy was expected to hold the southern bank of the river astride the Palasbari-Govindganj road with two companies and one company at Manoharpur road junction; and the fourth company was at Rampur road junction.

They were supported by tanks and field guns. I was grouped with "B" Squadron under Major S.C. Mehra to lead the outflanking manoeuvre. We set out just before midday mounted on the PT-76 tanks. The route chosen was Palasbari-Shahapara-Nakal-Kajla ferry crossing along the west bank of the river to Sripatipur-Shahpura. From Shahpura, our combat team was to peel off and establish a road block at Kamar road track junction. The reconnaissance troop of the regiment moved ahead with elements of Mukti Bahini that had successfully secured the crossing place at Kajla. In addition, an artillery observation post was established with the help of the Mukti Bahini at Magura that effectively engaged the enemy. We crossed the Karatoya River some 8 km downstream, east of Govindganj at Kajala at 1330 hrs and reached Shahpura by 1500 hrs. Thereafter while the battalion moved west to Govindganj, our combat team moved south west and was in position at Kamar by 1545 hrs.

This manoeuvre was remarkable in the sense that it exploited the capabilities of both the men and machines to the maximum in the battle that was to follow. This was the only instance in the whole campaign where mobile warfare actually came into play as a game changer. The PT-76 tanks swam through water obstacles, glided over marshes and soft ground with ease. Since this was the most unexpected route, we remained undetected. While this manoeuvre was going on, 6 Guards kept up the pressure on the enemy relentlessly from the north bank of the Karatoya River. When the attack went in from the rear by "B" Company with tanks in support, the enemy was taken by surprise and perplexed. They brought down uncoordinated artillery, anti-tank, and MMG fire on the assaulting troops. However, his resistance weakened under the weight of our fire as well as a determined assault by the infantry. He wilted and abandoned the defences in the confusion that followed to escape death and destruction. "B" Company had captured the road junction by 1700 hrs. "C" Company was also launched immediately thereafter. Both these companies were tasked to clear all the area east and west of the road, respectively. The enemy was in rout when the assaulting troops were closing in on the objective from their rear.

The enemy had no clue that "A" Company and "B" Squadron were waiting for them at a road block. At around 1800 hrs, a convoy of the enemy that was withdrawing entered the killing zone of the road block. It consisted of tanks, artillery guns and many trucks. Suddenly, all hell was let loose on them, both by the tanks and my company. We were deployed in a horse-shoe shape and the enemy had no chance of breaking through. The whole area was full of exploding vehicles and fleeing men. The withdrawing enemy abandoned their tanks, guns and vehicles to make good their escape on foot. One of the enemy parties trying to break through the road block fired at my position and a few bullets whizzed past, perforating my trousers. I narrowly escaped injuries by these bullets. The approaching darkness, sugarcane fields and groves came to the rescue of the fleeing enemy and many were lucky to escape while some hid in the groves and sugarcane fields. The enemy tanks, guns and vehicles stood abandoned. We did not care to count or collect the dead in this violent action. We also did not bother to take any prisoners. As darkness fell, the tanks were withdrawn to the inner circle for protection while my company took up the defence in the outer perimeter.

Lt. Babu Rao, the battalion intelligence officer came riding one of the PT-76s with a section to link up with me. Since I was coordinating the night defence between the tank squadron and my company, he joined me in one of the perimeter platoons. As we were walking back, one of the enemy parties hiding in that area fired at us. The automatic fire came right in my face and hit my helmet, grazing my neck and ears. My helmet rattled violently. I intuitively hit the ground for cover and thought for a moment that it was my end. Several bursts went over my head as the entire perimeter including the tanks had now opened fire. After a while the firing died down gradually. When the all-clear was sounded, I got up and so did my runner and radio operator but there was no trace of Babu Rao. After searching for a while he was found lying on the ground some yards from us. We thought that he had not heard the all-clear signal and one of the jawans shook him by the shoulder. He tried to get up but his intestines fell out and he slumped to the ground face down, dead. This was very sad. The enemy burst had caught him in the stomach before he could take position. We lost a very bold and fine officer. I sent his body back to the battalion on the same tank that he had come riding on to link with me. The next day, he was cremated with full military honours as one who had died for his country in the line of duty. His ashes and belongings were handed over to his mother and sister at Hyderabad by Capt. N.D. Sharief after the war.

At this juncture I thought I needed some rest as my head and right ear were throbbing with pain. I took off my helmet to wipe off the sweat that had soaked my neck and was trickling down the back. The palm of my hand felt very sticky and in the dim light of the torch I saw it was smeared with blood. I had been wounded in the right forehead and right ear. The nursing assistant removed the shrapnel lodged in my forehead, bandaged the wound and injected morphine. The pain subsided and I felt relieved. I informed Lt. Col. Dias about my injuries but refused to be evacuated. In the morning, I realized my helmet had taken the burst at an angle that had saved me. The bullets had perforated the sides and the brim with splinters injuring me in the forehead, upper ear and lobe. Blood had coagulated around the injuries. My scarf and collar of the shirt had been perforated by bullets on both sides and smeared with blood. I had escaped death miraculously. The regimental medical officer evacuated me to the ADS that was over flowing with casualties with severed limbs and gaping wounds awaiting treatment and further evacuation. I was only a walking wounded casualty among them. Our RMO, Capt. K.R.C. Prasad, assured me that he would take care of me better than the hospital. I thus refused to be admitted. In this operation, one officer and three jawans were killed and two officers, one JCO and seven jawans were wounded. We had killed approximately 80 enemy and taken 40 prisoners. Two Chaffee tanks were destroyed and four captured in addition to two 105 mm guns destroyed and five captured. Fifteen vehicles carrying ammunition and stores were also captured besides others. The prisoners revealed that the defences were held by 32 Baluch less two companies, one company of 23 Punjab Regiment, two troop Chaffee tanks, 60 Field Company Engineers, one battery of the 80 Field Regiment and 200 EPCAF personnel.

Battle of Mahasthan

After the defeat of 32 Baluch at Govindganj, it was presumed that the road to Bogra was open and both the armour and 5/11 GR that were available at hand could accomplish the task of contacting it by the evening of 12 December. Around midday the battalion was asked to resume advance to Bogra. After quick regrouping and replenishment, the advance commenced at 1500 hrs with a squadron of the 63 Cav (T-55) as the vanguard. "A" and "D" companies of 5/11 GR, mounted on PT-76 tanks of 69 Armoured Regiment were part of the main guard. The remainder battalion followed on foot. Contact with the enemy was established at about 1700 hrs when an enemy recoilless gun knocked out a tank of 63 Cav and heavy MMG and automatic fire was encountered from across the Ichamati Nala, a branch of the Karotya River. Any move by the tanks and infantry to close in with the enemy drew very heavy and accurate fire from the defenders. It appeared that we had hit a well prepared and coordinated defensive position. Perhaps this was enemy's last-ditch stand before the main battle at Bogra. "A" and "D" companies of 5/11 GR were given the task of securing the north bank of the Nala, east and west of the road, respectively. In the process, my company suffered a few fatalities. However, by 1900 hrs, we were able to fix the extent of defences and location of the enemy. We had also succeeded in securing a firm base astride the road on the north bank of the nala. Our patrolling and probing indicated that the enemy was holding the south bank of the nala with two companies covering the road axis at Malahar and Saulakhandi with a gap of about 200 to 300 yards. The inter company gaps and flanks were covered by RR and MMG fire. We had no knowledge of the enemy's depth companies but it was appreciated that he could be holding Nimarpara extending to Mahasthan Bridge in depth. There was no more information about the enemy.

After a brief discussion between the Commander and our CO, it was decided that night advance to Bogra must be resumed as early as possible. Since the tanks did not have night fighting capability, they could be used only at first light. It was therefore decided to infiltrate one company behind the enemy defences at night to isolate him and the opposition blocking the advance removed by an attack with infantry and tanks at first light.

This would ensure that the enemy could not reinforce Mahasthan defences and gained time to fight at Bogra. The order group assembled at 2100 hrs under a tree on the roadside, just out of range of enemy small arms fire. The CO briefed us about the situation and the orders from the brigade commander. Just then a volley of shells landed nearby throwing a lot of dust and debris but caused no physical harm to anyone. The orders were very succinct. Everyone understood the tasks allotted, their implications and the gravity of the situation. We dispersed as quickly and silently as we had assembled. "A" Company under my command was to infiltrate through the gap between the two forward enemy companies as I was best poised and knew the extent of the gap and layout of the ground. I was to establish a road block approximately three to four km behind the enemy positions on the road axis by 0300 hrs. "B" Company and "D" Company were to attack the enemy at Malahar and Saulakhandhi at first light or immediately after the road block was in position. "C" Company was reserve for both the tasks. The battalion would establish a firm base for a brigade attack if it could not clear enemy opposition.

The commanding officer gave me a free hand in planning and executing the road block. He asked me to inform him only of the start time and the time when I was in position at the road block. I was allotted all artillery in range with an FOO from 64 Mountain Regiment. I was ready by 2300 hrs and the infiltration commenced silently and stealthily. My plan was very simple but audacious. The key to my success was surprise. I had to do something that the enemy least expected under the circumstances. In the middle of the gap there was a bridge on the Ichamati nala over which the road passed. The road was the only geographical feature that could be used as a reliable navigational aid in the absence of accurate maps. I decided to infiltrate right under the nose of the enemy, keeping the bridge to my west. It was a risky plan but I was optimistic that it would succeed.

2/Lt. Teja Singh Bedi, an intelligent, brave, innovative and ingenious officer who had joined the battalion in July from the IMA led the infiltration with No. 1 platoon. While we waited anxiously some 200 yards from the nala, Teja Bedi, with a small reconnoitre party, found a footpath through the tall undergrowth that led to a foot crossing. This was some distance away, east of the bridge. Perhaps the crossing place was not known to the enemy and was therefore unguarded. It was pitch dark and we crossed the nala in sections, each man holding on to the other. The water channel was about 30 to 40 yards wide with a very soft bed and 2 to 4 feet deep. While we were fording, the enemy was engaged on the flanks with small arms fire and movements. Artillery and mortar fire was brought down on defensive positions to pin his head down and divert his attention from the infiltration. Crossing the water obstacle was not as simple as we had imagined it with full battle loads. Three feet deep water was enough trouble for a short Gorkha. Fortunately, no one was washed away or drowned. It took us an hour to cross the 40 yards. We were drenched and all our clothing and equipment was wet in the severe cold of December. The anxiety and tension was palpable on every face lest we were detected and mowed down.

After crossing the nala, we regrouped in platoons and headed towards the road whose silhouette was visible in the dim glow of the moonlight. The roads in East Pakistan were elevated and above ground level. This created a ditch running parallel to the road on both sides which was 5 to 6 feet deep and could easily hide a man walking in it. This ditch had knee-deep water and slush that drained into the river. I decided to move in the ditch so that we were not visible and our movements were not detected. The enemy would have never imagined that we would walk in the ditch along the main road, a direct route, right through his defences. We had walked for about two hrs until about 0200 hrs. I was amazed at the silence and stealth in which we moved, halting, listening and inching forward. Perhaps the darkness also helped us. As we moved away from the river, the depth of the ditch reduced and now our heads were level with the road. So far we had been lucky as our movements had not been detected and we were almost three to four km behind the enemy.

In the dim light of the waning moon, the leading section commander spotted two jeeps on the road and some men standing with maps spread on the bonnet. They were not clearly visible or audible but appeared to be discussing something in the glow of torchlight. Every one froze and I could make out that these men were officers on a visit to the defenders. They were barely 40 to 50 yards from us and easy targets. I decided to act before they noticed our presence. I ordered the LMG commander who was beside me, to fire at them. Alas! At that crucial juncture the LMG jammed and it would not fire in spite of repeated attempts. The slush and water had made it non-functional. The sound of repeated cocking and misfire alerted the enemy of our presence. They mounted their jeeps and fled towards Bogra. A few bursts by a replacement LMG were fired at the fleeing enemy but it was too late for any effect.

After the ceasefire, we learnt from Brig. Tajummal Hussain Mallick, Commander 205 Infantry Brigade, that it was he, along with Lt. Col. Tariq Anees, Commanding Officer, 80 Field Regiment, that we had missed killing or capturing on that occasion. They had come to visit 32 Baluch for discussing the operational situation and were trying to find their way to their battalion headquarters. In hind sight, we missed a high-value target and a great opportunity that could have averted much bloodshed and delay in the capture of Bogra later. I now realized that the surprise of our infiltration had been blown off. The enemy would react to our presence with speed and vengeance. So we established the road block astride the roade there with a clear killing ground. I asked the FOO to carry out silent registration of targets on approaches to the road block. To my surprise, neither the coordinates of our location, the target nor the location of the gun position were known to him. Therefore, silent registration was not possible so he asked my permission for active registration of at least one target. He informed the gun position that he was approximately 3 to 4 km from the river bank on the road to Bogra to indicate his approximate location and adopted the Bravo Tango-Oscar-Tango procedure to direct fire. The target chosen was a bamboo grove about 500 yards from our location. Fortunately, the first round fell in proximity of the target. He corrected the fire with two more rounds. We now knew our exact location. I admired the FOO's ingenuity in directing fire on a target in a totally unknown area at night. He carried out silent registration of the remaining targets as we did not want to alert the enemy before our road block was fully effective.

At this juncture, Sub. Dil Bahadur Tamang, No. 2 platoon commander, reported that an enemy party of four men carrying RR ammunition to forward companies had been intercepted by his platoon. They had been overpowered and slain with kukhris to maintain silence and surprise. I was very pleased with his presence of mind and achievement. But it dawned on me that enemy depth locations were close by. I told the platoon commanders to send out perimeter patrols and place listening posts and sentries so that we were not surprised. Fully confident and satisfied with our achievement, I sat down in my foxhole wrapped in a rain cape to rest before the main action started at dawn. It was bitterly cold and I was covered with sweat and grime all over my body; it made me very uncomfortable. The exertion, fatigue and anxiety made it impossible for a nap.

Just then, the perimeter patrol from No. 1 platoon located a telephone line, leading off the road. 2/Lt. Teja Bedi, along with about a section strength proceeded to investigate it. After walking about 500 yards, he found himself facing a group of bunkers, trenches, antennas and telephone exchange in what looked like a headquarters. Men were sleeping on the ground and sentries were facing away from him, perhaps also sleeping. There were no signs of life except a flickering of dim light in one of the bunkers. He alerted me about the situation in a hushed voice on the radio. I immediately ordered his remaining platoon to reinforce him. I also asked him to demonstrate that he was commanding a large force and assault the position if challenged. I followed him with some more men that I could muster immediately. After deploying his men, he, along with Nk. Bal Bahadur stealthily entered the bunker that had a light and found a Pakistani officer who turned around just then. Before he could react, Nk. Bal Bahadur pulled out his khukri and placed it on his neck.

Displaying exceptional presence of mind and courage, 2/Lt. Teja Bedi told the officer that his position had been surrounded. To his great surprise, the Pakistani officer told Teja Bedi, that he was Major Muhammad Ajmal, officiating commanding officer of 32 Baluch. (The commanding officer, Lt. Col. Raza Sultan Mahmud, had been killed during a counter attack on 2/5 GR on the night of 7/8 December at Pirganj). Teja Bedi who was in complete command of the situation, confidently and firmly reiterated to the major that his position had been surrounded by 5/11 GR and he had no choice but to surrender or get everyone killed in the ensuing fire fight.

Taken aback, completely confused and bewildered, Major Muhammad Ajmal disclosed that this was the battalion headquarters of 32 Baluch and offered to surrender if he and his men were not killed. Teja asked him to come out of the bunker, order his men not to offer any resistance and to surrender peacefully. By now the headquarters of 32 Baluch had come alive and there was commotion. Like their commanding officer, the men were also bewildered, confused and surprised to see the Gorkhas with weapons pointed at them ready to fire. Some of them attempted to man their weapons and positions. But Major Muhammad, emerged out of the bunker and ordered his men not to offer any resistance and remain peaceful. He explained that they were surrounded and would be killed if they resisted. Just then, the reinforcements for Teja Bedi arrived. The Pakistanis were now convinced that they had indeed been surrounded. The enemy was lined up, searched and disarmed. A total of 25 personnel surrendered. Teja Bedi quickly collected the officiating commanding officer, adjutant Capt. Muhammad Salim, RMO, Capt. Sherzaman, AMC, and the commanding officer's two radio operators with their sets and marched them to the company headquarters. Since it was not possible to control all the surrendered personnel with the about 20 men he had, and lest our bluff was called off; he turned them around and fired randomly. The Pakistanis fled away helter-skelter in the darkness of night to save themselves!

It was almost 0430 hrs when the officiating CO and four other POW were bundled up in the trenches of company headquarters with their hands tied. A quick interrogation revealed that the defences were based on the Ichamati nala with two companies holding the river bank and one company in the depth. It was now confirmed that my company was in the guts of the enemy battalion. I spoke to Lt. Col. F.T. Dias, and apprised him of the events. I requested him to link up with me as soon as possible. No sooner I had finished speaking to him, the enemy reacted violently to remove the road block and rescue their commanding officer. Some of the enemy personnel who had escaped from the battalion headquarters might have informed their depth company/brigade of the disaster that had befallen them. The removal of the road block was necessary for their survival and it had to be done quickly at any cost.

We had anticipated such a situation. Approximately one enemy company, most probably from the depth, had managed to close in against us, taking advantage of the darkness and the thick bamboo groves. We were in a dangerous situation. I told my men not to yield even an inch under any circumstances and fight it out till the last. At this stage, when we were under grave threat, I had no choice but to call for defensive fire 'RED, RED, RED' as the enemy was barely 200 yards away. The artillery reacted immediately to the FOOs orders and very heavy effective fire rained on the enemy that had formed up to assault us. The explosions, flashes and dust that accompanied were awe-inspiring. The Pakistani commanding officer was bewildered and ashen faced as if in shock when the ground around us began shaking. He wondered if he would survive the bombardment and intermittently cursed his luck and prayed with eyes closed. He looked miserable and pathetic. I told Major Muhammad Ajmal to speak on his radio and ask his men not to press the attack otherwise he would be shot by us. He immediately obeyed. Whether it had any affect is doubtful as his authority had ceased to exist. The shelling continued for about 15 minutes and much damage was caused to the enemy that was in the open. We faced a lot of shrapnel, dust and mud flying in our faces. After a feeble attempt to assault, the enemy faltered, broke line, and withdrew in disorder, leaving behind the dead. 5/11 GR attacked Saulakhandi and Malahar, the two forward companies at first light. The tanks of both 63 Cav and 69 Armoured Regiment provided fire support. "C" Company 32 Baluch at Saulakhandi put up a stubborn resistance but was eventually defeated. Many acts of bravery on the part of our men were recorded in this battle.

After the capture of Saulakhandi, the enemy realized the hopelessness of their situation. With the capture of their commanding officer and destruction of their headquarters, there was no central authority to command and control the battle. The defenders were demoralized and their survival instincts overtook them. "B" Company under Major T.B. Rai made light of the enemy resistance at Malahar who surrendered in large numbers. "C" Company under Capt. M.S. Pathania mopped up the remaining opposition by 1000 hrs from isolated pockets. He managed to rush the RCC Bridge on the river at Mahasthan before an enemy demolition party could fire the charges. Four hundred pounds of explosives to demolish the bridge was recovered. One member of the demolition firing party was killed and one JCO and four jawans were captured.

I sent PA-5511 Major Muhammad Ajmal, the officiating commanding officer along with PSS-8810 Capt. Muhammad Salim, adjutant, PSS-100992 Capt. Sherzaman, AMC, medical officer and the radio operators to headquarters after the link up. By 1200 hrs of 13 December, 32 Baluch had ceased to exist. It was a great humiliation for the battalion. This was 5/11 Gorkha Rifles' finest hour when they not only routed the enemy but had completely annihilated an adversary battalion by a bold infiltration and attack.

Battle of Bogra

The battle of Mahasthan had cleared the axis to Bogra. The GOC was now in a great hurry to capture Bogra before it was reinforced by remnants of the Pakistani 205 Infantry Brigade, 34 Infantry Brigade from Rajshahi or even 57 Infantry Brigade that had crossed the Hardinge Bridge on 11 December and were in Pabna. An early capture of Bogra would not only accomplish the tasks assigned to the division but also assist in capitulation of the strategic objective of Dacca. The battle of Bogra is unique in the history of the 1971 war as it was the only one that was fought in built-up areas. Ferocity of an unimaginable level between the two foes was witnessed. Every inch of ground was contested. Bogra was an important town, communications centre and a district headquarters. It had a large railway yard and an airstrip. HQ 205 Infantry Brigade and their logistics base were also located there.

5/11 provided a firm base for 340 Infantry Brigade's final assault on Bogra. In the afternoon of 13 December, 2/5 GR along with a squadron of 63 Cav (T-55) resumed advance along the Rangpur-Bogra road to capture the town from the north. 6 Guards with 69 Armoured Regiment (PT-76) bypassed it from the east and cut it off from the south. They attacked the town from the south and the southeast. 2/5 GR cleared the area north of the railway line by midday of 14 December against stiff opposition. 6

Guards also made steady progress from the south against determined resistance. 165 Mountain Brigade's thrust from the northwest had reached Khetlal but was still far away from Bogra. By the afternoon it was apparent that additional forces would be required to give an impetus to the operations, lest the strategic time frame was upset. Thus 4 Madras and 5/11 GR, along with additional artillery, were released to join the battle. Accordingly, at 1500 hrs on 14 December, 5/11 GR were tasked to concentrate in the Jaypurpara area, north of Bogra, by 2000 hrs. Around 2200 hrs, it was ordered to isolate Bogra from the west by first light and clear all enemy resistance west of the Bogra-Sherpur road by last light. The only avenue available for the enemy to be reinforced/escape was from Naogaon/Nator in the west/southwest. This had to be sealed by 5/11 GR to force early capitulation of the enemy.

Brig. Tajammul Hussain had taken command of the Bogra garrison. 4 FF (Hilli), 13 FF (Bhaduria), 32 Baluch (Mahasthan) and 8 Baluch from (Jaipurhat and Goraghat) had fallen back on Bogra. By 14 December, the town had strength of more than 2,000 all ranks. The Pakistanis could hold Bogra for more than a week with the resources at their disposal. After the war, Pakistani officers told us that Brig. Tajammul had gone around the entire town organizing the defences. Later, during the battle, he moved in his jeep with a loudspeaker exhorting them to fight till martyred. He was a fanatic and inspired his men by reciting the Koran. He was commissioned in 7 Rajput Regiment in February 1947 from OTS, Bangalore but opted to serve in Pak Army. He had volunteered to fight against the Indian Army even though he held a coveted appointment at the GHQ. He took over the Brigade on 17 November 1971 and refused to surrender even when his brigade had ceased to exist. He felt it was dishonourable for a Muslim to surrender. He attempted to flee to Nepal in disguise and then escape to Pakistan. He was apprehended by the Mukti Bahini while escaping and pleaded for mercy when battered. He was then handed over to the Indian Army. It is noteworthy that he was one of the few who were promoted after repatriation. He staged coups in 1977 and 1980 as GOC 23 Infantry Division. He was tried by court martial and imprisoned but pardoned in 1988 after the death of General Zia-ul-Haq.

As per our brigade plan, Bogra had to be sealed from all directions for the enemy's piecemeal destruction. 5/11 GR was tasked to capture the railway station, PS and Circuit House in the heart of the town. These three areas were the core of their defences. They were fortified and held strongly. The troops withdrawing from other areas had also reinforced the perimeter defence around these landmarks. We marched about 20 km from Jaypurpara cross-country at night, out flanking Bogra from the west. "B" Company established a road block at Sahardigi cutting off Bogra from Naogaon. The remaining battalion concentrated at track junction southwest of Bogra by 0500 hrs under the cover of darkness. We carried out our final preparations at this place and received orders at 0630 hrs. It was very quiet and not a single soul stirred. Stray dogs and abandoned cattle roamed in the streets. The civil population had fled the town or had gone into hiding, anticipating the looming danger of battle.

We commenced operations astride the Nator-Bogra road at 0830 hrs to capture our objectives. Heavy artillery fire was brought down on suspected enemy positions. Some buildings caught fire and some were demolished. It was an awe-inspiring and spectacular display of fireworks. We followed the artillery shelling at a distance. "A" and "C" companies secured Malgram by 0930 hrs without any opposition. It appeared as if we had entered a ghost town. There was no enemy but we noticed damaged buildings, maimed animals and bomb craters along our route. The atmosphere was eerie. Perhaps the enemy did not expect an outflanking move and attack from the southwest. He had thus left the outer perimeter undefended. After we had secured Malgram, "A" Company led by me was to capture the railway station and "C" Company under Capt. M.S. Pathania was to capture the Circuit House. "D" Company was in reserve. Both the objectives were about 3 km from our start point. The road bifurcated to these objectives from Malgram. We were now in a heavily built-up area. Bogra was remarkably similar to Siliguri or Malda across the border in India.

Here, it is important to explain the geography, layout and composition of the town so that the ferocity and savagery of the fighting; and the difficulties we faced in overcoming enemy resistance is understood in the right perspective. Bogra was a typical Bengal town. It was a combination of modern housing colonies and old township with narrow streets. Slums and shanties were intermingled with new colonies. There was no regular pattern of roads and streets. Some were wide with trees on both sides while others were very narrow and winding. Each colony had a mixture of colonial bungalows with large compounds, rows of low small houses as well as clusters of mud houses of the poor. The colonies were interspersed with ponds, groves, parks and playfields. There were also some tall structures like water towers and multi-level buildings. All in all, it was an ideal mixture, advantageous to the defender. He could fight from roof tops of concrete buildings. The tall buildings and towers gave him observation and a good field of fire. The bungalows provided him with open killing areas. The ponds and narrow roads, streets and alleys channelized our movement and bunching created good targets for him. Concrete houses had been fortified and automatic weapons effectively covered all movement. Placements for RRs, HMGs and other direct firing weapons had been made. Artillery fire caused damage to buildings but few casualties. The 75/24 howitzer was more accurate but less effective because the small shell caused little structural damage. Our best weapons were small arms, grenades, 3.5 in RLs and 57 mm RCLs. Every one carried Molotov cocktails as we knew that a Pakistani feared death by burning. They believed such a death would consign a Muslim to hell. He was thus mortally scared of this improvised weapon.

Before we set off from Malgram, I bid good luck to Capt. Pathania. He appeared a little anxious and apprehensive but we parted for our objectives with a smile and a victory sign. He had been appointed a company commander only four days earlier as a replacement for Maj. N. Bhasin. He came from an illustrious military family. His father had served in 6th Royal Battalion 13 Frontier Force Rifles as a VCO with General Muhammad Musa who later became COAS of the Pakistan Army. Pathania was the youngest of five brothers who were all officers.

I divided my company into two columns. No. 1 platoon under 2/Lt. Teja Bedi to clear all built up areas on the right of road and No. 2 platoon under Subedar Dil Bahadur Tamang to clear the area left of the road. No. 3 platoon under Subedar Madan Kumar Rai moved behind my group as reserve. No sooner had we covered a few blocks of houses when we came under intense auto fire from all directions. The battle commenced as we had hit the main enemy defences. We had to clear each house as part of our drill. This went fine in the early stages and the platoon commanders had some control over their men. But as the casualties started occurring and the intensity of enemy fire increased, cohesion broke. Some of the houses from where the enemy was engaging us had to be cleared from the back alleys or rear while the enemy was fixed on the front or roof top of adjoining houses. In one such action, Rfn. Kamal Rai and Man Bahadur Limbu jumped through a rear window and killed three enemies before the others scurried in fear to the next block. Sections leapfrogged from one house to another, physically evicting the enemy with grenades and Molotov cocktails.

The enemy put up heavy resistance in each encounter. He abandoned the building only when he was killed/wounded, trapped or isolated. Booby traps also put a break on our actions. Some of our sections lost cohesion and landed up with other platoons. Some continued to fight independently till last light. The enemy would allow us to close in and then bring down intense fire with all weapons, pinning us down or making us run for cover helter-skelter. We made very slow progress and by midday managed to clear only about a km or so of the area. I moved just behind both the platoons with enemy bullets flying all around, crouching and crawling along with the men. When Nk. Bal Bahadur Rai's men were held up by a HMG, the 75/24 howitzers came to our rescue blasting the enemy fortification. The 57 mm RCL was also effective in some such situations. An anxious commanding officer asked me to speed up the operations. He also launched "D" Company in the wake of "C" Company to give momentum to the operations. "B" Company was asked to join the battalion as reserve. Events were now moving fast and there was no time to think of life or death.

By now we were half way to the railway station-somewhere near a water tower. This structure was dominating the entire landscape. It was fortified at various levels to engage us successively at different ranges. We were effectively pinned down and could not move. We suffered two fatal casualties in quick succession while attempting to capture it. Rfn. Rum Bahadur

Limbu jumped the fence to enter the staircase of the water tower but was critically wounded by enemy fire. I asked Rfn. Kharka Bahadur Limbu from the same platoon who had taken a position close to me to neutralize the enemy firing at us. He took a hit in the abdomen as he dashed across. He looked towards me in pain and signalled if he could be rescued. We made several attempts to reach him under even cover of artillery fire but could not succeed in the face of heavy and accurate fire. This position was holding up two of my platoons for quite some time. All our attempts to move ahead were thwarted.

Finally, I decided to change the direction of the attack. While one section of No. 3 platoon continued to engage the enemy and protect the wounded, we bypassed the enemy further to the east and west of it. We faced stubborn resistance but somehow penetrated through the gaps. After about an hour, the enemy slowly gave way on the flanks of the water tower. He kept falling back towards the railway station. By 1700 hrs we were still at least one km from our objective. Realizing that it would be very difficult to fight at night, we decided to put in every ounce of our effort to reach our objective by last light. We used all the weapons and firepower at our disposal against each building occupied by the enemy that came in our way. We reduced it to rubble or set it on fire to flush him out. Many acts of bravery have gone unrecorded and unnoticed against the enemy during this time. The pulverizing effect of our fire and our bold and fearless actions took a heavy toll of the enemy and demoralized him.

Amazingly, our advance quickened. Perhaps the enemy realized that the situation was becoming hopeless every minute and fighting at night in isolated pockets would destroy them piecemeal. So they started falling back towards a safe area. Just before last light, No. 1 platoon under Teja Bedi captured part of the railway station while we were still some distance away in the west. It was a coup. Lnk. Man Bahadur's section surprised the Pakistanis holding the railway station who ran away along the railway line towards Naogaon without a fight. When the enemy found us in their rear they panicked and abandoned their fortified positions. They withdrew along the railway line towards Naogaon. We had breached the inner perimeter of defence and captured the whole railway station by last light. We quickly organized its defence. I did not pursue the enemy along the railway line but sent out an MMG detachment about 200 yards away under Hav. Kishore Chandra Pradhan to protect our flank. This area was part of the railway yard with a big shed close by. After securing the area, the gun was left with its gunners and the others went off to rest. Suddenly, there was firing; the gunners were killed and those resting were taken prisoners along with the MMG by the Pakistanis in the shed. I deferred any rescue action at that point of time as our priority was to secure the railway station against any enemy counter action. We had to regain control of the men who were still engaged with the enemy in isolated pockets. No. 3 Platoon was still at the water tower and found it difficult to move due to large water bodies and barricades all along its route. We had to also collect our casualties scattered at different places. Had the MMG detachment investigated the shed, the large concentration of Pakistanis there would have been revealed. All of them could have been killed by one or two artillery salvos.

I informed the commanding officer of our success as also about the MMG detachment mishap. I also told him about the presence of a large group of the enemy west of my location. My thoughts now turned to Rfn. Kharka Bahadur Limbu who lay helplessly wounded at the water tower along with other casualties. I was informed that the enemy had vacated the water tower quietly under the cover of darkness. Rfn. Kharka Bahadur had been rescued but he had lost a lot of blood and was very weak and feeble. Before he could be evacuated, life ebbed out of him. I contacted "C" Company to find out about their progress but was informed by Subedar Udai Prasad Rai that Capt. M.S. Pathania had been killed while assaulting an enemy position. I was very sad. Perhaps Pathania had a premonition about his death and that is why he was anxious and apprehensive that morning. I had four dead and about eight other casualties by nightfall. We were tired and fatigued. We spent the cold night on whatever food was left with us since the previous night. By 2030 hrs, all the objectives had been secured. However, we waited till first light to link up to avoid cross firing between our own troops. To our surprise, there was no enemy reaction against the railway station during the night. By and large, it was peaceful except for an occasional rifle shot/volleys in some distant area. At 0930 hrs of 16 December we learnt that a unilateral ceasefire had been declared by India and any Pakistani defence personnel who surrendered were to be taken as a POW. Those who continued to fight would be treated as enemies.

At about 1030 hrs, our sentry noticed some movement from the railway shed. First, a white flag was seen followed by a few jawans in khaki with their arms raised. We allowed them to approach. We also spotted two short persons in olive green among them. They were followed by about 200 other soldiers carrying their arms. They were asked to halt outside our defences and 2/Lt. Teja Bedi met them there. He informed me that there were 8 officers, 6 JCOs and 212 ORs. Hav. Kishore Pradhan, along with his gunners and MMG was also part of the group. They surrendered their weapons and belts. The group consisted of elements from 4 FF, 13 FF, 8 Baluch and other arms and services. We segregated them in groups of officers, JCOs and ORs. They surrendered 4 HMGs, 20 LMGs and a heap of rifles, sub-machine guns and pistols along with other military equipment.

They told me that two companies of 8 Baluch had been defending the perimeter around the railway station and one company was in the circuit house. They had been ordered to fight till the end. They had suffered continuous defeats and had been on the run since 8 December and had realized the hopelessness of the situation. Many of them were lying dead under the rubble and many others were sick. The Bengali population was baying for their blood. Thus they had no will to fight any more. When they heard the news of the ceasefire on the radio, they decided to ignore the orders of their commander and surrendered. The POWS were hungry, dishevelled, battle fatigued and demoralized. They informed me of the location of their rations, CSD and equipment store and a cook house very close by and sought permission to cook food as they were hungry since the previous day. I agreed to their request.

During this period, I interacted with the officers. There was one Muhajir major from UP now settled in Karachi. He was very worried, nervous and depressed. All the while he was keen to know the extent of damage caused to Karachi by our Navy and Air Force and concerned about the safety of his family. Then there were two Punjabi majors who were sulking and sullen in defeat. They were ignored by the other officers. Three other officers were happy that the war was over and that they were alive. They preferred to smoke and rest in a corner. Lastly, there were two lieutenants. War was a new experience for them and being POWS even more. They chatted eagerly and without any inhibitions. They ignored the Punjabi officers who felt uneasy because of their cosiness towards us. They told me that they were Rangars (Jat converts) who had migrated from Sonepat-Panipat. Their fathers were part of the Indian Army during the war in Burma and had been POW of Japanese. It was a coincidence that like their fathers, both of them were POW together, now in custody of the Indian Army.

They narrated a number of personal anecdotes of their life in PMA and their unit. They said that when the GOC had visited their battalion, a shoot was organized for him. They were asked to hide behind bushes with a cage full of partridges. There was a mix-up and the partridges were released before the arranged signal. The shoot was a flop and they were reprimanded for it by the commanding officer. The JCOs and ORs seemed happy that the war was over and were eager to return home. They praised the Indian Army in some way or other. All of a sudden, a large crowd of Bangladeshis and Mukti Bahini appeared to see the POW. They were taunted and jeered by them. Some of them brandished weapons, swords and knives at them. The Pakistanis seemed to be edgy and scared. The atmosphere changed dramatically and even the Punjabi officers pleaded for safety from the Mukti Bahini. I marched off all the POW under heavy escort to the battalion HQ before the angry and agitated Bangladeshis created a new situation.

Hav. Kishore Chandra Pradhan, the MMG detachment commander who had been captured by the Pakistanis told me that there was a clamour among a section of the Pakistanis to torture and shoot them in reprisal. But a major rebuked the hotheads and told them that they were surrounded and if these prisoners were killed, the Indian Army would not spare any of them either. The other officers supported him. Thereafter they were treated gently. After despatching POWs, we organized a proper military funeral for our fallen comrades. For us, the battle of Bogra was over when HQ 205 Infantry Brigade was captured. The BM, along with GSO 3 (Ops), CO 80 Field Regiment, 3 Engineer officers and 50 ORs surrendered disobeying orders of their commander. The battle honours of 8 Baluch were also captured. By the evening of 16 December, 14 officers, 6 JCOs and 262 ORs had surrendered. A formal surrender ceremony was held at Bogra on 18 December where Maj. Gen. Nazar Hussain Shah, GOC 16 Infantry Division, handed over his pistol and belt to Maj. Gen. Lachhman Singh, GOC 20 Mountain Division, in the presence of about 2,000 all ranks. The capture of Bogra was a landmark victory in which every soldier of 5/11 GR played a vital role against a strongly entrenched enemy. It was a classic battle in a built-up area where grit and determination combined with individual and collective gallant actions and military skills were on display. The pride of the Pakistan Army lay prostrate. They had been pulverized, humbled and reduced to a pathetic condition with no option but the ignominy of surrender.

War in other Sectors

By 7 December, the defence of East Pakistan in all the four sectors started crumbling under the weight of the Indian offensive. The Pakistani 9 Infantry Division in the SW sector had been ripped by 2 Corps. 107 Infantry Brigade had its back to the wall in Khulna and the 57 Infantry Brigade was pushed out of the sector across Harding Bridge by 10 December. 16 Infantry Division in the NW sector had been severed at the waist by 20 Mountain Division, when the GOC was ambushed on 7 December. The Rangpur-Dinajpur garrison was isolated and the 205 Infantry Brigade was trapped by the columns heading for Bogra. Due to the fast pace of the operations, 34 Infantry Brigade did not come into play at all. In the Northern sector, 93 Infantry Brigade collapsed when 31 Baluch at Kamalpur withdrew to Jamalpur on 5 December forcing the withdrawal of 33 Punjab to Mymensingh. In the confusion that followed they were ordered to withdraw to Dacca by 10 December. When Indian paratroopers landed at Tangail, the entire brigade disintegrated. In the NE sector, 14 Infantry Division had been rolled back west of the Meghna River by 8 December when Indian troops reached the river ports of Chandpur, Daukhandi and Ashuganj. All roads to Dacca from the east now lay open. Maulvi Bazaar had fallen by 7 December. Heli landing by 4/5 GR southeast of Sylhet had unnerved the enemy. Both 313 and 202 Infantry Brigades were trapped and under siege since 13 December when they ultimately capitulated. Similarly, after the capture of Akhaura, 57 Mountain Division advanced to Brahmanbaria and Ashuganj and in the process disseminated 27 Brigade that retreated to Bhairab Bazar on 10/11 December. In the SE sector, the 39 Infantry Division offered feeble resistance to our 23 Mountain Division that swept them out of the sector. They were in full retreat both from Comilla and Feni-Laksham by 10 December. Maj. Gen. Rahim Khan abandoned his HQ at Chandpur on 10 December and left for Dacca. By 12 December the division ceased to exist.

By 7 December, barely five days into the war, the Pakistani Eastern Command was heading towards defeat. Lt. Gen. A.A.K. Niazi was summoned by the Governor, Dr. A.M. Malik to brief him on the operational situation. Gen. Niazi accepted that his forces had suffered reverses in all sectors and the situation was grim. Formations were disintegrating and retreating. He saw the ignominy of defeat staring in his face and broke down, sobbing unashamedly[14] in front of all who were present. The news of Gen. Niazi sobbing spread like wildfire in his HQ which affected the already sagging morale of his force. The next three days were heavy for him as all his divisions had lost coherence and pushed beyond the line of penetration. To make matters worse, Pakistan had not made any gains in the west. From this point onwards, Niazi lost his confidence. He was despondent and a disappointed man who had no control over his command.

Dacca[15] was to be protected by an outer and inner perimeter defence system. Line Manekganj in the northwest, Kaliakair in the north, Narayanganj in the northeast, and Daudkandi in the east and Munshiganj in the southeast formed the outer perimeter. Formations were to fall back to occupy these positions. This did not happen as all these divisions were either disseminated or trapped by Indian forces. The line Mirpur Bridge, Tongi, Demra and Narayanganj formed the inner perimeter. 1,500 EPCAF personnel, 1,800 policemen and 300 razakars and other garrison troops were available for fighting. Major General Jamshed was in charge of the Dacca defences. By 12 December when he lost control of the war, Lt. Gen. Niazi, in consultation with Maj. Gen. Jamshed and Rao Farman Ali sent their recommendations for a ceasefire to Yahya Khan through the Governor.

On 14 December, the IAF attacked the Government House and a shaken Governor immediately resigned and moved out to Hotel Intercontinental that had been declared a neutral zone. From this point onwards, there was no government in East Pakistan and all the powers rested with Lt. Gen. Niazi.

On 14 December at 1530 hrs, Lt. Gen. Niazi was asked to hold on till a UN ceasefire was agreed to. So desperate and demoralized was Niazi at that time that he immediately set about to obtain a ceasefire and contacted the US consulate at Dacca for it. On 15 December, the Indian Army asked Lt. Gen. Niazi to surrender[16] unconditionally immediately if he wanted to stop further destruction and death of his army. The coordination for surrender could be done with HQ Eastern Command. GHQ Rawalpindi allowed Lt. Gen. Niazi to accept the ceasefire and by midnight of 15/16 December, the orders to formations were flashed. While all this was going on, it was realized that Dacca was unguarded as none of the troops were in their designated position when Maj. Gen. G.C. Nagra, the GOC 101 Area, appeared at Mirpur Bridge in the morning of 16 December to demand surrender.

The situation was so hopeless that Lt. Gen. Niazi, after consulting Maj. Gen. Farman Ali, Rear Admiral Sharriff and Jamshed immediately received Maj. Gen. Nagra as the representative of the Indian Army and gave him a respectful and warm welcome. At 1300 hrs on 16 December, Major General J.F.R. Jacob, COS Eastern Army, landed at Dacca with the surrender documents. Niazi was hesitant initially but he agreed meekly when Jacob told him that there was no choice with him under the circumstances. The same afternoon Lt. Gen. A.K.K. Niazi surrendered[17] to Lt. Gen. J.S. Aurora at 1655 hrs at a ceremony that was held at the Dacca Race Course. Bangladesh was born that instant.

A total of 93,000 Pakistani soldiers thus laid down their arms and were POW. However, many were worried about the trials of the war criminals among them. I visited the POW at Rangpur during dinner time and was surprised to see them drinking and singing as if it was the end of an exercise and not a POW camp of a defeated army. There was no sign of shame, remorse or guilt on their faces. Some of course did talk of revenge in the future disapproving the conduct of their colleagues. I was not surprised at their reasons for the defeat.

There were plenty of lessons to be learnt from this war on both sides. Good planning, sound logistics, bold execution, tri-service cooperation and maintenance of mobility were the major takeaways for us. The mobile warfare conducted by 20 Mountain Division was a decisive factor for the success. Once 66 Mountain Brigade had punched a hole in the defences Liddell Hart's theory of "The flowing torrent" commenced. The enemy was not given any time to regroup or reorganize his defences. The advance was continuous during day and night till we reached the final objective. The enemy was outmanoeuvred mentally and physically. His command and control mechanism was paralyzed. On our side some commanders showed timidity and were averse to risk taking. They were conventional, calculative and cautious. 202 Brigade kept bashing its head against prepared defences till the end of the war. Similarly, 66 Mountain Brigade exhausted itself by 6 December and was relegated to playing a secondary role thereafter. 165 Mountain Brigade remained in firm base and out of action. The IAF played a very significant role. INS *Vikrant* dominated the Bay of Bengal and blockaded East Pakistan effectively. The role of the Mukti Bahini in the war cannot be undermined. They created a fear psychosis in the enemy who was afraid to venture out of their fixed defences. It made the task of manoeuvring forces easy to defeat the enemy. The allegations of looting by the Indian Army cannot be denied. These cases were dealt with severely. Some senior officers were dismissed from service while others were denied promotions. Overall, the Indian Army conducted itself professionally.

In my opinion, the Pakistan Army personnel who had committed war crimes should have been tried. Many of them were rapists, looters and murderers. They committed inhuman and barbaric acts on innocent people and should have been made accountable. This was gross injustice to the Bangladeshis. Whatever the reasons, the Indian Government failed the Bangladesh people on this account. The second point that needs to be answered by the Government of India is why the 93,000 POW were returned to Pakistan without any quid pro quo. Why did India not extract the most advantageous solutions to the other problems that, Pakistan had created for us? The third point is why did India not negotiate realignment of the border with Bangladesh, particularly the security of the Kishanganj and Siliguri corridors, and an outlet to the Bay of Bengal through Tripura or Mizoram? The least it could demand was transit rights to the port of Chittagong. These questions will continue to haunt the conscience of the country. Many of us will continue to think whether our sacrifices went waste or was it worth it to let go of Pakistan and Bangladesh scot-free at the cost of our national security. If Mrs. Indira Gandhi had shown statesmanship, we would be a safer and secure country today. She failed both India and Bangladesh in spite of a brilliant victory.

NOTES

1. *Witness to Surrender* by Siddiq Salik, pp. 25-30. The Awami League had won all the seats in East Pakistan and was the largest party in the whole of Pakistan.
2. It was sponsored by Pakistan as per Pakistan judicial inquiry and *Witness to Surrender* by Siddiq Salik, p. 37.
3. *Witness to Surrender* by Siddiq Salik, pp. 71-90. Brutal execution of civilian population is narrated. *The 1971 Indo-Pak war* by Maj. Gen. Hakeem Arshad Qureshi, chs. 2 &3 narrate the events.
4. *Betrayal of East Pakistan* by Lt. Gen. A.A.K. Niazi, pp. 37-43. Yakub Khan was an aristocrat and son of the prime minister of the Nawab of Rampur. He opted to serve in the Pakistan Army after Partition.
5. *Witness to Surrender* by Siddiq Salik, pp 35-36. After the talks with Mujib failed, Yahya was hosted by Bhutto at his estate for a duck shoot and the conspiracy to deny the premiership to Mujib and the crackdown was hatched.
6. *Witness to Surrender* by Siddiq Malik, p. 92 and 94-96. Similar stories were narrated to us also by many survivors.
7. *A Tale of Millions* by Rafiqul Islam, pp. 226-229, 269-274. Atrocities committed by the Pakistan army.
8. Supported a coup against Mujib in 1974.and became President in 1977.
9. Died in a counter coup against by Zia-ur-Rehman.
10. *The 1971 Indo-Pak war* by Maj. Gen. Hakeem Arshad Qureshi.
11. *Betrayal of East Pakistan* by A.A.K. Niazi, p. 103.
12. *Liberation of Bangladesh*, vol. 1, by Maj. Gen, Sukhwant Singh, p. 82.
13. *Surrender at Dacca* by J.R.F. Jacob, pp. 69-70.
14. *Witness to Surrender* by Siddiq Salik, p. 194.
15. *Betrayal of East Pakistan* by A.A.K. Niazi, pp. 206-207. Gen. Niazi's assertions are figments of his imagination and his assessment of the Indian Army is wrong as he lived in delusion.
16. *Surrender at Dacca* by J.F.R. Jacob, pp. 137-138; *Betrayal of East Pakistan* by A.A.K. Niazi, p. 190
17. *Betrayal of East Pakistan* by A.A.K. Niazi, p. 235; *Surrender at Dacca* by J.F.R. Jacob, pp. 146-147.

Map 6: Bangladesh: Initial Deployment

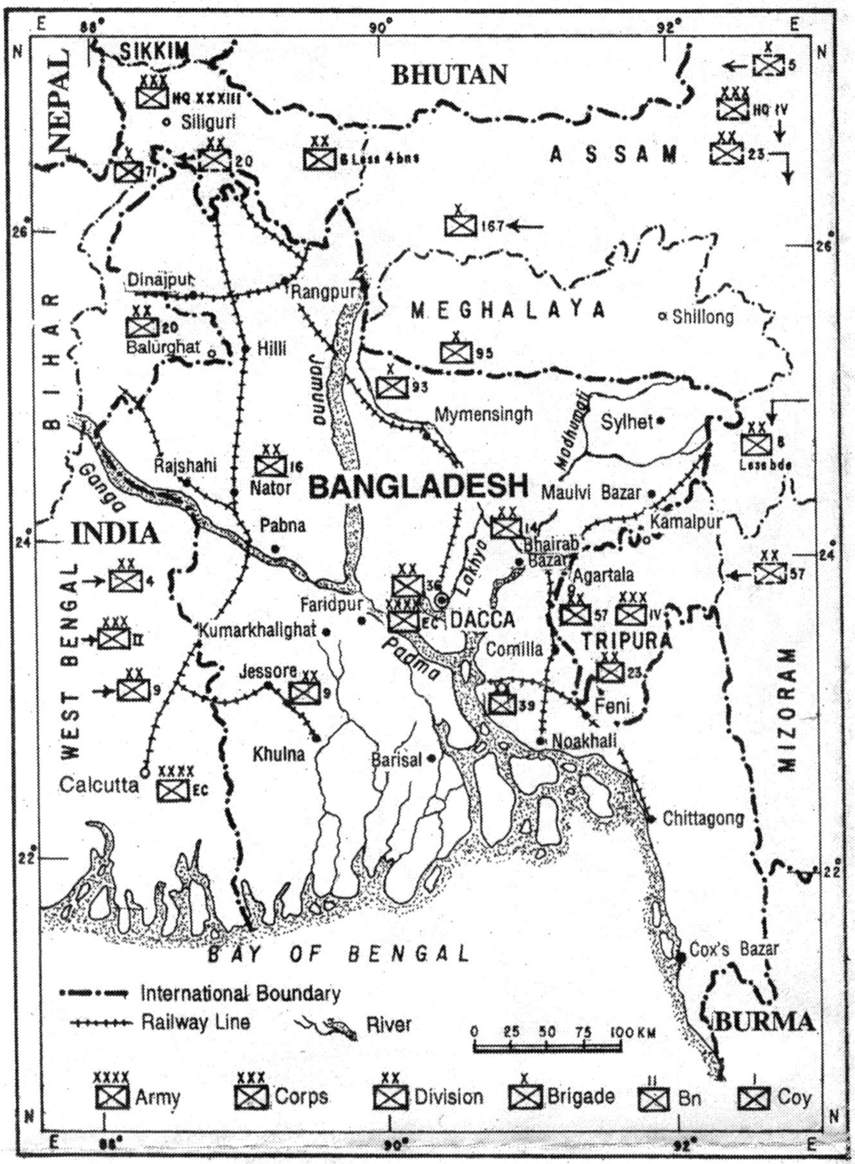

The external boundaries of India depicted in this map are neither correct nor authentic.

Map 7: North-West Sector

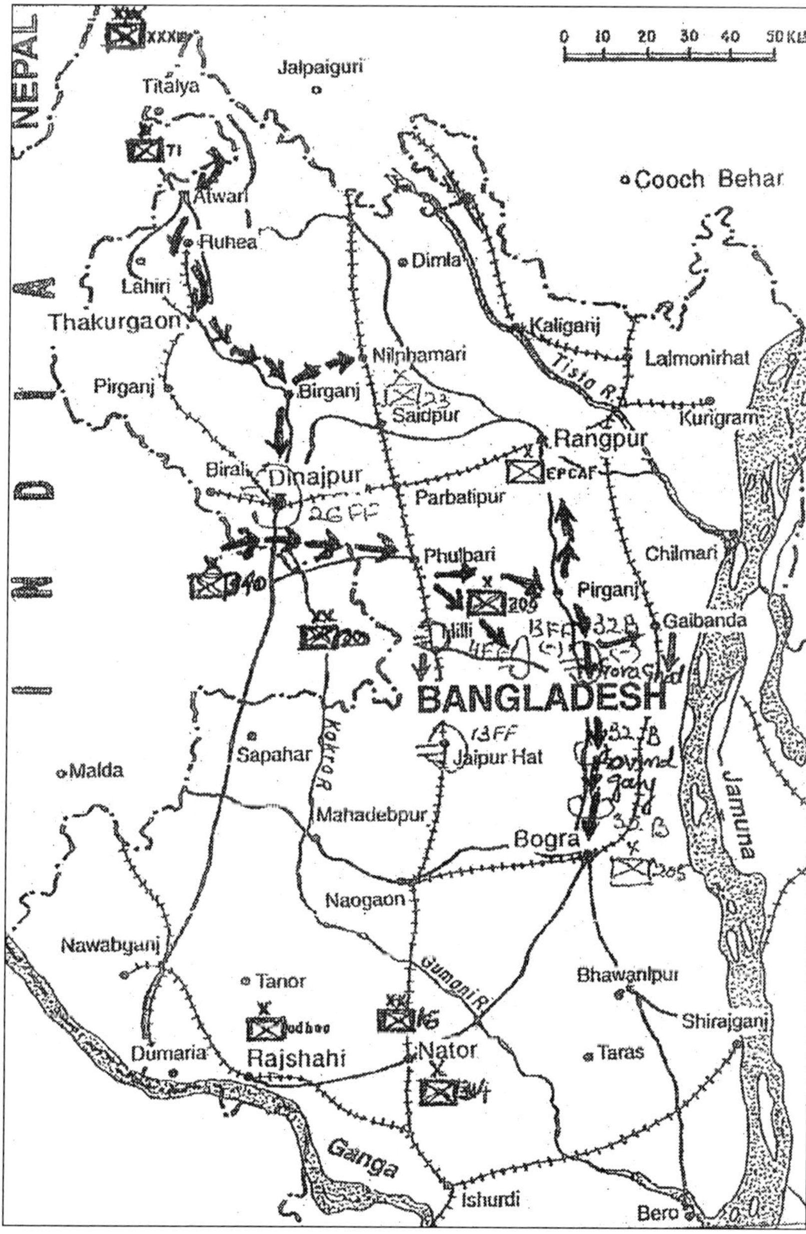

Map 8: 5/11 Gorkha Rifles: Area of Operations – Bangladesh-Bogra Sector, Nov-Dec 1971

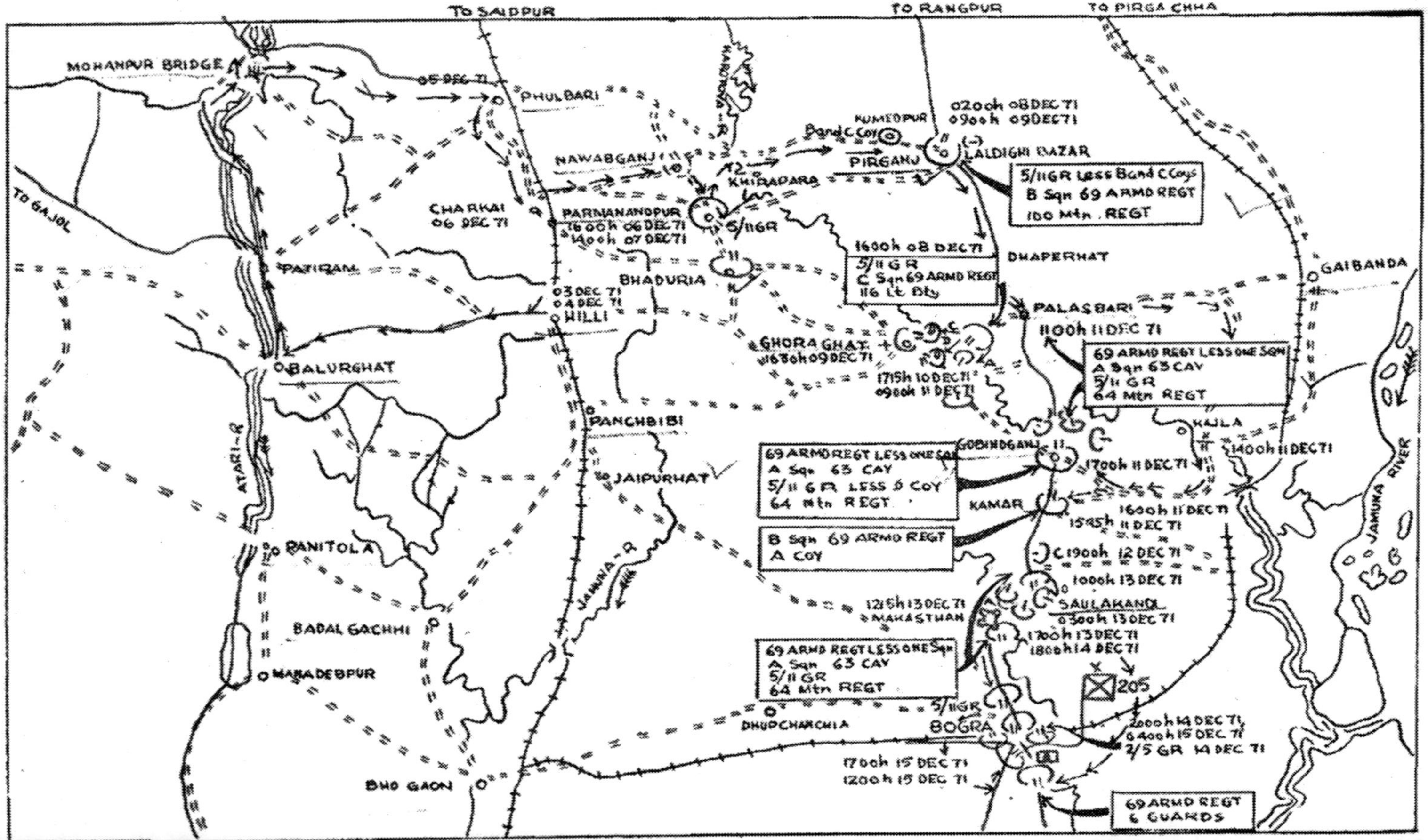

Map 9: Battle of Govindganj

Not to Scale

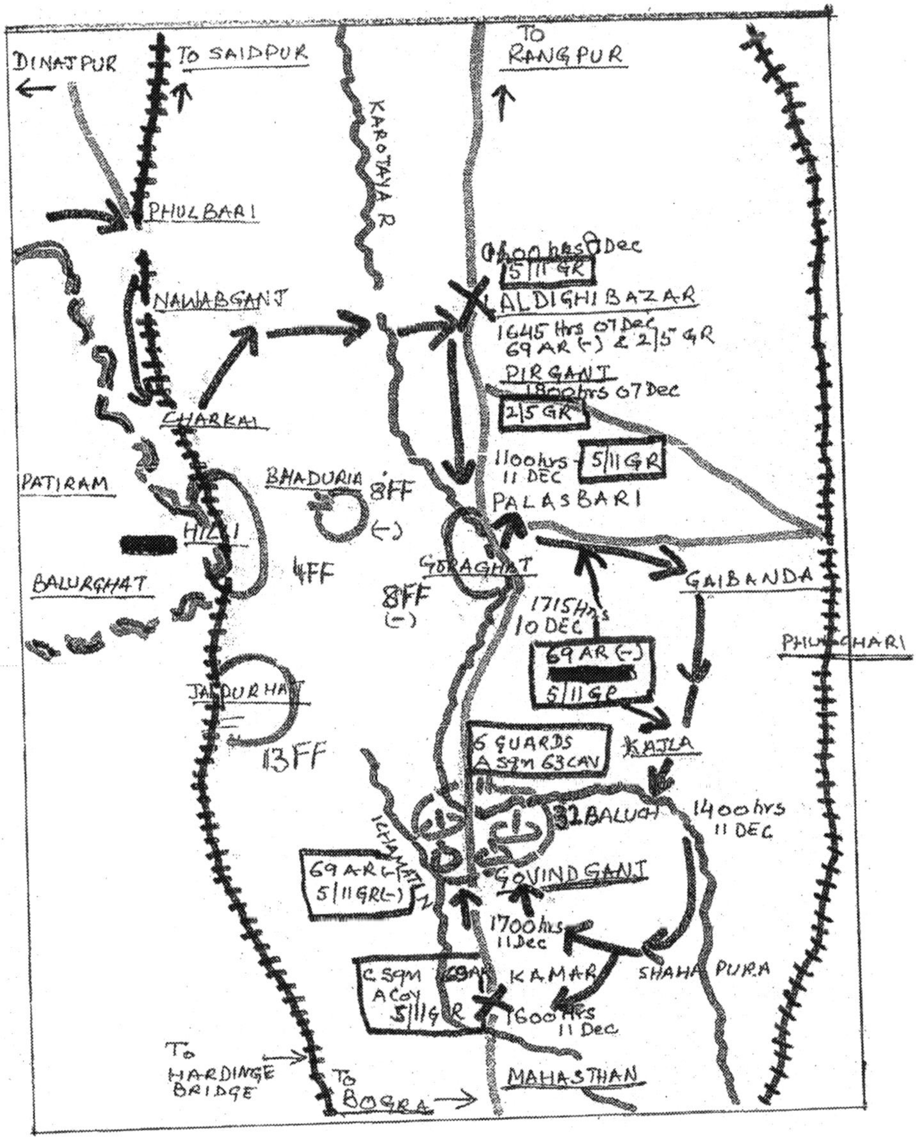

Map 10: Battle of Bogra: 5/11 Gorkha Rifles

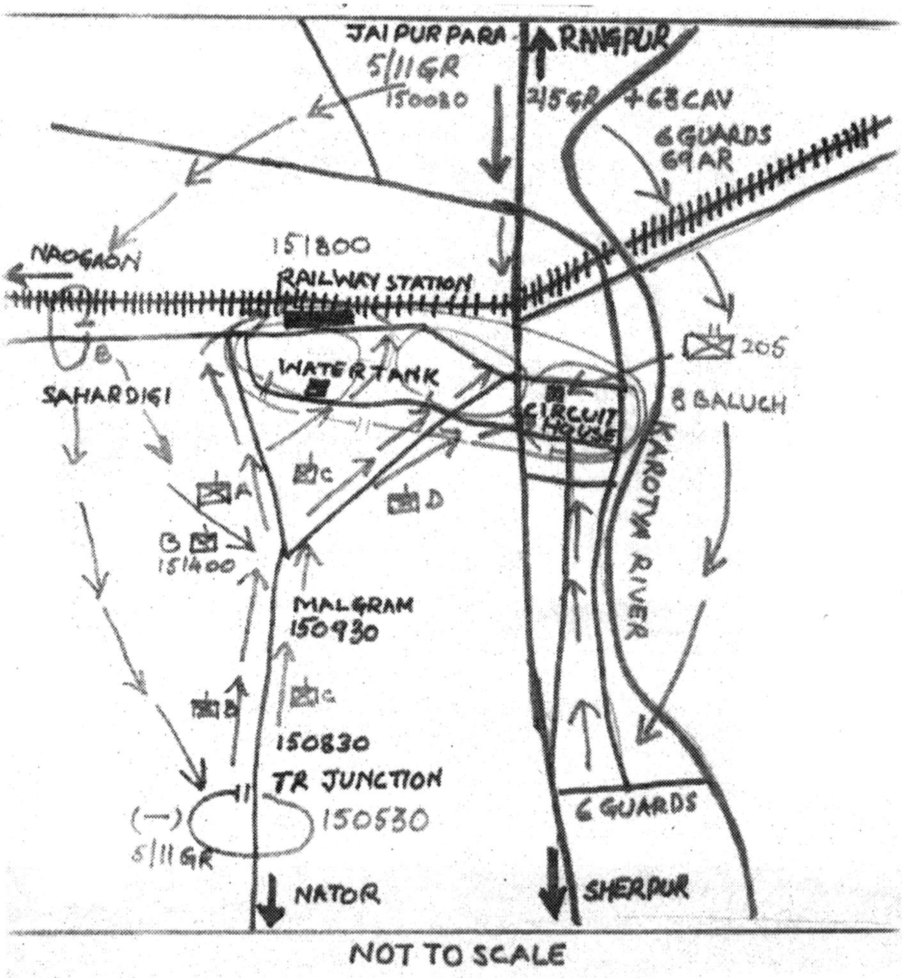

Chapter 4

The Intervening Years

Gujarat: The Western Front and Mhow

We moved to the Desert Sector on 25 December for our new operational role after the war ended. Major M.M. Walia, 4 Madras, Major B.M. Bali, 2/5 GR, and I were part of the advance party. We were feted by civilians at each station that our train halted. It was overwhelming and we were touched by the patriotism and adulations showered on us. The brigade concentrated at Jamnagar for operations in Kutch and Bhuj. Both the public and the ruler of Jamnagar hosted receptions in our honour. The ruler of Jamnagar was a Jadeja, a branch of the Bhattis/Yaduvanshis. A number of Ahirs reside in Kutch and Bhuj who are mainly agriculturists. They wear very colourful dresses and own large herds of cows, goats and camels. Gujarat was a very rich state and highly developed even in 1972. Gujaratis are entrepreneurs and businessmen by nature. Very few of them joined the army. The border areas and the Rann of Kutch are fascinating and full of wildlife. Herds of wild asses, camels, antelopes, and wild boars can be spotted easily. There was no dearth of partridges and other game in the countryside.

While at Jamnagar, we were informed that Lt. Col. Dias, Major A.S. Mamik and I had been awarded a Vir Chakra each while 2/Lt. T.S. Bedi and some others were awarded Sena Medals for gallantry. The award of Mahavir Chakra to the commander was a surprise as there were many officers and men who deserved this recognition instead. Lt. Gen. G.G. Bewoor, GOC-in-C, Southern Command, and the Colonel of our Regiment, also visited us. He was very happy with our performance during the war. We were shifted to Dharangdhara palace complex and after a short stay there to Kota in Rajasthan. Kota is located on the Chambal River and was an important princely state during the Mughal and British rule. It was carved out of Bundi and ruled by the Hada branch of Chouhan Rajputs. I was posted to MCTE Mhow as an instructor in the All-Arms Wing in April. I was not at all pleased with this posting that would contribute very little to my professional growth. At the same time, Lt. Col. F.T. Dias was posted to Bhutan as GSO 1. This was in recognition of his outstanding performance in the war.

Mhow suddenly came alive with commencement of training at all institutions located there. We remodelled the syllabus based on our war experiences and conducted outdoor exercises near the Narbada River. The Narbada, like the Ganga, is a holy river for Hindus. It originates in the Satpura and Vindyachal ranges and flows for 1,312 km east to west through the rift valleys in the states of Madhya Pradesh, Maharashtra, and Gujarat before draining into the Arabian Sea. It is dotted with places of pilgrimage such as Omkaleshwar, Maheshwar, Kaleshwar and Ankleshwar and many others. After one of the exercises, when it was a hot afternoon, I allowed the officers to swim in the river. I also decided to swim from one bank to the other. I was cautioned by the locals to avoid rapids and submerged rocks. I did not think much of their fears. I swam across the river through the rocks and small rapids without difficulty but during the return journey, I developed cramps and my legs refused to move. I sank in the water and was swept away downstream to a considerable distance. Death was staring in my face and I thought I would die. Suddenly I struck a submerged rock just near a rapid and gripped it tightly. I heaved myself slowly when a local swimmer who had noticed me drowning reached and pushed me up on the rock. After a little rest when the cramp subsided he guided me out of the river. I thanked my saviour and the Goddess Narbada for giving me another life. I enjoyed the peacetime routine at Mhow as it gave me enough time to reflect and study.

I also passed my Part C exam with distinction. On 28 January 1974, I married Neera at Rohtak. It was an arranged marriage though we had met on a few occasions earlier. At that time she was undergoing training as a doctor in the Govt. Medical College, Rohtak. She belonged to an illustrious family who had been bestowed a jagir of four villages and power to collect revenue of 45 villages with a title of jaildar by the rajah of Nabha. They were allowed judicial powers to hold court that lasted till the independence. Her grandfather was an alumnus of St. Stephen's College, Delhi, and held the post of a tehsildar and later retired as an IAS officer. Her father, Bikram Singh, was an alumnus of Hindu College, Delhi, and a brilliant advocate. Unfortunately, he died early. Neera herself was a brilliant student and had won a national scholarship. She graduated from King George's Medical College at Lucknow as an anaesthesiologist. She has been my constant and steadfast companion throughout our life.

Counter Insurgency in Mizo Hills and Defence College Wellington: A Temple of Knowledge

I was posted back to my battalion in April 1974 located at Trivandrum. Lt. Col. Pranab Dutt from 2/9 GR was our commanding officer. He was very intelligent, a good trainer and a natural leader. Major Sachinder Singh was our 2IC. They both ran a very happy and efficient team. Trivandrum cantonment was a legacy of the Travancore state forces and an ideal peace station. The Padamanabhaswami temple at Trivandrum is one of the richest temples and I visited often to pray. Kanya Kumari was a serene and peaceful place. No wonder Sri Vivekananda meditated there. Trivandram was also a cultural centre and we attended some outstanding performances of Bharata Natyam and Kathakali dances. Onam and annual boat races were very colourful and festive. Kerala is picturesque and famous for its backwaters. It is very hot and humid in the summers and receives torrential rains in the monsoons. Literacy in Kerala was very high and most people preferred white collar jobs. Money flowed in abundance from the Gulf where most Malayalis worked. The opulence was evident in big flashy dwellings that dotted the landscape. The communists ruled the state and the people were politically aware. Kerala had approximately 30 per cent each of Hindu, Muslim and Christian populations. They lived in harmony. Vasco da Gama in his pursuit to find India had landed at a spot near Calicut. The Portuguese, and later the Dutch, brought Christianity to Kerala. Tipu Sultan forced a large number of Hindus to convert to Islam.[1] Kerala Muslims are called

Moplahs and live mostly in Cannanor (now Kannur) and the north. The massacre of Hindus by Moplahs in 1920-21[2] is still recalled by the Hindus with bitterness. It was sad to notice that many of the attractive poor Moplah girls were married off to old Arabs as child brides. They were discarded and worked as house maids subsequently. The Portuguese and Dutch also forced conversions. Many of the poor Christian girls became nurses or nuns and worked in the Middle East or the West. The people were friendly and the men generally wore a white bush shirt and a mundum folded to the knees. The women wore the neriyathum mundum or sari and are attractive.

After my short stay at Trivandrum, we proceeded to Missamari in Assam in April 1975. Missamari was at the foothills surrounded by thick forests. It was an old Second World War US base that had been reactivated as a military station after the 1962 war. It was humid and hot in summer and very cold in winter. Monsoons brought torrential rains. Mosquitoes and snakes were our big enemies. The battalion was hauled up by the GOC for an inordinate number of malaria cases. Wild elephants, pythons, tigers and leopards were found in abundance in the foothills. We were part of 23 Mountain Division and 301 Mountain Brigade that were reserve formations for 4 Corps. Lt. Gen. S.L. Menezes, Grenadiers, Maj. Gen. M.C. Gupta, Engineers, and Brigadier M.N. Rawat, 1 GR, were our commanders. They were feared by everyone. It was said that one would be lucky to pass scrutiny of all the three at the same time. An atmosphere of fear and anxiety prevailed in the zone. But we survived them as we all worked very hard for each occasion. Major T.R. Prashar replaced Maj. Sachinder Singh who was posted out as the commanding officer of 7/11 GR. My company was trained for helicopter-borne operations with the IAF in MI-8 helicopters for any part of the theatre. We had to make load tables, be proficient in marking of landing zones, rappelling in and out of a hovering helicopter and operate behind enemy lines. Both the brigade and the divisional commanders tested us in a night exercise and were satisfied with our proficiency. The winter of 1975 brought bad news from home when my father suffered a stroke and Neera had to take care of him in my absence. It was tough for her to manage this in the midst of her final exam.

We received orders to move to Mizoram in February 1976 for anti-insurgency operations and spent four weeks at Counter-Insurgency School, Varangte, for training prior to induction. The CIJW School was an institution of excellence in counter-insurgency. Mizoram[3] is landlocked and about 250 km long and 135 km wide bordering both Myanmar and Bangladesh. The state is full of rolling hills, valleys, rivers and lakes. The altitude ranges from 3,000 to 7,000 ft. The climate is subtropical, hot and humid in summer followed by torrential rains and cold winters. Ninety per cent of the state is forested. The people of Mizoram are of mongoloid stock that migrated from neighbouring countries. Each tribe was governed by a tribal chief and they lived in autonomous villages. The British made their first contact with the Lushai Hills in 1840 and it became part of British India in 1895 after a series of expeditions.

Slash-and-burn or Jhum cultivation was the main occupation of the people. The area for cultivation was allocated by the village chief to each family. This resulted in large-scale destruction of the flora and fauna. The jungles abound in a variety of flora that includes tropical semi evergreens, tropical moist deciduous, subtropical broad -leafed trees and subtropical pine forests. Forty per cent of the forest comprises bamboo. There are a large variety of orchids and other flowers. Tigers, leopards, bears, antelopes, flying squirrels, monkeys and a large number of reptiles and pheasants live in the thick forests. In 1976, a two-way road connected Varangte, Aizwal and Serchip. Aizwal was connected to Champpai in the east on the Burma border. Free cross-border trade at this point was allowed with Burma. The railhead was near Varangte. The nearest airheads were Guwahati and Silchar. Most people are Christians. The people are hard working, disciplined, intelligent and religious. Many of them fought in both the great wars. The literacy rate is almost 100 per cent.

After independence the Lushai Hills became part of the state of Assam. Due to poor administration, lack of development and poor response of the government to the famine of 1959-60, protests by people started. The Mizo National Front headed by Laldenga, an ex-sergeant of the Indian Army, took birth, demanding independence from India. The protests turned into insurgency aided and abetted by both China and Pakistan. The army was deployed in 1966 to deal with the insurgency. The 1971 war and the emergence of Bangladesh was a big blow to the Insurgents as all their bases in East Pakistan were wiped out. Lack of external support could not sustain the momentum. Fatigue had also set in both among the population and the insurgents by 1976.

We were part of 57 Mountain Division and deployed along the Varangte-Aizwal road. We moved around frequently to conduct operations. Maj. Gen. Sushil Kumar was the GOC. He was responsible for controlling the insurgency that finally led to the peace accord. Mizoram was made a Union Territory and, with this, the administration and development of the area improved rapidly. Our battalion HQ was located at Aizawl and I was commanding "B" company. Information was received in March 1976 that one of the insurgent groups was returning from China with large quantities of arms and ammunition. I was tasked to intercept and destroy this gang on the Indo-Burma border north of Champai. It was an arduous seven-day trek through thick jungle and steep mountains to reach the deployment area. We camped for the night on the hill tops covered with forest to maintain secrecy. An old dugout covered with logs and sheets was my night shelter. We were struck by a severe thunderstorm followed by torrential rain and terrifying lightning at night while camping in this abandoned post. So severe was the intensity of the storm that the whole structure collapsed and I was buried under it. One of the beams struck my head and I fell with the centre pole by my side. I could not escape in time and it was a very fearsome situation. I thought I would die. I started digging my way out with the help of a wooden stave towards flashes of lightning I could see through one of the loopholes. After struggling for some time that seemed an eternity, I reached the loop hole through which I could breathe freely and see the trees in the lightning. I heaved myself up and jumped out of the loophole to land in a ditch full of water. At last, I was safe. I struggled to the nearest tree and to my relief found two of my men huddled under it. We searched for the others who had taken shelter under various trees, rocks and destroyed bunkers in the torrential rain. It was midnight when the storm ended; luckily all the men were safe with their weapons, ammunition and equipment. Once again Providence had saved me from death. We resumed our march the next day and reached 18 Jat at Ngopa commanded by Lt. Col. M.S. Kadhiyan. After a day's rest, the march was resumed with one company of Jats under my command and we reached the ridge separating India from Burma after another three days. We deployed platoon posts on the likely ingress routes over a distance of 12 km and remained so for about two weeks but no contact was made with the insurgents. Perhaps the news of our deployment had reached them. We were recalled.

On our way back, we met a number of Mizos who were friendly and provided us hospitality. Even in the border region, we found schools that were run by village committees. Every student paid the teacher a tin of rice as fee. There was plenty of fish in the jungle streams and we had no dearth of fresh vegetables from the forest. We met the deputy commissioner who was a Mizo, en route in a remote village. He was on an inspection tour. The village had prepared a feast for his welcome where dogs and monkeys were being roasted; they were considered delicacies. A cultural program by Mizo women in Puancheri and men in traditional Paw Kut dress was also organized where I was invited as the chief guest. We reached our base at 18 Jat after about a month. Our presence in the remote area signalled that the writ of the Government ran right up to the border. We were moved to Kolasib where Captain Madan Gopal, a paratrooper, joined as one of our platoon commanders. The battalion dominated the area very effectively and insurgent activities were under control. Great importance was given to fraternization with the local people that led to an active social life and many officers married attractive Mizo women. Lt. Col. Pranab Dutt was posted out in August 1976 and Lt. Col. R.P. Malhotra was posted as our new commanding officer. I had passed my DSSC examination and as such I was in and out of the battalion between August and December 1976.

Capt. Madan Gopal carried out a good operation against the insurgents on 6 December in Thingdawl near Kolasib. He launched a surprise raid on the hostile camp based on information from a source, after traversing thick jungle for six to seven hours in a dark night. The camp was located at Tuichieniui in thick jungle. The commander of the hostiles, a captain and his companion, was killed. One hostile was injured and captured while the rest escaped into the jungle. Capt. Madan Gopal was awarded a Sena Medal for this action. I was very happy with the performance of my company. I finally left the battalion at the end of December to join the Defence Services Staff College.

The college is located at Wellington near Ooty[4] in the Nilgiri Hills of Tamil Nadu. This region was ceded to the British by Tipu Sultan in 1799 after the battle of Srirangapatnam. Mr. John Sullivan, the collector of Coimbatore, fell in love with the beauty of this place in 1819. He described it as beautiful as Switzerland and built a cottage for himself around which the present town grew. The rich and some rajahs made their residences in this place. Thereafter, a convalescence home for British soldiers was established. It has a sub-tropical highland climate. Cool and breezy in summers, cold in winters and plenty of rain in monsoons. The entire area is thickly forested, abounds in lakes and springs with Doda Betta being the highest mountain at 7,000 ft.

The Indian Defence Services Staff College[5] was established at Wellington in the barracks vacated by the Madras Regimental Centre after Partition. The services of Major General Lentaigne, a British General of World War II fame were requisitioned to set it up. This is one of the finest military institutions in the world where staff officers and commanders are groomed. The faculty and students are the cream of the defence forces. Foreign officers are also part of the course on an exchange basis. Our course commenced in the bitter cold of January with the good news that Kanu Priya, our daughter, was born on 30 January 1977 at Medical College Hospital, Rohtak.

The course was divided into six tutorials starting with minor staff duties and ending with strategy. In between, we were put through international relations, economics, internal dynamics, war games, inter-services exercises, logistics and management capsules. Eminent persons, both from India and abroad, delivered lectures to us on specialized subjects such as economy, industry, nuclear doctrine, and management. The academic and social environment was very conducive to learning and professional growth. Five days a week was very hectic. Our instructors were very dedicated and thorough. Major General A.M. Sethana, the commandant, and Brig. B.C. Nanda, the deputy were outstanding. The weekends were full of social activities such as angling, sailing, fox hunting, cricket and golf.

I used to travel to Mattuplayam dam at the foothills for angling with other members of the club. It was an angler's delight and we were never disappointed. The Wellington Club, a legacy of the British, was also a popular place to socialize. Neera joined me in May. It was a welcome change for both of us and we set up our small home in a nice bungalow on a hill side. She enjoyed the break after the hectic life in the medical college. We visited Ooty and other places around Wellington during weekends with our friends. During the break, we travelled with Maj. G.S. Hooda and his wife, Milee, to Madras, Rameshwaram, Kanyakumari, and Trivandrum and back to Wellington via Coimbatore. It was a round trip that was memorable and interesting. It rained heavily resulting in landslides when we were 10 km short of Wellington. We spent the whole night with our little children confined in the car. It was dreadful experience with incessant torrential rain in the dense forest. We could reach the college in the afternoon of the next day after the landslide was cleared. I was posted as Brigade Major 45 Infantry Brigade after the course ended. Our stay in Wellington was like a dream and it ended too soon.

Jodhpur: A Legacy of Longewala

45 Infantry Brigade was part of 12 Infantry Division located at Jodhpur that was responsible for northern Rajasthan. We were looking after the territory of three erstwhile princely states of Bikaner, Jodhpur and Jaisalmer facing the states of Bahwalpur and Sindh in Pakistan. The history of these three states is fascinating. Jodhpur had become an important Army and Air Force base since 1965. The strategic importance of the desert had increased manifold with the Indira Gandhi Canal turning it green. It was also easy to sever Sindh from Punjab after traversing only 30 to 40 km of desert to reach the Indus and their green belt. Our infrastructure had been developed accordingly. It had nearly happened in the 1971 war when 12 Infantry Division was poised to strike deep into Pakistan through the Kishangarh Bulge towards Rahim Yar Khan, before it recoiled due to the

battle of Longewala. The battle of Longewala is a fascinating study of audacious planning, lack of coordination between the Pakistani army and the PAF, bad logistics and bad execution on the part of Pakistan.[6] It is a brilliant study of use of meagre air power by India to defeat a powerful armoured thrust in the desert. It is also a good study of poor leadership[7] on the part of the Indian Army. The history of the 1971 war would have been different if a divisional thrust had been launched into Pakistan once the battle of Longewala had been won by 5 December 1971. The battle raises many questions for both sides to answer.

I had presented the battle of Longewala several times during my tenure to all the senior visiting officers and important military delegations. I had travelled over the entire terrain on foot particularly along the Longewala-Kharo Tar track to BP 838. When I visited Longewala, the destroyed tanks, and the skeletons of recovery and other vehicles lay scattered along the track. The site of the AMX Indian tank that was destroyed in action and the location of a Pakistani tank near the helipad could be easily identified. The defences at the post were identifiable. The scene of the battle as on the morning of 5 December could be easily recreated with all the landmarks, features, destroyed tanks and vehicles and battle scars that were still visible on the ground in March 1978.

My presentations were result of extensive research, meant to drive home the correct lessons. The plan of GHQ Pakistan was to concentrate a force of 22 and 38 Cavalry regiments and 51 and 206 Infantry brigades close to the IB on the night of 02/03 December after covering a distance of 82 km from the railhead at Reti. The force was to debouch on the night of 03/04 December from BP 838 with 22 Cavalry and 51 Infantry Brigade leading along the Gabbar-Masitwari Bhit-Longewala track and by pass Longewala by first light. 38 Cavalry and 206 Infantry Brigade were to follow them so that they could continue on their march to capture Ramgarh, 59 km from the IB, by midday.

After capturing Ramgarh, the force was to take Jaisalmer which was another 70 km ahead. They got bogged down between the railhead and the forward assembly area and the launch was delayed by 24 hours as the force did not have desert crossing capability. The two columns got mixed up at night and could not follow the routes assigned to them. 38 Cavalry and 206 Infantry Brigade did not reach Longewala and got bogged down. I concluded that though bold, it was a foolhardy plan on part of the Pakistan GHQ. An impossible task had been thrust on Pakistan's 18 Infantry Division with no air support or logistic backing. The air base at Jacobabad was not activated for reasons of security. Actually, two out of four Hunter aircraft of the IAF, directed by the 12 AOP flight, were enough to destroy this force.

However, 18 Pakistan division was able to retrieve a few tanks of 22 Cavalry, most of 38 Cavalry and infantry due to sluggish counter-reactions of 12 Indian Infantry Division. We had destroyed 23 enemy tanks and captured one. A total of 138 vehicles including one field and 3 AD guns were destroyed/captured.[8] It must be said to the credit of Pakistan that they were able to keep this plan a secret till the last day and it was only by chance that an infantry patrol led by 2/Lt. Dharam Vir Bhan of 23 Punjab was able to detect the attacking force near the border on the night of 04/05 December. His report alerted 12 Infantry Division that was able to reinforce Longewala and destroy the intruders by midday with the help of the IAF directed by Capt. Sangha and Maj. Atma Singh of 12 AOP.

On the Indian side, 12 Infantry Division was to launch an offensive and capture Gabbar, Islamabad and Rahim Yar Khan. The Indian plans were sound and could have changed the course of the war if 12 Infantry Division had not panicked. Unfortunately, Major General Khambata was the most unsuitable and unqualified commander on the Indian side. The Indian plans and concentrations were known to Pakistan as it is believed that Pakistani agents had visited and stayed at our posts, including Longewala, in the guise of locals. 45 Infantry Brigade that was holding the firm base had failed in its task completely. The surveillance of prominent ingress routes to Longewala/Sadewala and Ghotaru-Rampur on the immediate flank of the planned offensive to Rahim Yar Khan had been neglected.

The AOP and the Air Force had not been tasked to keep the concentration/assembly areas near the border under surveillance where a large force of 90 tanks, two brigades and hundreds of vehicles had remained in the open since 3 December. There was a total failure of intelligence at tactical and strategic levels. The company commander stayed put on the post in the face of overwhelming enemy armour and infantry even though he could have withdrawn as an option. But his role has been vastly exaggerated. All that he had done was to lay scattered mines hurriedly with packing material and barbed wire lying in the open. The company also fired two RCL rounds that cautioned the enemy who retaliated with some tank fire on him but did not assault the post. It was revealed that the company had moved to the rear slope of the sand dune till the Air Force and reinforcements arrived in the morning. A fire fight between two AMX tanks of 20 Cavalry and tanks of 22 Cavalry took place around 0930 hrs when they suddenly came face to face near the helipad. The lead AMX was hit by the enemy and blown up like a match box. However the enemy commander's tank was also hit simultaneously by one of the AMXs. The crew abandoned it in running condition. The IAF not only halted but defeated the enemy by midday

The Indian reactions[9] after the enemy had been defeated were timid and cautious. The offensive towards Rahim Yar Khan was abandoned and 30 Infantry Brigade was now tasked to evict the enemy from Indian Territory. This was an easy task as the enemy was in full retreat and had vacated the area earlier. By 9 December, we were in possession of all Indian territory without suffering any casualties. The brigade could have continued to pursue the enemy as it was totally unbalanced and in disarray. We had 20 Cavalry and 6(I) Armoured Squadron, 330 Infantry Brigade and complete artillery to support this operation. We could have continued with our original plan of offensive towards Rahim Yar Khan with all the force available to us on 6 December when it was clear that the enemy had been defeated at Longewala and 18 Infantry Division of Pakistan was in total disarray. Instead, the Indian side was content with its achievements at Longewala. The third brigade took up defences at Ramgarh in depth and did not play any role. Thus, the higher commanders proved themselves inadequate to the challenges facing them.

Map 11: Indo-Pak War, 1971 - The Rivals' Plan

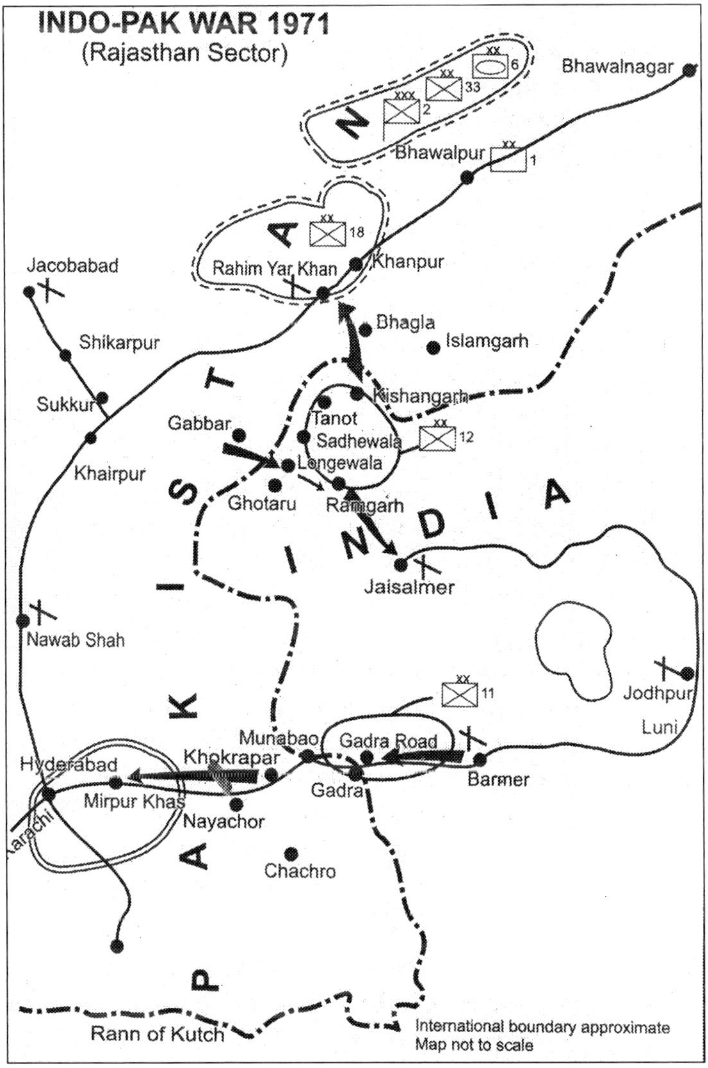

Map 12: Pakistan's Armoured Thrust

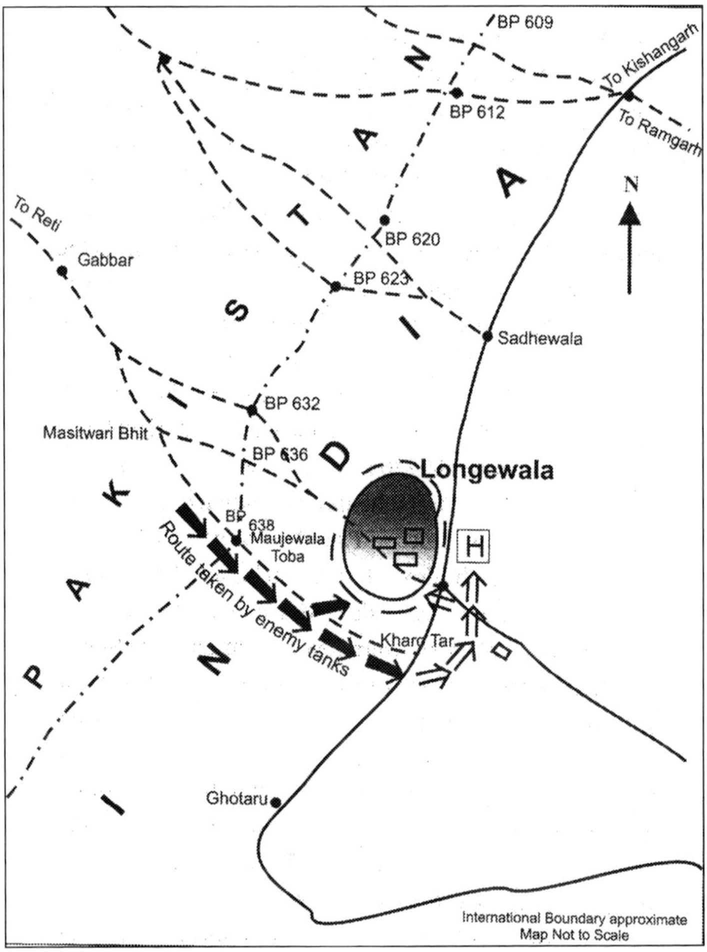

Map 13: Battle of Longewala, 5 Dec 1971

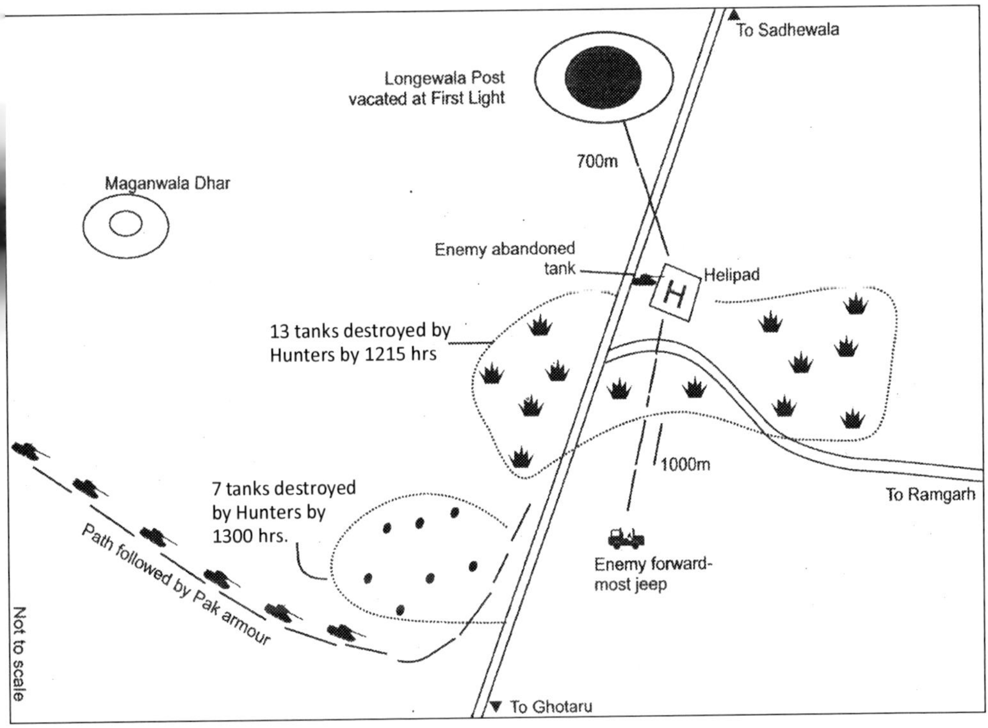

We had both defensive and offensive roles in the desert. The entire formation was out in the desert around Phalodi and Pokaran from October to February for collective training ending with field firing. The exercises involved an approach march of 40 km in one night along desert tracks to invest an enemy nodal point so that the depth objective could be contacted by the reserve formation the next night. The node was to be reduced by the third day to open an axis of maintenance. The advance would always be led by armour and mechanized infantry. The rest of the formation would follow in transport and be under camouflage by first light, before reaction by enemy air. The artillery, engineers and admin echelons were built up either the same or the next night. Much depended on surprise, correct navigation, track construction by engineers and water. The tasks were tough and exhausting and we barely managed to achieve them. Luckily the armour had night fighting capability and the troop/store-carrying vehicles had powerful engines with sand tyres. Navigating parties were inserted in enemy territory a night earlier. But battalions resorted to cheating and would mark the routes well in advance. Track laying for sustained traffic and digging deep bore water holes by engineers was critical, time-consuming and tedious.

These exercises decided the fate of senior commanders and the attrition rate was quite high. The defensive role envisaged occupying a strong brigade defensive node. Create an efficient and effective early warning and surveillance system ahead of the defences. Cause attrition in the enemy and daylight him so that the Air Force and armour could annihilate him. Once this was done, either take over the firm base or be part of a counter offensive. In fact, seven years after the battle of Longewala, the pattern of fighting in the desert on both sides of the border had not changed.

We rehearsed so that Longewala did not happen again and tried to reach the green belt on the other side that had eluded us in 1971. I gained a wealth of professional knowledge from the commanders I served under, particularly Brigadier Sardesh Pande, an intellectual and a soldier with an abundance of moral courage. He was a man of ideas. Life in Jodhpur was staid, very peaceful and enjoyable. Most of the time was spent on the border or in cantonment activities. The Rathores are very proud people. They love adventure and at one time the Maharaja's polo team was internationally famous. The Jodhpur forces contributed immensely during both the great wars. The Jodhpuri dress was designed by Maharaja Pratap Singh in 1890 during his visit to Britain and has become our national dress. Some of the Thakurs still retained their redstone palaces. They hosted us to lavish dinners with songs and music by Gauri Bai, a famous local artist. Mehrangarh fort, Umaid Bhavan palace and the royal cenotaphs at Mandore were a few of the famous landmarks of Jodhpur; there were many more that are steeped in history. Jodhpur has produced many great warriors including, Jaswant Singh, Amar Singh Rathore and Durga Das Rathore. Ajit Singh proclaimed independence from the Mughals. The last Maharaja, Hanwant Singh,[10] was a pilot and an Air Vice Marshal in the RAF. He was a controversial personality and died in an air crash in 1952. The people in the border areas lived in huts and neither electricity nor any modern facilities had reached them. They stored rain water in underground tanks called tankas that lasted them till the next rains. Cultivation was dependent on rains that were scanty. The entire landscape was treeless with a few desert bushes or khejeri trees.

We did lot of sand grouse shooting. The desert abounds with chinkaras, foxes, wolves, hares and snakes. The Bisnois do not allow hunting of chinkaras as they are considered holy by them. Many officers got into trouble for shooting this animal. Only the sheikhs from the Gulf were allowed to hunt the famous Great Indian Desert Bustards, an endangered species, as India could not displease them due to political exigencies. They would drive from the Pakistani side and set up a tented colony in the hunting area. Chartered flights to Jaisalmer would take care of their logistics. The beautiful fowl was hunted with hawks. They communicated with satellite phones that were not even heard of in our country then. My wife, Neera, did not enjoy her stay in Jodhpur as she was not allowed to practice or join the Medical College, being a non-domicile of the state. She joined Kasturba Gandhi Hospital in Delhi and later took up a temporary assignment in the MH.

Lucknow: Challenges of Command

Towards the end of 1980, we had completed our tenure of three years at Jodhpur. I was hoping to command 5/11 GR, the battalion I was commissioned in. Lt. Gen. R.D. Hira, the GOC-in-C and the Colonel of the Regiment, during his visit to Jodhpur told me to take over 7/11 GR in March 1981. He made light of my claim to 5/11 GR and refused to reconsider my request. He advised me to accept the challenge of commanding 7/11 GR that had gone through a period of turbulence. Deep inside my heart, I was sad. 7/11 GR had been an enigma for me. They had a splendid operational record. However, the battalion had courted controversies rather frequently that had affected its image and reputation. The battalion's tenure in NEFA had been extremely tenuous and it arrived at Lucknow on 12 November 1980. I realized that command of 7/11 GR was indeed going to be all together a different experience. This excited me immensely. I got over the disappointment of leaving 5/11 GR quickly and started preparing myself for the task ahead.

My arrival in the battalion in March 1981 was a non-event. Capt. R.S. Gosain, the Adjutant, received us at Lucknow railway station. He informed me that Lt. Gen. R.D. Hira was visiting the battalion and everyone was busy. Hence, no engagements had been scheduled for me till his departure. Secondly, Lt. Col. Bhanot's departure had been delayed sine die; therefore, I would have to assume the duties of second-in-command. Later, I learnt that Gen. Hira had come primarily to discuss the move of the centre from Darjeeling to Lucknow with Lt. Gen. W.A.G. Pinto, the army commander. His decision to shift the centre to Darjeeling had been a disaster. Fortunately, he succeeded to move it to Chetak Lines in Lucknow. We decided to stay in a rented flat just outside the cantonment in Awas Vikash colony, as government accommodation was not available. Neera joined King George's Medical College as a resident doctor from where she graduated as an anaesthesiologist. Kanu, our daughter, joined Loreto Convent School. I noticed that an atmosphere of fear and suspicion was palpable among the officers due to the uncertain command environment in the battalion. Everyone was apprehensive and insecure wondering how long the old order would continue and what would the new one be like? However, the change in the schedule turned out to be a blessing in disguise. Brig. Sawhney, the commander, fell sick unexpectedly and Lt. Col. Bhanot was designated officiating commander. I became the officiating commanding officer. Both of us got busy with a major brigade exercise with troops scheduled in April-May. This period gave me enough time to study the battalion's strengths and weaknesses. Lt. Col. Bhanot also had enough time to brief me. The brigade exercise gave me a firsthand feel of the fitness of the battalion. Finally, on 21 May 1981, I took over the command.

The first thing that I did was to speak to the officers who are the bedrock of a unit. I explained to them my philosophy. I laid down goals and objectives for everyone. I carried no baggage or malice/prejudice as I was new to the battalion. Team-making was thus easy. I explained to them that I was determined to lead them to success against all odds. My commitment, loyalty and trust were totally with 7/11 GR. I expected the same from everyone. All had a role to play and they were duty bound to play it positively and to their best. We had to achieve professional excellence. If we had the will to succeed, victory would automatically follow. Officers will always maintain professional and moral ascendency over the rank and file. I believed in leadership by example and to lead from the front. Every leader's motto henceforth would be "follow me". Responsibility, accountability, honesty and transparency were the essence of good leadership. This was applicable to the entire rank and file. Rewards and punishments would go side by side. Sound and efficient administrative back-up for operational and training events would be ensured. Welfare was important and adequate time and resources would be dedicated to it. Every activity should be result-oriented and end up in a high sense of satisfaction and achievement. There was no place for slackers and belly-achers.

I also explained my policy to the JCOs who are a very important component in a battalion; and finally spoke to the men in the durbar. I told the men honestly that for far too long we had been at the bottom of the ladder. We had the potential and talent to do well. It's time we found our rightful place in the regiment and the army. I found a positive and spontaneous response in the men. There was a glint in their eyes and positive body vibes. I had ignited their imagination. I was fortunate in having

Krishan Singh Rai as the subedar major. He was educated, a good manager, administrator and a dynamic leader. He was popular with the men, and enjoined their confidence. He not only encouraged and motivated the rank and file but ensured that they fell in line with the policy without any hesitation.

Life in a cantonment has both happy and difficult moments. Immediately on assuming command, as per the custom, I visited the unit mandir. The panditji, Sub. Chintamani Sharma told me that the battalion was under the influence of unfavourable constellations and was passing through a difficult phase. The omens indicated hard times ahead. These could only be mitigated if I performed certain religious ceremonies to neutralize their harmful influence. I was thus to fast on Sundays and offer prayers to the Sun God. I was also to perform a havan every month to keep the bad omens in check. I accepted Panditji's advice only to ensure that no harm came to anyone in the unit. I had to respect the battalion's sentiments, whatever be my own beliefs. I am not sure whether it was because of my prayers or because of some other factors that no harm actually came to anyone in the battalion during my tenure. We made the Sunday Mandir parade compulsory for everyone. Teachings from the *Gita*, episodes from the *Mahabharata* and the *Ramayana* relevant to war fighting were part of the sermons by the Punditji. We also deputed men from every platoon in rotation to perform morning and evening *aarti*. The aim was to provide spiritual strength and show the men that the path of *dharma* is important in the life of a soldier in the performance of his duties without fear and remorse. Religion also worked as a bulwark against evil thoughts and actions as the men's moral conscience was aroused. Sub. Chintamani was from Nepal who had obtained his Dharam Shastra degree from Varanasi. He was a learned man, who was both a religious teacher and a soldier.

The division organized a military history studies week at Allahabad. We were required to present the Korean War. Major B.J. Gupta, N.K. Pradhan, Capt. Lalit Rai, Lt. Inder Narain and the Intelligence Havildar, Tej Bir Subha, contributed immensely. Colonel Kuldeep Singh from the Brigade HQ, Major N.K. Gupta from 2 Rajput and Major Lakhani, 5 Assam, were also part of the team. We were adjudged the best syndicate.

Lt. Gen. W.A.G. Pinto, the army commander, in his concluding remarks said that we learn past history so that we can create a better future history. That made sense. This was followed by a division sand model exercise at Kanpur where I was the brigade syndicate leader. Once again, we were appreciated by Major General Sahdev Sehgal, the GOC, a very fastidious man.

We were part of 1 Corps that had an operational role in Punjab and semi-desert of north Rajasthan. There was thus great emphasis on speedy mobilization and offensive operations. In order to keep the battalion always ready for operations and mobilization at short notice, I worked out a training programme that ensured that the complete rank and file were put through battle physical endurance tests, obstacle course, firing, and drill once every week. No one was exempt and records were maintained for appraisals and improvements. Similarly, we practiced mobilization every month, both by day and by night. Company training cycles ensured that one company was ready for deployment at short notice anywhere. The program worked very well and both the division and brigade commanders were astounded by our efficiency and proficiency during their visit.

I believe that career planning of every officer, JCO and NCO was a command responsibility. We had many officers and men whose motivation levels were low and therefore were not performing optimally as progression in their career had been stalled. Every officer and rank and file had the potential to rise in his profession provided he was given an opportunity, guidance and a level playing field. Towards this end, we started counselling, coaching and training classes for officers, JCOs and men. Emphasis was given on improving communication skills, public speaking, essay writing and presentations. Officers were encouraged to study science, military history, leadership, administration and law. They were assisted in passing their promotion and competitive examinations. Those who had missed their chances were advised to study law, MBA or prepare for an alternate career. Talent hunting tests were devised to train and place the right man in the right job.

We thus ensured job satisfaction and optimum productivity in every individual. The results were apparent soon. The genius in every man was ignited and it triggered an urge to excel. Officers and men started performing well and obtained good results on courses. It opened avenues for them to qualify for Defence Services Staff College, postings to training institutions and good staff appointments. Many JCOs and NCOs were commissioned as officers in pursuant of this scheme. Subedar Prem Kumar Rai, Subedar Major Jit Bahadur Dewan, Subedar Padam Bahadur Gurung, Subedar Tejbir Suba, Subedar Karna Bahadur Pradhan and Subedar Amar Bahadur Rai were among them.

We carried out our field firing at the Rewa ranges every year in the winters. This was always a welcome and delightful break. All of us looked forward to this event eagerly. Rewa was an erstwhile princely state with vast pristine forests, mountains and the Rewa River. Rewa was famous for white tigers and gharial sanctuary in the river. The forest was teeming with wild animals such as sloth bears, deer, foxes, wolves, bison and a variety of pheasants. After field firing exercises, we fished in the river and hunted wild boar and small game for the camp fire. In 1982-83, there was a sudden squall followed by torrential rain and flash floods during the night. All the tents were uprooted and the entire camp was flooded and lay in ruins. We spent the night in the rain under an open sky. The field firing ended with an exercise by the brigade HQ. The return journey was a practice in long distance operational night driving. It was indeed gruelling and tiring. The 200-km journey had to be completed before first light which we successfully accomplished every time.

We also visited our operational area once a year in winter and travelled by road to Gurdaspur and thence along the Punjab border right up to Fazilka. These visits gave us a fairly good idea of operational and administrative necessities and training requirements. During the entire period, we had to ensure utmost secrecy about our movement and intentions. Internal security duties were yet another task that was important in a peace station, especially in an area where relations between Hindus and Muslims; Sunnis and Shias were not cordial. Tension simmered silently below surface that could erupt violently on the flimsiest pretext. We were responsible for the districts of Rae Bareilly, Amethi and Sultanpur. These areas were high-profile constituencies of the Nehru family and hence important. The civil administration was very efficient. Our visits to these areas every quarter, by themselves, were a sufficient check on the rogue elements. Except for one occasion when a company under Major K.K. Chaturvedi was mobilized for a flag march there were no incidents.

Gorkhas are very fond of playing games. Unfortunately, multifarious duties in a peace station did not allow most of them to participate. Our men were engaged in frivolous fatigues. In order to remedy this situation, we started inter-platoon competitions in sports. Football, boxing and cross-country runs were declared compulsory. This not only ensured more men on the play fields, but we were able to identify talented sportsmen. JCOs and NCOs were delegated the responsibility to organize the competitions. This helped us train them in organization skills, leadership, team spirit, initiative and ingenuity. Inter platoon competitions were extended to administrative activities as well. This concept was accepted with great enthusiasm by the men and was a great success.

Lucknow[11] is the state capital, full of historic places. It was a renowned cultural centre. It has a good climate and is well connected to all parts of the country, including Nepal. Religious places like Ayodhya, Prayag and Varanasi are in the close vicinity. We organized trips to these places which the men and families enjoyed immensely. The crocodile farm, museum, zoo, Residency and imambaras were popular tourist places. Hazratganj and Ameenabad were popular shopping centres. Dilkusha Kothi, the hunting resort of the nawabs, and All Saints Garrison Church, were within the cantonment. Topkhana and Sadar Bazaar were thriving little markets that met our daily needs. We also organized boating on the Gomti River which flowed close by.

The battalion was lodged in what is now called Nirbhay Lines. It was compact and a well maintained modern block of accommodation. Major Satish Chander and later, Chanderbal, was a very capable quartermaster assisted by L.D. Upadhaya and R.S. Sangwan as the mechanical transport officer. They ensured a very high standard of efficiency in their departments. The men liked the accommodation as it was functionally and administratively efficient and convenient. Officers' wives and families also participated in every regimental activity enthusiastically. They concentrated on adult education and skill generating programs among the families. Even though we had limited married quarters, no one was denied it. Family welfare activities benefitted many in self-employment back home or on retirement of their spouses. Officers' wives were encouraged to utilize their time and skills usefully and take up work that gave them gainful and dignified employment. These measures reduced frustration in the qualified and skilled ladies in our battalion.

Lucknow cantonment at Dilkusha was established by the British in 1858. Since then, a number of brothels and unauthorized liquor vends came up around it. They were a great source of trouble for the military authorities. In spite of strict vigil and precautions a few men still went astray. When I had been in command for some months, Subedar Major Krishan Singh Rai reported that four players from the battalion football team, who had won the command championship, had deserted and joined private clubs at Calcutta/Darjeeling. I considered this a gross act of indiscipline and disloyalty on the part of the men and lack of command and control on the part of the team captain. The JCO in charge was ordered to apprehend and bring them to the battalion or face severe disciplinary action. Two players were located and brought back to the battalion. The other two went into hiding in Nepal/Sikkim. Most were of the opinion that we should take a lenient view as these men had brought glory to the battalion in the past. However, I did not agree and ordered them to be tried by summary court martial. They were dismissed from service and awarded one year's rigorous imprisonment. For the first time, a promulgation parade was held to execute such punishment. This shock treatment was required to instil a sense of discipline in the battalion. A few weeks later, a NCO disobeyed and left the battalion without permission. He was also tried by a summary court martial. This time, the brigade HQ queried if such severe action was an answer to the problem. I replied that the battalion had suffered because misdemeanours had been swept under the carpet in the past and unless we sent a strong message to the rank and file, the situation would not improve. There were no more cases of indiscipline thereafter. Capt. Lalit Rai, the Adjutant, ensured that the level of discipline was at its best. The battalion prospered and we had a happy and peaceful tenure at Lucknow.

The financial health of the battalion was not robust when I took over. Regimental funds were meagre and all institutions running in lose. It was not possible to run a battalion in a station like Lucknow without sufficient funds or on deficit financing. Financial planning and revenue generation legally thus became a major priority for me. The unbridled activities of the unit baniya had also to be regulated to ensure that officers, JCOs and men were not in debt to him and compromised. We were able to generate sufficient funds by efficient management of institutions, especially the CSD. Havildar Karna Bahadur Pradhan was an amazing manager who ran one of the best canteens in the station with Hav. Sadhuram as a competent and efficient accounts clerk. By the time I left the battalion we were financially sound.

We had a combined brigade mess at No. 1, Bahadur Shah Zafar Marg. Our section of the mess was modest and austere compared to 2 RAJPUT, a century-old battalion with a hoary past. We did not have much to show. Lt. Col. Vishnu Sharma, the first commanding officer, contributed some priceless paintings and artefacts belonging to the Patiala state forces when requested. Some good silver pieces were presented by officers. We also procured a beautiful and rich woollen carpet from OCM, Amritsar. Capt. Krishnamurthy was instrumental in the improvements. We commenced dinner nights and a regimental dinner night once a month for all. The single officers' lives were now more regulated. They did not waste their time in frivolous pursuits and distractions which were in plenty at Lucknow. Our mess had become quite popular by now and we conducted all functions on behalf of the brigade and hosted many VIPs on more than one occasion.

A similar template was applied to the JCOs' mess where the duty officer dined with them once a week after attending their study period. Capt. Lalit Rai trained both the pipes and drums and the musical band. They attained a very high perfection in their performance and were in great demand in the station. They generated a good amount of funds which was used for buying new instruments and uniforms. Our MI room under Capt. Dr. Kamal Sen was adjudged the best in the station. He was highly competent and enthusiastic. Dr. Nandita, his wife, took care of the families. Capt. Ashok Hooda, another competent doctor, replaced him; he later retired as DGAMC.

We were allotted a temporary residence at 28 Cariappa Road in September, a fine bungalow with vast a estate around it. As per records, it was a sergeant major's residence during British times. It was located on the main road close to the command hospital. The house was blessed by punditji after a havan who predicted it would bring good luck to us. This house however had a horror history. Two of the earlier occupants had died in succession. Due to these unfortunate mishaps, no one had occupied it for some time. We did not know this before moving in. My wife was very apprehensive after learning of its legacy. The gods were however kind to us and our stay was indeed lucky. We were blessed with our son, Akshay, in this house on 19 December 1981 and had a comfortable time as predicted by punditji. Peacocks, golden eagles, partridges and a variety of birds abounded in the flora though they ruined the kitchen garden and the flower beds. During the nights, it was not unusual to spot a jackal, porcupine or a wild cat. The sighting of cobras and rat snakes was common in the foliage. We kept a big rooster and some geese to keep the snakes away. One day while sitting in the veranda at tea time, we saw a pair of cobras mating in our flower bed. It was a rare sight that very few would ever witness. The cobras were coiled to a height of about three feet and swaying rhythmically as if doing ballroom dancing. After mating they quietly disappeared in the tall grass beyond the fence. On another occasion, we saw a fight between a mongoose and a cobra in our kitchen garden. The cobra managed to escape.

Lt. Gen. Sushil Kumar, DGAR and Colonel of the Regiment, visited us on 6 December 1981. He was very pleased to see our all-round progress that we had made. Besides a regimental dinner night, we hosted a guest lunch in his honour, where all the officers of the command, brigade and sub area HQ were present. An outstanding musical concert was performed by our bands. Capt. Ram Singh Thakuri, who had composed the music and marching song tunes for the INA, gave an enthralling violin recital in honour of the chief guest. He belonged to 1 GR and had joined the INA under Subhash Chandra Bose after the British surrender at Singapore. He was now commandant in charge of the UP state police bands.

I Corps participated in Exercise Shiv Shakti in summer 1982. Lt. Gen. H.C. Dutta had planned and conducted this exercise to validate concepts for offensive operations in Punjab/semi desert. It was a massive exercise to practice opposed river crossings and break-out operations. The exercise was witnessed by a large number of senior officers, including Gen. Krishna Rao, the CAOS. 7/11 GR was part of the break-out force. We had practiced opposed river crossings on the Gomti River and had perfected our drills. After spending a few hours in the advance assembly area, we moved to the bridgehead over the Yamuna River past midnight. We broke out of the bridgehead with armour in the face of stiff enemy opposition at first light. All the visiting officers and the umpires descended on us to see our reactions and performance. We fared well in spite of the fatigue and gruelling nature of the work for the past 48 hours. Our final objective was a nodal point in depth some 30 km away. We were continuously on the move for three nights and days and went through extreme privation. The exercise finished near Bharatpur. We were tested in tactical manoeuvres, battle drills and limits of our mental and physical endurance. By and large, we had done well and returned to the cantonment fully satisfied with our performance. It was a landmark exercise. Exercise Shiv Shakti was followed by a sand model exercise at Jhansi by the armoured division. Once again, we, as the brigade syndicate, excelled. Lt. Gen. H.C. Dutta, was appointed army commander and moved to Lucknow in July that year.

In August 1982, Sub. Major Hony. Capt. Krishan Bahadur Rai retired and Sub. Major Wakh Bahadur Rai took charge. He was an outstanding sportsman and a great asset to the battalion. He was trustworthy and dependable and worked tirelessly. Another person who needs a mention here is Sub. Clerk Pritam Chand, a dedicated head clerk; under his watch no one suffered because of erratic documentation. We participated in a number of competitions during the year and did very well in football and boxing, our traditional games. Mr. Douglas, an Anglo Indian coach of repute, trained our boxers who performed very well in army, YMCA and state-level tournaments. Similarly, our football team performed well. They played tournaments in Sikkim and UP where they earned a good amount of gate money that was used to equip and train them. Capt. Inder Narayan was posted out in November 1982 as an instructor in the infantry school and Capt. Pramanik took over his duties of intelligence officer. Both were outstanding in their job.

Dusshera celebrations in October 1982 were a big event when Lt. Gen. H.C. Dutta, the army commander, was the chief guest. I was out with Brig. H.S. Choudhary, JAT, our commander on that day. Major Samuel had supervised all the arrangements in my absence that were excellent and flawless. In the evening when the function commenced, Brig. Choudhary was very agitated and upset with the seating. He should have been seated next to the army commander as per protocol. He was however inadvertently ushered to a seat away from the chief guest. I had to bear his immediate displeasure and reprimand. He refused to be pacified even after an apology was tendered and the error rectified. All guests, including the army commander however had enjoyed the function and conveyed their best wishes and compliments on the occasion. In spite of my apology, Brig. Choudhary issued a show-cause letter the next day, as to why the lapse in protocol should not be taken cognizance of and action taken against those responsible. An inadvertent act had become a serious issue that threatened to jeopardize our entire working relationship. I explained to the commander that though the lapse was inadvertent, I take the responsibility for it. Only the commanding officer could be held responsible for whatever happened in his battalion, more so if it concerned a commander. The commander appreciated my moral courage that I would protect my command whatever the consequences. He dropped the matter thereafter.

In May1983, we once again participated in a major exercise. This time we had to affect an opportunity crossing over a major canal and provide a bridgehead to the breakout force. The exercise was held on the Betwa canal in Bundelkhand. We had trained well for the task and were confident of executing it. However during the exercise, the water level in the canal dropped to less than three feet below the banks and the flow increased to more than 1.5 knots. These were extreme conditions. One platoon each from the two assault companies had to secure an opportunity crossing by swimming across the canal in their battle order. However, due to the water level and speed of the current some of our men drifted downstream. After a hard struggle and anxious moments, a few under 2/Lts. Y.V.K. Mohan and R.V. Ramana were able to scramble up the steep bank and secure it. The rest were rescued with great difficulty. The initial assault waves also met similar difficulties. The boats drifted downstream and docked on the far bank with great difficulty. The men managed to climb the slippery and steep far bank with the help of rope ladders. It was chaotic and a flop show but the enemy was surprised as we had landed up in the un-held gaps by default. We did not suffer any casualties or loss of equipment and quickly built up on the breach provided by the platoons with captive rafts and ferry. Initially, there was a lot of confusion and chaos but by first light everything was in order. Majors Samuel, B.J. Gupta, N.K. Pradhan and I.S. Sharma worked tirelessly the whole night. All the four rifle companies had secured their objectives and were organized before the enemy could react. Immediate first echelon stores were also inducted along with the tactical battalion HQ. The engineers built the assault bridges and armour induction took place well before first light.

Brig. B.M. Bammi, 4 GR, the assistant chief umpire, who witnessed the entire action commended our effort to bring order out of the disorder that followed the contact battle. He ignored our mistakes and appreciated the perseverance and determination of the men in crossing a formidable obstacle. He also praised the flexibility and confidence in each level of command. We were organized when the enemy armour and aircraft attacked us at first light. Our armour was able to break out in time and we followed in their wake the next morning in transports and later by speed marches. Finally, the depth node was invested and captured. The battalion had undergone extreme privation and endurance. Everyone had done his task well and our performance was appreciated. There were lessons to be learnt in executing an opportunity crossing over a wide canal with a fast flowing current. Primitive/improvised equipment and sheer willpower alone could not win battles under such conditions.

My eventful tenure came to an end when I received my posting order as GSO 1 MT-3 Army HQ, immediately after the exercise. I handed over the battalion to Lt. Colonel K.R. Chandran from 1/11 GR on 12 June 1983. I was more than satisfied and leaving 7/11 GR fully conscientious that we had achieved all our targets. I was proud of these achievements and carried cherished memories of a short eventful period.

I reported to Army Headquarters in July. We were allotted accommodation in Kotah House that was once a palace of the rajah. It had deteriorated considerably and I was not happy living in it. Consequently we shifted to Battle Honours Mess on Sardar Patel Marg. This was a more congenial place where many like us with families had been lodged temporarily. MT-3 at that time dealt with concepts and doctrines. Colonel Vinod Sehgal, Poona Horse, was my director. He was an acknowledged military thinker. After brainstorming on important topics every day, we sat down to research and write on them. It was a great experience.

The work was exciting and challenging but our working conditions were poor. We worked in small cubicles. There was no air conditioning or heating. Toilets were unhygienic and the cafeteria was shabby. The civilian staff was inefficient and always reported late for work and left early. Office tables were piled with dusty files and corridors were blocked with cupboards filled with old documents. The Indian military liaison officer UK, military attaches, Indian delegations and officers on course to foreign countries provided us most of the inputs for our research papers. We also found that since Pakistan was part of the Western alliance and the OIC, their officers had better access and exposure to military concepts and technology than us. Our socialist policies and dependence on USSR had made us paranoid. I was able to break this bias and we commenced sending officers selectively to Western countries. This benefitted us broad basing our inputs. The annual military training conference was a major event organized by us and all points pertaining to concepts, doctrines and annual training directive were discussed. By October, I rented a house in Prasad Nagar. I commuted by a military bus. Kanu was admitted in the Army Public School at Dhaula Kuan. Neera also started working as an anaesthesiologist in Jeevan Hospital that was close by. I was informed sometime in January 1984 that I had been selected to proceed to Malaysia as a military attaché in the Indian High Commission. We were of course very happy as few officers ever get an opportunity for such assignments. Brig. D.K. Khanna, Kumaon, to Pakistan, Lt. Col. Madhav Aron, Engineers, to Poland, Lt. Col. D.N. Sabarwal, Signals, to Japan, Lt. Col. C.M. Mehta, Guards, to Burma, Lt. Col. S.S. Sohal, Sikh LI, to Iraq and Lt. Col. Bhupinder Singh, Rajput, to Ethiopia were also selected along with me.

Our training was conducted at the United Services Institute, located in Kashmir House. We were given lectures on international relations, Indian foreign and defence policy, Indian economy, defence production, Indian heritage, cultural, art, literature and social structure, military diplomacy and co-operation. We were also taught social graces, diplomatic nuances and a host of other topics. The lectures were taken by eminent personalities like Dr. Karan Singh, historian Romila Thapar, officers from the MEA, professors from JNU, ambassadors, ex-military attachés, and officers from RAW and DGMI. Ladies also joined the common lectures. We attended classes in foreign languages specific to our country of posting in the afternoons in the School of Foreign Languages.

Malaysia: Defence Diplomacy and More

We boarded an Air India flight to Kuala Lumpur from Delhi international airport what is now T1. It was then very small. Our flight was routed through Bombay and Madras to Kuala Lumpur where we were received by Colonel Vijay Oberoi and his wife, Daulat. We stayed in Hotel Hilton. The High Commission was located in a building near Jalan Masjid—the old commercial hub of Kuala Lumpur. The Royal Selongor Club was located close by. Our High Commission was not in the best of places and the building was unworthy of it. After four days of briefings and visits to the Malaysian armed forces Headquarters where I called on the Malaysian Deputy Defence Minister, Dato Abang Abu Bakar, the DGMI, Lt. Gen. Dato Abdullah and other senior officers, the Oberois left. All my predecessors had left their mark and now it was my duty to carry forward their legacy.

Malaysia is located just north of the Equator. It consists of the mainland peninsula and Sabah and Sarawak on the island of Borneo. The climate is equatorial, hot and humid with plenty of rainfall from both the northeast and southwest monsoons. The terrain is hilly with dense evergreen rain forests with an average height of 1,000 ft. Genting High Lands and Fraser Hill are popular hill stations at 7,000 ft established by the British to escape the heat and humidity. We visited these often as they resembled Ooty in the Nilgiris. The flora is among the richest with several thousand species of vascular plants and more than 2,000 varieties of trees as well as parasitic monster flowers and carnivorous pitcher plants. A large variety of animals including elephants, tigers, gaurs, rhinoceroses, tapis, wild boars and mouse deer exist in these forests.

We spent four days in Taman Nagara, a national park, where we not only saw most of the fauna from hides at night and also the Orang Asli or aborigines at close quarters. They looked like the Jarawas of Andaman and Nicobar Islands. Crocodiles, monitor lizards, pythons and cobras are also found in these jungles. The orang-utan is special to the forests of Borneo. The green sea turtle and giant leather back turtles are also found in the coastal areas. Sabah and Sarawak[12] are called East Malaysia. The kingdom of Brunei, floating on oil, is sandwiched between the two. The Philippines are to the immediate north of Sabah. The province of Kalimantan, belonging to Indonesia, is to the east of both. These parts of Malaysia abound in minerals, oil and forest products.

The population shows great ethnic, linguistic, cultural and religious diversity like India. The indigenous people including those of Sabah and Sarawak are called bhumiputras. All Malays are Muslims whereas the Chinese are either Christians or Buddhists. Indians are mostly Hindus. Malays were about 50 per cent and the Chinese and Indians 25 per cent each at the time of independence. Due to discrimination a significant number of Chinese and Indians have migrated to Australia. A recent survey shows that 61 per cent Malays, 21 per cent Chinese, 7 per cent Indians and 11 per cent others compose the population of the country.

Malaysia is located on a strategic sea lane for international trade. The history[13] of Malaysia is thus interlinked with both India and China. Hinduism and Buddhism dominated its early history. Hinduism peaked during the Sumatra-based Sri Vijay civilization. The Chola empire, when at its zenith, had outreached till Indonesia and Malaysia and had very strong trade and cultural ties with it. Later, Islam travelled through Malabar traders. It made inroads when Premeshwara, the rajah of Malacca and Sumatra, accepted the religion. The people converted to the new religion when his son, Rajah Ram Vikrama, accepted Islam in 1414 AD. Many Hindu practices and customs continued to be part of the Malay culture till the Islamic revolution of 1979. The Portuguese captured Malacca in 1514 AD followed by the Dutch in 1614. They brought Christianity but it did not find much acceptance.

The British took over Malaya in 1824[14] following the Anglo-Dutch treaty. Malaya remained part of the East India Company till 1867 and was governed from Calcutta. Thereafter, it became a crown colony and was governed from London till its independence in 1957. The British exploited the minerals, mainly tin and oil, and developed the ports of Singapore, Penang and Port Dickson. Large areas were brought under rubber, tea and palm oil plantation from 1880 for commercial purposes. Singapore, that controlled the strategic Malacca Straits, became the most important port and town. Indian labour from Tamil Nadu was brought in large numbers to work on the plantations. They still continue to do the same job and live in clusters of labour colonies. Their lifestyles have not changed and they still remain the poorest segment of Malaysian society.

Sikhs from Punjab were preferred for settlement in Malaya, basically for police and security duties as they were considered sturdy, disciplined and loyal. The Chinese came in large numbers mainly to work in the tin mines and as businessmen. The Malays were considered lazy and lacked enterprise by the British. They were left alone to be governed by the sultans. During World War II, the Japanese overran Malaya[15] after landing at Kota Kinabalu in a short campaign from 8 December 1941 to 15 February 1942. Nearly 15,703 Indian and British soldiers were killed and 130,000 made prisoners. The battle ship *HMS Prince of Wales* and the battle cruiser *HMS*

Repulse were sunk by the Japanese. Lt. Gen. Arthur Percival,[16] the force commander, surrendered at Singapore on 15 February.

The Japanese weaned away the Indian POWs and they formed the first Indian National Army under Mohan Singh in April 1942. Rash Bihari Bose was also used in this effort. However, this force was disbanded due to differences in employment between the Japanese and Indian officers. The second Indian National Army was formed under Netaji Subhash Chandra Bose at Singapore in 1943. The operations of the Indian National Army[17] against the British in Burma contributed substantially to the independence of India. An office of INA existed in Kuala Lumpur in 1984. This was run by the survivors and one of them was Dato Mahima Singh of Seremban. He was a stately and prominent figure in the Sikh community then. He was a member of parliament under Tunku Abdul Rehman. I met him several times in his home. He was a repository of history before the war, during the war, the INA and life in contemporary Malaysia. After World War II had ended, the British returned and the Malayan Union was formed in 1946.

Communist Chinese insurgency broke out immediately after the return of the British. It could be controlled only after Lt. General Gerald Walter Templer[18] took charge. The emergency was lifted in 1960. The Malaysians were inspired by the independence struggle of India and three main political parties, the United Malay National Organization, the Malaysian Chinese Party and the Malaysian Indian Congress, came into existence. Malaya achieved independence on 31 August 1957 with Tunku Abdul Rehman as the PM. Malaysia became a federation on 1 September 1963 when Sabah, Sarawak and Singapore joined. However Singapore broke away and became independent in 1965 under Lee Kuan Yew.

Islam was recognized as the main religion as the Malays are a majority community. The government system is modelled on the Westminster parliamentary system and the legal system is based on common law. The head of the state is the king called Yang-D-Pertuan Agong. He is an elected monarch chosen from among the hereditary sultans of the nine Malay states every five years. Thc head of the government is the PM. The official language is Malay with English as the second language. When Sabah and Sarawak were integrated with Malaya, tension broke out with the Philippines and Indonesia over territory and border issues. However, peace was restored but the problem still festers.

India and Malaysia had a very cosy relationship up to 1970, when Tunku Abdul Rehman was the PM. Tunku supported India in its war with Pakistan in 1965. India helped Malaysia build its railways, transport, infrastructure, education and health sectors. Indian goods dominated the market. Indian academics, finance and law experts, engineers and technicians worked in every field to help develop Malaysia. Malaysian defence officers and personnel were trained in large numbers in India. Thousands of Malaysians were granted scholarships to educate and train in India. While the plantations were dominated by Indians, the Chinese dominated the mining sector. The Indians, who were more educated, also dominated the administration. The Malays who were less educated were mostly agriculturist or served in the lower ranks in the services. Thus, the Malays were resentful of the prosperity and power enjoyed by the Chinese and Indians. Due to these and other politico-economic reasons, racial riots[19] broke out on 13 May 1969 and emergency was imposed for the second time.

This was the turning point in Malaysian history. Tunku Abdul Rehman, who was a democrat, secular and tolerant leader was replaced by Tun Abdul Razak, a hardliner Malay. Malay supremacy over the other races was established. Many Indians and Chinese left Malaysia for Australia, Singapore or Taiwan/Hongkong. Ultra chauvinist leaders like Mohammad Bin Mahathir emerged and they espoused the cause of the Malays, berated the other communities and religions and despised the Chinese and Indian economic supremacy. He professed "New Economic Policy" and published it in his book "The Malay Dilemma" in 1970. Most of his ideas were implemented post the 1969 riots. The Malaysian economy is export oriented. It is one of the largest exporters of tin, palm oil, forest products, oil and gas. Flushed with foreign exchange surpluses, it made rapid progress in all fields and by 1980 its per capita income was among the highest in the world.

Malaysia had the most modern transport, health and education system, a booming economy, a stable political system and a high HRD index. It was counted among the most progressive, developed and prosperous countries. This was given further impetus when Mohammad Mahathir became the PM in 1981. The Japanese invested heavily in the country and the manufacturing sector grew rapidly. Malaysia was a prominent member of the ASEAN and Five Power Defence Arrangement and fully aligned with the West. The Russian presence in Vietnam and the Kampuchean crisis pushed it further into the US camp. Relations with India declined rapidly after the race riots. As Malaysia progressed rapidly and due to its new religious orientation, its dependence on India declined in favour of its Western allies and the rich Arab/Islamic countries. Our relations received a further setback when Mahathir became the PM and we supported Vietnam on Kampuchea. Indian relations with Pakistan and China also had a great influence on our relations with Malaysia. There was an obvious tilt towards Pakistan as both were members of the OIC and firmly in the US camp. An improvement in USA-China relations also influenced the Malaysian policy towards India.

We settled down quickly at our new residence in Ampang Jaya in the suburbs of Kuala Lumpur. It was a modest house. A number of rich Indian doctors and Chinese resided in this area. One of them, Dr. Krishnan, had married a Malay and had converted to Islam as it gave him the bhumiputra status. The Bangladesh First Secretary Counsellor, Mr. Alam and Saida, his doctor wife, were one of our neighbours. Alam was a Mukti Bahini Jodha who was trained in India and had participated in the 1971 war of independence. Mr. Badawi, a senior cabinet minister, had a palatial house in the same area.

I reported to the High Commissioner and the DMI at Army HQ, New Delhi. My staff consisted of Havildar Nair who was my Assistant and Subedar Clerk Bawa Ditta and later T. Vasudevan. Mr Ranjit Sethi, a career diplomat, was our High Commissioner. He was very intelligent and knowledgeable. He spoke Mandarin and French. His wife, Indu, was a charming lady. Both made an ideal team for the job. Sethi was however intellectually arrogant and had the habit of pontificating. The Malays, particularly the PM, did not like to be told what their foreign policy towards India or any other country, especially Pakistan and China, should be. This made him unpopular in the Malay political hierarchy. Thus India-Malaysia relations suffered.

When Mr. Preet Singh Malik and his wife, Aruna, replaced them, the relations improved dramatically. Mr. Malik was also a career diplomat with great skills. He, being a Sikh, was also an advantage to win the confidence of the community. I was briefed by both Colonel Vijay Oberoi and Mr. Sethi not to ever discuss five subjects with the Malays. They were Islam as the state religion, the bhumiputra policy, the primacy of the Malay language, NEP and the hereditary sultans. I adhered to this advice and never courted any controversy throughout my tenure. Mr. B. Jai Shankar was the First Secretary, Press and Information. He had a scholarly look, was suave, friendly and popular. He was later replaced by Mr. Suresh Goel, an equally good and efficient man. His wife, Shalini, was Neera's friend from their college days and we had a great equation with them. Mr. Jyoti Pandey was First Secretary, Commerce. He was married to the beautiful daughter of Mr. V.C. Shukla, once CM of MP, and a powerful cabinet minister. Pandey had an estranged relationship with his wife as the two were not intellectually and economically compatible. He was very talented but due to his domestic problems could not give his best. Mr. J.D. Bell and his Swiss wife replaced them. We had an adverse trade relationship with Malaysia with a huge palm oil import bill. Even though we were the premier exporters of beef, rice and other food products, the trade gap kept rising. We lost the Malaysian market for technical and engineering goods to Japan and Korea as we could not compete in quality. We also lost construction projects and the consultancy and service sector due to the same reasons and our inability to access and influence the decision makers.

Therefore, we had to resort to counter trade. This had some effect but our products were dumped as necessary waste in contempt. Indian industrialists including the Birla and Thapar groups were given land and other facilities to set up ventures in Malaysia to promote a trade relationship. Sham projects with second-hand machinery were set up by them. All the projects failed, further eroding confidence in our country. The First

Secretary, Consular, was responsible for visas and consular work. He had full time work with a large Indian Diaspora. Mr. Chawla, a Sikh from RAW, handled this job. He would exaggerate the Sikh and Tamil anti-India activities and file fake or worthless reports. His performance was subpar. He was replaced by Mr. B. Peerumal Swamy, an IPS officer. He and his wife, Sowdhamani, did a great job and restored the image of the department. Mr. T.G. Ramamurthi was Head of the Chancery. He looked after the administration, security, pay and allowances; and the budget. He was efficient and worked silently. There were a number of second secretaries and attachés. Most of them were good at their job but their prime concern was to save as much money as possible so that they could lead a decent retired life and settle their children well. Subedar Raghubir Singh was our cipher in-charge. He was extremely good at his job and most reliable. The entire high commission staff lived like a family. Neera was popular with not only our embassy but also other military attachés, Malays and Indians as she could counsel them on medical and stress-related problems. This relationship provided a support system to all of them.

The military attaché corps in Malaysia was very small with a footprint from 14 countries. The ASEAN and Five Power Defence Arrangement countries had very close and special working relationship with the hosts. The Japanese and Koreans were next due to their close economic and defence interests. The Turkish and Pakistanis were also included in the favoured list due to close religious affinity. India's position was decided mainly because of its Diaspora and the huge market for Malaysian palm oil. The last and least favoured were the Russians.

Relations between the attaches were friendly. We made many friends in the diplomatic corps as well as with Malaysian officers. My non-intrusive approach put them at ease and dispelled the notion that I was collecting information or intelligence. They opened up on their own and would discuss every subject connected with security in the region and what they expected from India. The High Commissioner allowed me to become a member of the Royal Selangor Golf Club as this helped me to interact with influential Malaysians. It was a well-known fact that most of the ministers, bureaucrats, businessmen and other influential people in ASEAN countries played golf and such interactions helped in transactions and important decisions. The Indians ignored this forum.

I quickly established a good working relationship with the Malaysian Defence HQ, particularly the DGMI, Lt. Gen. Abdullah and later Lt. Gen. Mohd. Yusuf Din. Brig. Raja Abdul Rashid bin Raja and Brig. Abdul Rehman bin Haji Khamis of the MI directorate were also good friends. I was allowed a meagre amount of $ 200 as entertainment allowance that I spent on organizing interactions with Malaysian officers. The High Commissioner and other officers also joined. Malaysian officers followed the British army traditions and ethos and this commonality helped. Many of them were secular and modern. By the time we left, the Islamic influence had started taking roots. Ladies also started wearing the hijab and officers avoided drinking in public. I organized lectures by Mr. Preet Malik at the Malaysian Staff College and other institutions that improved our interaction in the higher echelons. I visited the Institute of Strategic Studies and International Studies regularly and interacted with the defence scholars there. The institution was established in 1983 and was housed in a beautiful colonial building. It had a good research and learning environment.

The Malaysian defence forces consisted of 4 infantry divisions, a small Navy and a few squadrons of the Air Force. The Malaysian Army had its origin in the Penang Rifles raised in 1861. The first Malay battalion was raised in 1938 and the second in 1941. Both battalions played important roles in World War II. Seven more battalions were raised in 1950 to fight the communist insurgency alongside British and Gorkha battalions. The army also consisted of combat support and service elements on the pattern of the Indian Army. The Rangers, the Special Forces Group, a Para Brigade and two squadrons of Army Aviation also existed. The armed forces had a special status and they were looked after well. Although the communist insurgency was dead and no neighbour posed any threat to the country, the Malaysians had plans to deal with threats from all of them.

The communists operated from sanctuaries in Thailand in Malaysian territory. The Muslim radicals operated from the Malaysian side in Thai territory. Similarly, the Moro piracy and the insurgency in Mindanao Island were used by both countries against each other. Pakistan supplied arms to the Muslim insurgents in Mindanao Island through Malaysia. Singapore was apprehensive that Malaysia could strangulate them by cutting off freshwater supplies from Johor or easily invade them across the causeway. They had a very effective mobilization plan to deal with the threat. The Indonesia, confrontation in 1963-66 was still fresh in the minds of the Malays and it played on their sub conscience.

We had built up a very strong and healthy relationship with the Malaysian army and so it was easy for me to reinforce the same with the Chief of Defence Forces, General Mohd. Ghazali bin Hj Che Mat, and the Army Chief Tansree, General Hashim Mohamad Ali. Hashim had an impressive personality. He was trained at Sandhurst, Camberley and at the National Defence College, New Delhi. Although he had a healthy respect for the Indian armed forces he did not think much of India like his brother-in-law the PM. He was succeeded by Gen. Yacob bin Mohd Zain. His deputy, Lt. Gen. Nik Mahmood Fakhruddin Kamil, had been trained in India and was very friendly. Among the many other Malay officers, Brig. Borhan bin Hj Ahmad, the commander of 21 Special Forces group was outstanding. He was also trained at the DSSC, Wellington, and the NDC, New Delhi. He rose to become the CDF.

The Chinese and Indian officers had great talent, but the bhumiputra policy came in their way of promotions. Rear Admiral Thanabalasingham, CNS, was the last and only senior officer of Indian origin. The Chief of the Royal Malaysian Air Force, Air Chief Marshal Ungha, was also a good friend of India. He was a graduate of the National Defence College, New Delhi. He visited India and later Air Chief Marshal La Fontaine reciprocated the visit. Both remained good friends. Similarly, we were able to build up a close relationship with the Royal Malaysian Navy that had a large number of officers and other ranks trained in India.

Indian naval ships visited Malaysia regularly. I handled three visits by our ships that were whole-heartedly welcomed by the Malaysians. The ships were opened to the public and thousands of people visited them. Vice Admiral Abdul Wahab bin Hj Navi, the CNS, Rear Admiral Haron bin Dato Mohd Salleh, the Chief of Naval Operations, and Rear Admiral

Dato Mohd Sharief bin Ishak, the Fleet Commander, would always attend the receptions. The administration, fuelling, supplies and transport for on-shore movement of the officers and sailors had also to be arranged by me. We used the services of the Malaysian government, PETRONAS and port authorities to avoid malpractices and corruption and got the best rates which no other navy could manage. Only the visit under Captain Madanjit Singh created a problem for us. The ship's logistics officer demanded some gratification from the suppliers, failing which he rejected the fuel and fresh supplies. The sulphur content in the fuel was re-examined and it was found well within the acceptable limits. The visit under Captain Sushil Issac in 1987 was remarkable. He was a good polo player and on my suggestion brought the naval polo team on board. They played polo matches at Penang against the teams of the sultans of Johor and Brunei. Our team fared well against Penang and Johor but was not successful against the formidable team of Brunei that had a line-up of the best Argentineans. At both places we were feted and received by the sultans with affection.

Our ships also visited Port Kinabalu in Sabah for the first time. The visit of *Trishna*,[20] the Indian round-the-world sailing boat by Indian sappers to Malaysia was another remarkable event. They were led by Col. T.P.S. Choudhary with Lt. Col. K.S. Rao and Maj. A.K. Singh as members among others. They halted at Penang from 29 November to 5 December 1986. They were received by Mr. P.S. Malik and his wife, Aruna Malik along with many prominent officials and dignitaries. Professor Chattar Singh and Dr. B.S. Manocha played prominent roles in giving them a civic reception and organizing their visit to various places.

The officers and their families were hosted by the Malaysian Army in its officers' mess. A courtesy call by them on Tenku Abdul Rehman was indeed memorable. The National Defence College students also visited Malaysia every two years as part of strategic neighbourhood studies. They flew in an IAF Dakota and thereafter the Malaysians took charge. The Malaysians were always happy to receive them and interactions took place at the highest level. The Malaysians were quiet frank and open during the discussions about their economic progress, internal stability and peace with all neighbours and the factors that could cause turbulence in the future.

The two points that worried them the most was the revival of insurgency and racial disturbances. The first visit in August 1984 was headed by Vice Admiral Awanti and the second in August 1986 by Air Marshal P.K. Puri. During the second visit, they allowed us to visit Malaysian border areas with Thailand and Sarawak which were generally not open to visitors. Brig. Rony S. Mahendran who was the brigade commander, gave a very good presentation on the security situation in Sarawak. The Malaysian Air Force facilitated a visit by the officers to Singapore as well. The IAF Dakota took off from Johor Air Force base with great difficulty due to overload of duty-free goods purchased there.

The only significant political visits that took place were that by Mr. P.A. Sangma, the Commerce Minister, Mr. K. Natwar Singh, the Deputy Foreign Minister and Mr. Balram Jakhar, the Speaker of the Lok Sabha. They were covered in small print in the local press. Gen. V.N. Sharma, later COAS, Lt. Gen. H.C. Dutta, 8 GR, Lt. Gen. Sushil Kumar, 11 GR, and Lt. Gen. M.K. Ghosh, Signals, Col. Chandran and Samuel were some of the many officers who were hosted by us as private guests in our beautiful big house in Damsara Heights. We also took the opportunity to visit Brunei, Thailand, Indonesia and Singapore. Singapore was a world trade hub and favourite tourist destination for Indians who would throng Mustaffa Stores on Buffallo Road and carried bundles of electronic and other consumer items, of which India was starved. The smuggling was on a massive scale and well organized with the connivance of customs officers.

Collecting intelligence is a specialized job mainly in the domain of RAW officers. Military attachés' are not normally involved unless specifically instructed to. But I had to deal with one peculiar case when an officer from the Pakistan Army contacted me to sell some highly classified documents. The MI Directorate and the High Commissioner allowed me to handle the case with Mr. Perumal Swami as my back up. I met the officer in a hotel lobby. He told me that he wanted to sell the plan of defence of the Kahuta nuclear establishment that he was responsible to guard as he was in urgent need of money. He allowed me to scan the handmade layout and notes. He answered my questions confidently even though there were gaps in his narrative which caused suspicion and doubts about the authenticity. He demanded a hundred thousand dollars for the documents. I was amazed at his imprudence. I told him that I needed time to think about the deal and would like to study the documents once again. He refused to part with the original but gave me sketchy notes. The entire conversation was taped and witnessed by Perumal Swamy who was sitting a table away. I briefed the High Commissioner and advised him that the deal was not worth more than a few hundred dollars and we should let it pass. Later, we learnt that he had tried the same trick at Singapore and Bangkok where also his offer had been rejected. Whether it was the ingenuity of the officer or a trick of the ISI to fool us cannot be confirmed. The entire act and deal was bogus.

One of the tasks given to me by the High Commissioner was to handle the alienated Sikh community post Operation Blue Star in June 1984. They were not only unfriendly but at times publically hostile much to the delight of the Pakistanis and some sections of Malaysian society. There was no doubt that the Sikhs had celebrated the assassination of Indira Gandhi and a majority of them were sullen and angry. They boycotted the High Commission. We could not afford to keep a large and influential section of the Malaysian Sikh community alienated in our national interests. I was happy to take on this challenge. I planned an outreach to them through various channels individually and with help of common Indian and Malay friends at multiple forums and levels.

All the prominent Sikh residents including serving officers were more than happy to meet me and Neera when we contacted or invited them. They discussed the Punjab problem with me openly and were convinced that the movement had degenerated from the true ideals of Sikhism resulting in a political mess. Some Malaysian Sikhs had also been affected and they had contributed to funds raised by the Khalistanis. They had nothing against the country as Mrs. Gandhi had already paid the price for her mistakes. The hard-core Khalistanis in Malaysia were listed and we tackled them individually. By and large, all the Sikhs had relations in India and I facilitated their visits without harassment by the visa section. We also helped the Sikh Diaspora in many other ways that opened the gates of goodwill. They found in me a friend and an ally and thus the relationship with the High Commission was also gradually re-established.

This relationship got a tremendous boost with the posting of Mr. Preet Malik. Col. Dr. Mohan Singh, Dr. Niranjan Singh, Dato Mahima Singh and Dato Professor Chattar Singh and many others were a great support and help. Dr. K. Mahinder Singh, who was president of the Sikh sangat and was virulently anti-India also eventually welcomed me to the gurudwara and became a friend. The Sikh sangat gave me a rousing farewell on my posting back to India which I still cherish. A small number of Tamils were also unhappy with us due to the Sri Lankan problem; otherwise they were a friendly lot. Mr. Sammyvellu, a senior minister and Mr. Padamanabhan, a minister of state, were community leaders and great friends of India but they carried little weight with Mahathir on relations with India.

India had a long history of arms and ammunition manufacturing and had a huge defence industrial complex. However, as a policy, the country had decided not to export/sell arms. I always thought our policy was wrong and we were wasting our production capacities and a great source of foreign exchange. A small opportunity arose in 1985 when the High Commission, in conjunction with the Ministry of Trade and Commerce, decided to hold a trade fair to boost trade with South-East Asia. Unmindful of the government policy, I requested the High Commissioner if a stall by the MOD could also be put up. He was amused but agreed if the MOD consented.

A small cell in the MOD under a Director, Defence Export Organization, dealt with the proposal. He out rightly rejected the proposal as export of lethal equipment was against national policy. I convinced him that many non-lethal items produced by our ordnance factories could be exported and thus we would not violate the policy. He agreed to process the proposal. When I had almost given up hope, the Director rang me up to say that it had been decided to participate in the trade fair with non-lethal items as an experiment. The High Commissioner was both surprised and glad when I broke the news to him. We had a modest presence from the OFB, HAL, BEL, BEML, and the DRDO when the fair opened. The

OFB displayed parachutes, fire-fighting equipment, machine tools, and photographs of a range of vehicles, transporters, water trucks, troop carriers, ambulances, and other items that could not be displayed. The BEL, HAL, BEML and DRDO also displayed models of equipment produced by them. Our stalls drew a large number of visitors and inquiries. It's a different matter that we were not prepared for such an overwhelming response and went through a sham drill of negotiations and taking orders when we did not even have a price list or knew whether such orders would ever be executed.

The MOD, the High Commissioner and the participants were more than satisfied with the success and the experience we gained. Three orders followed the exhibition through Mr. Kimis, a Malaysian Indian, for spare parts for Alouette helicopters, 5.5–in. naval gun ammunition and spare parts for L-60, 40 mm AD gun, stocks of which were held only by India. Each order was worth $ 10 million. Luckily, the MOD agreed and the deals materialized after some hiccups and faux pas. This was perhaps the first commercial sale of defence items by us. A Singapore-based company called Defence Services Asia organized an arms exhibition in Putra Trade Centre, Kuala Lumpur, in 1986. I recommended our participation which was endorsed by the High Commissioner. This time the MOD readily agreed to send both lethal and non-lethal items for display. The Indian stall was most visited and popular. Our indigenous 105 mm IFG was the centre of attraction with 120 and 81 mm mortars, the complete range of infantry weapons, the communications equipment including radars and models of other weapons and equipment on display. There were ready orders for 105 mm IFGs but they were declined as the production capacity was already booked. The ministry was not yet a clever exporter. They could have easily accepted the orders over domestic demand and adjusted the deliveries. There was a ready market for ammunition and spare parts but we failed to cash in on it as there was no incentive or motivation for the OFB or PSUs to sell.

Also, we were not as suave and clever as the old established dealers. The sleazy side of this business was not known to us. Our stall manager did not have the training for negotiations or art of holding presentations.

They did not have enough funds for entertainment or hosting prospective buyers. But this participation opened the doors for the Defence Export Organization to enlarge its activities. Major General V.K. Kapoor, and later Brigadier Swinder Singh, organized bigger participations in subsequent exhibitions in Singapore, Turkey, West Asia and other parts of the world. I am happy that now India holds these exhibitions regularly aimed at $ 5 billion export target.

I was also accredited to the kingdom of Brunei and visited it along with Mr. P.S. Malik when he presented his credentials to the Sultan in 1986. The history of Brunei[21] is very well documented. It was a most peaceful, rich and happy country with an enlightened ruler. There was no disparity in distribution of wealth and the whole country lived like a contented family. The Sultan, Sir Muda Hassanal Bolkiah,[22] was educated in the UK and trained at Sandhurst. He had a modern and progressive outlook. Though the country had embraced Islam, much like Indonesia and Malaysia under similar circumstances, it was extremely liberal in its outlook. Its main revenue was from oil and the assets were protected by the British. They had a British Gorkha battalion to guard royalty and these assets. There was another Gorkha battalion composed of retired personnel from Indian GR battalions that looked after domestic security. The Grand Chamberlain organized a tour of the palace. It was dazzling, especially the inner living chambers whose walls were embedded with gold biscuits. The toilet taps and other fitments were also made of pure gold. Before we were ushered into these areas, we were cautioned not to touch the walls or other fittings. We thought we were in real Disneyland during that tour. The Sultan is friendly to India and has visited the country many times.

My tour of duty ended in December 1987. It was a memorable tenure where I was able to contribute substantially. The posting was a great experience in defence diplomacy and an exposure to South East Asia.

Counter Insurgency in Nagaland

I reported to HQ 8 Mountain Division at Zakhama near Kohima as Colonel Quartermaster in January 1988, after settling Neera and the children at Pratap Chowk, Dhaula Kuan, New Delhi. 8 Mountain Division raised in

1963 had successfully controlled insurgencies in the NE since then. My father passed away on 28 March. It was a great setback to the family. He had a great personality with intellect and strength of character. Getting over this loss was not easy as we loved him dearly. A large multitude from all the surrounding villages attended his funeral. It was a befitting tribute to him.

The division was deployed from Khonsa in Arunachal Pradesh to Manipur in the south with 192 Mountain brigade at Khonsa, 56 Mountain brigade at Mon and 81 Mountain brigade at Chakabama. The battalions and companies were deployed in a grid. Some of the posts were air maintained while the majority were maintained by mules or trucks. My job was tough as the supply chain was vast and its supervision even more difficult. After the battle of Kohima, the town had grown haphazardly without any planning or vision. Development was poor and corruption and inefficiency was rampant. Had the government focused on good governance and development, the insurgency would have died long ago. I served with major generals H.S. Talwar, Sher Amir Singh and V.P. Malik. Life in Zakhama was hectic as we spent most of our time solving operational and logistic problems. The station came to life in summers when families and children could join us for a few weeks. The arrival of Lt. Gen. B.C. Joshi, the new Corps Commander, infused new vigour in the formation. On 19 December 1989, General V.N. Sharma, the Chief, visited Zakhama and ordered the division[23] to move to J&K. It was a big surprise as such a contingency had never been visualized.

The internal and external situations for India were grim towards the end of 1989. The militancy in Punjab had not abated and terrorism in Kashmir had raised its ugly head with vengeance. The internal turmoil and the Sri Lanka fiasco had sapped our national energy and resources. The USSR had been defeated in Afghanistan. The Afghan and other terrorists were now available to Pakistan for battle in Kashmir. Flushed with its success in Punjab and Kashmir, they were now ready to challenge India for a military showdown. Thus, Army HQ had no choice but to move 8 Mountain Division to the western front to cope with the emerging threat. Orders for de-induction[24] were received in early January 1990. It was a herculean and challenging task that had to be planned and executed by me. For 27 years since its raising, the division had moved out of its location only once for the 1971 war. It had become a static formation without any experience in contemporary warfare. We were not prepared for such a contingency and no plans existed for mobilization of this scale. We were told to plan to move by air, train and road or a combination of two or all three modes. Three challenges faced us. To reel in all posts on foot and mule tracks to company bases. From there on jeep tracks to the battalion base and then move to brigade concentration areas at road heads. Then move to different air bases/entraining stations from roadheads. Similarly, move from different de-training stations/airfields to different areas for operations. Then we had to hand over the permanent assets created since 1963 to the relieving formation.

Major General V.P. Malik, our GOC, had a clear vision, positive attitude and exuded great confidence that percolated right down the chain. My team consisting of Lt. Col. P.S. Dutta, Major Rajiv Vasudeva and Capt. Dilip Nambiar worked many nights and presented our movement plan to the GOC by the end of January. By mid-February the plans were approved by HQ 3 Corps and sent to Eastern Command. The final presentation by me at Eastern Command took place from 21 to 24 February. It was not easy to convince both the Corps and Command HQs who questioned our requirements of aircrafts, mechanical transport and trains. It would require the battalions to reel in and concentrate at one place in 14 days and from there to the entraining stations and mounting bases in another three days. While the entraining stations were Rangia and Guwahati, the detraining stations were Mukerian, Chakki Bank, Pathankot and Brahmana di Bari. The air mounting bases were Jorhat, Chabua, Guwahati and Imphal. Our requirement of air transport for only the reconnaissance and order groups was six IL-76s, 55 AN 32s, 25 Boeing 737s and nine-Air Bus planes. We were allotted only one IL-76 that carried the advance party of division headquarters. We required 910 vehicles to ferry troops and stores to various entraining stations with 15 days' dry, and 7 days' fresh rations, all stores, ammunition and personal baggage. Control HQ was established at Zakhama till 29 April and then it moved to Narangi till the completion of our move on 15 May. A regulating HQ under Major Rajiv Vasudeva was established at Narangi to liaise with the railways and ensure that the rolling stock was positioned at entraining stations on time. Staging areas were established at Dimapur, Misa, Johrat, Rangiya and Guwahati to provide accommodation, supplies, refuelling and maintenance of vehicles. We required 36 trains but we used only 29 as large rear parties had to be left behind to guard the defence and other stores till they were taken over by Assam Rifles.

The move commenced on 10 April along four routes and the last convoy reached the entraining station on 10 May. Route A, Mariani-Jorhat-Misa-Rangiya-Guwahati; Route B, Chakabama-Dimapur-Misa-Tejpur-Rangiya; Route C, Khonsa-Johrat-Misa-Rangiya-Guwahati; and Route D, Zakhama-Dimapur-Misa-Tejpur-Rangiya/Guwahati. Four trains moved from Rangia to Brahamana di Bari, six from Guwahati to Mukerian, 11 from Rangia to Chakki Bank, 11 from Rangia to Mukerian and four from Rangia to Chakki Bank. Trains that had brought 57 Mountain Division from Srilanka were used by us. The last train reached its destination on 15 May.

The move from detraining stations was under Northern Command; as such we did not face any difficulty. However by the time 8 Mountain Division started arriving in J&K, the war clouds had receded. The USA and Western countries had realized that both India and Pakistan were very close to war that could escalate to the nuclear domain. A high level US delegation consisting of Roberts Gate and Richard Hess shuttled between Pakistan and India in April 1990 that perhaps defused the situation. Some reports suggested that the V.P. Singh government was pressurized by them not to precipitate the situation in spite of Pakistan's involvement in Punjab and Kashmir. As soon as 81 Mountain Brigade under Brigadier V. Mahalingam arrived in J&K, it was inducted in the Valley under 15 Corps. 192 Brigade under Brigadier Surinder Verma was deployed at Surankot in 25 Mountain Division. 56 Brigade under Brigadier Rajiv Pandit was deployed at Jindra. The divisional HQ and divisional troops were deployed in Udhampur.

The move of the formation from Nagaland to J&K was remarkable. It was a multi-mode move. There were no accidents. The schedule was adhered to. The railways and the "Q" staff passed the test in planning, organizing and executing it. A large number of lessons were learnt by us. Logistic exercises are as important as operational rehearsals. Large-scale deficiencies should not be allowed to accumulate. The shortage of transport was particularly worrisome and it affected our mobility. The uncertainty of the mode of move till the last minute created great suspense and extra work. A large number of rear parties had to be left behind. They took about a year to fetch up. It was a large move that was difficult to conceal. No sooner the USA got wind of, it compromised India's actions. Pakistan was chastened as soon as it realized that India was ready for a response.

As time passed we all were frustrated with the ambiguity. In the meantime, families were allowed to visit Jammu. I visited the holy shrine of Vaishno Devi for the first time with Neera and the children who had come to Dalhousie for their summer holidays. The trek had to be completed between sunset and sunrise as it was the peak of summer. At that time, only a mule track existed and we climbed 13 km on foot in six hours. There were a few tea shops and water points en route. The shrine was managed by hereditary pundits and under control of the maharaja who paid scant attention to conveniences for pilgrims. All this changed when Mr. Jagmohan became the Governor. It is now managed very efficiently. We crawled through the old cave in ice-cold water for the final darshan. It was the most exhilarating experience standing in front of the three images of the goddess. We started the descent after midnight and were at Katra army camp by 0600 hrs. It was a fulfilling spiritual journey. By this time, I had received my promotion order and posting to Jallandhar as commander 350 Infantry brigade.

NOTES

1. *Tipu Sultan as known in Kerala* by Ravi Varma, pp. 468 & 508; *Tipu Sultan Villain or Hero* by Sita Ram Goel.
2. *Mopalah Rebellion* by Puja Mondal; *Dr. Ambedkar on Moplah Rebellion in Malabar,* pp. 183-184.
3. *Making of Mizoram* by Chatterjee Suhas.
4. *History of Ootacamund* by Sir Fredericks Price.
5. *History of Wellington* by Sqn. Ldr. R.I. Seshan, *Three Decades of DSSC* by P.K. Raghupathy, *The Owl* 1977, p. 20.

6. *The Way it Was* by Brig. Z.A. Khan.
7. *Defence of Western Border* by Maj, Gen, Sukhwant Singh, pp. 189, 194, 214, 219 & 220.
8. *Defence of the Western Border* by Maj. Gen. Sukhwant Singh, p. 222.
9. *Defence of Western Border* by Maj. Gen. Sukhwant Singh, pp. 219-220 & 239; *Rajasthan Campaign*, pp. 178-245. The author has severely criticized Lt. Gen. G.G. Bewoor, the Army Commander, and Maj. Gen. Khambata, GOC.
10. *The Last Days of British Raj* by Leonard Mosley.
11. *Lucknow: The City of Heritage and Culture* by Vipul B. Varshney; *Lucknow: Memories of a City* by Violette Graff,
12. *The White Rajahs of Sarawak* by Robert Payne.
13. *India and Malaya Through the Ages* by S. Durai Raja Singam.
14. *A History of Malaysia and Singapore* by N.J. Ryan.
15. *The Malayan Campaign* by Falk Stanley L.
16. *Percival and the Tragedy of Singapore* by John George Smyth.
17. *The History of Indian National Army* by Kalyan Kumar Ghosh; *The Rani of Jhansi Regiment* by Joyce C. Lebra.
18. *Templer, Tiger of Malaya, The Life of Field Marshal Sir Gerald Templer* by John Cloake.
19. *Race War in Malaysia, Time Magazine* 23 May 1969.
20. *Trishna* by Dom Moraes, pp. 186-88.
21. *A History of Brunei* by Saunders Graham; *British North Borneo* by Arthur Owen.
22. *Brunei Dausaallam* published by Brunei Shell Petroleum Company.
23. *Forever in Operations: History of 8 Mountain Division*, vols. 1 & 2, by Brig. S.P. Sinha.
24. *Forever in Operations*, vol. 2, by Brig. S.P. Sinha, pp. 6-18.

Chapter 5

Punjab Insurgency

I moved to Jallandhar and took over command of the 350 (I) Infantry Brigade from Brig. Jai Shankar, Mahar Regt. Lt. Gen. B.K.N. Chhibber, 9 GR, took over as the Corps Commander from Lt. Gen. B.T. Pandit, VrC, Engrs, at the same time. Gen. Pandit's parting advice to me was that I was now a commander of an all-arms force of more than 3,000 men. "Think all arms and think big," he said. He was right. I was now a general cadre officer and my brigade was composed of all arms, with a role in the entire 11 Corps. His advice has stood by me well throughout my service career. In the wake of Exercise Zarb-e-Momin and posturing by Pakistan, the entire western front had been mobilized. While all formations were deployed on the border, my brigade, consisting of 2 Dogra, 10 Garhwal Rifles and later 21 Rajputana Rifles at Jallandhar and 3 Assam, at Ludhiana remained as reserve. I had inherited a well-knit team of officers.

We moved into No. 2, The Mall, Flag Staff House. Kanu and Akshay were admitted to the Army Public School along with Sameer, their cousin. Neera also joined a hospital. We were together after more than two years. The militancy in Punjab was still raging and the entire cantonment was like a fortress. I was responsible for its security. During our stay, only one terrorist incident took place in the city when militants fired at the vehicle of the chief signal officer. I improved the existing plan to ensure that it was effective and our responses and reactions were quick. The worst the militants could do was to crash through the barriers with an explosive-laden vehicle. However this did not happen due to our vigil.

Operation Desert Storm[1] between the US-led coalition forces and Iraq was launched as soon as I had taken over. The war was over by February

1991. Since it had thrown up a large number of lessons, I was asked to make a presentation to all the officers of the Corps by Lt. Gen. B.K.N. Chhibber. The Iraqis had occupied Kuwait on 2 August 1990 after a short battle of six hours. This created an international crisis that affected India as well. Iraq had been a steadfast friend of India among the Arab nations and not only did it meet our oil imports, we also had a very strong defence relationship with it. A large number of Indians worked in both Iraq and Kuwait. The development of events there was very important and we watched every action closely. Saddam Hussain had overplayed his hand. Iraq's hegemonic conduct was not acceptable to Saudi Arabia and Egypt.

Mrs. Margaret Thatcher, the PM of UK, feared that if no action was taken against Iraq, it would create more problems in the Gulf and oil supplies to the West would be threatened. The USA also realized that Saddam in fact could destabilize the Middle East. The UN imposed economic sanctions on Iraq on 6 August 1990. The UN and later the US-led coalition asked Iraq to withdraw from Kuwait without any preconditions and the counter-proposals by Iraq were rejected. The best option for Saddam was to withdraw and negotiate peace with his neighbours. His arrogance led to the war. Thirty-five nations including Pakistan and Bangladesh joined the war in a UN coalition led by the USA. Pakistan provided a brigade as a reserve. Bangladesh provided two ambulance companies. Russia was not in a position to help Iraq after its breakup and the retreat of communism from Eastern Europe. China would not intervene as it was undergoing economic reforms. The Non-Aligned Nations were a defunct lot.

The Iraqis were therefore friendless. Within a period of six months the coalition forces led by US Central Command under General Norman Schwarzkopf were ready to strike in Iraq. The initial plan to defend Saudi Arabia was called "Operation Desert Shield" and the offensive plan to liberate Kuwait was called "Operation Desert Storm". "Operation Desert Storm" lasted from 17 January to 28 February 1991. This was the most high-technology war where smart weapon platforms, precision guided bombs, missiles and anti-missiles, control of electromagnetic spectrum and space-controlled command communications and intelligence, and the electronic media played a very prominent role. The progress of the war was shown live in drawing rooms across the world. The Iraqi forces could not withstand the ferocity of the air operations of the coalition forces that was carried out for five weeks from 17 January to 24 February and the blitzkrieg-type ground operation that lasted for another four days. They capitulated by 28 February 1991.

The war was fought in two phases – the air campaign and the ground campaign. The Iraqi air force consisted of more than 550 operational aircraft protected in 594 hardened shelters. They had 16000 surface-to-air missiles and 154 SAM sites. They also had 2,404 fixed air and 6,100 mobile AD guns supported by 478 early warning radars, 75 HF radars, and 154 acquisition radars. A C2 computer system was used to integrate the entire air defence system at the national air defence operational centre located underground in Baghdad. The coalition force had 2,250 aircraft of which 1,600 belonged to the USA, including F-117 Stealth fighters, A-10 Thunderbolts, B-52 bombers, E-2, E-3A, and P-3 Orion AWACS, AH-64 Apache, and AH-1 Cobra attack helicopters. Tomahawk cruise missiles, maverick optical guided missiles and high speed anti-radiation missiles, TGM, laser guided, cluster and napalm bombs were used. Satellite imagery, GPS-based systems and even special forces personnel were inserted to locate targets and guide the attacking aircrafts.

The air campaign was conducted in three phases. In phase I, the anti-aircraft systems, radar sites, missile launching pads, HQs, command posts, command control, communications and intelligence systems were destroyed. In Phase II, 259 aircraft were destroyed. 115 to 140 Iraqi aircraft managed to escape to Iran and could not take part in the war thereafter. In Phase III, the infrastructure, including the presidential palace, government buildings, airfields, TV stations, and military installations, supply bases, electric power plants, oil refineries and defence factories were targeted. The Iraqi air force was wiped out within a few days, the IADS made ineffective and the country pulverized. The Iraqis fired 88 Russian-made Scud missiles mainly at Israel and Saudi Arabia but they failed to achieve any significant result except for a few casualties of US soldiers and Israeli

The Family - Faizabad 1950
The author is standing extreme left
with his parents and sibling

25th Course K Sqn NDA Khadakvasla Jan 1961
Sitting L to R. AR Raikar, 4221-K, JBS Yadava (author), Chhiller (ACS) SC Carriapa (SCC), HS Bopparai (CS), A K Sarwate, SS Sidhu. Mid Row. Kohli, SC Bakshi, V Kaistha, P Ramani, RB Menon, R Verma, A Malhotra, DC Nayyar, AN Sinha, S Kalmadi. Top Row. LM Bhatia, Kushwant Singh, HS Kang, Kasturia, I Das, DV Dongre, LK Anand

IMA Dehradun 1964
IC 16095 2/Lt JBS Yadava on Commissioning

East Pakistan 1971
Before the Battle of Govindganj (Centre)

East Pakistan Battle of Bogra 16 Dec 1971
Author with Bandage with Sub Dil Bahadur Tamang and personnel from A Cay with captured weapons

East Pakistan: Battle of Bogra 14-16 Dec 1971
2/Lt Teja Bedi on extreme left, author with Bandage with Pak Officers captured in battle. PA 7058 Maj Syed Fakhar ul Islam, 32 Baluch; PSS 8421 Maj Touqir Hasan, 8 Baluch; PSS 11163 Capt Muhammad Afzal 80 Fd Regt; PSS 9875 Capt Shah Jehan, ASC; PA 12748 2/Lt Sharafat Ali, 32 Baluch; PA 13332 2/Lt M Jehangir Khan, 32 Baluch; PA 13340 2/Lt Tariq Amin Gilani, 8 Baluch

Felicitations by Smt Indra Gandhi, Prime Minister of India

Investiture Ceremony – Rashtrapati Bhavan Awarded Vir Chakra by Sh VV Giri, President of India

Neera as a Bride 28 Jan 1974

Commanding Officer 7/11 GR, Lucknow, May 1981

Kaula Lumpur 1986

With Tunku Abdul Rahman First Prime Minister of Malaysia Mr. PS Malik, HC, Extreme left and Smt Aruna Malik second from right

Punjab Insurgency - 1992 with Mr KPS Gill

Kashmir Insurgency 1996-98,
as GOC 8 Mountain Division

Kashmir-Wangat 1997, with
Mian Altaf Hussain and
Mian Bashir

Lucknow Dec 1998, with
Mr Beni Prasad Minister P&T,
Mr Mulayam Singh RM (author)
Lt Gen SS Sangra, GOC-in-C and
Col KVS Lalotra

Investiture Ceremony Rashtrapati Bahvan - April 1998
Awarded AVSM by Mr KR Narayan, President of India

Nepal – Dharan 1999
With Mr Jaswant Singh, Foreign Minister of India

Jammu - Rajouri 2002 with Mr George Fernandes – LoC

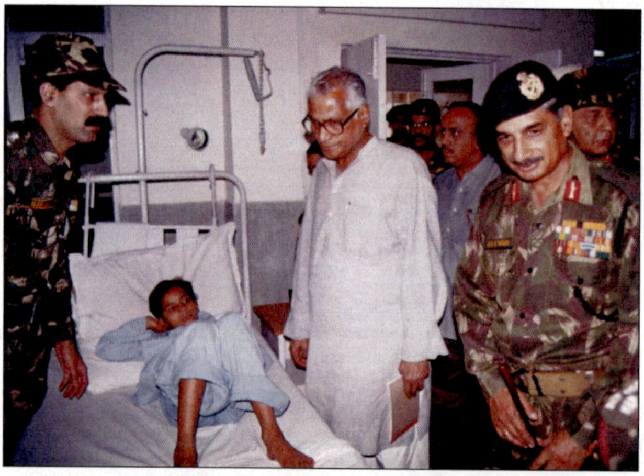

MH – Jammu - May 2002 with Mr George Fernandes, visiting casualties of terrorist attack Kaluchak.

With Mr Robert Dean Blackwill, US Ambassador Jan 2002

As DCOAS – 2002

France – School of Armoured Corps – 2003

Losetho – Africa
with Defence Minister and COAS Losetho Army
Brig Padam Badhwar TT Leader extreme left

Zambia – 2003
with General JSA Chisuzi, Army Chief

Fort Leavenwrth USA. With Lt Gen William S Wallace, Commandant Combined Arms Centre.

Lebnon – 2003
Visit tò Indian UN Contigent

Investiture Ceremony Rashtrapati Bahvan – 2003
Awarded PVSM by
Sh Abdul Kalam Azad,
President of India

The Family – 2001
With Akshay and Kanu Priya

Akshay – 2018

Agastya, Kanu Priya, Dr Ajay Yadav – 2024

Thimpu Bhutan – 2004
With HH Jigme Singye,
The King of Bhutan

Dhaka, Bangladesh – 16 Dec 2017
With Mrs Sheikh Hassina, PM. Neera on the left

civilians. The US deployed Patriot missiles in response in Israel, Turkey and Saudi Arabia with satisfactory successful interception rate.

A three prong blitzkrieg like ground operation completely outmanoeuvred the Iraqis. The coalition ground forces consisted of XV11 Airborne Corps, V11 Corps and Marines from the USA. The French and UK contributed one armoured division each. Saudi Arabia, Egypt, and the Gulf States contributed substantial troops. Prince Khaled bin Sultan Al Saud, a member of the royal family and former deputy defence minister of Saudi Arabia was the force commander of these troops. The UN force launched a three-prong offensive on 24 February. XV11 Airborne Corps operated as the western thrust, its flank was protected by the French. The V11 Corps was in the centre with the British I Armoured Division under command. The Arab contingents operated on the eastern flank. The Marines were also on this flank. The ground operations lasted four days from 24 to 28 February before the Iraqis capitulated. The Iraqi defences were well organized with extensive mine fields, anti-tank screens, fortifications and strong points that were systematically destroyed by the air operations. The Iraqis were overwhelmed by the coalition forces and had no will to fight when the offensive commenced. Electronic and psychological warfare also played a major role in their collapse. The western thrust went deep into Iraq, completely outflanking the enemy. The 101 Airborne Division landed 249 km behind enemy lines. Four hundred helicopters transported 2,000 troops in this operation. They trapped the retreating Iraqis including the elite Republican Guard. The Marines in the east launched an amphibian assault threat and tied down a substantial number of Iraqi troops.

The central thrust did meet resistance by the Iraqis that was overcome easily. The road from Kuwait to Basra which was the main supply line was interdicted and a large number of Iraqis were trapped and killed. It was called the road to death. Kuwait was liberated and Saddam Hussein was defeated and humiliated when the UN, vide resolution 687, declared a ceasefire. He was however allowed to retain power. The Iraqis lost five of their seven divisions and the Republican Guard was completely destroyed. 25,000 Iraqi soldiers were killed, 75,000 were wounded and 60,000 surrendered. The naval operations were carried out by two naval task forces

Map 14: Offensive Plan

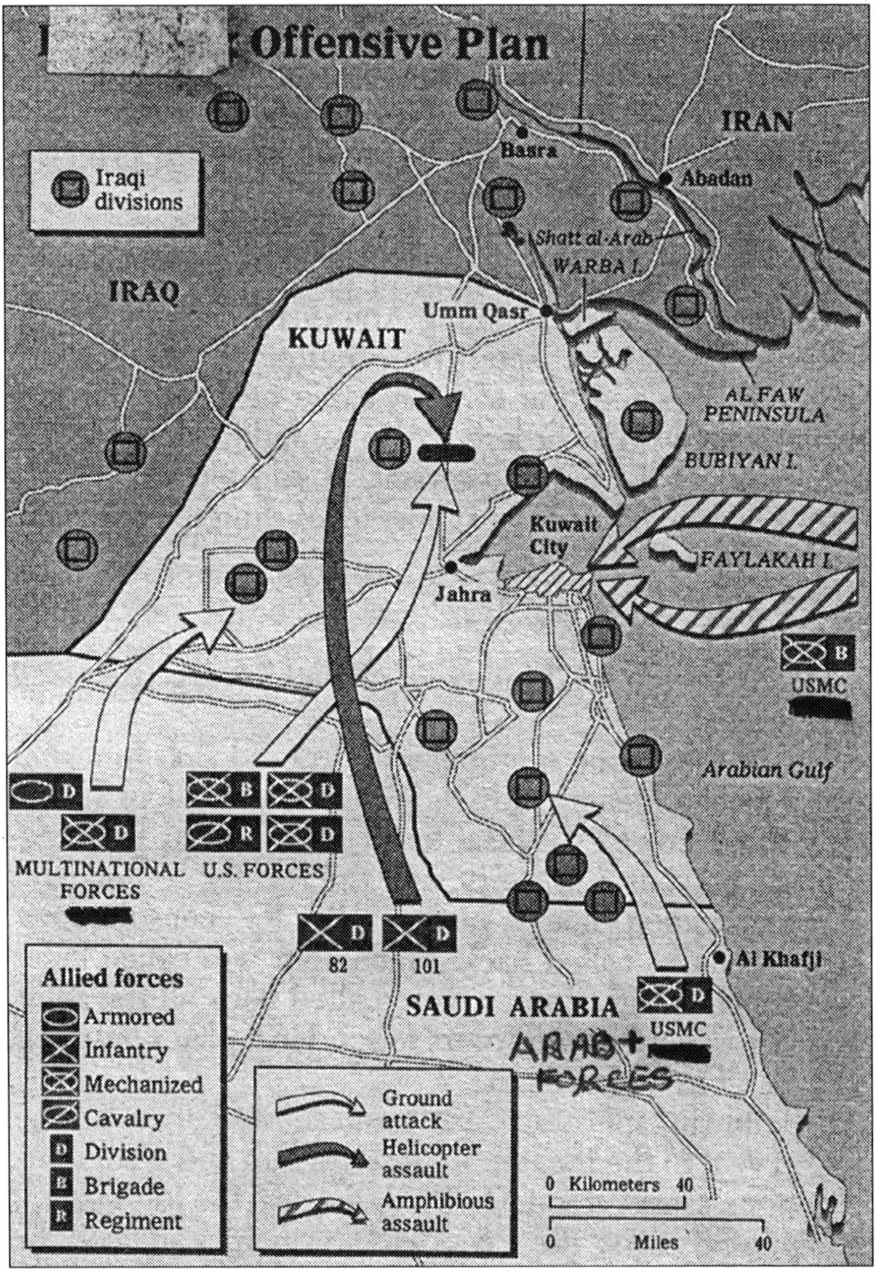

from 6 Carrier battle groups. Besides, the naval blockade, they destroyed the entire Iraqi Navy. The carrier groups also contributed substantially in the air offensive.

The independence of Kuwait was restored. Iraq had set all the 737 Kuwaiti oilfields on fire and that became an environment nightmare for many months thereafter. The UN imposed sanctions against Iraq. Northern Iraq was declared a no fly zone. Iraqi Kurdistan was granted autonomy. The war cost the US$ 60 and Saudi Arabia US$ 32 billion. The success of "Operation Desert Storm" had revolutionized warfare. The lessons learnt from the war made a great impact on military experts all over the world.

The advanced technology employed by the USA broke the will of the Iraqis to resist and fight the war. The major lessons that this war brought home were: 1. Decisive leadership, particularly that of President H.W. Bush and Gen. Norman Schwarzkopf; 2. Management of political cooperation at international and UN levels; 3. Innovative and effective strategy including strategic surprise and deception, bold planning and execution of war; 4. Use of revolutionary high technology weapons; 5. Well-trained forces; 6. Good planning and sound logistics with strategic sea and air lift; 7. Good coordination between contingents from different countries; 8. Air power and its use in shaping the battle environment; 9. Use of missiles and anti-missiles during the war; 10. Important role played by electronic media. The CNN gave live coverage of the war; 11. Space-based command, control, communications and intelligence capabilities; 12. Role played by psychological and electronic warfare. The victory can be attributed to technological advantage that enhanced the conventional military superiority of the coalition forces and the clever application of manoeuvre warfare. The Iraqi forces were poorly led, trained and technologically inferior. Technology had impacted every war but this was astounding. There was no doubt that the revolution in military affairs would also affect us in future wars and the presentation was a learning step in that direction.

When I had joined 350 (I) Infantry Brigade, the complete Western Command was deployed on the border as part of "Operation Rakshak-1" against Pakistan. The deployment had to a great extent reduced the infiltration of militants from Pakistan and their free movement. The militant activities however continued in the towns and rural areas. It was decided to terminate "Operation Rakshak" after the midterm elections in June 1991. In May 1991, the offensive formations were withdrawn and my brigade was deployed to relieve 61 Infantry Brigade at Taran Taran. We were placed under 23 Infantry Division with effect from 13 May 1991. Our primary task was to guard the DCB, prevent infiltration, and be ready for operations against Pakistan at short notice. Anti-Militancy, assisting police against militants and area domination was a secondary task.

Our area of responsibility extended from the DCB in the west to the Beas River in the east and from the Ravi River in the north to Kalra in the south. We occupied the stadium at Taran Taran as our HQ. 2 Dogra was located at Taran Taran on the road to Goindwal, 21 Raj Rif was located at Thaththian Mahanta and 3 Assam at Chabal Kalan. However, anti-militant operations gained primacy within a short time as militant activities affecting us increased with the withdrawal of troops. Militancy in Punjab was born in the districts of Amritsar, Taran Taran and Gurdaspur. Taran Taran became the hub. Historically, the old Mughal route from Lahore to Delhi passed through Sarai Amant Khan – Taran Taran – Goindwal to Ludhiana and thereafter along the present GT road to Delhi. The people of this area were predators by nature as they lived off the loot from various caravans that passed through this route. The Mughal chronicles describe them as bandits and plunderers who preyed on caravans passing through their areas. It is said that they also looted the baggage of Nadir Shah and Ahmed Shah Abdali when they were returning home after sacking Delhi. The Jat Sikhs of this area had two contradictory traits. The noble and brave that encompassed, chivalrous, loyal, generous, compassionate and the negative were overbearing, arrogant, vindictive, easily hurt and aroused. The British realized that they made excellent soldiers and could be ferocious against an adversary. After the Khalsa army was disbanded, they recruited most of them in the British army. They also laid a vast network of canals that kept the others busy as cultivators. Predatory qualities had re-emerged among the unemployed youth and they joined the militant ranks in large numbers. It is relevant to revisit the genesis of the problem in Punjab here.

Militancy in Punjab started in 1970 as a militant Sikh nationalism known as the Khalistan movement. In the 1980s, it developed into a secessionist movement under Jarnail Singh Bhindranwala. The movement also has its origin in the then Punjab politics between the Akali Dal and the Congress. It was also one of the most virulent terrorist campaigns in the world. Groups of bigots who discovered their justification in the perversion of the Sikh religious identity, promoted and conducted it, supported by opportunist politicians. The movement consumed 21,469 lives before it was defeated in 1993. The Akalis, after their defeat, in the 1972 elections brought the Anandpur Sahib resolution that demanded autonomy for the state that was secessionist in parts. It is alleged that Bhindranwala[2] was a creation of the Congress-Akali politics. He was financed and propped up by the Congress against the Akalis to defeat them in the SPGC elections in 1978. It is said that Giani Zail Singh and Sanjay Gandhi were directly involved and Bhindranwala helped the Congress win the 1980 elections. His religious and political influence grew with time and when the Congress tried to tame him, he joined the Akalis and led a 'dharam yudh' to implement the resolution and to even declare a separate country of Khalistan.

He is credited with the launching of Sikh militancy with training and support from Pakistan. He also adopted an antagonistic attitude towards Hindus for one reason or the other. He led the *jatha* in the massacre at the Sant Nirankari convention held at Amritsar on 13 April 1978 against the so-called enemies of the Sikhs. The Babbar Khalsa and All India Sikh Federation also joined him. On 24 April 1980, Baba Gurbachan Singh Nirankari, was murdered. In order to avoid arrest, Bhindranwala took up residence in the Golden Temple.

The green revolution had brought prosperity to Punjab. Cheap labour from Bihar and mechanized farming had released the youth from active farming as all of them could now afford both. The Centre had been hesitant to establish heavy industry in the state due to the high strategic risk. Both these reasons created massive unemployment among the educated youth. This led to drug addiction and alcoholism among them. Many of them were thus attracted towards the agitation under Bhindranwala and subsequently the militancy. However as per Mr. K.P.S. Gill, the Khalistan movement was not a collective unfulfilled aspiration of the Sikhs but a creation of venal politics, unscrupulous manipulations and brazen jockeying for political power. This kind of politics between the Congress and Akalis not only created the problem but nurtured it till 1988.

The ISI of Pakistan took advantage of the restiveness and sowed the seeds of a Sikh-Hindu divide as well. Zulfiqar Ali Bhutto had politically always supported the idea of Khalistan. The Pak support to the movement became prominent and obvious under Zia-ul-Haq to revenge the 1971 defeat. Zia-ul-Haq and Lt. Gen. Hamid Gul, the Chief of the ISI, believed that the destabilization of Punjab and J&K would lead to the breakup of India. Like the USSR had been defeated in Afghanistan, India could also be defeated through religious extremism in these states. The ISI created a special cell to support Sikh militancy. Training camps were opened at Lahore and Karachi. Field intelligence units were located close to the border to support and direct the militants. The Bhindranwala Tiger Force, Khalistan Commando Force, Khalistan Liberation Force and Babbar Khalsa were the main militant groups that received their support.

Pakistan had planned to execute the operation in three phases. Phase-I, to alienate Sikhs from the rest of India. Phase-II, subvert government institutions and organize mass agitations. Phase-III, create mass terror and violence leading to secession. Pakistan also co-opted the Sikh Panthic Committee in India as a partner. They also approached the Shiromani Gurudwara Prabandhakh Committee. Sikhs and gurudwaras in Pakistan were actively involved in the plan to host militants and propagate secession. Gurudwaras on both sides of the border were used for recruitment of militants, and storing and supply of arms and ammunition. Wadhwa Singh, chief of the Babbar Khalsa International, Lakhbir Singh Rode, the chief of the International Sikh Youth Federation, Param Jit Singh Panjwar, the chief of the Khalistan Commando Force, Gajinder Singh, the chief of Dal Khalsa International and Ranjit Singh Neeta, the chief of the Khalistan Zindabad Force were some of the prominent militants based in Pakistan who coordinated operations in Punjab and the rest of India from there. However, a later survey indicated that only 5 per cent of the Sikhs were in favour of Khalistan and the majority of the militants were hard-core criminals, drug traffickers and smugglers.

The political rivalry between Sardar Darbara Singh and Giani Zail Singh also had its affect on the functioning of the Punjab government. Political interference by both the Congress and Akalis had made the police ineffective and they were completely unprepared for the emerging challenges. Between 1980 and 5 June 1984, the day "Operation Blue Star" was launched, 25 major incidents of killings by the militants had taken place that included the killing of the chief of the Nirankaris, Lala Jagat Narain of the Hind Samachar group, killing of DIG A.S. Atwal, threat to Asian Games 1982, mass killing of Hindus[3] after pulling them out of buses and trains, bombing of Hindu weddings and processions, Hindu-Sikh clashes and murder of Harbans Singh Manchanda, president of the Delhi Gurudwara Management Committee in broad daylight in New Delhi. Sixty-eight Hindus were killed in a period of 11 days.

After Bhindranwala had taken residence in the Golden Temple, he made the sacred complex an armoury and his HQ for the establishment of Khalistan. The total casualties were 410 killed and 1,180 injured so far. Intelligence reports said that prominent leaders of the Khalistan movement, Major General Shahbeg Singh,[4] Balbir Singh and Amrik Singh had made at least six secret trips to Pakistan between 1981 and 1983. It is also said that the KGB tipped off RAW that the CIA and ISI were planning to destabilize India through an operation called "OP GIBRALTAR". RAW also learnt that Pakistan was planning to infiltrate SSG personnel to assist Bhindranwala in the creation of Khalistan.

All these inputs led Mrs. Indira Gandhi to order "Operation Blue Star"[5] to flush out the militants from the Golden Temple. The use of the army against the activities of Bhindranwala and the militants was not accepted as an option by Lt. General S.K. Sinha as the army commander and General K.V. Krishna Rao when he was the COAS as it was considered imprudent. The matter had to be resolved politically and by the use of the state police or central police forces. However, by 1984, it was apparent that the situation was grave and the state was unable to handle it. General A.S. Vaidya, the COAS, and Lt. General K. Sunderji, the GOC-in-C, accepted the task. "Operation Blue Star" is a dark chapter in the history of the Indian Army. Both these commanders not only failed to appreciate the political and strategic implications of the operation but conducted it badly with grave consequences. Indira Gandhi ordered the army on 1 June 1984 to clear the Golden Temple Complex of all militants. Maj. Gen. K.S. Brar, GOC 9 Infantry Division, was assigned this task. General Brar, a Sikh officer, totally misread the situation politically and militarily. He did not have intelligence about the strength of the militants; types of weapons held by them, the nature of the fortifications or even a detailed layout of the complex. He grossly under-estimated their fighting potential. Reconnaissance was carried out hurriedly in civilian clothes. A siege was laid of the complex which was thronging with pilgrims. Announcements were made to the militants to surrender and to the pilgrims to vacate the complex by 1700 hrs 5 June. The militants not only refused to comply but were defiant and contemptuous. The pilgrims in the complex were held hostage.

The army moved in at last light and clashes commenced immediately thereafter between them and militants. The severity of coordinated automatic fire and rocket launchers compelled the army to use tanks. There was great destruction to the complex, especially to the Akal Takht. Except for the Harminder Sahib, almost all buildings were damaged. The Army had 83 dead and 249 wounded. Nearly 493 civilians, including militants, died and 1,592 were wounded. Among those killed were Bhindranwala and Maj. Gen. Shahbeg Singh. "Operation Blue Star" was followed by "Operation Wood Rose" to flush out militants from all gurudwaras in the state. This was conducted even more inaptly. Many innocent Sikhs were apprehended and humiliated in the process. Operations "Blue Star" and "Wood Rose" were severely criticized by all Sikhs within and outside India. It was considered an assault on their religion. So much so, many Sikhs in the army revolted and deserted their units to fight for their faith and religion.

The situation was controlled with great difficulty. The Sikh community felt humiliated and hurt. Many prominent Sikhs in the Congress and government resigned in protest. Even Giani Zail Singh, the President and a trusted follower of Indira Gandhi, is said to have been sullen and greatly disturbed by the army action. The sacrilege and destruction caused to the Golden Temple complex traumatized every Sikh and impacted their psyche. Mrs. Gandhi was assassinated by her Sikh guards four months after "Operation Blue Star", on 31 October 1984. General A.S. Vaidya was also assassinated by Sikh terrorists at Pune on 10 August 1986. Mrs. Gandhi's assassination caused another upheaval; more than 3,000 Sikhs were killed across India in the riots that followed. Most of the killings took place in Delhi and its neighbourhood. It is said that celebrations and illumination of gurudwaras by the Sikhs on the eve of her assassination was a catalyst for the riots.

A provocative statement by Rajiv Gandhi was a signal to his workers to attack Sikhs. People were pulled out of their houses and lynched. Their shops were gutted. Sikhs, including army personnel, were pulled out of trains and buses and murdered. The riots were organized by Congress workers. Rajesh Tytler, Sajjan Kumar, H.K.L. Bhagat and Kalpnath Rai were in the forefront of the rioting as per inquiries conducted by the government later. The army restored peace and order after much damage had been done. As many as 20,000 Sikhs were displaced. Some of my colleagues in the army were victims of these riots which were unfortunate and pained us greatly. "Operation Blue Star" and the attack on Sikhs were the two major factors that promoted the militancy most, to the great satisfaction of the ISI. Pakistan had achieved its aim of creating a Sikh-Hindu divide, at least for the time being.

Post "Operation Blue Star," militancy in Punjab gained momentum[6] as even those who were against or neutral now supported it. The Sikh Diaspora in the USA, Canada, UK, Australia and Malaysia, where they were an influential segment of society, came out openly in support of Khalistan, morally and financially. The political moves by Rajiv Gandhi post 'Blue Star' created more militancy as the Akali government under Mr. Barnala not only shared the political philosophy of the militants but was ineffective. From 1984 to 1986, militancy continued to gather momentum and the Golden Temple was once again under the control of extremist Sikh organizations. The killing of Hindus commenced more vigorously. AI flight 182 from Canada to India was bombed by Canadian Sikh militants when it was flying over the Atlantic Ocean on 23 June 1985. All the passengers, who were mostly Hindus perished. Sant Harcharan Singh Longewala was assassinated on 20 August 1985 for signing the Longewala accord with Rajiv Gandhi. Operation 'Black Thunder-1' had to be undertaken to flush out the militants on 30 April 1986.

About 200 militants had been occupying the Golden temple for the last three months. The police action took place when the radicals announced the proclamation of the independent Sikh nation of Khalistan. About 300 Black Commandos stormed the Golden Temple complex supported by 700 BSF personnel. No resistance was offered by the militants who had taken shelter in the sanctuary of the Temple and they surrendered. The operation lasted for eight hours and was ordered by Mr. Surjit Singh Barnala. The situation continued to deteriorate and President's Rule was imposed on 11 June 1987. An ineffective anti-militancy policy was followed even when Mr. Siddharth Shankar Ray was the governor and Mr. Julio Ribeiro, the DGP. Mr Ribeiro may have earned his spurs as Commissioner of Police in Bombay but he was ineffective in Punjab as he was unfamiliar with the ground realities.

The police was rudderless and ineffective. The militants occupied the Golden Temple for the third time in April 1988 and 'Operation Black Thunder-2'[7] had to be launched on 9 May to flush the holy temple clean of militant. By this time, Mr. K.P.S. Gill, a renowned IPS officer with vast experience in anti-insurgency operations in Assam and Punjab, was appointed as the DGP of the state. He planned, ordered and supervised the execution of the operation. The logistic support to the complex was cut off and all entry and exit points sealed. NSG personnel were posted at vantage points from where the activities of the militants could be observed day and night by high resolution telescopic and night vision sights and devices. They were equipped with high precision sniper rifles to target the militants.

The militants were constantly harassed by sniping and starvation. Forty-one militants died by the sniping and by 18 May they were worn out. About 200 of them surrendered. Thus the operation ended successfully without any sacrilege or damage to the Temple. The media was allowed to cover the operation live. Therefore, the whole operation was transparent and under public scrutiny. Some of the militants with females had hidden themselves in the sanctum sanctorum. They had defecated and soiled the area with excreta. The misdeeds and defiling of the sanctum sanctorum by the militants was exposed to all Sikhs through this live coverage. The blockade with the use of high-technology weapons and devices, live media coverage, use of minimum force and no collateral damage proved to be highly successful. *Kirtan* in the temple was resumed from 23 May. The operation gained the people's applause and was a great setback to the militants and their cause.

Between 1988 and 1990, the intensity of killing and militant activities eased a little when Mr. K.P.S. Gill took charge of the anti-militancy operations. He reorganized the police, trained them for the operations and put in place an effective coordination mechanism with the Central Armed Police Forces. The police was equipped with weapons and equipment to match the firepower, mobility and communications of militants. The police officers led all operations from the front. The rivalry and gang wars between various groups and panthic committees headed by Dr. Sohan Singh and that by Manochal for control of the movement also helped. The people of Punjab realized that the idea of an independent nation was unrealistic. It would be a land locked country sandwiched between two antagonistic neighbours. The new state's agrarian economy would be unviable to sustain it. The Sikhs were a prosperous community spread all over India who held high status and respect in society; they would be uprooted on the creation of a new state. The holocaust of 1947 was still fresh in their minds.

Khalistan, as a country would be dependent and at the mercy of Pakistan that was most unreliable. They also realized that there was much more to lose than gain and Pakistan was using them as a proxy to settle scores with India. The militancy had also degenerated into the narcotic trade, gun-running, extortions, land grabbing, and murders to settle enmity. The illegal power and status enjoyed by the militants led to access to women, abductions, free food, liquor and vehicles. Thus, a number of prominent and common Sikhs and, to a large extent, even the Akalis, disapproved of the activities of the militants and disassociated themselves. They hoped that somehow peace would be restored. The militants started abducting and killing police personnel and their families to demoralize them. Mr. Gill ordered counter abduction of families and relatives of militants. This had an immediate effect on the militants who ceased this practice.

By the end of 1989, significant success had been achieved against the militants and their influence was restricted to only the border areas. The parliamentary elections in December 1989 saw Mr. V.P. Singh of the Janata Party as the PM, replacing the corrupt Congress and Rajiv Gandhi. V.P. Singh was very soft on terrorism and talked of healing hearts rather than dealing firmly with rogue militants. The elections also saw 10 MPs who supported militancy enter Parliament. Simranjit Singh Mann was among them. The militants now had a voice and platform in Parliament to execute their agenda. Pakistan held Exercise Zarb-e-Momin on the Indian border to scale up the sagging militancy. The Indian Army deployment as a response was a blessing in disguise as this greatly curtailed the movement and activities of the militants. Though the army was not involved in operations against militants, the villages and towns where the army was deployed were relieved of the menace.

After the Janata Party government fell, Mr. Chandrashekhar, as the PM, continued to follow the policy of appeasement. So much so that Mr. K.P.S. Gill was posted out of the state under pressure from Simranjit Singh Mann and others. Militancy came to the centre stage again. It shifted from the border areas to interior Punjab. The militants imposed the Panthic code of conduct on the public which, though resented, was meekly followed as a weak government could not enforce law and order. About 506 people were killed during 1990. After the fall of the Chandrashekhar government, midterm elections were announced. Mr. Rajiv Gandhi was assassinated near Chennai during an election campaign on 21 May 1991. High alert was sounded by the government and we were deployed.

Immediately after our deployment, an encounter with the militants took place at village Kot Sivia on 13 May 1991. We mobilized columns from both 3 Assam and 2 Dogra but the militants, including Paramjit Singh Panjwar, slipped away and we learnt some new lessons. In our second encounter, 2 Dogra battalion killed four militants in an operation at Sanga village,[8] three km from Taran Taran, on the road to Goindwal. On the night of 25/26 May 1991, the SP Ops, Mr. Kubhi Ram, informed us that militants were reported seen in the notorious village of Sanga and military assistance was requisitioned. A cordon of the village was established by 2 Dogra under Colonel B.C. Lagwal by 2330 hrs. At about 0445 hrs, a horse cart followed by a pickup truck without lights emerged from the gurudwara and tried to break through the road block. A fire fight ensued in which the head granthi, Sardar Kabul Singh, was killed. He was armed with a 12 bore gun and a belt of cartridges. The other occupants ran into the village under the cover of darkness. In a second attempt to escape, two of the militants who were following a scout from the village again ran into the second block. In the fire fight that followed, one militant was killed and the other consumed cyanide and died. In yet another attempt to escape, two more militants tried to swim through the UBDC (Kasur branch). Both were shot dead and the body of one of them was later fished out of the canal. When the search of the village commenced in the morning, three bodies were found without weapons. No one from the village identified them.

It was widely rumoured that innocent villagers and a granthi had been killed by us. The Deputy Divisional Commander, Brigadier Mishra, also arrived at the site to verify the encounter. However Mr. Kubhiram and the officers of 2 Dogras were sure that they had killed the militants and at least one more was hiding in the village. Repeated searches yielded no result. Finally, suspicion was aroused in a house, where a wedding ceremony was in progress. Sepoy Raj Mal of the search party observed that the bride was rather masculine and she was wearing male sandals. The game of the terrorist masquerading as a bride was finally up when 'she' was asked to be interrogated by the lady police. He consumed cyanide and died instantly. He was identified as Harbhaj Singh, Bhaja, a self-styled lt. gen. of the

Bhindranwala Tiger Force. The other militants killed were Bhai Hardev Singh, alias Titoo, an area commander, Kashmir Singh, alias Kala, Balwinder Singh Sanga, younger brother of notorious terrorist Sukhvender Singh Sanga, in whose memory the gurudwara was being constructed and the granthi, Kabul Singh Sanga.

A GPMP, belonging to Harbhaj Singh and other weapons were recovered from a heap of dung, where they had been hidden by the militants. Thus, the operation ended successfully vindicating our stand. There was no collateral damage or harassment of the villagers. A few more such operations were conducted by us with success at Kassel, Kaler, Taran Taran and Gidri Gagrain villages. We dominated the area by random checks of suspected militant hideouts in villages and farm houses. Roving road blocks and multiple area ambushes were established both during day and night to restrict the movement of militants. They avoided us but continued killing suspected collaborators and those who failed to obey their dictates. At least one or two killings were reported every day in Taran Taran district.

The most significant killing was that of an ex MLA at Khadoor Sahib on 2 June. While Major General S.C. Vohra, the GOC, was happy with us, the corps and the army commander were not as they apprehended that my brigade might unduly get sucked into these operations. The army wanted to stay clear of any involvement in anti-militant operations after their bitter experience of "OP Blue Star". I explained to them that we were not carrying out anti-militancy operations but operating against those who threatened our security. We continued to assert our presence in the area. The GOC, Major General S.C. Vohra visited us on 3 June. I briefed him on the status of militancy, area domination for the elections and our operational preparedness. He visited the DCB as well and was fully satisfied with our performance.

All other formations were withdrawn except my brigade by the end of June after the elections. Mr. P.V. Narasimha Rao became the PM in June 1991. My brigade was now deployed on the DCB from Rania in the north to Buchcher headworks in the south. We were placed under 15 Infantry Division. The deployment on the DCB was tedious, monotonous and boring. We were supposed to rest during the day and be deployed during the night as most of the border crossings by militants took place during darkness. Even though a fence had been erected, lit at night and patrolled, it only acted as a deterrent and the militants still managed to cross it. They employed ingenious methods like digging tunnels, or jumping over the fence with the help of ladders.

Our northern flank held by 2 Dogra rested on the Ravi river. The river had numerous fordable channels with small islands full of tall elephant grass. The fence along the river had gaps and was difficult to patrol. It was an ideal area for trans-border illegal activities. Pakistan rangers provided the logistics and intelligence to the militants in every case. Even in the monsoon, crossings were possible and attempted with inflatable tubes or swimming with help of buffalos. However, we devised an effective surveillance system and incorporated the villagers to thwart the crossings. Crossings could not take place without their help in the vicinity of the DCB. The weather was very hot and humid due to rice cultivation. It was as bad as Bengal. Mosquitoes and snakes were a deadly menace. We had a number of snake bite casualties some even fatal. The deployment also had physiological changes in the jawans as their body clock was disturbed. Every one detested this deployment but we endured it.

The other problem that we encountered on the DCB was illegal border crossing by Bangladeshis into Pakistan with the aim of reaching the Gulf countries or Saudi Arabia as their final destination. Every week a large group would be apprehended and handed over to the BSF for repatriation to their country. But, in fact, no one went back and they all melted in rural Punjab. So the BSF, seeking an easy solution, would allow them to enter Pakistan. This migration was in fact a big national security threat and a study was carried out by us and submitted to the Corps HQ. A number of studies and seminars on illegal migration[9] from Bangladesh into India have since been carried out validating our findings. In fact, this was a well organized plan and very precisely executed.

The BSF at the Indo-Bangla border were accomplices in this illegal migration. Poor peasants in Bangladesh were lured by agents for greener pastures to Saudi Arabia. A heavy fee was charged by them with the promise of a safe journey. These people then crossed the border in connivance with the BSF on the Indian side and handed over to the Indian agent who travelled with them up to Patna, Banares or any other convenient station and then abandoned them to their fate. Touts would pounce on these unsuspecting innocents and force them into bonded labour, housework or prostitution. This poaching game would continue till they reached Punjab. Some of them would realize the miserable state that they were in and would abandon the journey and merge with the local population to settle in crowded Muslim areas.

Those who reached Punjab would be rounded up at the stations by labour agents and herded to villages. They were employed as farm labourers and released when not required. These hapless and helpless people would then resume their journey to the 'promised land' and towards the border entry points. They would halt for the night near a gurudwara for food and go along the canals and drains flowing towards the border. It was easy to cross the border when the fence had not come up. Those arrested by BSF would push them into Pakistan to be arrested by Pakistan Rangers or farmers on the other side. Most of the women were sexually exploited by the Rangers or the villagers and then sold for prostitution or retained as labourers. Others would settle down in crowded cities in Pakistan. Hardly anyone reached their dream destination. We felt sorry for these people, especially the women. Only 30 per cent of the group managed to reach Pakistan.

Later, when the situation became difficult because of the fence, they crossed over either through Kutch or the Jammu border. In subsequent years, when the complete border was fenced, the number of crossings became negligible and most of them settled in India. They are in a substantial number in Ludhiana and are employed in hazardous chemical industries. Delhi itself has lakhs of them. Ever since this migration commenced in the 'Eighties, the demography of the border areas in Assam and West Bengal has drastically changed to a Muslim majority. They are in substantial numbers in states like Bihar, Odisha, Delhi, UP and Maharashtra and in smaller numbers in almost all states. The menace has become a national security issue and a point of discord between India and Bangladesh. Most housemaids and rickshaw pullers in Indian cities are these illegal migrants.

Lt. Gen. B.K.N. Chhibber, the Corps Commander, visited us on 10 July. By now we were responsible for 1,400 sq km of area consisting of 400 villages. Taran Taran and Amritsar districts were the most notorious. Almost all the militant groups operated in this area. We had churned up the whole area with our aggressive patrolling. I briefed him on our operational role, the effectiveness of the fence and the defensive potential of the DCB. I also highlighted the illegal migration of Bangladeshis and its impact on security. There was a need for an effective policy to either stop it or they be allowed to cross over to Pakistan as repatriation was a futile effort. I apprised him of the status of militancy, performance of the police and future trends. I also flagged that the main reason of sustenance of militancy was support by Pakistan, lack of effective policy and coordination of operations. People by and large were fed up with the militancy and a concerted and coordinated effort was needed.

I also brought to his notice that our deployment on the DCB should not be for more than three months due to the physiological side effects on the men. The GOC travelled with me from Kakkar in the north to Bucher Head in the south. He was an acknowledged authority on Punjab. Nothing could escape his scrutiny. He was an astute commander with a sharp intellect and instincts. He accepted my recommendations and complimented the officers and the men for their work. The Corps Commander visited us again on 24 September to assess whether or when elections could be held in the state. During this period we had also conducted operations against terrorists at Bachiwind, Pindori and Sarai Amant Khan villages. The BSF had foiled two attempts by infiltrators near the fence. The crime rate was rather high with 15 murders.

The civil administration was still ineffective. There was very little development which was a key issue of the people and the main cause of militancy. There was rampant corruption and inefficiency. Lower-level functionaries took advantage of the prevailing militancy to fleece poor peasants. The police harassed vulnerable farmers[10] to extort money from them. The simple method was to arrest a prosperous farmer on suspicion of links with militants and then negotiate a deal. Some farmers even sold their land to raise money for the release of their dear ones. The judiciary was thoroughly corrupt. They were either bribed or intimidated into submission by the militants for judgments in their favour, bail or postponement. Thus, most militants who were apprehended were eliminated and not put on trial by the police. The police and CRPF were still not fully trained to fight the militants who were now equipped with GPMGs, AK-47 and RPGs.

There was a lot of collateral damage and unnecessary casualties of both the police and civilians. The public was very happy with the presence of the army as it provided them a vent for their grievances and some security. However they still obeyed the diktats of the militants that were published in the vernacular papers like *Ajit*, conveyed through letters or orally. Therefore, much more was needed to be done to win their confidence for participating in the state elections. We also recommended that elections should be held as early as possible but the ground had to be prepared by relentless operations against the militants. The army was needed to assist the police in this matter as they were incapable of creating a favourable environment. Later, I learnt that our inputs to the Corps Commander were used for planning the elections. We were de-inducted on 8 October 1991 after a fruitful tenure.

Finally the new government under Narasimha Rao decided to take a tough stand against the militants as the option of a political solution had ceased to exist. The Akalis had been marginalized and Mr. Simranjit Singh Mann had been forced out of the elections. Harminder Sandhu of the AISSF was murdered by Khalistan Commando Force militants (Dr. Sohan Singh Panthic Committee). There was no other leader of stature left to hold talks. Post "Op Rakshak", killings had increased. In November 1991, the government decided to end the militancy once and for all. Mr. K.P.S. Gill was recalled as DGP Punjab Police on 11 November 1991. The security forces (Army, Central Armed Police Forces and Punjab Police) were mandated to enforce law and order and prepare the ground for elections in mid-February. A coherent strategy was formulated to restore peace in the state so that all institutions that had been paralyzed could be revived and a democratically elected government functioned.

What emerged was a unique experiment in multi-force counter militant operations and integrated command structure. An operations room was established at each of the Corps HQ at Jallandhar, Bhatinda and Ambala with an officer of IGP rank attached to them. Brig. Narayan Chaterjee, AD, was in charge of the operations room at 11 Corps HQ. An SP was placed with each brigade HQ and a contingent of police and central police force was attached to each battalion for coordinated operations at short notice. Army intelligence personnel were placed at each police control room to share information. Thus, there was complete coordination without any sub group or force loyalty. The entire state was saturated with security forces giving no space to the militants. We were redeployed on 12 November 1991 with this philosophy and mandate.

I was given the old area of Taran Taran and placed under 9 Infantry Division. The brigade HQ occupied the stadium. 2 Dogra was deployed in its previous area near Taran Taran on the road to Goindwal, 21 Rajputana Rifles in the Thathian Mahanta and Naushara Panwan areas. 3 Assam was deployed in Chabal Kurd. Mr. M.S. Bhullar (IG Border Range) and Mr. Bhatti IGP were part of operational planning. Mr. Ajit Singh Sandhu, the SSP, was placed under us. We also dealt with the SSPs of Amritsar, Ajnala and Goindwal. Mr. Khubiram, Assistant Commandant, was SP Operations. Mr. Kalra I.P.S. ASP, a probationer, was also attached. Ajit Singh had been recruited as an ASI and had risen to the rank of SSP as his performance against the militants had been commendable. He was reliable, competent and sincere. However, I learnt subsequently that he was involved in extortions,[11] land grabbing and extra-judicial killings of both militants and civilians who did not do his bidding. After normalcy had been restored in the state, he was hounded by human right activists and dragged to the courts and held guilty. He committed suicide some time in 1997 because of the humiliation he had suffered in various courts and by the relatives of victims.

I was sorry to know about this as I had a good opinion of him. He did his job well under us. Kubhiram was from western UP. He was from the CRPF. We found him very intelligent, who could coordinate information from all the police stations and convert it into actionable intelligence. He was bold and daring. Mr. Kalra was a young officer, keen to learn and always present at the site of operations. All the SHOs were good in their work. We were also given 75 and 236 battalions CRPF with 10 and 8 companies each. In actual fact they were operating with 50 per cent strength. The strength of police personnel was 1,590, including 567 SPOs and 774 home guards. Twenty militant groups were operating in our area with an estimated strength of about 200. They were headed by three deputy chiefs and one head of the Panthic Committee. Six groups operated in the vicinity of Taran Taran.

I told all the police officers that we had to finish the militancy once and for all and create a favourable environment for elections at all cost. Their task was to get actionable intelligence. The army would carry out aggressive operations and assist them whenever needed. There would be no harassment of civilians, human rights violations and minimum collateral damage while carrying out operations. Mr. Sarabjit Singh Sandhu, Deputy Commissioner, and all his officers in our area were also co-opted into the planning and execution of development projects and civic actions conducted by us. All the three organs developed a perfect and harmonious relationship with each other for the next 10 months that we were together. The Army took three more steps to improve functioning with the police. They were allowed to claim in full the bounty that the militants carried. The police was given full credit in every operation that they participated in. The army trained the village guards and special police officers who were enrolled to supplement police resources.

We divided the operations into three phases. In phase-I, we were to carry out intense operations against the militants so that the elections were held without fear and interference, smoothly and fairly. In phase-II, we were to provide security cover during the elections to create confidence and faith in the people in the constitutional process; and ensure a large voter turnout. In phase-III, we were to consolidate the gains in the post-election period. 8 Dogra under Colonel Gungesh was also placed under us. Maj. Gen. S.K. Sharma, GOC, 9 Infantry Division, allowed us full freedom of action in planning and executing operations and was a source of inspiration. We carried out a number of successful operations during this period and the whole area was under our effective control by mid-February. As we succeeded, the people gained confidence and information about the militants started flowing.

Lt. Gen. B.K.N. Chhibber visited us on 6 December and Mr. K.P.S. Gill, the DGP, on 7 December 1991 to appreciate the quantum change in the environment that our operations had made. Finally, General S.F. Rodrigues, the COAS, accompanied by Lt. General B.C. Joshi, the GOC-in-C also visited us on 13 February 1992. By now we had carried out 14 major operations and achieved significant success. Three of them are described in succeeding paragraphs to indicate their ferocity and complexity.

Operation Rataul-Kotli on the Taran Taran-Jandiala Guru road, was launched on 2/3 December 1991. 2 Dogra was mobilized at 2330 hrs on 2 December based on information from a reliable source and laid a cordon around the area from multiple directions. The militants fired at the search party and disappeared towards Kasur Nala. The tracker dog with the unit lost the trail near the nala. Due to the vastness of the area, difficult terrain and crops, two companies of 3 Assam were also pressed into the operations. By the morning, five companies of the CRPF and police also joined. The whole area was combed minutely and a fire fight with the militants ensued that continued till the afternoon. Finally, four militants were killed. They were armed with 7.62 SLR (Belgium), Dragnov sniper rifle (Russian) AK-47, RPG and a Mauser pistol. A large quantity of food items, ammunition and medicines were also recovered. It will be seen that the militants were armed heavily and put up a serious fight till they were killed. The quantum of troops employed indicated the vastness of the area and the requirement of troops to search minutely without suffering casualties and causing any collateral damage. Intelligence was key to success which came from a source in the village. It was a message to the militants and the public that the state would use all its resources to enforce law and order.

The next operation was carried out in Gagubua village[12] from 9 to 11 December 1991. Colonel M.S. Kauchar had established a good relationship with the villages in his area, particularly ex-servicemen. An ex-serviceman's two beautiful nieces were being sexually abused by the notorious militant, Balwinder Singh Gagubua. His gang had terrorized the people and preyed on defenceless women. The ex-serviceman could not bear the dishonour of the family by this rogue. He took the courage and confided in Kauchhar his predicament. He was given a wireless set and codes to give us information. Thereafter it was easy to track the militant's movements. His presence was reported on 9 December and a cordon was laid immediately around the village by 3 Assam assisted by the police. The search throughout the night did not yield any result. It was frustrating, as the militants could have escaped under the cover of darkness. However one of the women accomplices of Balwinder Singh was interrogated by the police in the morning who indicated the house where he could be possibly hiding. By now, additional police and CRPF had been added to search the village while the army tightened the outer cordon. Repeated searching of the house did not yield any result. Since the operation had been prolonged beyond expectation, I decided to supervise its progress and reached the site around lunch time. The women accomplice, under sustained interrogation led us to a trapdoor leading to a concealed bunker in the house where the terrorists had taken refuge. The search party asked the militants to surrender. When they did not respond, his mother was sent inside who earnestly pleaded with him to do so. He refused to listen to her also.

Grenades were then lobbed into the bunker by the police to flush him out. Presuming that the militants had been wounded or killed, the search party entered the bunker to be greeted by a volley of automatic fire. In the confusion that followed, Balwinder Singh and another militant emerged out of the bunker blazing away with his AK-47. Balwinder's mother and 2 CRPF personnel who were blocking his path were mowed down by him; three others were injured. The courtyard of the house had become a battle ground. I also missed a volley of bullets that whizzed past me. When the cross-firing intensified, we climbed onto the roof. We had no choice but to jump from there when it became unsafe and in the process I broke my ankle.

In the confusion and crossfire that followed, one militant was killed. Balwinder was able to break the inner cordon and was about to make good his escape when a sniper from 3 Assam felled him 67 metres from his house. Thus ended the life of Balwinder Singh, self-styled lt. gen. and deputy chief of the KCF (W). Although the CRPF and police suffered casualties in this operation, it was a big blow to the militants and a great relief to the villagers. The moral depravation and viciousness of the militants were exposed. The militant had no remorse in killing his mother. Good intelligence, cooperation of the villagers, coordination with the police and good drills had won the day for the SF. The state could not be challenged any more by militants.

Yet another good operation that needs mention was carried out by 2 Dogra on 7 January 1992 at Upal, Gil Kaler, Sarai Talwandi and Mianwind villages. Information was received on 2 January that militants were present in them. However, they managed to escape. Subsequently, the grandfather of a young girl, Daljit Kaur, confided that she was missing from her school from 6 January. He feared that she had been abducted by the militants. A second cordon-and-search of these villages was launched on 7 January. The militants fired at the search parties and tried to break through the cordon. Intense cross firing took place. However, Balwinder Singh, one of the militants who was trapped in the crossfire lost his nerve and surrendered. It led to the surrender of another four of them.

Balwinder Singh and Chilmal Singh revealed that they belonged to the BTKF (Manochal) and had managed to escape on 2/3 January. That night, they had locked up all the male members of the family of Gurpal Singh and raped his wife, Paramjit Kaur, and niece, Balwinder Kaur, in the adjoining room. They had also extorted Rs. 20,000 from the villagers. They also confirmed that Daljit Kaur had been abducted from her school by him and kept in a hideout in Amritsar as he had taken a fancy for her. They had planned to take her to Bombay against her wishes. Daljit Kaur was recovered from the hideout and restored to her parents. She and her grandfather agreed to make a statement against the militants and their debauchery on TV. This particular episode exposed the ugly face of the militants and created an anti-militant atmosphere. Other victims were now emboldened to cooperate in their destruction in the subsequent operations that followed.

After suppressing militancy to an acceptable extent, we embarked on phase-II to motivate the public to participate in the electoral process. The militants had imposed a boycott of the elections. They and their mentors in Pakistan, UK, USA, Canada and other countries, believed that a boycott would either lead to postponement of elections or a low turnout will prove to the international community that it was a sham. A turnout below 10 per cent would vindicate their stand and prove to the world that it was a referendum in their favour. They did not allow the Akali Dal, except the unknown Kabul Singh faction, to participate in the elections. Dr. Sohan Singh was the only militant who advocated participation but he was threatened by his gang and had to flee for safety to Pakistan. The entire state was saturated with posters, leaflets, and press notes through selected newspapers and warnings of reprisal to election officers who acted against militant diktats.

We held meetings in each village in our area of responsibility and explained to the people the importance of the elections, their constitutional right and a chance to elect a government of their choice. It would also be a befitting reply to the militants who had held every one hostage to their nefarious designs. We also highlighted the futility of Khalistan and its impracticality. The people responded favourably even though the fear of militant reprisals was lurking in their minds. We also enrolled the support of ex-servicemen, government servants, educated youths, local leaders and eminent people of the area. Many were fence sitters till the last day. A few villages openly supported the elections at the same time; some frankly admitted their apprehensions and compulsions even though they wanted the elections to be held. One elderly lambardar went to the extent of telling me that his village had decided not to participate in the elections but they respected and were proud of the army and would not like to disappoint us. Therefore, he along with four more would ensure that the ballet box did not go empty. He kept his word. Only four votes were cast in that village.

The police provided three tiers of protection to the candidates. Their personal security while canvassing; security to their family members; and security at campaign venues. Not a single candidate could be killed by the militants. The army undertook active operations to ensure that the militants were on the run. On the day of voting, while the police provided the inner security to the polling booths, the army provided the outer cordon. The militants imposed total curfew on 18 and 19 February but people still came out to vote.[13] The voter turnout in Taran Taran was about 30-35 per cent; it was high, contrary to expectations.[14] The overall voter turnout in the state was between 40 and 45 per cent and the Congress under Mr. Beant Singh managed a comfortable majority in the assembly. People had rejected the militants and their supporters. The militants had misread the mood of the people and they realized their mistake belatedly.

The Akali Dal was the biggest loser in this entire game. The Beant Singh government did not take long to lay down a policy against the militants which was in line with the directions of the central government. The people now had a platform to resolve their grievances and development of the area through their elected MLAs. They started thronging to them. The SF had a clear mandate to finish militancy as early as possible. The militants and their supporters stood exposed of their misdeeds as the government initiated legal action against each of them. Their skeletons of misdeeds came tumbling out of the cupboards. The militants had no political voice and could speak only through bullets or guns of which the people had enough.

Phase-III commenced now. We ensured that all government offices and institutions like schools, dispensaries, veterinary hospitals, electric substations, PWD departments, canal department and roadways functioned on a regular basis. We conducted a number of civic actions such as free eye camps, medical camps, vocational classes, and recruitment training for medically fit boys. We also repaired some tracks, community centres, culverts and bridges. We organized sports competitions. At the same time, all-out operations were launched against the militants. We launched immediate operations against any militant act in our area as per the new directions. This response would invariably result in an encounter and killing of the perpetuator. We now focused on the militant leadership. They were tracked and hunted down one by one. Night operations were given primacy as all militants moved in before midnight and moved out before dawn. Under this policy, Major K.J. Singh of 2 Dogra tracked an important militant in Amritsar who was arrested in broad daylight when he went to meet his accomplices at the bus stand. Similarly, 2 Dogra tracked down another important militant in Muzaffarnagar, UP, and arrested him with the help of the UP police. The militants now realized that they were no more safe anywhere.

Another operation that brought out some good lessons for the police and CAPF was conducted at Behla village[15] on 8/9 June 1992. Information was received by the police that some important militants were holding a meeting at Behla village in the house of an Akali ex MLA. It was a big double-storey house with a large compound and a high boundary wall. This gave it inherent defensibility. Surjit Singh Behala who was deputy chief of the BTKF (Manochal) and next to Gurcharan Singh Manochal, Madan Singh or Chota Behla was among the militants present. Mr. Ajit Singh, the SSP, along with Mr. Kubhiram and a police force of about 20 personnel reached the house and conducted a preliminary search. The militants engaged the police during this search. Two policemen who were at the entrance were killed and most of the members of the search party escaped onto the roof of the house on the second floor where they were trapped. Kubhiram and the rest of the personnel continued to engage them. CRPF reinforcements were unable to rescue the SSP and he requisitioned army help. Two companies each of 2 Dogra, 3 Assam and 21 Raj Rif were despatched and the operation was taken over by Colonel B.C. Langwal.

In the meantime the police collected the relatives of Surjit Singh, including his sister, to ask the militants to surrender. The militants fired at them killing two and injuring four including the sister of Surjit Singh. In the fire fight that ensued, two CRPF jawans were injured. The trapped police personnel were rescued by the army. Thereafter, an intense fire fight commenced between the two sides. Rocket launchers were used for the first time to flush out the militants. The operation lasted 28 hours when all the seven militants were killed. The intelligence and immediate response of the police was good. The SSP did not follow the correct search drills and landed himself in a very precarious situation. The Akali-militant nexus was exposed. The hard core top militants were ruthless and fought till death. The operation once again sent a strong message about the resolve of the state to handle militancy firmly.

By 11 April, when Lt. Gen. B.K.N. Chhibber visited us, 20 groups still operated in our area even though we had killed 17 top militants by then. We had conducted 35 operations and killed more than 40 militants and captured large quantities of weapons and ammunition. Manochal, Panjwar and Gurmukh Singh Nagoke were most prominent of those still operating in our area. The BTKF and KLF had been mauled considerably. The modus operandi of the militants had not changed. Reprisals against soft targets were on the increase to assert their influence but the people were no longer terrorized and cooperated willingly with the SF. We recommended that the present pace of operations must continue till the end of June and no dilution of deployment should take place as was being planned. 8 Dogra should remain under our command. Surrenders should be encouraged. The elected MLAs should be asked to visit their constituencies frequently to interact with the public. The induction of Rashtriya Rifles had commenced who would eventually replace us. It was decided that 9 Infantry Division would be de-inducted in May after the corps commander's visit and we were placed under 15 Infantry Division on 1 May. Thus an eventful period came to an end.

Maj. Gen. J.S. Laskar, GOC 15 Infantry Division, visited us on 14 May and then again on 17 June. The pace of operations continued and under intense pressure from the SF, the militants either fled the area or surrendered. 2 Dogra also participated in a big operation along with police in the Mand area from 1 to 3 July 1992 as the militants would normally take shelter in this vast marsh land formed by the Beas River. A number of hideouts were destroyed and some militants were killed in this joint operation. By June, 46 militants had given up the gun,[16] and they were all rehabilitated under generous terms. Lt. Gen. B.K.N. Chhibber visited us once again on 28 July before our de-induction in mid Aug. Another batch of 27 militants surrendered on 13 August 1992 bringing the total to 73. By now, a body blow had been given to the KCF (Wassan), KCF (Panjwar) and BTKF groups. It was rumoured that while Manochal still operated in the area, other top guns like Wadhwa Singh of the Babbar Khalsa, Paramjit Singh Panjwar of the KLF had fled to Pakistan. Gurcharan Singh Manochal was also finally gunned down in village Rataul in January 1993.

The militants were now demoralized and willing to surrender. Their recruitment had dropped to zero. Shops and markets opened. Night activities commenced. People refused to comply with the dictates of militants. We now focused on training of the police and CRPF to make them more effective after our departure and not repeat the mistakes that they had made at Behla. Under this scheme, we trained 29 ASIs, 282 special police officers and two CRPF battalions. Our tenure of duty finally came to an end on 15 August and we returned to our cantonments. Rashtriya Rifles under Brig. A.J.B. Jaini, replaced us. It had been an eventful, rich and fruitful tenure. Col. Prakash Choudhary was replaced by Mukesh Sethi in June, and B.C. Lagwal by Dadwal. Our efforts had put the final nail in the coffin of militancy in Taran Taran, the hub of militancy. We were rewarded richly for our contribution in ushering peace in Punjab. Colonel M.S. Kauchhar was awarded a VSM, B.C. Lagwal a SC, Dadwal and Gungesh with SMs. Officers and men of each battalion had received a fair number of awards. All the four battalions received COAS commendations on Army Day 1993 in recognition of their services which was a unique distinction.

Lt. Gen. B.K.N. Chhibber was posted out as Chief of Staff HQ Western Command in September. He was an adviser to the CM for a short time before his appointment as the governor. He and Mr. K.P.S. Gill were the main architects of terminating militancy. Lt. Gen. V.P. Malik was now the corps commander. He consolidated the gains made by us and continued with the proactive policy. Finally, in December 1992, my tenure ended. I was awarded a VSM and nominated to attend the National Defence College Course at New Delhi. Militancy in Punjab was declared dead in 1993.

The end of militancy in Punjab is one of the very few success stories in the world. The cardinal principles for its defeat were the removal of perceived grievances of the people, employment generation and ensuring good governance. These aspects were addressed seriously in June 1991. By the middle of June 1992, recruitment for militancy had dropped to zero. The external support and financing by Pakistan and mentors of the militant elements in the USA, UK, Canada and other countries was also effectively neutralized. Border fencing also impacted on the physical movement of the militants, and supply of arms and ammunition. For the first time since 1970, the central and state governments took a determined stand against militancy and formed a comprehensive and coordinated policy.

This policy was executed through joint command HQ and they were allotted adequate resources. The police and CAPF were trained, equipped and led from the front. Legislative measures such as the National Security Act, 1980, Anti-Hijacking Act, 1982, Armed Forces Special Power Act, 1983, Punjab Disturbed Area Act, 1983; TADA and POTA, Prevention and Misuse of Religious Institutions Ordinance, 1988, were applied seriously against defaulters. Many supporters of militancy, both overt and covert, were held accountable for their actions. Public opinion and perceptions were also transformed by effective psychological operations and the media played a positive role in achieving it. The use of technology to intercept and jam communications nets of militants and track their movement also played a prominent role. Elimination of top militant leadership led to the collapse of command and control of militant organizations within one year. The MEA also played a vital role in neutralizing foreign interference and propaganda against human rights violations at the international level. Lastly, Mr. K.P.S. Gill played a central role in achieving success. It was he who sowed the seeds of success and stamped out the curse of militancy with the help of the army.

I joined the National Defence College, New Delhi, in January 1993. The college is located at no. 6, Tees January Marg, in an imposing palace-like building. This building was constructed in 1935 and was owned by Khan Saheb Tej Muhamad Khan of Badarshi, NWFP. It had Victorian architecture and vice regal splendour. It was acquired by the government for an officers' mess in 1939 during the war. The college was established in 1960 on the pattern of the IDC/RCDS, UK. Lt. Gen. K. Bahadur Singh was the first commandant. We were 70 senior officers from the three services, the Indian Foreign Service, Indian Administrative Service, Indian Police, Railways, Postal, Revenue and other allied services. All officers were of joint secretary level. There were 20 foreign officers as well from all the important countries of the world. The one-year sabbatical was a great learning experience in strategy, international relations, economics, and political, social, technological and industrial aspects of national security. The study of internal and external threats; foreign, economic and defence policies of other countries that impacted the security and development of India was also part of the syllabus. We were exposed to knowledge-sharing with internationally renowned experts, ambassadors, senior politicians and other eminent personalities.

Air Marshal S. Kulkarni, the commandant, was an excellent mentor. The college faculty consisted of one senior directing staff from each of the three services and the IFS and IAS. We undertook tours to various states in India to study their political, socio and economic models. I was team leader during the visit in Bihar, the most backward, underdeveloped, volatile state, rife with corruption, caste politics and little or no law and order. We had the opportunity to interact with Shri Lalu Prasad Yadav, the maverick CM. Bihar is a very important state but very poor due to bad governance. An interaction with the CM was very enlightening. We found him very intelligent and communicative. He answered a wide range of questions including his plans for the development of the state. Unfortunately, he did not achieve what he projected but the people were happy with his policies. He was from a poor backward family and had found ready acceptance by them. His policy theme was social justice for the backward and dalits. He was mired in financial scams and later convicted by the courts. He spent many years in jail but his party has flourished.

We also visited the tribal areas, Bodh Gaya, the centre of Buddhism, and the ruins of the ancient university of Nalanda. This famous university was destroyed by a barbaric Muslim marauder Muhammad Bakhtiyar Khan Khilji, in 1202. All the scholars and students were killed and the country lost a treasure of knowledge forever. I was part of the foreign tour to Italy and Switzerland. This tour was of little value from both the security and international relations point of view. However, it exposed us to the EU/ NATO and the developed world. I also took the opportunity to visit Prague, Vienna and London along with Brig. P.K. Renjen. Prague was still recovering from the effects of communism. I was a paying guest of a retired school teacher. The old lady was very gentle and lived alone. She made additional money for herself by renting out one room of her small flat. We stayed with the Indian ambassador at Vienna and were able to visit all parts of this famous ancient historic city. Our visit to Southall in London was most memorable as it transported us back to Karol Bagh in Delhi with all the desi flavours.

We also visited the Andaman and Nicobar islands as part of internal security studies. It was one of the most interesting tours that took us to the closest point to Indonesia, Malaysia and Burma. The strategic importance of Andaman-Nicobar has been belatedly recognized by India. Environment protection was at the top of the agenda of the government. The flora and fauna exists in its pristine form. The famous Cellular Jail is now a national museum. The ruins on Ross Island have been preserved to remind us of British imperialism. The signs of Japanese occupation also exist. My thesis on Technology and Terrorism was approved by Madras University and I was granted the degree of M. Phil.

I was posted as DDG Discipline and Vigilance at Army HQ. I was not happy with this posting as it was out of line with my profile. Due to a spurt in cases of indiscipline in the army, this directorate had suddenly become important. The MS rejected my representation for this reason. The origin of the discipline and vigilance directorate is traced to World War II when a large number of corruption cases came to be noticed in supply contracts and procurements for the defence forces. Thus, the white collar crimes had to be detected, investigated and prosecuted. After independence, the civilian component became the CBI and the army component remained under the AG's branch. It was one of the smallest directorates in Sena Bhavan. Our subordinate staff was composed of civilians. I worked very closely with the MS Branch and the Judge Advocate General. I also attended important court cases at the Supreme Court along with the attorney/solicitor generals.

Maj. Gen. Sampath Kumar was the ADG who later became Military Secretary to the President. He was replaced by S.G. Vombatkhere. Both handled the directorate expertly. Lt. Gen. Suri and Vinay Shankar were the Director Generals. They allowed me total freedom in the course of my work. Both retired as DG Artillery. Similarly, Lt. Gen. M.M. Lakhera and later K.N. Seth as Adjutant General allowed us total independence of thought and application of mind in all cases. I made a monthly presentation to the COAS on the state of discipline in the Indian Army. My analysis brought out three distinct trends. The first was service-related offences. This was restricted to officers with less than 10 years of service. The cases related to them were mostly in the form of altercations, assaults and affrays with other government department officers or civilians whenever the rights, entitlements, precedence or dignity of the defence personnel or their families were in question such as misdemeanour of seniors, misconduct by policemen, railway staff, civil administrators or civilians. Normally, such cases were the outcome of high moral values, high standards of work ethics, and noble traditions of the Indian Army in conflict with disrespectful, corrupt, inefficient and indifferent government officials or civilians. The assault and affray between a Gorkha battalion and railway staff at Meerut and between YOs at Mhow and the police fell in this category. Such offences would be disposed off with an advisory.

The second trend was career-related offences by officers between 10 and 20 years of service. These involved cases related to career progression such as cheating, fudging, appeasements, acquiescence, malfeasance, misuse of government property, manpower or other facilities and gratification for the sake of their careers. Since such officers were future senior commanders, their offences were dealt with seriously ending in court martials or severe administrative action that would retard their prospects of promotion.

The last was related to impropriety, financial corruption, misuse of power and authority. These were related to senior ranks that had vast administrative and financial powers. The local and emergent purchase powers, supply, hiring of transport, labour and animal contracts; and operational works provided ample opportunities to these officers to go astray. They exploited the vulnerabilities of subordinates and even women officers. Once again, a serious view was taken of such cases. New trends were emerging with the changing socio-economic environment, such as marital discord, stealing the affection of a brother officer's wife, promiscuity among male and female officers, change in moral values and increase in cases related to stress. Increase in suicides, fratricides, drug abuse, and depression/anxiety among both officers and families were also noticed. Marital discords were due to intellectual and social incompatibility between husband and wife. The women officers desire to find a suitable husband and settle down before their five-year terms of service ended led them to promiscuous relationships with fellow male officers that, in many cases, ended in sexual misconduct.

A case of sexual misconduct between a male and female officer at ASC Centre, Bangalore, made a most sordid case resulting in the dismissal of both. Cases related to senior officers were difficult to finalize and a determined effort was needed to conclude them successfully. They used multiple ways to delay, derail and escape. The famous case of financial impropriety in 33 Corps involved the corps, division, brigade and the commanding officer of the engineer regiment. We were able to prosecute all of them in spite of protracted delays and attempts to derail the prosecution. However, we were unable to bring to book a divisional commander who rose to become an army commander when he transported four trucks of building material meant for defence works from his division in the east to his residence in Kasauli and Punjab. Later, there were numerous cases of transporting foreign goods from Dula Bari on the Nepal side of the border to his residence.

Yet another army commander did the same from Lucknow to Secunderabad. There was one Major General who was allowed to retire after forgery was detected in his date of birth and another was allowed to be promoted to Lt. Gen. due to his proximity to the higher hierarchy and MOD. Another officer was sentenced to life imprisonment for extortion and murder of a businessman in Punjab during OP Rakshak. He was close to the home minister who wanted to grant him parole that he was not entitled to and remit his sentence. The HM tried to pressurize me but I refused and my recommendations were upheld up the chain. Many convicted officers waited for an opportune time to seek relief. Normally, as time went by, the facts of the case would be forgotten and a campaign to play a victim would be launched to dilute the offence, gain sympathy and create a favourable lobby. It would also enable their mentors or sympathizers in power to help them. I had plenty of such cases that kept me busy. Studying such 10 to 20 year-old cases was tedious and even though they had been filtered by a very fair and robust system, many would get underserved relief due to proximity to the COAS or someone in the MOD.

The case of Brigadier Pritam Singh, Kumaon Regiment that occurred in 1947 was revived for relief by some of his relatives. A known criminal was sought to be resurrected by a Presidential pardon. This was a travesty of justice and a wrong precedent. The COAS had been approached by the vested party but when the facts were put up, the case was rejected outright. I also had many cases of misdeeds related to senior officers in my custody; some were convicted and some others allowed to retire. It was impossible to prosecute all of them. The resources and time consumed would be immense. Therefore, I recommended to the COAS to prosecute only those that would send a strong message to the environment and act as a deterrent. One of the senior officers of the Ordnance Corps escaped from custody and resurfaced when the provisions of AR 123 lapsed. We took special sanction of the Supreme Court to prosecute him. He was dismissed from service and jailed. A powerful message had been conveyed to all.

Similarly, four major generals were dismissed from service under Army Rule 19 for misconduct. Even though I did not like the job, yet I learnt a lot of the darker side of the Army. I was fully aware of the weaknesses and how the crooks operated and manipulated the system. Col. B.S. Yadav, D.V.S. Malik, Mr. Chandershekhar and Mrs. Arti Srivastav, both SCSOs, were a great help in the performance of my work. My tenure concluded in June 1996 when I was informed by General S. Roychoudhary, the COAS, that he had selected me to command 8 Mountain Division in the Srinagar Valley.

NOTES

1. *It Does't Take a Hero* by General Norman Schwarzkopf.
2. 'How Congress Built up Bhindranwala,' *The Caravan,* 8 June 2019.
3. *Amritsar: Mrs. Gandhi's Last Battle* by Mark Tully.
4. Maj Gen Shahbeg Singh belonged to Amritsar district and studied in Khalsa College Amritsar and Govt College Lohare before his selection as an officer in IA in 1942. He fought in Burma during WW 2 with Garhwal Rifles.. Was transferred to 1 Para Battallion and later commanded

3/11 GR with distinction during 1965 war in J&K. After commanding a brigade he fought the 1971 War for Liberation of Bangladesh with Mukti Bahini with great distinction, He was promoted Maj Gen but dismissed from service on charges of corruption. He joined Bhindranwala as his adviser during the Punjab Militancy after his dismissal in frustration, against humiliation he had suffered and due to his perceived grievances. He was mastermind in fortification of Golden Temple. He died along with Bhindrawala and his daughter who had also joined militancy during OP Blue Star. His three sons were in the army then and served the country loyaly till their retirement.

5. *Operation Blue Star, The True Story* by Lt. Gen. K.S. Brar.
6. *The Siege Within* by M.J. Akbar.
7. *Operation Black Thunder. An Eyewitness Account of Terrorism in Punjab* by Sarbjit Singh.
8. *The Times of India* 27 May 1991; *The Tribune*, 28 May 1991; *Punjab Kesari*, 27 May 1991.
9. *Illegal Bangladeshi Migration to India. Impact on Internal Security* by Anand Kumar. IDSA Papers, January 2011,
10. The SHO of Chabal Kalan had arrested the only surviving young male member of a family that owned more than 100 acres of land and demanded money or transfer of part of the land to him from his mother for his release. Fearing for his life, the mother confided her dilemma to Colonel M.S. Kauchhar. I ordered the SSP to release the boy and post out the SHO or it would be taken up with the DGP. Thereafter such misdeeds stopped.
11. *The Punjab Monitor, Ajit Singh Sandhu–A Criminal in Uniform* by Kulwinder Sandhu and Simran Sidhu. It was established that Mr Ajit Singh was involved in extra-judicial killings.
12. *The Tribune,* News Beat, 5-11 January 1992, 'Eyewitness' by R. Sharma. A detailed account by the reporter.
13. *New York Times*, 19 February 1992, 'Sikh Militants in Punjab Impose Boycotts in Voting' by Sanjoy Hazarika.
14. *Washington Post*, 20 February 1992. 'Threats Curtail Turnout in Punjabi Vote' by Steve Coll. *India Today*, 29 February 1992, 'With Militant Scare and Akali Boycott, Punjab Elections may be Damp Squib' by Ramesh Vinayak.
15. *Indian Express,* 10 June 1992, *The Tribune*, 10 June 1992. The operation has been described in detail.
16. *The Tribune,* 5 April 1992. *Indian Express* 5 April also covered the event prominently.

Chapter 6

Insurgency in the Srinagar Valley

I reported for duty at Srinagar on 5 July 1996. Parliamentary elections had been held but the ground situation was still far from normal. The gun still ruled. Very few shops opened during the day and there was a virtual curfew during the night as if ghosts ruled every village and town at night. Only army patrols or terrorists moved at night. The quietness of the night was frequently disturbed by gunfire of encounters between the two. My task was to carry forward the unfinished agenda of the Government; to create a peaceful environment for the state assembly elections to be held in September. General Shankar Roychowdhury, the Chief, had told me that he had selected me as the GOC, based on my experience in Punjab, and he expected similar results in the Valley. Lt. Gen. J.S. Dhillon, the Corps Commander, also laid down the same mandate. I also met General Krishna Rao, the Governor, Lt. Gen. B.D. Shaklani, his advisor, Mr. Ashok Kumar, the chief secretary, Mr. S.S. Bloeria, the home secretary and Mr. M.N. Sabarwal, the DGP, shortly thereafter.

They briefed me on various facets of the prevailing situation. A welcome dinner was held in my honour by the J&K IAS, IPS, and CAFP senior officers at the Amar Club in Srinagar. The general atmosphere was upbeat after the elections but apprehension and uncertainty about the future still prevailed. The dinner was over by 2100 hrs to allow all the participants to reach their destinations before it became unsafe. The club was like a fortress and every participant moved out in a convoy of escort vehicles. I was advised to stay put in Srinagar for the night for the same reason. I refused the suggestion and undertook the night journey back to my HQ to make my defiance clear to the enemies of the state. I ordered that henceforth all moves would be conducted during day and at night without restriction and fear of terrorists. All formations and units would dominate their areas effectively by day and night and no space would be given to the terrorists. Before I proceed with my narrative, a recount of the events that had taken place so far and reasons for the current state of terrorism is necessary.

Srinagar was the cradle of Hindu civilization[1] and a great centre of learning till 1339 when it came under Islamic rule.[2] Shaivism came to the fore after the visit of Adishankaracharya in the eighth century. The Shiva temple on top of the Shankaracharya hill[3] in the heart of Srinagar is living testimony of that glorious period. Kashmir was also famous because of the Sharda Peeth, a famous university and centre of great learning. This university with its treasure of knowledge, scripts, and documents was destroyed by the Muslim rulers. A large number of ruins of ancient temples dot the Valley. Famous among them are the Martand sun temple at Anantnag, Avantiswami temple at Avantipura, Shankara Gaurishavra temple at Pattan and Wangath temples in Ganderbal. I had the opportunity to visit all of them. Sadly, they are in a state of ruin and neglect. The mountains of Harmukh, Hari Parvat, Amarnath, and all the lakes and rivers are also associated with Hinduism. The Jhelum was called Vitasta in olden days and is still known as Vyeth locally. The last Hindu King was Udayanadeva. His wife, Kota Rani, is said to have been a good administrator who dominated the court.

Islam spread into the Valley through Sufi saints. The early saints came from Persia and Central Asia but the later ones were mostly Muslim converts. Sufism in the Valley is a continuum of the Hindu rishi tradition. There are more than 200 Sufi shrines dedicated to them. The prominent among them were Sayyid Bulbul Shah, Sayyid Ali and Mir Mohammad Hamdani, Lalded, Rupa Bhawani, Nund Rishi or Sheikh Nuruddin and Hazrat Makhdoom Shah. Islam spread between the 13th and 15th centuries but the importance of Hindu and Buddhist civilizations was not lost as the majority of the converted were either Hindus or Buddhists. Mir Shah, who was a minister of the last Hindu king, usurped the throne to become the first Muslim ruler in 1339. His son, Sultan Sikandar, was most brutal of all the rulers in that dynasty. He massacred pundits in thousands, destroyed a highly developed Hindu society, culture, temples and ancient scripts. He was called Bhut Shikan or destroyer of idols. The Shah dynasty lasted till 1586 when the Valley was captured by the Mughals.

The Hindus suffered again under the tyrannical rule of Aurangzeb. The Mughals were replaced in 1747 by the Afghans. This was the darkest period in the history of Kashmir, marked by exploitation and destruction. Both the Hindus and Muslims suffered under their rule and they invited the Sikhs to liberate them from Afghan tyranny. The Sikhs ruled the Valley from 1819 to 1846. Gulab Singh was appointed the rajah of Jammu in recognition of his services to the Sikh empire. General Zorawar Singh, an outstanding military leader and commander of the Dogra armies, extended the frontiers of the Sikh empire to Ladakh and Baltistan. After the Anglo-Sikh wars, Kashmir, Ladakh and Baltistan became part of his state under the treaty of Amritsar signed on 16 March 1846. Gulab Singh paid Rs. 75 lakh to the British for taking permanent possession of this territory and proclaimed as the maharaja.

Thus began the Dogra Hindu rule after a lapse of 400 years. The Dogra rule brought peace and development to the region but the British realized the strategic importance of the region and the role it could play during the great games between the Russians and the British belatedly. Thus, their aim now was to have a firm control over the maharaja and bring about efficient administration and development to serve their strategic aim. They forced a British officer as officer on special duty on the Maharaja in 1852 for the purpose. Maharaja Gulab Singh was a firm and just ruler who pulled the Valley out of anarchy and chaos. He provided security and stability and the rule of law. Maharaja Ranbir Singh succeeded him in 1856 and was a good administrator, learned and tolerant. The Ranbir canal on the Chenab River was constructed in his time. He had a good relationship with the British and allowed them to establish a trade agency at Leh in 1867 to control trade with Central Asia.

Maharaja Pratap Singh succeeded his father in 1885. The British appointed a political agent in 1884 and a permanent resident in 1889.[4] Mr. Walter R. Lawrence,[5] one of the ablest British officers, took this post and did a great service to the state. Gilgit Agency was created in 1889 that came under the direct control of the British political agent. With the arrival of Mr. Lawrence, a council of regency was established to assist the maharaja in the administration of his state. The revenue system was put in place and extensive reforms were undertaken in all fields. The state was connected to the rest of India with an all-weather road from Rawalpindi to Srinagar. As per accounts left by Lawrence, no princely state in India progressed as rapidly as Kashmir during that period under the first three rulers.

Maharaja Hari Singh, the nephew of Pratap Singh, succeeded him in 1925. His rule is characterized with more agricultural, educational and administrative reforms. Political awakening also marked this period with the formation of the All Jammu and Kashmir Muslim Conference under Sheikh Abdullah that later became the National Conference. Political activities in the state kept pace with those in other parts of the country. The maharaja also leased the Gilgit Agency to the British Government of India for a period of 60 years in 1935 for a sum of Rs. 75,000. The British were now responsible for defence, foreign affairs and communications and the state for administration of the region.

With the passage of the Indian Independence Act, 1947 by the British Parliament, all treaties and agreements between the British and the princely states lapsed on 15 August 1947. It was expected of all the princely states to accede to either India or Pakistan. Maharaja Hari Singh was undecided on this issue and perhaps flirted with the idea of an independent state. His proposal of a standstill agreement to maintain the status quo was accepted by Pakistan but India did not. In the meantime, Pakistan started pressurizing the maharaja to accede to them by blocking communications and imposing an economic blockade. Failing that, the invasion of the state was planned with the help of Pashtun tribes. 20 lashkars, consisting of 1,000 tribals each, were recruited and trained by the Bannu brigade. They were equipped by PAVO Cavalry (11 Cavalry)[6] with rifles, ammunition and grenades by September 1947.

Ten lashkars were launched through Muzzafarabad into the Valley and ten through Poonch, Bhimber and Rawalakot for the capture of Jammu. Colonel Sher Khan of the Pak MI directorate was responsible for the planning and Akbar Khan[7] for its execution. Mr Liaquat Ali Khan, the

PM, General Sir Frank Walter Messervy,[8] C-in-C the Pakistan Army, and later Gen. Sir Douglas David Gracey,[9] were privy to the plan. Revolts by Muslim troops of the state forces were engineered at Muzzafarabad, Domel and Poonch. The attacks by the tribals commenced on 22 October who overran the garrisons at Muzzafarabad, Baramulla, Domel, Kotli, Mirpur, Rawalakot and Jhangar quickly. The Hindus and Sikhs at these places were massacred and their women abducted. They looted plundered, and killed all those who came in their way from Muzzafarabad to Baramulla. The state forces under Brigadier Rajinder Singh were unable to stop them and he was killed in action. By 24 October, the raiders were in Baramulla. The maharaja, at this critical moment, requested military help from India and signed the instrument of accession on 26 October 1947.[10] Indian forces landed at Srinagar on 27 October and were able to prevent the capitulation of Srinagar. In a series of battles that followed, Indian troops under Brigadier L.P. Sen[11] were able to push them out to Uri by the middle of November 1947.

Early snowfall, long lines of communications and administrative difficulties prevented the troops from advancing further to Muzzafarabad. The Hindu troops of the state forces held out during the winter at Naushera, Mirpur, Kotli, Domel Poonch, Rajouri, Leh and Skardu against the raiders who were supported by the Pakistan regular army. The winter gave enough time to Pakistan to occupy areas not held by the Indian Army with regular troops.

The Maharaja had appointed Brigadier Ganshara Singh as the governor of Gilgit Agency. He reached there on 15 August to assume his duties as the lease of Gilgit Agency had expired. These parts were defended by the Chitral and Gilgit Scouts under Major W.A. Brown[12] and Captain Matheson, who incited Muslim troops to revolt and instigated accession with Pakistan. They hoisted the Pakistani flag on 4 November 1947. The disloyalty and treachery of these British officers resulted in the imprisonment of Brig. Ganshara by the rebellious Muslim troops of the Scouts and 6 J&K Infantry battalion and the massacre of all the Hindu and Sikh soldiers of the battalion. Major Sherjang Thapa of the same battalion at Leh occupied Skardu with 2 officers 2 JCOs and 75 jawans in

December 1947. He was reinforced by two batches by 10 February bringing his strength to about 285.

A second attempt to reinforce Skardu by Brigadier Faqir Singh failed as he was ambushed by the rebels on 15 March 1948, 32 km short of Skardu at Gol. He retreated after suffering heavy casualties. The third attempt was made by two columns under Lt. Col. Krishan Singh and Lt. Col. Sampuran Bachan Singh and Major Coutts in April. The information of these reinforcements was known to the enemy. They were continuously ambushed during their advance. For some inexplicable reasons, this task was abandoned and the columns were recalled half way under orders of General Thimayya. No attempt was made to link up after our troops had occupied Zozilla, Drass, Kargil and Leh, which again is inexplicable. The garrison finally capitulated in August 1948[13] when the Indian Army could not link up with them. The inmates were massacred and the women were taken as slaves. Lt. Col. Sherjang Thapa and his orderly were spared as he was known to General Sir Douglas Gracey, the C-in-C, Pakistan Army. They both belonged to 1 GR and were together at Dharamshala. It was a sad day for India. In hindsight it was a great military failure on part of the Indian Army. Whatever may have been the compulsions, its strategic ramifications have been great. The fault lay at both the political and military levels.

More Indian troops were inducted into the Jammu region and valley for the spring offensive of 1948. The troops in the Jammu sector were commanded by Major General Atma Singh and those in the Srinagar sector by Major General Thimayya. Jhangar, Naushera, and Rajouri were recaptured and a link with Poonch established by the end of summer 1948. However, all the area west of this line including Mirpur and Kotli were lost. Perhaps they did not have the resources to reclaim the remaining areas as Pakistan army troops were now deployed against them. Similarly in the Valley, while no significant progress could be made towards Muzzafarabad, the Indian Army was able to capture Tangdhar and all the area up to Kishanganga. Guraiz and Keren were also secured.

After the battle of Zozilla, communications with Kargil and Leh were established. By this time, the Hindu-dominated Jammu, the Buddhist area of Leh and the Valley had been secured. Both the Pakistan and the Indian armies faced each other and it became a slugging match between the two. The British also felt that Pakistan was now strategically secure and India could be prevailed upon to stop the offensive.[14] India fell into the trap and agreed to the ceasefire and UN resolution. What was supposed to bring about a permanent solution became a festering wound that continues to bleed India.

The British had realized the strategic importance of Kashmir, Gilgit, Baltistan, Ladakh and Tibet since the Afghan and Sikh wars. Whoever controls this area dominates Tibet, China, Central Asia and Afghanistan. Whoever controls this area controls the water reservoirs of South Asia and Southeast Asia as the waters of all the rivers flowing in Pakistan, India, Nepal, Burma (now Myanmar) and Southeast Asia are stored in the glaciers of this region. Whoever possesses this area also possesses the rich and rare mineral resources hidden in it. The British were able to keep the Russians away from this region till World War II. Once the Independence of India was decided, they felt that an Indian state would not toe their line on strategic matters but were sure that it was possible to manipulate a weak state like Pakistan. With this in view, they wanted Pakistan to hold the Gilgit and Baltistan areas that could sustain them. Thus it was ensured that the Indian Army did not cross the Jhangar, Rajauri, Poonch, Uri, Thangdhar, Kishan Ganga, Kargil and Leh line. This gave enough depth for the defence of Pakistan, secure its communications and water resources.

The question that now arises is that when the political and military leadership in Pakistan knew the strategic importance of J&K, why did the Indian political and military leaders not realize the same and progress operations to that end. Why did they allow themselves to be blinded by Mountbatten, Auchinleck and Bucher? Why were operations not progressed towards Muzazzarabad after the capture of Uri? Why was Kotali abandoned and no attempt made to retake Mirpur and Domel after linking up with Poonch. Why was Skardu allowed to capitulate after it held out with just a company for one year?

The Indian Army was three times larger than the Pakistan Army; what was the hurry to accept the ceasefire? It is however plausible that since the ceasefire was in the offing since 21 April 1948 UN Resolution, the Indian side presumed it would get the area vacated of the three Pakistan brigades facing it without further fighting. Clearly, it was naïve to think so and a political and military blunder for which the country is paying dearly even today. The UN resolutions of 21 April and 13 August 1948 governed the ceasefire agreement that came in effect on 1 January 1949. The salient points of this resolution were:

(a) Pakistan agreed to withdraw its military forces from the territory of J&K.

(b) Pakistan agreed to withdraw non-regular combatants and non-residents of J&K from the occupied areas.

(c) All efforts were to be made to ensure normalcy is restored in the state, and India was to maintain its military presence to ensure this.

(d) Once normalcy is restored, a plebiscite was to be held to decide the final accession of the state to India or Pakistan.

The Indian Constitution was adopted on 26 January 1950, hence the jurisdiction exercised by the maharaja over the state ceased. J&K was irrevocably brought under the territorial and constitutional jurisdiction of India. It was however granted special status under Article 370. The UN resolution did not solve the J&K problem. Rather, as time passed, it became more complex and embroiled in international power politics. Kashmir was important to both India and Pakistan strategically; all other arguments for its merger with either of them were peripheral. Since Pakistan, did not execute the first two clauses of the UN resolution of 13 August 1948, no plebiscite could be held. Both sides thus dug in their heels and continue to bleed each other in the process.

Pakistan launched a combination of irregular and conventional war to annex J&K, a second time in 1965. But their calculations went awry with the Indian riposte in Punjab. They had almost lost the war had not another ceasefire brokered by USSR been accepted. It was hoped that after the third war between the two countries in 1971 that Pakistan lost and was considerably weakened, peace would prevail between them. The Shimla

Agreement 1972 was a step in this direction. However, Pakistan's obsession with Kashmir and its desire to avenge the humiliation of the 1971 defeat negated the treaty and Pakistan once again stoked fire in the Valley in 1989 in a big way. The situation in the Valley worsened by the end of the year to such an extent that 8 Mountain Division had to be moved from Nagaland to bring it under control.

The state of J&K had a generally peaceful period from 1 January 1949 to 1984. The Plebiscite Front under Mirza Afzal Beg and Maulvi Mahmood Farooq, the Mirwaiz and leader of the Muslim Conference, had continued to raise a subdued voice of dissidence in the absence of Sheikh Abdullah while he was in prison on charges of treason since 1953. The Indira-Sheikh Accord once again brought back the chastened Sheikh Abdullah as the CM in February 1975 till his death. The Plebiscite Front became the National Conference. Farooq Abdullah, his son, became the CM in September 1982. Farooq was a liberal and easy-going person. Even though he was not a good administrator or as shrewd as his father, he was popular with the people and won the 1983 state elections by defeating the Congress. They were miffed and destabilized his government through defections.

This was the beginning of the trouble in the state. Ghulam Mohammad Shah became CM from July 1984 to March 1986. After the Rajiv-Farooq Accord, Farooq again became the CM from November 1986 to March 1987 and thereafter the National Conference and the Congress came to power with an absolute majority in 1987 through rigged elections. As a result, the Muslim United Front that was the people's choice won only four seats. Mr. Jagmohan, an able and efficient IAS officer, was the governor of the state from 1984 to 1889 but his role in toppling the Farooq government in 1984 and then organizing a rigged election negated his achievements and tarnished his reputation. Pakistan took advantage of the unstable political conditions, the resentment, and the disenchantment of the people and tried to annex the state, this time by organizing a revolt from within.

Pakistan had started planning the destabilization of the state since 1984. The plan was conceived by the ISI Chief, Lt. General Akhtar Abdul Rehman, under orders of President General Zia-ul-Haq.[15] The dissatisfaction and unfulfilled aspirations of the people were used to engineer an internal revolt. The JKLF, a popular political outfit that rooted for an independent Kashmir, became the main instrument of executing their plan. Pakistan started locating, recruiting, training and infiltrating people of the Valley to organize mayhem and revolt. The unstable political conditions in India then also helped Pakistan in this operation. Punjab was on the boil, Indira Gandhi had been assassinated, and Rajiv Gandhi was embroiled in Sri Lanka followed by the Bofors scandal. India was going through a bad phase politically and economically. A bomb blast at the Srinagar telegraph office on 31 July 1988 by the JKLF officially started terrorism in the state.

By early 1989, the violence and subversion by anti-national elements had increased dramatically. Regular bandhs, hartals and violent protests exposed the weakness of law enforcement authorities. The emboldened anti-national elements started targeting political leaders of the NC, Congress, and BJP and killing government officials and security forces personnel openly. There was a complete boycott of parliamentary elections in 1989. Dr. Rubaiya, daughter of Mufti Mohammad Sayeed, the Home Minister, was kidnapped by terrorists on 8 December 1989, creating a new phase of terror. The release of five top terrorists in exchange for Dr. Rubaiya was a gross mistake that exposed the weakness and vulnerability of the state. The law and order situation nosed-dived and the terrorists had now the upper hand. The reappointment of Jagmohan as the governor led to the resignation of Farooq Abdullah as the CM and imposition of President's Rule. The appeasement policies followed by the V.P. Singh and Chandrashekhar governments led to daring killings and cleansing of Hindu pundits from the Valley.

For some reason Mirwaiz Maulvi Farooq fell out of favour of the ISI and was shot dead by terrorists on 21 May 1990. His death created a sudden anti-terrorist sentiment among the people that could have been a great advantage to India. It was however grossly mishandled and that led to firing by the CRPF in panic resulting in the deaths of about 50 mourners. The whole Valley seemed to be in revolt after that. Jagmohan's inept handling of the situation in J&K led to his replacement by Mr. G.C. Saxena, an IPS officer, in May 1990. This was the time when 8 Mountain Division was inducted into J&K. The situation continued to deteriorate as there was no coherent and coordinated political or military policy to deal with the situation. The state administration, judiciary and police were non-functional just like in Punjab in the same period. The army, CAPF and local police all worked in their own tight compartments. Similarly, there was no one to coordinate the working of the intelligence agencies. After Mr. P.V. Narasimha Rao became the PM in June 1991, a clear policy on Kashmir like that in Punjab was expected to emerge. But it took him more than a year and half to formulate one and find the right person. General Krishna Rao was brought back as the governor in March 1993 with a mandate to restore the rule of law, bring normalcy, make the defunct intuitions functional and restore democracy.

The Punjab model was available to him as a success story. Unfortunately, General Krishna Rao did not have a DGP of the calibre of K.P.S. Gill or the intelligence agencies and bureaucratic set-up that could measure up to the challenge. Lt. Gen. Z.A. Zakki and Mr. Ashok Jaitly, an IAS officer, were his advisers. Sheikh Ghulam Rasool was the chief secretary and Mr. Wajahat Habibullah was the divisional commissioner. Though capable they proved grossly inadequate to the challenges facing them. Mr. M.N. Sabherwal, the DGP, was ineffective and a flop. He had no control over his force and could not inspire them to perform. There was no will or vigour to fight the terrorists and their supporters. Unlike in Punjab, the army could not field troops that were required to hunt down terrorists in an all-out operation. India had also failed to check Pakistan and other Arab and Muslim countries supporting the terrorists directly or through international mechanisms. A war against terrorists cannot be won unless external support is neutralized. The terrorists on the other hand had the support and unlimited funds from Pakistan, Arab and Muslim countries for the jihad.

General Krishna Rao however created a Unified HQ to coordinate operations of the security forces. 39 Infantry Division was inducted into the Valley to supplement the effort. Vigorous operations were launched against the terrorists by Major General R.S. Mavi and later by S.S. Grewal that resulted in gaining control over the main centres of Shopian, Anantnag,

Srinagar, Sopore and Baramulla. However, when the situation seemed to improve, terrorists occupied Maqdoom Saheb and Naqshband in September 1993 to incite religious sentiments. They occupied the Hazratganj mosque on 15 October 1993.[16] The aim was to create a Golden Temple-like situation that led to Operation Blue Star but the security forces and the Government did not fall into that trap and a protracted standoff with the terrorists freed it on 15 November. Even though the Governor tried very hard to rein in the terrorists and hold elections in the state, his efforts did not bear fruit due to the unfavourable security situation and conflicting political interests.

Pakistan had been trying to create political organizations to execute its agenda since 1984. The JKLF was selected and it was allowed to open an office in POK. The Muslim United Front under Maulvi Mohammad Abbas Ansari was formed in April 1986 to fight the elections of 1987. Later, the All-Party Hurriyat Conference was created on 27 December 1992 comprising all the secessionist leaders. When Pakistan found that the JKLF was adamant on an independent Kashmir and the Muslim United Front and Hurriyat had failed in achieving the agenda set for them, a new fundamentalist organization called the Hizbul Mujahideen was created. This organization comprised Pakistan, Afghan, and radical Kashmiri terrorists.

On the Indian side, the Rashtriya Rifles (RR) was inducted in J&K and HQ V force RR was located at Avantipur with the responsibility for south Kashmir. Due to the relentless pressure of security forces, the terrorists started cracking up, resulting in large surrenders and defections. It appeared that elections could be held in 1994. General Krishna Rao was of the view that Farooq Abdullah was the best bet for India; however, the Congress and intelligence agencies wanted that an alternative leadership also be developed. Yasin Malik, the JKLF leader, was released in May 1994. Gilani and Lone of the Hurriyat were also released on an assurance that they would help restore the democratic process. However, this move backfired. Not only was the National Conference unhappy with this arrangement but the released secessionists also backtracked following threats from the ISI.

Towards the end of 1994, reports were received that foreign terrorists had been infiltrated into the Valley. Three major incidents that made international headlines were created by them in 1995. The bombing of the Republic Day function in January 1995 at Jammu presided over by the Governor was the first. The timing and actual location of the Governor had been compromised in minute detail for its planning and execution by ISI moles in the police, administration and the Governor's staff. It was later revealed that these devices were prepared in Pakistan and terrorists had been successful in planting them undetected.

The second incident related to the holy shrine of Charar-e-Sharif that was venerated by both Muslims and Hindus and visited by almost all Kashmiris at least once a year. Since the fundamentalists did not subscribe to Sufism, they targeted these shrines for religious reorientation of the Kashmiris and strengthen radical Islam. A group of Afghan terrorists led by Mast Gul occupied the shrine in March 1995 that was protected by the BSF. The army was requisitioned when it became obvious that the terrorists could not be handled by the police and the BSF. The shrine had to be saved at all costs keeping public sentiment in mind. The terrorists however set the shrine ablaze on 10 May and made good their escape in the darkness and the melee that followed. The SF could neither save the shrine nor punish the perpetrators. Nearly 23 terrorists including nine foreign ones were killed and Abu Jindal, a Pakistani terrorist, was apprehended who authenticated the involvement of the ISI in the destruction of the shrine. But this achievement was a small consolation.

The third incident pertained to the abduction of foreign tourists. On 5 July 1995, Donald Fred Hutchings and Johan Childs, both US nationals, and Keith Mangan and Paul Seymour Wells, both British nationals, were visiting Kashmir as tourists when they were kidnapped by terrorists. On 8 July, Hert Disket, a German and Otto Hans Christian, a Norwegian, were also kidnapped. A terrorist group called Al Farran claimed responsibility for the kidnappings. They sent a note to the US Embassy at Delhi demanding the release of 16 terrorists held in the custody of Indian security forces in lieu of the release of those they had kidnapped. Johan Childs made good his escape on 9 July and was rescued from the forests of Sheshnag. He revealed that the terrorist group consisted of 16 Pakistanis or Afghans and two local guides. They had sophisticated arms and communications. Their aim was to force the Indian Government to release all the top Pakistani terrorists such as Mohammad Masoor Azhar, Nasarullah Mansoor, Mohammad Ahsan Dar, Mustaq Ahmed Bhat and Sajad, all protégés of the ISI. The countries of the abducted tourists were informed by India to ask Pakistan to release their citizens as the terrorists were under their control. The mutilated body of Otto Hans Christian was found in Chattal forest of Anantnag district on 13 August. The negotiators refused to come face-to-face and thus the Government refused to relent. After some time all the leads went cold and no trace of the four tourists was found. They were presumed to be killed and that the terrorists had escaped to Pakistan. Thus an impression that the situation was still not conducive for holding elections was formed. The opposition, the Congress and the Home Ministry also did not show enthusiasm. President's Rule was extended by one year, ending speculation of elections at least in 1995.

In spite of the turbulence, discussions with political parties in the state to hold elections continued. A parliamentarian team visited the state to assess the situation. So did ambassadors of the USA and European countries, Iran and UN Human Rights Organisations. The Election Commission announced parliamentary elections including those in J&K on 19 March. The state elections were however deferred. This was not acceptable to Pakistan that somehow wanted to queer the pitch again. This time they found Shabir Siddiqui, President of the JKLF, who had been flirting with Indian agencies as well, to be their henchman for a considerable sum of money. He, along with his group, occupied the Hazaratbal mosque. This time the public was not with him and when negotiations failed to yield any results, he was killed in the operation along with 24 others.

Vigorous operations against terrorists were launched. A Large number of terrorists who had been fatigued since 1995 surrendered. This not only depleted the terrorist ranks but also affected their morale. When it became apparent that other political leaders like Sabir Shah, Gilani, Lone and Mirwaiz were not openly opposed to the elections, the Government decided to provide them security against threats from the ISI. Their movements and activities were now under 24 hour surveillance. However the government incurred huge expenditure on their safety, residences, medical and other travel expenses even though they continued to indulge in anti-national activities. The elections in J&K were scheduled from 9 to 30 May. The Awami League, a new party, joined the fray along with the, Congress, BJP and the Janata Dal. The NC made a grave mistake like the Akalis in Punjab of not participating. The Congress won all the four seats in the Valley and Ladakh, the BJP and the Janata Dal won one each in Jammu. The voting was 41 per cent in the Valley and 51 per cent in Jammu. The results of this election encouraged the Government to announce state assembly elections in October 1996. I took over command of 8 Mountain Division at this juncture on 8 July with the mandate that the democratic process had to be established by October.

The Kashmir Valley with which we are presently concerned is bounded by the Pir Panjal range in the south and west. It is protected by the Karakoram range in the north and the Zanskar in the east. The Valley is about 150 km long and 80 to 100 km wide. The Lidder Valley in Pahalgam district, the Sind valley extending up to Zozila Pass and the Lolab Valley in Baramulla are also of significance. The Valley is surrounded by the Harmukh mountain that separates the Jhelum from the Kishan Ganga in the north, the Burzail mountains separate it from Ladakh, and the Amarnath mountains are near Pahalgam. The Vitasta or Jhelum is the principal river that flows through the Valley towards Baramulla and thence to Muzzafarabad and Pakistan. The main tributaries of the Jhelum are the Vishav, Lidder and Sind rivers. There are five main lakes in the Valley. The Wullar Lake is the largest which is 16 km long and 9.6 km wide. The Jhelum flows through it. The forests around the lake known as kandi are ideal hiding places for terrorists. The Dal Lake is within the city of Srinagar and a tourist attraction. It is 8 km long and 6.4 km wide. The Anchar lake is astride the Sind river and is 8 km long and 3 km wide. The Mansbal lake is in Safapur. It is 5 km long and 1 km wide. The Harvan lake has shrunk to the size of a pond. Similarly, the Hokarsar lake is now a swamp. Many small lakes are hidden in the mountains. The Gangasar and Kisansar lakes at a height of 15,000 feet in the Harmukh Mountains are considered holy by Hindus. Similarly, the Konasarnag lake in Shopian district which is the source of the Vishav river is also important.

These lakes abound in marine life and sustain most of the population. The Valley abounds in flora and fauna. The hillsides are full of dense forests of deodar, pine and fir. Walnuts, almonds and apples are grown in huge orchards. Willows grow along the river valleys. The hill sides abound in a wide variety of flowers during summer. The Shalimar, Nishat, Chasm-e-Shahi, Pari Mahal, Achabal and Verinag gardens are famous for their flowers. Tulips and saffron are also grown. Wild animals such as snow leopards, deer, wild sheep, both the black and brown bear and musk shrew abound in the forested areas. Ducks, geese, partridges, chakor, pheasants and water pigeons abound in and around the water bodies and forests. The Valley is extremely fertile. The main crops are rice and maize. Almost all vegetables are grown. The national highway runs from Jammu to Baramulla through the Jawahar tunnel. Another national highway connects Srinagar with Leh over the Zozila pass. This road is closed during winter. The towns and villages are connected with roads. There is an international airport at Srinagar. The Valley is divided into 10 districts for administrative purposes. They are Anantnag, Pulwama, Kulgam and Shopian in the south; Srinagar, Budgam, Bandipore, Ganderbal and Baramulla in the centre and Kupwara in the north.

The Valley is inhabited by Kashmiris whereas Gujjars and Bakarwals occupy the hills. Till 1342, the Valley was inhabited by Hindus and Buddhists with a small number of Muslims. Following successive waves of conversions since then, there are 97 per cent Muslims in the Valley now. The remaining 3 per cent are Hindus, Sikhs and Buddhists. The Gujjars and Bakarwals who identify themselves with the Hindu Gujjars of north India are 100 per cent Muslims and follow soft Islam. Kashmiri Muslims[17] are divided between Sunnis and Shias. Those who derive their lineage from pandits are Bhat, Dhar, Mantu, Gannai, Mattoo, Pandit, Razdan, Kaul, Sapru, Yatoo, Munshi, Wani, Ganju, etc. Most of these Muslims also call themselves 'sheikhs' because they are associated with priesthood and connected with the teaching, practice and administering religious laws, leading the prayers, etc. They may be divided into Kazi, Mufti, Rishi or

Maulvi. Then there are Saiyads who are also men of religion. Some Muslims claim to be of Mughal or Pathan origin but there is no distinction between them and the other Muslims. There are some inferior Muslim tribes such as Dums or village watchman; Galawans are horse or mule keepers, Chaupans are shepherds, Bhands are minstrels, Hanjis are boatmen or fishermen, Watals are gypsies and Nangar are menials. Carpenters, blacksmiths, potters, weavers, butchers, washermen, barbers, tailors, bakers, goldsmiths, porters, dyers, milkmen, cotton cleaners, oil-pressers and snuff makers also fall in this category. There are faqirs whose profession is begging though they hold land and property. There are no inter-marriages between Sheikhs/Sayyaids and inferior Muslims or between Gujjars and Bakarwals.

The Kashmiris are fair and their physical features resemble Aryans. They have a prominent hooked nose like Jews. The inferior Muslims, agriculturists and labourers tend to be dark. The women of higher strata are fair and pretty but the others are far from pretty and wither away under the weight of work and repeated early pregnancies. The dress of all Kashmiris is simple in appearance with very little difference between that of men and women. They both wear effeminate gowns that are drab, not attractive or functional. The Hindus also wear a similar dress with some modifications to differentiate themselves from the Muslims

Kashmiris of all faiths and tribes do not enjoy a good reputation. Moorcraft, an Englishman, felt they are selfish, superstitious, ignorant, supple, intriguing, crafty, dishonest and false. Drew, another Englishman, also admitted that they are false tongued, ready with a lie and given to various forms of deceit. They are timid, exaggerate events and are loud and voluble. They however found that in terms of intellect,[18] a Kashmiri was superior to other native Indians but they were weak hearted and soft. A Kashmiri can be industrious, an entrepreneur,[19] excellent cultivator, weaver and craftsman when his interest is involved. By nature, he is a loving husband and a father who cares for his family. A Kashmiri wife plays a dominant role in running her family and men are known to live in awe of their consorts. Lawrence, while commissioner of Kashmir, observed that the city men were more effeminate, lazy and helpless. It was their opinion that the duty of the state was to feed them and provide them subsidized fuel, health and education while he himself was unfettered by any obligations to the state. Some psychologists feel centuries of subjugation and an instinct for survival is responsible for the state of their psyche. I tend to agree with these British administrators, travellers and missionaries based on my dealings and working with Kashmiris. Basically, a Kashmiri has not changed even after 70 years of independence.

The economy of Kashmir is export oriented and flourishing but it is controlled by a few affluent and politically powerful families. Kashmir exports fruits, wood, forest products, and metal handicrafts. It also exports pashmina shawls, gems, jewellery and carpets. It produces surplus hydro power that is sold to other states. The tourist industry is a big revenue earner. More than one lakh Hindus visit the Amarnath cave shrine every year. However, the Kashmiris are habituated to live on subsidies and very few pay taxes with the result the state revenue is negligible and they perpetually live on central grants. The planning commission allocates funds four times more than its entitlement. These do not trickle down to the poor or used for economic growth and development but gobbled up by corrupt bureaucrats, politicians and contractors. Economic disparity is very wide, even though no one is poor. Large Diasporas of rich and influential Kashmiris live in the UK, USA and UAE. Almost every Kashmiri family has at least one member in government service.

I familiarized myself quickly with the area, deployment and challenges facing the formation. The division HQ was located at Sarifabad, a raised flat ground with good all-around observation and defensibility. It was about 15 km from Srinagar on the road to Baramulla. It is close to Sheletang where the Pakistani invaders were defeated in 1947. All factories in the industrial area were completely destroyed by the terrorists. Suibug, the village of Sallaudin, the HM commander, was in the vicinity. He is based in Pakistan since 1990 and waging terrorism against us. The Hokarsar lake nearby is full of migratory birds during winter. It was once a private duck hunting reserve of the maharaja. There were plenty of golden foxes, jackals and hares in the wild growth. The GOC lived in a captain's accommodation that was requisitioned for his residence. The Signal Regiment under Colonel S. Bhatnagar was co-located with us. The Aviation Base commanded by

Colonel D.S. Yadav, a very competent and experienced officer, was part of our formation. The area was guarded by Sikh and later Garhwali troops of the defence and employment company. Hooch, my personal guard dog that had been gifted by the Gujjars, was very ferocious and part of the guard. He guarded the area zealously and no one dare come near his post. We lived in a totally operational environment where there was no room for laxity or comfort. The division operations branch was headed by Colonel Avdesh Kumar, a very competent officer with a sharp and analytical mind. He was assisted by Lt. Col. Krishnan and later by D.K. Ghosh and Capt. Babu who were outstanding in their work. The logistics and administration were headed by Colonel J.P. Singh, an Armoured Corps officer, ably assisted by Lt. Col. A.B. Shivane, who were ingenious and innovative. The entire team was dedicated and competent.

The ASC battalion under Colonel M.C. Chauhan, the DOU under Colonel B.K. Singh, the EME battalion under Col. B.B. Sharma, and the 308 Field Ambulance under Col. G.C. Vinayak was at the old airfield and 408 Field Ambulance under Lt. Col. A.S. Kandalla and later S.S. Pangalia was at Pattan. 13 Engineer regiment under Colonel Balwinder Singh was at Haft Chinar. 108 Engineer Regiment replaced them.

- 56 Mountain Brigade under Brig. R.P. Saini and later Amar Aul was at Badgam with responsibility for the area astride Srinagar-Baramulla highway from Srinagar to Ziran.
- 12 Sector RR under Brig. R.S. Ranawat was also at Badgam with the responsibility for Badgam and all the area up to the Pir Panjal in the west and Ziran-Tangmarg in the north.
- 8 Artillery Brigade under Brig. S.B. Singh and later J. Koshy was at Tangmarg in both artillery and infantry roles with the responsibility for Gulmarg and Tanmarg.
- 192 Mountain Brigade under Brig. D.K. Ghosh and later M.P.S. Bajwa was located at Pattan with the responsibility for Sopore and all the area north up to Baramulla and west of Manasbal and the Wullar lake.

- 5 Sector under Brig. P.N. Mehra was located at Manasbal. The areas of Manasbal, Safapura, Ganderbal and Badipura were their responsibility.
- 11 Sector RR under Brig. Surjit Singh was located at Wusan. All the area east of Gandebal up to Zozila was under their jurisdiction.
- HQ 70 Mountain Brigade under Brig. R.K.S. Shivrain and later Devinder Singh was inducted for operations in 1997. Their area of responsibility was Safapura heights, Ganderbal, Dachigam and Wussan.

The naval commandos (MARCOS) were at Wattal and responsible for the Wullar and Kandi belt. I thus had seven brigades under my command.

When I took over, terrorism had already crossed three phases. The pre-1989 phase—the build-up for an outbreak of insurgency; the 1990-93 phase—domination by insurgents; and the 1993-95 phase—when the initiative was seized by the SF. We had now entered a new phase with the parliamentary elections in May 1996. There were approximately 5,000 terrorists including 2,000 foreigners in the Valley then. The Hizbul Mujahideen (HM), Lashkar-e-Taiba (LET), Al Jihad, Al Burq and Muslim Mujahideen (MM), were the main pro-Pakistan groups while the JKLF, Al Umar and Ikawan-ul-Musalmeen (IUM) were pro-independence. The Jamaat-e-Islami, JKLF, Peoples Conference, United Peoples League, Quami Mahaz-e-Azadi, Muslim Conference, Kashmir Liberation Council and Awami Action Committee were the main anti-India political parties.

Our first task was to create a peaceful environment for holding elections to the State assembly. It was well known that Pakistan would try its best to thwart the elections. A low turnout would prove that people were against us and that the elections were a sham. The terrorists, their supporters, anti-national parties like the Hurriyat and hostile elements in the media who were their tools had to be neutralized. There was no doubt that we had to carry out very vigorous and intense operations so that the rule of law could be enforced, confidence of the people regained and all the fence sitters came over to our side. All institutions and instruments of state were to be revived. The fear of terrorists had to be driven out of the minds of the people before their confidence in the democratic process could be restored.

People were the centre of gravity in this war against terrorism. I visited each formation and unit during July and August to ensure that these tasks were achieved and we were firm in our resolve. Operations were to be carried out round the clock but with minimum inconvenience to the people and collateral damage. The hearts and minds of people had to be won. Simultaneously, we reached out to the masses and assured them of their security and their democratic right to elect a government of their choice. I personally spoke to people at every place that I visited. So did all the commanders down the chain. This created a bond and relationship of faith and trust between us.

The EC visited the Valley on 7 August and announced that the elections would be held between 7 and 30 September. There were four main elements opposed to the elections. The Hurriyat and JEI as political organizations gave a call for a boycott of the elections. They imposed bandhs and intimidated the people who supported the elections. Both legal and military action was taken against such elements. Then there were religious fundamentalists who controlled the mosques and used them against the elections. It was a difficult and sensitive task but we ensured that the religious places were not used for political purposes. The hostile and unfriendly media, particularly the Urdu local dailies that advocated a boycott of the elections and spewed venom on the SF, had to be handled firmly. They were chastened legally and by arm-twisting. Lastly, terrorists had to be physically eliminated and their underground supporters who issued threats through leaflets, advertisements and notes to the candidates and people had to be neutralized. The Ikhwanis were mobilized against the anti-election lobbies. Doordarshan, AIR Srinagar and national media effectively countered the hostile local and foreign media. Mr. Farooq Nazki and Mr. and Mrs. B.A. Malik played a great role in this regard. The BBC also started reporting more objectively after Jaffar Miheraj and their local reporters were handled strictly and their nexus with the anti-nationals and their lies exposed.

All suspected anti-national elements were taken into preventive custody and denied the opportunity to create violence and disrupt the elections. Over 31,000 CAPF and 12,000 election staff were inducted for the smooth conduct of the elections. The election staff was given one month's pay as an incentive and insured for Rs. 5 Lakh against any accident. About 42 observers were appointed to see if the elections were conducted fairly and properly. A three-tier security ring was created for the conduct of the elections.

The candidates and their families were provided personal security by the police in the first tier. Security was provided for canvassing and election rallies in the second tier. Lastly, the election staff and polling booths were physically protected by the CAPF in the third tier. The army dominated the area of responsibility and provided the outer ring at polling booths. The NC, INC, BJP, JD, CPI, independents and a new party called the Awami League were in the fray. The Gujjars under Mian Altaf Ahmed and the Shias under Moulvi Iftikhar Hussain Ansari threw their lot with the NC. Itfikhar Hussain Ansari was a prominent Shia leader, businessman and politician. He was president of the All J&K Shia Association. This boosted the pro-election elements. The Governor and Lt. Gen. Padmanabhan, the Army Commander, visited us to assess the status and they were satisfied with the state of readiness and arrangements.

All eyes were on the elections in the Valley. Foreign media and election observers from all over were present. All constituencies in the Valley were sensitive or hyper sensitive. Violence could erupt in any area. On the day of the elections, people defied the boycott call of the Hurriyat and came out in large numbers to vote. Like in Punjab, they only had to be nudged.The mosques also urged the people to participate in the voting after some nudging. They knew which side the wind was blowing. The foreign media was given free access to the polling booths and observe the conduct of the elections. There was only one grenade lobbing and three minor IED incidents each in Ganderbal and Badgam. The rest of the Valley was peaceful. There were five cases of re-polling. The lowest polling (4%) was in Habbakadal in Srinagar under the BSF. In the area of 8 Mountain Division, polling was as high as 62 per cent in Kangan and 50 per cent in other areas but the average came down to 30 per cent because of the city.

The NC won 43 seats out of 46 in the Valley and 57 out of 87 in the state. Dr. Farooq Abdullah was sworn as the CM on 9 October in a ceremony held at the Sher-e-Kashmir international convention centre. Ghulam Mohi-ud-Din Shah, Pyare Lal Handoo, Mohammad Safi, Abdul Rahim Rather, Mustafa Kamal, Ajat Shatru Singh, Moulvi Iftikhar Hussain Ansari and Mian Altaf Ahmed were administered oaths as ministers. A large number of dignitaries from Delhi including Mr. V.P. Singh, former PM, Sitaram Kesri, president, INC, Harkishan Surjeet, general secretary, CPM and Mr. C.M. Ibrahim, minister for aviation, were among them. I represented the Army at the ceremony. Mr. Kukka Parrey was the lone Awami League winner. It was a great victory for democracy and a defeat for Pakistan and their lackeys.

There were three major challenges post the elections. One was whether the Government would be able to keep the faith reposed in them by the people. It was a herculean task for the NC. The people had given them a second chance, forgetting their 1983 and 1987 misdeeds. Their major task was to provide good governance. The complete administration from patwari to the secretary had to be toned up. Corruption had to be rooted out, transparency and efficiency given priority. The police had to be overhauled and made responsive, effective and accountable. A defunct judiciary had to be reactivated. Focus had to be placed on development, education, health and transportation as a first challenge. The second challenge was job creation and rehabilitation of the surrendered terrorists including the Ikhwanis who had contributed substantially to the smooth conduct of the elections. Commercial and economic activities that generated jobs and revenue had to be revived. The government had to be innovative and sincere in reviving various industries that had been badly affected by terrorist activities. The third and last was to defeat efforts by Pakistan to disturb and derail the democratic process set in motion by us.

I met the Governor and the CM at their residence once a month to review the security situation. These meetings were very useful to discuss sensitive issues. I requested the CM during our first meeting that he should continue with the Unified HQ[20] and preside over the meetings to harmonize the functioning of all agencies. I cited the example of Punjab where terrorism was rooted out successfully by the doctrine of "Security and Development". Security was handled by the coordinated effort of all the forces. They ensured peace was restored that was essential for development. The chief secretary handled development and ensured that all targets were achieved by the institutions and departments of the state. He also headed the psychological operations through the media, radio and TV. The activities of all the three were to be supervised by the CM every month. Mr. M.N. Saberwal, the DGP was replaced by Mr. G.S. Jagat, an IPS officer of the UT cadre who was efficient and vigorous but not of the calibre of K.P.S. Gill. Mr. Ashok Kumar, the CS, was replaced by Mr. Ashok Jaitly, another efficient officer. Mr. S.S. Bloeria continued as the home secretary. He was an ex-army officer from Jammu. Mr. Apa Sahib Alur as IG BSF was responsible for Srinagar town and was effective. Mr. P.S. Gill, IPS, was IGP Valley who was able to restore the confidence, proficiency, efficiency and loyalty of the police.

The security situation in the Valley depended on four factors. The first was good governance and internal stability, a responsibility of the CM and the state government. The second was the quality of centre-state relations. An adversarial relationship could be harmful. It was hoped that the two would work in harmony. The third was the state of Indo-Pak relations in this case too, an adversarial relationship always created a war-like situation. This was not likely to improve and we had to cater for even a higher level of Pak mischief than before. The proxy war was a result of that bad relationship. The fourth was the status of India's relations with the USA, the West, China and the OIC as Pakistan drew encouragement and sustenance from these blocs against us. Pakistan had an edge over us as they were a frontline state and a strategic ally of the USA and the West after the Afghanistan war. It had a good relationship with China as well that was using it as a limpet to weaken India.

For us, the most important task was to finish the residual terrorism so that the democratic process in the state could be consolidated. We had the people's support after the elections. Vigorous CT operations were launched. Infiltration routes were blocked. All guides who helped foreign terrorists navigate the LoC were rounded up. A strict vigil was launched on all underground supporters. No respite was given to the terrorists during the winters. By the end of the year, we had killed 327 terrorists, apprehended 238 and accepted the surrender of 92. Nine officers, one JCO, and 32 ORs were killed and 10 officers, nine JCOs and 120 ORs were wounded on our side. Post elections, the strategy adopted for counterterrorism operations was similar to that in Punjab. We conducted joint operations with the local police and the special operations group/special task force. The Ikhwanis became our eyes and ears and played a very active role. Grievance cells were also activated at the district level as well as at all battalion HQs so that immediate relief could be provided to the aggrieved people. We assisted the government in activating institutions in our areas. Local MLAs and functionaries were co-opted for all such activities.

A big function to celebrate the anniversary of the liberation of Kashmir from the raiders in 1947 was held at Sopore on 27 October 1996. This day is also celebrated as Infantry Day. Sopore, the epicentre of terrorism and stronghold of the Hurriyat, was deliberately chosen as the venue to send a message that the Government's writ now prevailed in every corner of the Valley and no anti-national activities would be tolerated. Sopore is also the biggest apple exporting market in the Valley and money-laundering centre for terror. Apple merchants made unprecedented profits that year because of the peace and very few cases of extortion took place. An unimaginable crowd participated in the function with a number of cabinet ministers including Moulvi Itfikhar Hussain Ansari, Mian Altaf Ahmed, Abdul Qayum, Basir Ahmed Kichloo and Ali Mohammad Sagar. Martial arts, folk dances from different parts of the country, patriotic songs by school children, motor cycle display and mass PT display by school children were the main attractions. The call for midday prayers from the mosques went unheeded due to the enthusiasm of the crowd that indicated their acceptance of the new government and the beginning of the end of terrorism.

A similar function was held in Srinagar in 1997 with a larger scope. The crowd was unprecedented and the stadium overflowed with people. Ghulam Mohiudin Shah, the senior-most cabinet minister, was the chief guest. Abdul Qayoom, Basir Ahmed Kichloo, Ajat Shatru Singh, Surjit Singh Slathia, Ali Mohammad Sagar and Basir Ahmed Nengroo—all ministers—along with many MLAs also attended. Lt. Gen. Krishan Pal, the corps commander, presided. Participation of people in these functions was unimaginable a year earlier.

It is necessary to acknowledge the contribution of the Ikhwanis and the Awami League, its political wing, here. Managing counter groups was not new to 8 Mountain Division. However, it was applied more imaginatively and aggressively in J&K due to the peculiar operational environment. The Ikhwanis were known as pro-government/sarkari militants and renegades by their opponents. The status and future employment of the Ikhwanis[21] or counter groups was a subject of intense debate post elections. Those who were conversant with the ground realities in the Kashmir Valley were in no doubt that they had played a significant role against the HM and other Pakistan-sponsored terrorists and helped the SF in achieving normalcy. Their detractors also grudgingly agreed that the resounding success that we achieved was largely because of them.

The Ikhwan-ul-Musalmoon, headed by Mohammad Usaf Parrey also known as Kuka Parrey, was a splinter group of the Ikhwan-ul-Musalmeen (IUM) headed by Hilal Hyder, affiliated to the JKLF. After short shrift by Pakistan, they were short of funds, arms and ammunition and at the receiving end of the HM. The HM or armed wing of the JEI had become supreme under the patronage of Pakistan. Power went to their heads and their highhandedness, excesses, brutalities, rape and abduction of women they fancied alienated the people and other groups. A large number opposed to their misdeeds were eliminated in reprisals. The internecine war between the HM and IUM led to the killing of Mansoor Nawabate, an important leader of the IUM and close associate of Kuka Parrey.

In order to avenge the assassination of Mansoor and retain their primacy and territorial control of Sumbal, Bandipora and Safapora, it had become necessary for Kuka Parrey to take the HM head on. The IUM had no choice but to approach the SF for assistance at this juncture. A secret relationship developed between Colonel H.S. Gaur, CO, 10 Bihar and Kuka Parrey against the HM. Colonel Gaur provided necessary help to Kuka Parrey in his fight against the HM in September 1994. Kuka Parrey started assisting the army in reciprocity. When Kuka Parrey's association with the Army came to the knowledge of Hilal Beg, he was expelled from the Ikhwan-ul-Musalmeen. From that moment, he became independent and the Ikhwan-ul-Musalmaan[22] received full patronage of the army. The army provided him financial assistance and 50 weapons in April 1995. After the death of Colonel Gaur in an operation, Brigadier Devraj Singh, Commander 5 Sector, continued to patronise and played a key role in making them an effective force. Kuka Parrey was provided additional weapons, radio sets and finances and allowed to keep the weapons that his cadres had captured from the HM. The results of the operations against the HM brought spectacular success and it was decided to raise more IUM groups to cover the entire Valley. Liaquat Khan (Hilal Hyder), Javed Shah, Ghulam Nabi Azad and Papa Kishtwari who had all been part of the JKLF and bitterly opposed to the HM, decided to join Kuka Parrey. It was also realized by them that independence was only a chimera and the JKLF was motherless and dying. Their survival depended on joining the IUM under Kuka Parrey and protection of the SF. All of them joined Kuka Parrey[23] with their groups and became IUM leaders in their respective areas. Javed Shah was a police constable from Nadhial, Bandipura, before joining the terrorists. Liaquat Khan aka Hilal Hyder had been a second-year student from Anantnag when he joined terrorism. He was articulate and a good organizer and climbed the hierarchy rapidly. Similarly, Naba of Anantnag, Papa Kishtwari of Pulwama and Samad Khan of Dooru belonged to the south. They were from humble and poor backgrounds. Javed Shah controlled the area of Bandipora and was very useful. He fell to an assassin's bullet in August 2003 at Greenway Hotel, Srinagar. The rank and file of the Ikhwanis consisted of young boys from poor or inferior Muslim communities of Kashmir. They were all unemployed and exploited with nothing but a bleak future to look forward to. The call for Azadi was an attractive option for such boys and they became part of the movement. A gun gave them respectability and status in society and was a source of income.

However, after some time, they were disillusioned. A life of privation, insecurity, hardship and constantly under fire did not suit their temperament. Fatigue set in and survival became difficult. Joining the IUM gave these homesick boys a ray of hope. A force of 1,500 IUM cadres was created by early 1996. They were integrated into the SF including the police, SOG, BSF and CRPF. After the state elections, the NC and all other established political parties saw the IUM and Awami League, its political wing, as a potential threat to their election base and hence wanted them to be disbanded.

However, terrorism had not been totally stamped out of J&K and vigorous efforts by Pakistan to destabilize the state necessitated their existence. They were still a force multiplier for the SF. Not only could they fight the HM, and conduct special operations, they were also good in intelligence collection, as guides and spotters. Insurgency and counter-insurgency is a fight for control of the minds of the people. This was the force that neutralized the radicalized JEI, pro-Pakistan cadres and their influence over the people of the Valley in 1994-96. Abandoning this cadre would have been a great betrayal. I thus recommended very strongly the continuance of the Ikhwanis as counter groups and their gradual rehabilitation. Their primary task was to fight the HM, neutralize anti-national elements like the JEI and gather information for the units they were affiliated to. Their secondary role was to dominate their area of responsibility and carry out covert operations. Any move to disband or disown them would force them into joining other terrorist groups for their survival.

However, the antipathy of the government was obvious after a few months in power. They refused to pay or rehabilitate them. The JEI warmed up to the elected MLAs and instigated the Government to hound the Ikhwanis under various criminal charges. This led to some demoralization and desertions. No doubt a few Ikhwanis had turned rogue but it did not diminish their utility. We organized the IUM sector-wise and those on our payrolls were fully accounted for. Twenty-five Ikhwanis had been killed fighting the HM and 39 had deserted during 1996. Anyone who did not walk the line was dismissed and those who performed their duties well were rehabilitated in J&K Police or BSF. We rehabilitated 205 in BSF, 18 in CRPF and 73 as SPOs in police from our area by August 1997. Some others were absorbed as village guards and home guards. Those found medically or educationally deficient were given vocational training and rehabilitated as self-employed. The army created home and hearth TA battalions in 2003 to rehabilitate more. I met Kuka Parrey, Captain Tikoo, his deputy, and other leaders almost every month to take stock of his force and status of operations. He was a bulky man, of average intelligence but simple and sincere. He had been a folk singer with a very humble background and no formal education. He lived in a humble dwelling but was a great leader-sort of Robin Hood. It was later alleged that he had acquired properties in Srinagar and Jammu. Mughal Durbar, a restaurant in Jammu, belonged to him. His inner circle consisted of Abdul Rashid Parrey aka Billa (cousin), Manzoor Parrey aka Wafadar (cousin) and Gulam Rasool Parrey. Kuka Parrey was the only elected member of the assembly from his party. He did not know the hurly-burly of politics and was at sea. However he was popular and remained a threat to the other parties. He was assassinated on 13 September 2003 by ISI agents. I paid my tribute to this man who had done a lot for the country. His son, Khurshid Parrey, donned his father's mettle after his death.

Much of the credit for successful elections in September 1996 should rightly go to 8 Mountain Division. We had played a significant role in creating a conducive environment to hold them. In view of the decline in terrorism, Pakistan was quick to introduce many changes in its strategy to fight the proxy war. More battle-hardened, better-trained foreign terrorists were inducted to reinforce the HM and LET. They were equipped with missiles and RPGs. The IEDs were more sophisticated with timers and remote controlled devices. They carried digital communications equipment with hopping frequencies and encrypting capabilities. They shifted from population centres to dense forests and mountain caves to avoid detection. They avoided direct confrontation with the SF and operated from well fortified and carefully sited hideouts.

Accordingly, we also changed our concept of operations. We used sophisticated direction finding, interception and jamming equipment. Computers that were quick and accurate were used for decoding terrorist messages. 13 Engineer Regiment had created teams that could not only detect and deactivate the most sophisticated IEDs remotely or with robots but also re-use them against the terrorists. Instead of large CASO, we now operated in small clandestine groups with sniper rifles and night vision devices to hunt down terrorists near their hideouts. The terrorists were mortally scared of the flame throwers, phosphorus and stun grenades that we used during encounters in built-up areas. We used firepower, time and resources to our advantage during encounters. The terrorists were worn out and killed. Reappraisal of important operations was carried out every quarter with the commanding officers. Each was analyzed in depth for its strength and weaknesses as part of learning and improvement. This exercise proved very useful as our collective wisdom was utilized to evolve new tactics and operational art to defeat terrorism.

The marine commandos or MARCOS were inducted into the Valley in 1996. They were employed in the Kandi belt around Wullar lake, an ideal hiding area for terrorists due to its inaccessibility. The MARCOS operated in conjunction with 5 sector in the west and north of the Wullar and with 70 Mountain brigade in the east and south. They carried out a number of successful operations under Lt. Thakur, IN, and achieved total dominance of the belt by 1998. While most of the area of responsibility of 8 Mountain Division was effectively covered by a counter-insurgency grid, the areas of Ganderbal, Safapor, Dachigam, and Wussan were not, especially after the de-induction of 3 and 10 AR from 11 sector without replacements.

70 Mountain Brigade was loaned to us during the summers of 1997 and 1998 to fill the void in CI grid in Ganderbal. They were located in Ganderbal. Dachigam RF was a perfect hiding place for terrorists due to its remoteness. It was a pristine beautiful valley full of wildlife and trout. The maharaja's hunting lodge was located here that was used exclusively by state guests. The original lodge had been burnt down but an equally elegant luxury rest house had been built in its place. The exclusivity was still maintained. I spent some memorable days in this lodge with Neera and Akshay when they were on holiday. 8 Mountain Division launched all-out counter terrorist operations from October 1996 onwards. Some of the important operations carried out during this period are described in the succeeding paragraphs to illustrate the intensity and tenacity of the fighting.

In 5 Sector, 13 RR commanded by Colonel R.S. Jamwal, carried out an outstanding operation on 2 November 1996 in Haphruda forest that had been dominated by the terrorists. This forest area was used for rest and recuperation and as a supply base by the terrorists. It had become necessary to destroy it. Three columns moved out at night and cordoned off the area by first light. Immediately thereafter, fighting commenced and one column under Lt. Col. S.S. Rana, located the terrorist camp protected by outposts. He killed three foreign terrorists. The fighting continued for six hours. Some eight to 10 terrorists made good their escape taking advantage of the forest cover and some gaps in the cordon. Rana was fatally wounded in this encounter. A big stockpile of explosives, rations, stores and medical stores was recovered. The operation cleared the forest of terrorists and it was never used by them again. Lt. Col. S.S. Rana[24] was awarded the Ashoka Chakra, the highest award for bravery.

13 RR continued to perform well under Colonel R. Kulkarni. 14 RR under Colonel S.V. Bhide and later Colonel R. Chaudhary found a huge cache of arms in Kemahghat on 9-10 October that included 24 rifles, 35 grenades, one Pika machine gun, a radio set and 30 kg of explosives. 17 Bihar under Colonel Pradeep Rathi carried out many successful operations. In one such operation, they killed four terrorists in Wandahom village on 20 October 1997 in a pitched fight and recovered four AK rifles. Some of the operations carried out by 17 Bihar lasted 10 hours. Almost every company commander of 17 Bihar was wounded in the operations. The operations by 13 RR, 14 RR and 17 Bihar cleared the area completely of terrorists in Sumbal, Bandipura and Safapura by 1998. Colonels Jamwal and Bhide were awarded VSMs while Colonel Pradeep Rathi was awarded SC for meritorious service and bravery.

In 192 Mountain Brigade area, 5/9 GR under Colonel George Mathai and later 13 J&K Rifles under Colonel Jasbir Singh cleared Sopore of all terrorists and the influence of the JEI and Hurriyat was neutralized. Sayeed Ali Gilani was marginalized and lost his grip over the people forever. This epicentre of terrorism was henceforth peaceful. 15 RR under Colonel Stanley Samuel and R.S. Jasrotia at Hamre and 5 Mahar/3/3 GR at Pattan wrested control of the area from the terrorists and the JEI. Operations by 13 JAK Rifles and 3/3 GR on 15 September in village Pethsir resulted in the killing of three terrorists and recovery of three AK rifles, three pistols and a passive night vision device. 13 JAK Rifles again killed three terrorists in Adipur village on 29 November 1997. Gilani lamented his defeat privately when people paid no heed to his bandh calls. People wanted to reinvent their shattered lives and make use of the peace provided by the democratic process for development and progress. They were more interested in economic prosperity and the wellbeing of their families than in destructive activities espoused by the JEI and the Hurriyat.

The area of 12 sector had been a hotbed of terrorism as it was on the ingress route of terrorists across the Pir Panjal. 34 RR under Colonel R.J.S. Dhillon at Beeru killed six terrorists at Gogaldhara on 17 November 1996. 35 RR under Colonel K.K. Chopra at Badgam killed three terrorists at Hiwandor village on 25 March 1997. 34 RR, now under Colonel S.C.S. Pathania and 36 RR under Colonel A. Verghese in a joint operation killed three foreign terrorists in village Phakarpur on 11 June 1997. In a spectacular joint operation, 34 and 35 RR, now under Colonel D. Nagarajan, killed 16 terrorists in a single operation on 21 September 1997 at Latun[25] village. The operation was witnessed by the HC course visiting the formation. Mr. Kamal Mustaffa, the cabinet minister from Tanmarg, accompanied them. This was one of the finest operations without any collateral damage. The performance of these RR battalions was commendable. Col. R.J.S. Dhillon was awarded a VSM for his meritorious services. K.K. Chopra was selected for a staff course in the USA.

56 Mountain Brigade with 13 Guards under Colonel Man Singh at Zainkot and Dangarpur killed a number of terrorists. He was awarded a VSM for his meritorious services. They were later replaced by 2/8 GR. 20 Grenadiers killed four terrorists in a bold and innovative operation in the Hamidania-Narakur area in the same period. They also killed three terrorists at Cherahar on 8 August 1997. They were replaced by 18 Grenadiers in February 1998. 7 JAT, who were later replaced by 25 Rajput, also dominated their area effectively. The area of operations of 56 Brigade fell astride the NH from Srinagar to Ziran. Accurate intelligence and meticulous planning was required for every operation that we conducted to avoid collateral damage in this densely populated area. The terrorists eventually vacated this area as they were now unsafe due to our effective domination.

The 8 Mountain Artillery Brigade was located at Tanmarg with 11 Field Regiment. 42 Field Regiment was deployed at Ziran. 167 Fd Regt was at Dachigam and the Lt Regt at Kangan. The brigade was in an infantry role and carried out their duties effectively. All the units also carried out their annual field firing at Toshai Maidan to remain fit for their primary role. Dr. Kamal Mustaffa, brother of the CM and a minister, lived in a palatial house at Tangmar. He was an aristocrat and intelligent man. He was very friendly with the army and we visited each other frequently.

11 Sector at Wussan had 3 and 10 AR, 167 Field Regiment at Dachigam and the light regiment at Kangan. Their main task was to keep the NH open up to Zozila and ensure that terrorists did not infiltrate across the Harmukh Mountains. 10 Mechanized Infantry Battalion ex 3 Mountain Division was located at Sonamarg during the summer to reinforce the security of the NH during the stocking period. Gujjars who lived in the upper reaches were employed by the terrorists as guides for infiltration. They did not participate in terrorism but were not averse to making some extra money as guides during the idle winter months. Surjit was able to enlist the support of Gujjars in this area that facilitated his task immensely. All those suspected as guides were quarantined in their homes during the infiltration period. And those who had been coerced to guide the groups normally abandoned them in unknown territories and informed the SF. They thus made money from both parties.

These lost and disoriented terrorist groups were easy to detect and destroy by the SF. In a joint operation, 3 and 10 AR killed four terrorists in the Pachigam-Sonamarg area on 7 July 1997. The area was free of terrorists by mid-1997 enabling us to open the Srinagar-Baltal route for the Amarnath yatra and Sonamarg for tourism and adventure activities. The Gujjars under Mian Bashir Ahmed and his son Mian Altaf Ahmed were a great help in this effort. They benefitted immensely with the opening of the route to Baltal as it provided them job opportunities and income. Mian Bashir Ahmed Laavir was a patriot and staunch nationalist, a prominent religious and political leader of the Gujjars in the entire J&K. He was proclaimed a caliph of the Islamic sufi order. Gujjars from all parts of the state congregated at his ziarat-cum-residence at Kangan for the annual Urs. It was believed that the talismans given by him to his devotees possessed magical powers to heal and bring good fortune.

I had developed a close relationship with him and that helped in enlisting community support against the terrorists. I visited Mian Bashir Ahmed on numerous occasions when he talked of his heroic deeds against the raiders in 1947 and how his Gujjars had rallied behind the army and helped them in the 1965 and 1971 wars. Mian Altaf Ahmed, his son, had been targeted by the terrorists for not throwing in his lot with them, and they severely damaged his leg in an IED attack. Since then, the holy man had vowed the destruction of these ungodly terrorists. Altaf would take me and Akshay, my son, deep into the valleys and forests on his horses to show us the beauty of Harmukh Mountains. I was also able to visit the lakes of Gangasar and Kishansar at 14,000 feet, considered holy by the pundits who believed that the departed souls of their ancestors rested there. These lakes are pristine with pure blue and green waters.

70 Mountain Brigade was commanded by Brigadier R.K.S. Shivrain, a very energetic and intelligent paratrooper. His HQ was located at Zakurah and later at Kangan. 6 Sikh was located at Hafizbagh. They were replaced by 1/11 GR in July 1997. 9 Dogra replaced 1/11 GR when they were de-inducted for Siachen. They carried out some spectacular operations and were able to cleanse the area of terrorists by the middle of 1998. 3 Kumaon killed two foreign terrorists on 6 May 1997. 1/11 GR carried out an outstanding operation on 20 July in Nawshera village under Lieut. Puneet Dutt.[26] This operation lasted 10 hours and culminated in killing three foreign terrorists and recovery of their weapons along with 10 kg of explosives. Puneet was fatally wounded in this operation and awarded an Ashoka Chakra for gallantry. I was proud of their achievement both as the GOC and the COR.

Puneet was a second-generation officer. His father Lt. Col. P.N. Dutt had also served in 1/11 GR. Puneet had an outstanding record and excelled professionally. His dedication and commitment resulted in the discovery of the terrorists and subsequent encounter. When the operation was not making headway due to effective and heavy volume of fire from the terrorists, he led the assault team and eliminated the three terrorists before succumbing to his injuries. It was a shining example of courage in the face of the enemy. 3 Kumaon and 1/11 GR killed four terrorists in Pandachh village on 8 August and recovered a UMG and 12 grenades besides the personal weapons of the terrorists. 3 Kumaon under Lt. Col. Sudhir Uppal killed yet another four foreign and two local terrorists on 27 August.

Pakistan was rattled by our success against its proxy war. The foreign terrorists hiding in Safapura Heights were now directed to carry out a sensational act of mass killing of Kashmiri pundits in Wandhama[27] village in Gandherbal constituency in reprisal. This horrendous massacre of 12 pundit families comprising 23 members that included women and children took place on 25 January 1998, two days before the inauguration of the National Winter Games at Gulmarg and one day before Republic Day. The aim was to trigger social disharmony, indicate that the situation was not normal and that the sway of the terrorists still existed. The reverberations of this massacre were felt in Delhi and Mr. I.K. Gujral, the PM, visited the families of the victims to share his grief in the tragedy and confirm the resolve of the Government of India to bring those responsible for it to justice. I received the PM along with Mr. N.N. Vohra at the Ganderbal helipad and assured him that the perpetrators of the crime would be punished within four weeks.

70 Mountain Brigade with 3 Kumaon, 9 Dogra, 17 Bihar and 13 RR were given the task to search and destroy the terrorists who were hiding in the caves of Safapura Heights. The place is a dominating hill feature with thick forest, and rocky and numerous caves. The terrorists had the advantage of observation, concealment and escape routes. The location of the terrorists had been bracketed by interceptions and information from sources. Operations were launched from multiple directions to establish a cordon by first light of 13 February. The search and destroy operation lasted two days. All the suspected caves were systematically demolished by engineer parties before flushing operations. Intense cross firing was exchanged with the terrorists. Seven foreign terrorists were killed in this operation on 15 February.[28] One UMG, five AK-47/56 rifles, one grenade launcher, two radio sets and a large quantity of assorted stores were recovered. One of the seven terrorists was a serving ISI major and one a captain of Al Badr. Safapora Heights was a classic search and destroy operation in snow-covered hills at 11,000 feet and very difficult terrain. Bold leadership, planning, tactics, physical fitness, tenacity and use of technology were the reason of success.

The SF had redeemed their pledge and a strong message was conveyed to Pakistan and all anti-national elements that lawlessness would be not be tolerated by the state.

From 1996 to 1998, 8 Mountain Division had killed 689 terrorists, apprehended 441 and took the surrender of 166. They captured 790 AK rifles, 391 pistols, 35 UMGs, 3 GGPMGs, 53 RLs/RPG, 10 Pika guns, 14 sniper rifles and 227 radio sets. The formation was awarded two Ashoka Chakras, five Kirti Ckakras, 33 Shaurya Chakras, 179 Sena Medals (Gallantry), two AVSMs and 12 VSMs.

Among the many causes of terrorism in the Valley, the growth of radical Islam[29] was prominent. It sowed the seeds of destruction. A peaceful and progressive state and society was in turmoil since 1977 when radical Islam took hold of it. Islam had entered the state in 1342. In the next 500 years 80 per cent of the population was forced to convert. These Muslims, though victims of violence and forced conversions, continued to follow sufi traditions and many customs of their Hindu ancestors till the entry of the JEI in 1945. From 1989 onwards, terrorism has taken religious-secessionist contours. Pakistan could not have unleashed its proxy war nor could terrorism have assumed the sinister form and proportions it did without the role played by the JEI.

The influence of the JEI is all pervading on the lives of the people in the Valley. It implemented its well thought out plan in a very organized and systematic manner. The Kashmiri Muslim was systematically brain-washed to disown his Hindu ancestry, identity, and heritage and sufi beliefs. The virus of hatred was planted against kafirs and jihad became a slogan. This organization is evil and terrorism hinges on the potential and fate of this sinister organization. The JEI established its HQ in Lahore in 1941 after moving out from India. It is the most influential party in that country with branches in all most all the countries of South Asia. It is the nerve centre of pan-Islam and follows the most violent policy of implementation.

It was established in Kashmir at Shopian by Maulvi Ghulam Ahar in 1945. It strictly follows instructions from Pakistan and is fully supported by their people and the government. It has been opposed to the accession of Kashmir with India and supports its merger with Pakistan. It has fought elections in the Valley only to reverse the accession. The women's wing, called Dukhtaran-e-Milat, is headed by Asiya Andrabi, a rabid proponent of strict Islam. HM, the militant wing of the JEI, was created in 1989. The JEI operates through the Kashmir cell at Lahore. Ghulam Mohamad Sofi and Safi of Baramulla crossed over to Pakistan and were actively coordinating the activities of all the terrorist groups in the Valley. Kashmiri expatriates like Dr. Ghulam Nabi Fai, Ayoub Thakur, Prof. Md. Asraf, Md. Yousaf Nasim, Abdul Majid Dhar, Ali Md. Dhar, Mustaq Ahmed Wani and Bilal Wani were prominent supporters of terrorism. They were funded and guided by the ISI. They raised funds, organized demonstrations, seminars, and protests and the bogey of violation of human rights at every international forum against India.

The JEI had a structure starting at the village or ward level called the Nizam-e-Halqa, and then came the Nizam-e-Markan who was in charge of a group of 10 to 15 villages, followed by Nizam-e-Tehsil at the sub district level followed by Nizam-e-Zila at the district level and finally Nizam-e-Alla at the state level. JEI activities, though low key till the 1970s, took their inspiration from Pakistan and followed Deobandi/Wahabi Islam. The impetus came after the 1977 revolution in Iran. Large numbers of Deobandi/Wahabi preachers were imported from Pakistan, Iran, other Arab countries, UP and Bihar who took charge of the mosques. They systematically brainwashed the gullible Kashmiris into believing that Kashmiriyat and Sufi Islam was haram and they could be good Muslims only by following Wahabi Islam and discarding everything that was associated with their Hindu past.

The indoctrination of innocent young Kashmiri youths commenced in social meetings/clubs, madarsas, maktabs, dargahs and during Friday prayers in the mosques. The concept of Darul-ul-Islam, Darul-ul-Harb, jihad against kafirs or Hindus and the creation of a Nizam-e-Mustafa or Islamic state were preached. The JEI gained acceptability and power between 1980 and 1989. They organized international Islamic conferences, occupied Hindu temple lands, destroyed Hindu temples, shrines, institutions, libraries and coerced many Hindus to either leave the area or abandon their properties. They also dictated the government to alter the school syllabus and align all activities in the state, universities and other institutions with the sharia.

By December 1989, the JEI had become so powerful that it started the Azadi rebellion and the Valley plunged into serious terrorism. The call for the cleansing of Hindus was given on 19 January 1990 by the JEI and by March, approximately 100,000 out of 140,000 pundits fled the Valley. Between 1989 and 1995, the JEI reigned supreme and was in the forefront of terrorism. They had a complete hold over the vernacular media and that ran under its diktats. Even the government media was subverted and most of the AIR relay stations were burnt down and staff coerced not to function. Government schools were burnt and Islamic education propagated through madarsas and private schools. The indoctrination of women was undertaken by Dukhtaran-e-Milat vigorously and they were forced to follow strict Islam, shun Western education, dress and liberal thoughts. The JEI encouraged forceful occupation of temple land, houses and property of Hindus who had fled the valley. Mosques were made the HQ of all activities and fatwas by the maulanas were rigidly implemented. They collected taxes and Sharia courts were established to punish those who did not obey the rule of Islam. The JEI became the main recruiting agency for terrorism. Young men were selected and sent to Pakistan for training.

We had come to the conclusion that the influence of the JEI had to be neutralized politically, legally, socially, administratively and militarily. This organization was banned by the government and simultaneously marginalized. Old parties were revived and alternatives created. This was evident during the parliamentary and state elections. The JEI members and the Hurriyat did not participate in the elections as they had lost much of their credibility and stood exposed of their misdeeds. After the elections, they lost more political ground.

The Hurriyat leaders including the Mirwaiz were now under government radar and could not indulge in any anti-national activity without inviting action against them. Once the democratic process had been revived, the judiciary and police became effective and accountable.

Legal actions were initiated against a large number of JEI operatives who were booked under various acts for violence, money laundering, inciting the public and causing law and order disturbances. The law caught up with many of them and this greatly curtailed their nefarious activities. All government employees who were either JEI members or sympathizers were weeded out. No one wanted to lose his job so most of the sympathizers distanced themselves from the JEI. De-radicalization of the youth was necessary to free them from the suffocating stranglehold of the JEI.

No madarsa was allowed to function without registration. They had to follow the government-approved education curriculum. All maulvis were registered and their activities monitored. A FIR was registered against those preaching hate or radical Islam. The units and formations organized activities that promoted healthy mental and physical growth in the young. Cultural events and musical concerts were revived and organized for the public at Nishat, Shalimar Bagh and other recreational places. Both the soft and hard approaches were adopted by the army. The activities of JEI members were under our surveillance and monitored at every level. The Ikhwanis were also used against the JEI operatives who were their sworn enemies to discipline them. The media was freed of their stranglehold. Once the JEI lost control over the media and press, their misdeeds and corrupt life was exposed.

Improvised explosive devices or IED[30] was one of the most effective and widely used weapons in the hands of terrorists against their opponents. Terrorism was heralded in the Valley by bomb blasts in various places in 1989. Since then, the use of IEDs kept increasing and the quality improving. It was clear that if the SF had to defeat terrorism in the Valley then the IED war had to be won. An IED created a terrific physical and psychological effect on the target and hence it was a popular weapon in the hands of the terrorists. Every blast was a victory for them. It made headlines, caused casualties and demoralized the opponent at no cost. The terrorists blew up the office of the DGP on 24 January 1992. The TV towers, communications, government property and infrastructure were systematically destroyed. SF convoys were regularly targeted. They were equally successful in targeting the Governor on 26 January 1995.

The IED blasts echoed in every corner of the Valley every day till 1995. Nearly 148 IEDs were detected in 1992-93 While 114 were detected from November 1993 to December 1994; 129 IEDs were neutralized in 1995. These were manufactured from locally procured chemicals to sophisticated explosives smuggled from Pakistan. They were triggered from simple-pull-and-pressure switches to sophisticated timer mechanisms and remotely controlled devices. They were fabricated in wooden, metal or plastic containers, pressure cookers, gas cylinders, car bombs or undetectable casings buried deep underground.

They were laid under culverts, hill slopes, tracks/roads, office buildings and venues of official functions and fitted with anti-lifting devices or in tandem up to seven in an area for maximum damage and effect. A number of terrorists had been trained in Pakistan specially to wage IED warfare. They manufactured the IEDs in clandestine factories, and trained people to assemble, lay and activate them. The more sophisticated IEDs were smuggled directly from Pakistan. We carried out a detailed analysis and took remedial measures that ultimately defeated the terrorists at their game. All units and sub-units carried out terrain analysis and identified areas that were tactically suited for laying IEDs; vulnerability assessments were carried out and such targets were provided adequate protection and counter-measures taken.

Finally, threat analysis gave an insight of enemy tactics, equipment, technology used and methodology. It was seen that before an IED, signal traffic in the target area would increase while the physical activity of the locals would drastically decrease as a threat indicator. There were many other threat indicators that an expert eye could discern. We countered the threat of IEDs both by physical means and use of technology. All important lines of communications were fully secured physically and kept under surveillance. Sniffer dogs were used extensively. Vasgar ECM2 jammers, EVD 3000 explosive detectors, and Super Brooms to detect electronic devices and non-metallic electronic devices, bomb suits, search inspection kits, optical inspection kits, Doppler or electronic stethoscopes, DIMM vehicles to sweep for buried mines and Ferex Search instruments were some of the items that we used.

The most effective measure was incorporation of the local population in this war. Every village was given an area of responsibility to ensure that no IEDs were planted in its jurisdiction. If the terrorists did manage to plant one, they were equally responsible. The reward–and-punishment method had immediate effect. With these in place, terrorists could blast only two IEDs in our area during 1996-97. Colonel Balwinder Singh, 13 Engineer Regiment, and his men played a very vital role in defeating the IED war. They reverse engineered many of these defused IEDs to be used against terrorists to very good effect.

Winning the Hearts and Minds (WHAM) of people is an important principle of counter insurgency/terrorist operations. This had always been part of the policy of the Indian Army whenever and wherever it was deployed. Successful application of this policy during 1996-98 was one of the main reasons for the defeat of the terrorists. It was important to understand the basics of the problem before it could be implemented. The Kashmir problem has existed at three levels. It is an internal problem at the first level because the people of the Valley wrongly perceived that they have been denied the right of self-determination. It is a regional dispute between India and Pakistan at the second level on the basis of the two-nation theory. At the third level, it became an international issue.

Kashmiri terrorism is not based on any specific grievance against India but the tragedy is that in spite of secularism since 1947, Indian Muslims still feel a fatal attraction for the concept of an Islamic state. This affects their psyche. Yet another factor that affects them is Kashmiriyat. People of the Valley feel highly insecure outside the Valley or of the presence of people from outside. Sir Aurel Stein, a noted authority on Kashmir who spent many years in the Valley, stated that the geographical features have determined the culture and psyche of the people. As a consequence of its geographic features and kaleidoscopic mosaic of the past, there grew a common culture, native pride, a togetherness and mutuality between all those who live in the confines of the Valley that is called Kashmiriyat that generates the need to safeguard their identity. It has a strong emotive content.

Kashmiris were always unhappy with subjugation whether they were the early Muslims, Mughals, Afghans or Dogras as it hurts their identity and pride. This fear of subjugation of their identity was being exploited by Pakistan that had led to terrorism. The aim of WHAM was to remove insecurity and alienation in the general public. Many schemes and programs were initiated at the national and state levels. However, 8 Mountain Division could address the problems at only the field level. These were categorized as those that affected the people on a daily basis, those that accrued midterm benefits and those with long-term benefits to them. All these were translated into immediate remedies through grievance cells, integration, skill development, employment generation, health education, communications and welfare.

Groups of children were sent on study tours to different parts of the country to understand the concept of unity in diversity and the democratic, secular and federal concept of governance. They were exposed to the glorious past of the country and the making of a strong and modern India. Every unit set up skill generation centres in schools that made children capable of self-employment. About 246 children were given training in 1996-97. Coaching classes for recruitment in the Army, sports institutions, computer training and competitive examinations were organized for students. Almost all government schools that had been destroyed by the terrorists were rebuilt and made functional. About 30 playgrounds were constructed in them. All village dispensaries were made functional and 10 free medical camps were organized. Over 700 patients were treated by army and civil doctors in a single camp organized by 8 Mountain Artillery Brigade. 5 Sector also organized an eye camp in Watlab from 20 to 22 May 1997. Similarly, veterinary services were reactivated. 13 Engineer Regiment constructed two floating bridges,[31] 36 Bailey bridges, and a number of culverts at Yaripora, Zaina in Shopian, Mamat, Soibug and Tunjiheran. They also constructed several kilometres of tracks and two kilometres of anti-flood bundhs. The division opened the Baltal route for the Amarnath yatra creating employment for hundreds of people. Thousands of people were rescued in Srinagar during the 1996 floods in the Jhelum. Every company adopted one village and one child from a poor family. We co-opted local bodies and people in planning and executing all WHAM programmes and that ensured their success. A special bond was created between the people and the SF as the feeling of "We Care for Them" spread.

Psychological warfare and perception management are also important aspects of CT operations. Pakistan had been more successful than us in the Valley on this account. The revolt and subsequent terrorism was a product of their psychological war. The JEI controlled the vernacular press and the national and foreign media was subverted both by coercion and funds from Pakistan and Muslim/Arab countries. Foreign media had outsourced news supply to local correspondents who fed biased information to their principals. Yussof Jameel and Zaffar Mehraj, BBC correspondents, Tariq and Bilal Bhatt of ANI, from the Valley were in the forefront of spreading falsehoods. They were on the payroll of foreign intelligence agencies and lived in palatial houses. We utilized DD and AIR Srinagar to counter them with live programs in which children, ladies, surrendered terrorists, academicians, intellectuals and common folk participated. They brought out the changes and benefits their lives had experienced due to our indulgence. Live appeals and messages by mothers, sisters and relatives were sent through TV and AIR to terrorists to return home and live a safe and graceful life.

The *Kashmir* and *Srinagar Times* (Urdu) owned by Mr. Ved Bhasin, a Mirpuri Hindu, was grossly biased. Masood was one of their most virulent reporters and a champion of false reporting of human rights violations. It was reported that he was funded by the ISI. They seldom reported the misdeeds of the JEI, Hurriyat or terrorists. *Greater Kashmir* owned by Rashid Makhdoomi was also a popular English daily; the group also published the Nawa-e-Jhelum and *Kashmir Uzma,* both Urdu editions. Faiz Ahmad Kaloo and Qayoom, their reporters, were generally biased. There were reports that this paper also received funds from outside agencies. The *Excelsior* owned by Rohmetra and Ahmad Ali Faiz, their correspondent, was more accurate and balanced than all the other papers. Faiz and a few other reporters covered operations live unlike most who constructed events sitting in their offices.

Asha Kosha, a Kashmiri pandit, and her husband, Joseph, were very active. They had interviewed terrorist leaders like Sallaudin and Mustgul. They were investigative journalists and generally accurate. Ifthikar Gilani, son-in-law of Sayeed Ali Shah Gilani, was the Delhi bureau chief of *Kashmir Times* and *The Nation Pakistan*, both published in Pakistan. We had instituted a press briefing after every major operation and civic action event. I held a monthly press briefing for the entire press corps. We thus established a good working relationship with the media and ensured transparency. The tide turned against the terrorists and the JEI when the media was free of fear and commenced reporting in an unbiased manner including the misdeeds of terrorists.

By October 1997, Farooq Abdullah's government had completed one year. There were many achievements to their credit. Terrorism was well under control. All government institutions functioned well. People had resumed normal life. Commercial activities including tourism were flourishing. The Winter Olympics at Gulmarg was a great success. I interacted frequently with the CM at his residence on Gupkar Road and most of the cabinet colleagues, including Ajat Shatru Singh, son of Dr. Karan Singh who lived in his palace, Karan Niwas. It was located on Gupkar Road with a breathtaking view of the Dal Lake. He was married to the daughter of General Srinagesh. He was intelligent and honest but not made for Kashmiri politics.

While the government had settled down and there were many achievements to its credit in this short period of one year, there were reports of corruption, nepotism, favouritism, financial impropriety and embezzlement of funds and grants. Loans from J&K banks were granted on recommendations of the CM or influential ministers. There were many irregularities under Mohammad Yussaf, the MD, with doubtful credentials, and loans were never recovered. There were also reports of ministers and MLAs with links with terrorists. Col. Awasthi, CO, 36 RR, personally searched the house of Mr. Abdul Raheem Rather, the finance minister, on confirmed information. This became a political issue in the state assembly.[32] But we held our ground and were proved right. The CM spent more than

Rs. 4 crore on constructing his dream project, the "Srinagar International Golf Course". This was certainly not a priority project.

MLAs sold vacancies for employment for huge sums of money. The people were getting impatient and resented the lavish lifestyle of the ministers and MLAs. All of them had prime properties in Srinagar, Jammu or Delhi and business interests in the Middle East or Europe/USA. There were also rumours that the CM and Moulvi Iftikhar Hussain Ansari were linked to Jet Airways. All the cronies of the ruling party were elected as MLCs. It appeared that sooner or later the NC would get back to its old ways and all the gains made so far would be wasted. By now, Lt. Gen. Krishan Pal had taken over as the corps commander. He had a sharp mind and an acute strategic knowledge. He allowed us the same freedom of action as Lt. Gen. J.S. Dhillon had done before him.

Battle stress is quite common during intense operations. Prolonged battle fatigue manifests in fratricide, running amok, depression and anxiety. It is demoralizing and affects unit morale. We took adequate measures to provide psychological and social support to our men. The officer-men relationship was the key to high morale. I was convinced that if our men had faith in their commanders, in their weapons and equipment and were backed by strong logistics, they would not crack up. Their spiritual and emotional needs had also to be satisfied. They were convinced that if terrorists were waging jihad they were fighting a dharma yudh. We suffered only one case of running amok in 15 RR. This was also due to inept handling of the situation by his commander. There was yet another case of indiscipline that led to the court-martial of Major Yaspal Naggar of the Intelligence and Field Security Company. He had done some great work in intelligence collection that led to the elimination of many terrorists groups. Over a period of time, his network of sources went rogue and became criminals. They used to abduct rich businessmen for extortion, indulge in arms smuggling and illegal sale of stolen vehicles in other parts of the country. When a spate of such incidents was reported, the source of origin was traced to Major Yaspal Naggar and his safe houses in the city. I had no regret in court-martialling this officer who was cashiered and jailed.

The United Front Government led by Mr. I.K. Gujral collapsed when the Congress withdrew its support. Fresh parliamentary elections were thus held in February 1998. There was a lot of enthusiasm and willing participation this time. However, we took all precautions that we had taken during the state elections in September 1996. No terrorist activity of significance took place and the voting percentage in the Valley was 41 per cent. Mr. Saifuddin Soz and Omar Abdullah, son of Mr. Farooq Abdullah, from the NC won from Baramulla and Srinagar, respectively, while Mr. Mufti Mohammad Sayeed from the Congress won from Anantnag. With this, the third generation of the Abdullahs entered politics. Mr. Soz was a seasoned politician but people wished that Mr. Muzaffar Hussain Beg, an independent candidate, had won. Mr. Beg was educated at Harvard University and had a clean image. He was practicing lawyer in the Supreme Court of India. I was much impressed by his knowledge, grace and personality. Omar Abdullah was a new-generation politician, different in thinking and approach. His vision of the Valley was vastly opposed to the older politicians. His opponent, Ghulam Hassan Mir, was a seasoned and honest politician. Mir also impressed us with his dedication to the people of his constituency. He interacted with us frequently. 8 Mountain Division once again had played a significant role in ensuring the smooth and fair conduct of the elections.

Memorials to soldiers who made the supreme sacrifice are erected by all countries. The aim is to honour the brave hearts and to inspire future generations. Honour guards are mounted and wreaths laid on these memorials. Many sacrifices have been made by the Indian Army in J&K since 1947. My division had played a very significant role in CT operations since 1990. I thought it appropriate to create a unique memorial to honour all our gallant soldiers who had contributed to peace and tranquillity in the Valley. Lt. Gen. Krishanpal, the GOC, allowed us to construct one in Badamibagh near an ancient Hindu temple. 13 Engineer Regiment drew up a beautiful design that reflected the ancient heritage, multi-culture of the Valley and valour of the jawans. The landscaping and the memorial merged with the temple complex and enhanced its beauty. The stone and marble carving was done by local artisans. All ranks of the division had stood by their post in most critical times, done their duty under extreme circumstances and had kept the faith of the country in great adversity. This sentiment was etched on the front stone in an epitaph by Mr. B.S. Malik, a Kashmiri poet. The J&K Government donated Rs. 5 lakh, the cost of the memorial, in gratitude to the soldiers who had laid down their lives. This beautiful memorial was dedicated to the nation by Gen. K.V. Krishnarao, the Governor, in the presence of Mr. Farooq Abdullah, the CM, Mr. Iftikhar Hussain Ansari, the PWD minister and Lt. Gen. Krishan Pal on 16 March 1998. The Governor was overwhelmed with emotion and so pleased with the design that he dedicated it to all the soldiers who had laid down their lives in the Valley since 1947. 8 Mountain Division's memorial thus became the Chinar memorial.

My tenure in the Valley came to end immediately after the elections and I was posted to HQ Western Command. It was a most satisfying tenure packed with action. I was given an affectionate farewell by both the Governor and the CM. I left the Valley after paying my gratitude to all my fallen colleagues and those who had stood with me during those trying days.

NOTES

1. *Rajatarangini* by Kalhan gives the dynastic and political history of Kashmir up to the 8th century and a study of *Nilmata Purana* by Dr. Ved Kumari, published by J&K Academy of Art provides the social background of that era.
2. The history of Kashmir as narrated in the book *My Frozen Turbulence in Kashmir* by Jagmohan.
3. Fundamentalist Muslims claim it as Takth-e-Sulaiman.
4. *Danger in Kashmir* by Josef Korbel, p.-15. Maharaja Pratap Singh was temporarily suspended in favour of his brother, Amar Singh. He was restored in 1905.
5. *The Valley of Kashmir* by Walter R. Lawrence.
6. *Kashmir 1947-1965. A Story Retold* by Manoj Joshi.
7. *Raiders in Kashmir* by Akbar Khan.
8. Messervy was commissioned in Hudson Horse and was GOC-in-C, Western Command, at Rawalpindi. He was C-in-C, Pak Army, from 14 August 1947 to 10 February 1948.
9. Gracey 1 GR was CGS, Pak Army, under Messervy and C-in-C, Pak Army, from 11 February to January 1951.
10. *Integration of Indian States* by V.P. Menon, ch 20, p. 390.
11. *Slender was the Thread* by Major General L.P. Sen.
12. *Gilgit Rebellion* by W.A. Brown.
13. *Fall of Skardu* by Col. T.K. Tikkoo, Vivekananda International Foundation Papers, July 2013.

14. The military line and radio communications in J&K were routed through GHQ at Rawalpindi. The British were also privy to the codes for crypto messages they thus shared operational plans of the Indian Army with Pakistan.
15. *The Lost Rebellion* by Manoj Joshi, p. 16.
16. *In the Service of the Nation* by Krishna Rao, pp. 456-461.
17. *The Valley of Kashmir* by Walter R. Lawrence, ch. 12, *Castes and Tribes,* pp. 302-318.
18. *Kashmir Sunlight and Shade* by C.E. Tyndale Biscose. He was a missionary and head master of Kashmir Mission School, Srinagar during 1921 and has described the life and people then. The pundits were intellectually superior.
19. *Travels in Kashmir, Ladak, Iskardoo* by G.T. Vigne, pp. 124-134. He describes the Pashmina shawl trade.
20. The first meeting was held on 10 December 1996 and covered by *The Daily Excelsior,* 11 December 1997.
21. *The Greater Kashmir,* 12 November 1997. An Interview by me on responsibility to rehabilitate the Ikhwanis.
22. Interview of Kuka Parrey by Harvinder, *India Today,* December 1995.
23. *An Untold Story* by Praveen Swami, *Frontline,* 15 November 1996.
24. *Forever in Operations: A History of 8 Mountain Division,* by Brig. S.P. Sinha, p. 127.
25. *The Indian Express,* 23 September 1997. The group was detected by electronics and human intelligence.
26. *Forever in Operations-A History of 8 Mountain Division,* by Brig. S.P. Sinha, p. 130.
27. *Times of India,* Chandigarh, 15 February 2021, by Bikram Singh, an eye witness account.
28. Reported in *The Times of India*, *The Hindu*, *The Tribune* of 16 February and *Daily Excelsior,* 18 February 1998.
29. *A Report by 8 Mtn Division,* "Growth of Radical Islam in Kashmir and its Effects on Society and Terrorism".
30. From a Report on this subject prepared by a team of Officers from 13 Engineer Regiment.
31. *Kashmir Times*, 29 April 1997, 15 August 1997, 3 September 1997; *Daily Excelsior,* 6 September 1997.
32. The issue was raised as HR violations by the SF in the State Assembly. *Kashmir Times* 12 and 16 June, 1997.

Map 15: Jammu and Kashmir

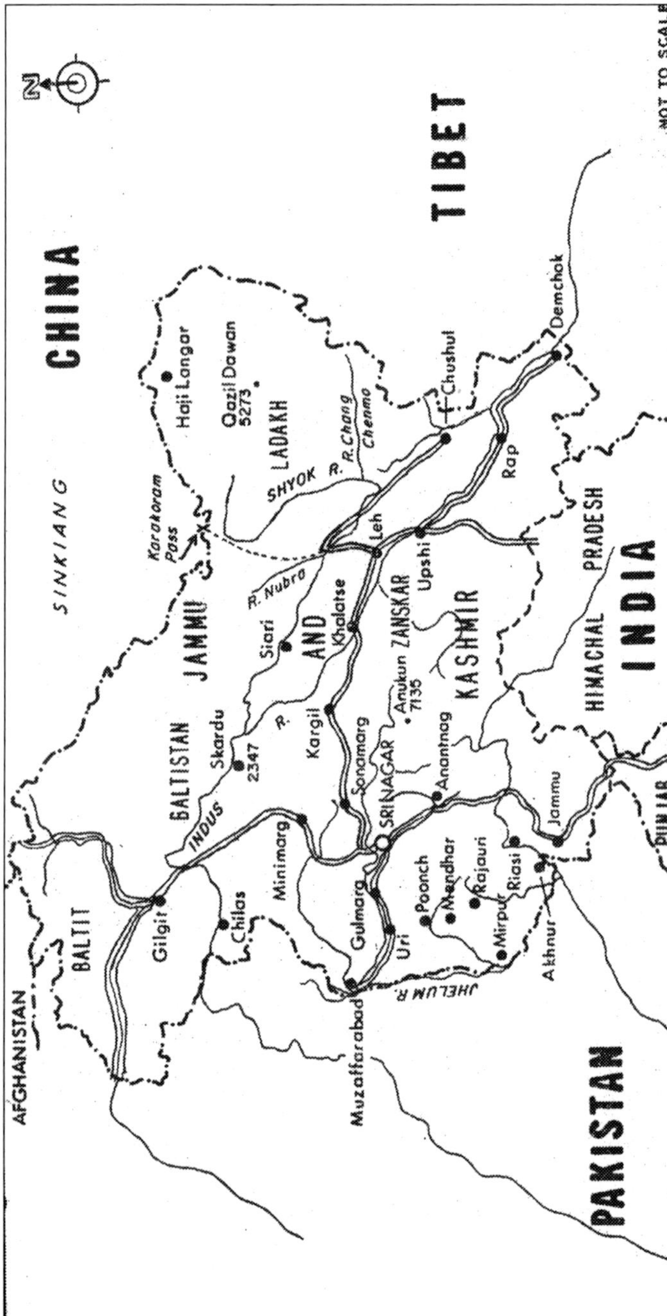

Map 16: Area of Operation of 8 Mountain Division

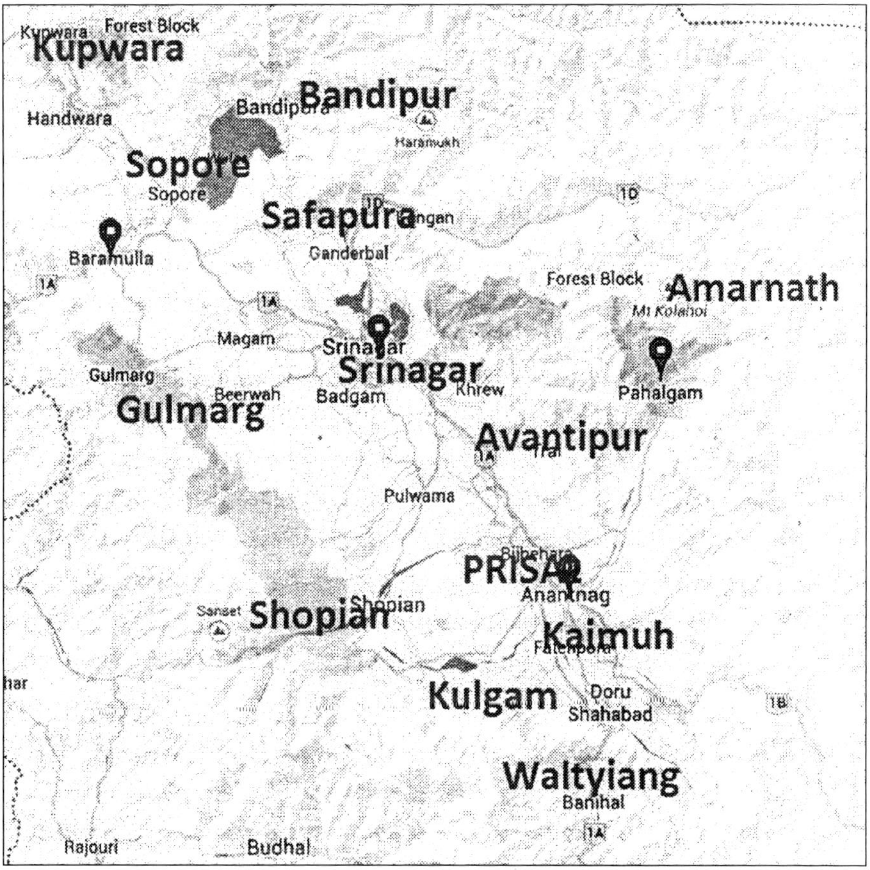

Chapter 7

Back to Punjab, Kargil and J&K Insurgency

I was posted to HQ Western Command at Chandimandir in April 1998 as Head of Operations. This HQ was re-raised in August 1947 at Shimla when HQ North-Western Army at Rawalpindi became GHQ Pakistan. It was responsible for the security of Delhi, Rajasthan, Punjab, Haryana, Himachal, and J&K. When Northern Command was created post the 1971 war, J&K was taken out of its jurisdiction. They moved to Chandimandir in 1985. Lt. Gen. H.B. Kala was the GOC-in-C. 10 Corps, was responsible for North Rajasthan while 11 Corps was responsible for entire Punjab. The HP-Tibet border was the responsibility of 36 Sector. 2 Corps was mandated for offensive operations. Illustrious officers of the army had been GOC-in-C of this command since its raising.

The command, from its inception, had fought all wars and performed well except for "Operation Blue Star". It had contributed substantially to bring peace to the state after "Op Rakshak-2", when a democratically elected government under Mr. Beant Singh took office in April 1992. Peace has endured since then. Most of the time after 1993 was thus spent in routine peacetime activities. India carried out its second nuclear test at Pokharan from 11 to 13 May 1998. Pakistan followed suit by carrying out five simultaneous nuclear explosions in the Ras Koh Hills of Chagai district in Balochistan on 28 May 1998. The strategic dynamics changed overnight with the emergence of two nuclear armed hostile neighbours. Nuclear warfare now became a reality and was taken seriously in all training and administrative exercises.

Our defence preparedness was impacted by US sanctions, a cut in the defence budget and our involvement in CT operations. The government enhanced age of retirement by two years that impacted both service conditions and promotions and many of us were affected one way or the other. By and large, the decision was welcomed although it was detrimental for the organization. The young age profile of the army was disturbed. Commanders were now physically and mentally not as agile as their younger predecessors earlier. They tended to be cautious, risk averse, indecisive, lacked aggressiveness and boldness. The age profile of a battalion commander suddenly increased to 44 years from 37. Senior officers looked grey, tired, and haggard. This increase was resented by those affected by delayed promotions but many found the extension beneficial as it gave them additional years to serve.

The Kargil War in 1999 abruptly disturbed our peacetime routine. A strategic analysis of the development was carried out during the first and second weeks of May 1999 when it became somewhat clear that the Pakistan army had intruded into Kargil and efforts to evict them by local formations had failed. Air strikes were launched and all formations put on alert after the CCS meeting on 24 May when Pakistan's complicity was confirmed. At the international level, the reaction of the USA and EU was generally positive and favourable towards us on the Kargil issue. However they would not support us on expanding the conflict beyond the area in dispute which gave us better options for war fighting. Even the selective mobilization of the defence forces was frowned upon. Russia however supported us like always in the past.

China was silent like our neighbours; Arab and Muslim countries were either neutral or silent. It was expected that in case of a war between India and Pakistan, the USA and the West would pressurize Pakistan to restore the sanctity of the LoC leading to de-escalation by both. Failing which they would cut off all military assistance and impose more sanctions. Russia was expected to support us both diplomatically and militarily while China would support Pakistan. Saudi Arabia, Libya, Jordan and Turkey were expected to openly help Pakistan. As per our assessment, the immediate aim of Pakistan was to (a) internationalize the J&K issue, (b) ensure third-party intervention in the dispute, (c) involve other countries militarily like in Kosovo and Afghanistan, and (d) ensure a strong bargaining position on Siachen/future Indo-Pak talks.

The Pak military strategy was (a) be proactive in J&K, tie down the Indian Army and wear it out, (b) localize the conflict to Kargil and sever the Valley from Ladakh, and (c) adopt a defensive posture in the plains of Punjab and other areas. In response to this, our military aims were quite clear. (a) To evict the enemy and capture maximum territory in J&K, and (b) while retaining an overall strategic balance, be reactive in the plains and the desert with a swift campaign with conflict termination in our favour politically and militarily. It was necessary for us to ensure that we fought a one-front war; all war preparations were done well in time; and minimum nuclear deterrence was in place to achieve our aims.

Punjab on both sides of the border was a very sensitive theatre of war. Loss of territory was not acceptable. The density of troop deployment was very high on both sides. On the Pak side, 8 Infantry Division and 19 Armoured Brigade as part of 30 Corps was opposite Gurdaspur. 1 Corps was in depth for a riposte. 4 Corps with 10 and 11 infantry divisions and 3 (I) Armoured Brigade was deployed in the Lahore Sector. 31 Corps with 14 and 35 divisions, 10 (I) Armoured Brigade, 14 (I) Armoured Brigade and 44 (I) Mechanized Brigade were deployed in Suleimanke, Bahawalnagar and Fort Abbas area. 2 Corps was also deployed in this area for a riposte. The Ravi river was an obstacle in the Gurdaspur sector for both sides. The Ichogil canal on the Pakistani side was a well-known obstacle. India had also constructed a formidable ditch-cum-bundh opposite it. The obstacle system in the Fazilka sector was mainly based on irrigation canals on both sides.

Operations during the monsoon were difficult except in the desert which was suitable for mechanized warfare. The depth areas in Punjab were riddled with irrigation canals that could be used as part of the defences in depth. Every inch of ground would be contested and fought for as high-value targets were located very close to the border. Ditches, canals, and bunds on both sides were laced with concrete bunkers. Enclaves across the Ravi and Sutlej rivers had to be defended. Some of them could also be used for launching offensive operations. We had water flushing schemes in extreme eventualities necessitating coordination with the irrigation department. Co-ordination had also to be done with the transport department to move formations, civil defence, health, police, para military forces, state home department, home guards, etc., in case of total war.

We took immediate action to defend all the enclaves and forward zones so that we would not be caught by surprise. Early warning systems were activated and formations partly mobilized while others were at short notice. The COAS, CAS, AOC Western Air Command, all commanders, including the GOC-in-C, Central Command, and ARTRAC were briefed by us as part of the co-ordination. However, it was found that we were deficient in critical equipment, especially in 2 Corps. This grossly affected the war fighting capability of the formation and the Corps Commander, was apprehensive of attaining his operational objectives if war broke out. Procurement agencies at the national level were galvanized and Lt. Gen. J.S. Dhillon, the MGO, made frequent trips to our HQ to ensure that the deficiencies were made up quickly.

The conflict was restricted to Kargil only and an all-out war was averted under pressure from the USA on both sides. The war ended by 27 July. This was very unfair to India. While we were made to shed blood to regain our own territory, the guilty had been let off without punishment. The army commander and I visited all the formations including HQ 1 Corps that had moved to Punjab to ensure its fitness for war. The quick fallout of the limited Kargil War was that we were all shaken out of inertia and now all our effort was devoted to battle readiness at all times. Our operational directives and logistic plans were updated, duly validated, approved by the army commander and issued.

Had war broken out, we would have succeeded without doubt as the new plans were based on surprise, high mobility and unexpected multiple thrust lines. A lot of innovation and ingenuity had gone in drafting these plans. Provision for adequate artillery and administrative build up was catered for under supervision of Maj. Gen. Purshotam Vig MGIC Adm. Plans for 36 Sector were also revised. Offensive operations were given primacy. We were confident that our troops would have made substantive gains against the Chinese had they interfered in a war with Pakistan. Lt. Gen. Vijay Oberoi replaced Gen. Kala after the Kargil War. He was a great thinker and military strategist of repute. A tri service model exercise was conducted by him to validate our concepts of offensive operations immediately on his arrival. This was followed by mobilization of the formations for a full-scale exercise with troops.

We practised the concepts of vertical envelopment, vertical pivots and transfer of live battle field images and data on TV screens in the operations room for the first time. Col. S.P. Kochhar, who later became the SO-in-C, ensured connectivity and continuous data and image transfer from the front lines to the operations room. Satellite images were transferred from DIPAC to the exercise area. The nuclear aspects were also factored in. General V.P. Malik, the COAS, along with Air Chief Marshal A.Y. Tipnis, the CAS, attended the exercise with troops and were highly appreciative of the effort made in conducting this event. Only a person of the vision and genius of Lt. Gen. Oberoi could have conceived and conducted such a massive exercise that incorporated technology and the modern concepts of war.

Gen. Oberoi's tenure was rather short and he moved to Army HQ as the Vice Chief soon after the exercise. However, he left a lasting impact on all of us. Lt. Gen. S.S. Sangra, who replaced him, was very competent professionally and humane by nature. I was thus fortunate to gain wisdom from three most eminent commanders of the Indian Army. The command experienced massive flash floods in the Sutlej River on 31 July and 1 August 2000, causing extensive damage to life and property. It was speculated that these floods had been caused by China but these reports were baseless. The river had been blocked by landslides creating a temporary mud dam that burst under the pressure of water causing flash floods. The area of Sumdong was badly affected and so were the NJ hydel projects under construction. Grouping and co-locating formations closer to their operational areas was one of our major achievements. Our formations and units were located in UP, Himachal and Delhi. Some were split in two to three places within the command that caused admin and mobilization problems. We were able to pull everyone within the command jurisdiction and created homogeneous formations within one station. This improved our operational readiness and deployment.

We had very harmonious civil-military relations with all the three states of Punjab, Haryana and HP. Mr. Prakash Singh Badal, the CM of Punjab, and Ch. Bansilal and later Om Prakash Chautala, CM of Haryana, were ever forthcoming in help. Lt. Gen. B.K.N. Chhibber, as the Governor of Punjab, was very helpful to the Army. Mr. George Fernandes, the RM, visited our HQ and later all the border areas. He was a remarkably simple man, very sharp, attentive and positive. He travelled in an ordinary compartment of the Shatabdi train to various locations. Being a socialist, he wore simple attire, carried his small bag and lived frugally. He was accompanied by only his personal assistant, Mr. Ashok Kumar, without bodyguards or escorts. He mixed with the troops freely and loved to have his meals with them.

My tenure as MGGS ended in March 2001 when I was posted as GOC 16 Corps on promotion. I had a very professionally rewarding and educative tenure. It was one of the few peace tenures where we were able to live together as a family and make many friends. Kanu Priya, my daughter, was now a medical student in Medical College, Rohtak. Akshay passed his secondary school and joined the economics stream in Delhi University. Neera was also able to work as an anaesthesiologist in the Knee and Hip Joint Hospital, Panchkula. Chandigarh and the surrounding areas had a very large veteran fraternity that gave us an opportunity to meet some very old colleagues and friends. Col. H.S. Boparai, who was our course in charge in the NDA, and Maj. Gen. H.S. Talwar and S.P.S. Kochhar were some of them.

I was promoted Lieutenant General and posted as GOC 16 Corps at Nagrota, Jammu, on 1 April 2001. It was the largest formation in the Army, both geographically as well as in number of formations under its command. It was responsible for the strategically sensitive areas of Jammu and had both offensive as well as defensive roles. When I took command, the Jammu region was in the grip of terrorism that added yet another dimension to the operational situation. The region extends from the Ravi river in the south to the Pir Panjal range in the north and the IB and

LoC in the west to the Himachal boundary in the east, an area of 26,293 sq. km.

Geographically, it can be divided into outer plains, the Shiwaliks and the Middle Himalayas. The outer plains are a continuation of the northern Indian plains and are fertile lands. The Shiwaliks are 200 km long from the Ravi river to Janggar and beyond and 20 to 25 km wide with heights of up to 1,000 mtrs. Numerous seasonal nalas flow from the Shiwaliks; the Ujah, Deg and Basantar are among them draining into the Ravi. The Middle Himalayas also run from Ravi to Muzzafarabad. They are about 400 km long and 10 to 60 km wide with heights ranging from 3,600 to 4,600 mtrs. The Trikuta mountains, Pir Panjal and Dhaula Dhar ranges are part of the Middle Himalayas. The Chenab river cuts across these mountains. The Pir Panjal, Badli and Banihal passes connect the Srinagar Valley with Jammu. The Poonch river, Manawar, and Jammu Tawi originate from these mountains and are perennial sources of water. The Kandi belt exists between the Shiwaliks and the Middle Himalayas.

The region has been divided into 10 districts of Poonch, Rajouri, Reasi, Ramban, Doda, Kishtwar, Udhampur, Jammu, Samba and Kathua. The population consisted of 63 per cent Hindus, 30 per cent Muslims and 7 per cent of the rest. Poonch, Rajouri, Ramban, Doda and Kishtwar are Gujjar and Kashmiri dominated and the rest is Hindu dominated. The area is divided into 37 state and two parliamentary constituencies.

Relations with Pakistan continued to deteriorate even after the Kargil War in 1999. General Musharraf had seized power in Pakistan in October 1999 and had further upped the ante against India. Terrorists attacked Red Fort, the symbol of Indian authority, on 22 December 2000. The Agra summit between Mr. Atal Bihari Vajpayee, PM of India, and General Pervez Musharraf, President of Pakistan, from 14 to 16 July 2001 ended in failure. Pakistan became more obdurate and terrorists aided by them continued to strike with new vigour at sensitive targets in J&K and beyond. The attack on Twin Towers in the USA by the Al-Qaeda in September 2001 brought retribution from the US-led NATO alliance against the Taliban government in Afghanistan for supporting Al-Qaeda.

As in 1979, Pakistan was once again propelled into the reckoning with the NATO countries and became a frontline state of the alliance in its fight against the 'Axis of Evil.' Sanctions against the country were lifted and large-scale economic and military aid resumed much to the consternation of India. Surprisingly, the epicentre of terrorism was now a frontline state in the fight against terror. This quick turnaround did not change Pakistan's policy towards India. In fact, it pursued its agenda of proxy war with more vigour than before with the USA downplaying India's concerns. Militant camps in POK continued to proliferate. Infiltration of terrorists from Pakistan also continued unabated despite enhanced vigilance at the LoC and IB. New routes through Nepal and Bangladesh were opened. Firing incidents at the LoC and IB also intensified. It appeared that all the gains made after the Kargil War had been neutralized and terrorism in J&K was at its zenith once again.

The arrival of the Jaish-e-Mohammad (JeM), a foreign-heavy militant group supported by Pakistan in J&K in 2000, brought in the spectre of 'fidayeen attacks'. Taking advantage of the changed geo-political situation, terrorists unleashed attacks all over J&K including the state assembly in October 2001. When terrorists struck at India's Parliament on 13 December 2001, "Op. Parakram" was launched that brought the two countries to the brink of war. Terrorists attacked the Kaluckak military station near Jammu on 14 May 2002. All military establishments in J&K quickly transformed into armed fortresses. India's defensive mindset was at its best. The war was averted due to US intervention as it did not want Pakistan to be attacked when they were conducting operations in Afghanistan against the Taliban.

With 25 Infantry Division at Rajouri, 10 at Akhnoor, 26 at Jammu, 29 at Mamun and 39 at Reasi, HQ Delta Force in Doda, HQ Romeo Force in Rajouri, HQ Uniform Force at Reasi, the army switched over to the 'grid system' of deployment to combat terrorism in Jammu. 27 Mountain Division from the east and 9 (I) Mountain Brigade from the Western Command were also moved in January 2002 for "Op Parakram". Later, they were deployed in Rajouri as part of the grid. The corps was indeed an army command with nine major formations and many independent brigades. My tenure was thus very hectic and I had to deal with both terrorism and the impending war. My first priority was to roll back terrorism beyond the formation boundaries as briefed by Lt. Gen. G.S. Sihota, the DGMO. There was no doubt in my mind about our task and we followed a very robust and aggressive policy to achieve it.

One of the tenets of counter-terrorism is to neutralize the source or sponsors of terrorism. The USA and Israel had been following this policy. However, due to political and geostrategic reasons, we could not do this to Pakistan. This was a big handicap for us. Our counter-terror or CI philosophy was primarily based on the principle of peace and development. Ensure peace by eliminating the terrorists and remove perceived or genuine grievances of the people by development. We had successfully applied this concept in the Punjab and in the Northeast. The same policy had achieved satisfactory results in J&K also in the past but poor governance and the deep involvement of Pakistan had not allowed us to achieve the desired end results. Since we were not allowed to cross the LoC, the best option to punish the sponsor was by artillery or rocket fire on their known bases or carry out attacks on their forward posts. The five infantry divisions, three RR Force HQs and the DIG BSF along with the police force under IG Jammu were synergized under the Unified HQ by me and within a short time we were able to score major successes in Rajouri, Poonch, Reasi, Doda and Kishtwar, notwithstanding some high-profile terrorist acts against us.

The terrorists killed five Hindus in Mahore Reasi on 4 June 2001, 15 Hindus were killed in Kishtwar on 4 August 2001, 10 passengers were killed at the Jammu railway station on 15 August 2001, four civilians were killed in Petha Dyalgon on 4 November 2001, and 11 SF personnel were killed in Ramban on 17 November 2001. Raghunath Temple in Jammu was attacked on 30 March 2002 where 11 devotees were killed and 20 injured. I presided over the Unified HQ where all the GOCs, Mr. A.K. Suri, the DGP, along with IGP R.B. Raju and DIG Shesh Paul Vaid, Mr. Vijay Raman IGP, BSF, Mr. S.C. Kukereja, IGP CRPF and Mr. Massood Choudhary, IGP, Railway Protection Force, attended as part of the security forces. Mr. C. Phunsog, the Home Secretary, Mr. Anil Goswami, Commissioner, Jammu, along with the DC, Mr. R.K. Goyal and later Rohit Kansal and other officers attended as part of the State Government.

Mr. K.M. Singh, the IB chief, and Mr. Chatroo Sinha from the RAW, also attended and provided vital intelligence inputs. I reverted to the practice of meeting the CM and the Governor once a month to brief them of the security situation as head of the Unified HQ.[1]

It did not take the formations long to clean up their areas of responsibility with the Punjab and Kashmir Valley experience behind us. 25 Infantry Division under Maj Gen NS Pathania and later Randhir Sinh kept a tight control on the LoC. HQ Romeo Force under Maj. Gen. Richard Khare with Brig. K.S. Yadava commanding 6 Sector RR, scored some spectacular successes and cleared the entire depth area of 25 Infantry Division of terrorists. The notorious area of Hill Kaka was addressed and cleared of terrorist bases. Nearly 103 terrorists were killed in 2001 and 47 in 2002 in this area.[2] Similarly, 39 Infantry Division under Maj. Gen. Balbir Singh cleared the Reasi and Pirpanjal areas of terrorists. Later, HQ Uniform Force under Maj. Gen. Rajeshwar Singh continued with the momentum. HQ Delta Force under Maj. Gen. M.P. Bhagat and later Prakash Choudhary brought the entire Doda-Kishtwar-Badherwa area under control. Brig. G.K. Bakshi, Commander 9 Sector RR, was most energetic in this enterprise. The formations pursued the terrorists in Hill Kaka, upper reaches of Pir Panjal and in-depth areas of Doda–Kishtwar and hunted them down in large numbers.

As a result of these intense operations, Naik Rambeer Singh Tomar of 15 Kumaon serving with 26 RR was awarded an Ashoka Chakra for his bravery on 17 October in Doda area. Subedar Surinder Singh of 3 Sikh was also awarded an Ashoka Chakra for his bravery on 3 March 2002 in Rajouri. When the ISI-guided terrorists targeted Raghunath temple, and some vulnerable points in Jammu, we took the battle to their bases in Kotli; we even bombarded suburbs of Sialkot with great success. A large number of terrorists hiding in mosques in Kotli were killed by our artillery fire attacks. There was no hesitation by us to carry out massive fire assaults on training camps, terrorist rest areas and launch bases. This had a great impact on the civilians in POK who bore the brunt because of terrorists and consequently dissuaded them from entering their villages to avoid retaliation from us. The new surveillance system consisting of ground sensors, electronic devices, night vision devices and aerial platforms was made operational. It was integrated with control centres at Battalion HQ.

It was very effective. Interceptions, digital decoding and jamming also helped us. Very few terrorists could now infiltrate in our territory and those who attempted to were killed before they could cross over. Information started flowing when the local population sensed the tide had turned. Terror financing was also targeted to a large extent by surveillance of suspected bank accounts but we were not entirely successful. The ISI activated the IB sector when infiltration became difficult through the LoC. Initially, a few groups were successful to infiltrate as the fence had not yet been completed and they managed to sneak through the border posts taking advantage of the nalas and tall elephant grass. Usually, they used the gaps between Kathua-Hiranagar-Dhamaal-Samba and Birpur. However, we did not hesitate to punish the enemy with equal ferocity in this sector as well. They were easily identified by the Hindu population and tracking them was easy in hunting down these terrorists. Mortars and guns were used in this sector as well in retaliation that caused great economic and infrastructure damage to the Pakistanis in the Shakargarh Bulge. Pakistan had to now open new routes through Nepal and Bangladesh.

Terrorism dies its natural death when the people are against it. As in Punjab, we involved the people of Jammu in our operations against the terrorists. The Gujjars and Kashmiris were being exploited by the terrorists in the name of religion that fell hollow when terrorism degenerated into rapes, murders, settling personal feuds, extortion and carving areas of influence. Foreign terrorists were not welcomed because of their demanding nature, debauchery, rape and uncouth conduct. The Gujjars in particular were against them. We revived the village defence committees to co-opt people in this fight. Such committees had functioned well in the 1965 and 1971 wars against saboteurs. We recruited volunteers consisting of ex-servicemen, ex-central police forces, police and civilians. Important villages along the IB and depth areas were selected. The VDC consisted of 10 to 15 personnel who were armed with licensed .303 rifles.

They were registered with the DM and SPs and worked under the supervision of the army and local police. The village sarpanch was responsible for their conduct. They were trained by local army units in firing, patrolling, ambushes, information gathering and fighting and holding terrorists till reinforcements arrived from the army or police. The system worked very well and the terrorists felt unsafe entering these areas between the Ravi river and Akhnoor. Once the system proved a success, it was formalized. The VDCs were given the status of SPOs and a stipend of Rs. 1,500. We distributed 2.500 to 3,000 rifles among these volunteers. Later, the Home and Hearth territorial battalions were also created for this purpose.

As I mentioned earlier, Pakistan needed to be punished for using terrorism as an instrument of state policy. This realization had existed in the army since the Punjab problem but all governments since then had been reluctant to take such a decision. We had followed a policy of "Reactive Counter Terrorism" instead of "Proactive Counter Terrorism". No insurgency or terrorism can be defeated that enjoys inviolate sanctuary. The sanctuaries, training area, launch bases and routes of ingress have to be hit hard. Our passivity emboldened Pakistan and terrorism continued to escalate. Terrorism was at an all-time high after General Musharraf seized power in Pakistan. Something bold had to be done to make Pakistan pay for its intransigence. We hoped that the BJP government would support the army plan of action after its bitter experience of war in Kargil.

Sometime in June 2001, a decision at AHQ was taken for punitive action against Pakistan. The aim was to put an end to infiltration and demonstrate the high cost of waging a proxy war. I had always advocated this and assured Lt. Gen. R.K. Nanavatty, the Army Commander, that shallow intrusions in selected areas were possible to capture tactically important areas across the LoC to improve our operational posture. Like in the period preceding the 1965 war, when the Indian Army captured the Haji Pir and other areas that were used by Pakistan for 'Operation Gibraltar', we could do the same on a broad front from Chhamb to Poonch in my Corps zone. A similar operational situation as in August 1965 existed and we had a reason to retaliate. 16 Corps units had carried out successful raids on enemy posts in Chhamb, Akhnoor, Mender, Kotli and Poonch areas between January and August 2000.

It was also an opportunity to do a Kargil on Musharraf. Battalion and brigade size actions from Chhamb to Poonch would not lead to an all-out war as these were within threshold levels. Such local actions were manageable within our resources. Surprise and speed was possible in all these actions that were most essential for success. We pulled out units and formations from the inactive CI grid and put them on training for these tasks. All operational requirements were coordinated without divulging the actual tasks to maintain secrecy. Reconnaissance and briefings had also been completed on a strictly need-to-know basis by the end of August. Artillery ammunition had been dumped secretly and FDCs had been identified. We were sure orders would be received after the failure of the Agra talks between Mr. Vajpayee and Musharraf in July 2001. September was the expected period of these operations. Unfortunately, the orders never came. It was a big disappointment to all of us.

The BJP, particularly Mr. Jaswant Singh, the FM, felt that in spite of all the setbacks suffered by India at Lahore, Kargil, Kandahar and Agra and knowing fully well that Pakistan was engineering terrorism, diplomatic efforts for peace had to continue. Peace had no alternative was a dictum held close by him. It is believed that the 9/11 airstrikes against the Twin Towers in the USA by Al-Qaeda were the reasons for abandonment of these plans. My belief is that the Vajpayee government did not give it political clearance. Basically, the trio formed by Vajpayee, Jaswant Singh and Brajesh Mishra did not have the political courage to give orders in spite of all the bluster as events proved later during "Operation Parakram". Thus, "Operation Kabaddi"[3] was consigned to the archives and a great opportunity to punish Pakistan was missed. India expected the USA to restrain Pakistan in its proxy war with India. This did not happen as the USA did not consider Pakistan's terror against India as part of its fight against international terror in Afghanistan. Pakistan thus continued to bleed India blatantly. The attacks on the Kashmir Assembly followed by the attack on Parliament and then Kaluchak on 14 May 2002 are some of the high-profile terrorist acts that took place under the direct supervision of the ISI.

Since Kaluchak[4] fell in my area of responsibility, the terrorist attack on this target needs to be described in some detail. Our anti-terror operations had succeeded beyond expectations and the punishment through cross-border firing had a telling affect, especially in the IB Sector. This forced Pakistan to launch a terror attack that would put the Kashmir issue on centre stage through shock and publicity. The target chosen was a thinly guarded military station. They managed to infiltrate three terrorists who were staged through Zaffarwal and infiltrated the IB near Vijaynagar. These terrorists were dressed in army combat uniforms and thus remained unsuspected and merged with the locals easily. The Indian Army had been mobilized due to "Operation Parakram" and the garrison of Kaluchak was thus thinly guarded with only families residing there.

The terrorists boarded a Himachal Pradesh bus travelling to Jammu. As they reached Kaluchak, the driver and bus conductor were shot dead and indiscriminate firing killed seven passengers and wounded 15. The army guards of the Kaluchak military garrison that is located on the main road near the bus stand fired at the terrorists who retaliated and managed to enter the garrison. In the ensuing fire fight, the terrorists ran helter-skelter into the family lines and moved from quarter to quarter killing who ever came in their way. They killed 18 family members including 10 children who were getting ready to go to school; 12 were wounded. Children who were hiding under their beds and in bathrooms were killed in cold blood. The pleas of wailing mothers went unheeded by these ruthless bloodthirsty murderers. Ultimately, all the three were killed. Three army personnel were also killed and 12 wounded in the fire fight. A total of 31 people were killed and 47 wounded.

The Pakistani terrorists were identified as Abu Suhail of Faisalabad, Abu Murshed (Mohd Munir) of Salamatpura Gujranwala and Abu Javed (Amzad Salam Bin Mohd Gisha) of Guda Girya Gujranwala. This carnage was condemned and publicized worldwide. Pakistan had achieved its aim. Mr. Vajpayee, the PM, called it "most inhuman and brutal'. Mr. Jaswant Singh, the FM, mentions in his book that this terror act nearly brought the two countries to a war. Mr. George Fernandes, the Defence Minister, visited Kaluchak and the Military Hospital to pay his condolences to the families and interact with those wounded on 15 May 2002. He mentioned to the public and press that Pakistan would not go unpunished for this dastardly act.[5] He evaded the question whether punishment meant war.

Mrs. Sonia Gandhi from the opposition followed suit after a day. Neera my wife conducted her. She was visibly upset and tearful while interacting with the affected families in their quarters and in the hospital. This was one opportunity that should have been used for crossing the border to punish Pakistan as a legitimate response. We were already deployed and it was possible to do so. However, the BJP government did not have the guile and they were ever obliging to the USA to even accept the shame of an attack on Parliament and an army garrison to go unpunished. We were disappointed with the Government's response and the US attitude towards terrorism in India. The Garrison Commander was taken to task for laxity and poor response to the terror attack. I counselled GOC 26 Infantry Division, Maj. Gen. Mohan Pandey as well for this lapse. Over a period of time, Muslim colonies had mushroomed around the city from where underground agents helped these terrorists. Muslims were also allowed to settle on government land along some well-defined infiltration routes as part of a deliberate plan to change the demography of the area. Both the NC and the PDP were part in this plan.

Terrorism cannot be eliminated by active operations alone. Civic actions, development and psychological warfare are important parts of the overall policy. My request to Mrs. Sushma Swaraj, the Information Minister, resulted in repair and reactivation of all AIR relay stations in the Jammu region; they had been burnt down by terrorists. The AIR station at Bhaderwa was inaugurated by Mr. Chaman Lal Gupta, the MOS Defence and BJP MP from Udhampur on 14 July 2002. AIR FM relay stations were also activated at Poonch, Rajouri, Naushera and Kathua. Seven more were planned to cover the entire area. We distributed FM transistor sets to every household in the border belt with fixed channels that could only receive Indian broadcasts to counter Pakistan propaganda. Brig. A.J.S. Lamba, the Chief Signal Officer, conducted the psychological operations very competently and effectively through print and electronic media. Our media cell issued regular bulletins of each operation and activity that we carried out. Monthly briefings of the media were done after each Unified HQ conference. With the 24x7 availability of our media officer, the passage of information to the media was continuous with no scope of speculation by the foreign or national media.

I regularly invited the media heads to our HQ for exchange of views. I was also in regular contact with the local academia, senior retired bureaucrats, service officers and influential community leaders. Mr. Khajuria, ex DGP; Lt. Gen. Wadhera and Maj. Gen. Govardhan Jamwal, all senior retired officers; Mr. Balraj Puri, a renowned intellectual; Mr. Ghosh, a historian in Jammu University; Mr. Raumitra of the *Daily Excelsior* and Mr. Ved Bhasin of *Greater Kashmir* were all helpful in providing us feedback and advice. Mr. Lal Mohd Sabri, Choudhary Mohd Aslam, MP, and Mr. Masood Choudhary IGP, were prominent Gujjar leaders who were a great help in connecting us with their community.

We held a horse show[6] for the first time in Jammu where Mr. Girish Saxena, the Governor, was the chief guest. All the MLAs, ministers, bureaucrats and the gentry of Jammu were present. It was a stupendous success with spectators overflowing the ground. We also celebrated Vijay Diwas[7] on 16 December where Mr. Moiudin Shah, the senior minister, was the chief guest. The locals from all corners of Jammu region participated in the celebrations. Thus, our reach out to the civil population at all levels and good civil-military relations went a long way in eliminating terrorism. Brigadier Y.K. Jain, Chief Engineer, implemented the civic action programme that consisted of creating model villages, hydro-electric projects, construction of health centres, roads and tracks, vocational and computer training centres and electric supply.

We spent Rs. 300 crore in 2001-2002 and Rs. 556 crores in 2002-2003 on these schemes. Sogra and Palma were created as two model villages at a cost of Rs. 80 lakh each as pioneer projects. Every village wanted to be covered under this scheme after the successful completion of these two pilot projects. Fifty schools were renovated, 10 vocational centres were created, five primary health centres, 25 community halls, and 32 toilets were constructed. Eight villages were electrified. One lift irrigation water scheme along with water supply to 30 villages was completed. About 47 km of road were constructed. Brigadier Khuda Baxsh Public School that was run by the Gujjar Desh Charitable Trust was given a functional computer-cum-language laboratory under this scheme. The civil administration and local people were co-opted in all these schemes and the joint effort went a long way in providing good governance that earned us great goodwill.

We sponsored and assisted Jammu University in conducting a seminar[8] on "Jammu & Kashmir: The Way Ahead" on 31 October and 1 November 2001. This was the first of its kind in the entire state where think tanks, defence analysts, politicians and other stakeholders converged on a single platform to discuss the problems that the state was facing and to find the best way to solve them. This was possible because we were able to create a peaceful environment in a short period of six months and now the people were ready to take charge of their destiny. Dr. Mrs. Rekha Choudhary gave the introductory note that was followed by a welcome address by Mr. R.R. Sharma, the VC. Lt. Gen. R.K. Nanavatty, the GOC-in-C, Northern Command, delivered the keynote address that was followed by an address by Mr. Farooq Abdullah, the CM, who was the chief guest. The inaugural address was delivered by Mr. G.C. Saxena, the Governor. The theme of the first session was 'Search for a Viable Solution: Problems and Prospects'. Mr. Salman Haider, ex FS, Mr. Kanti Bajpai, an academic and international affairs analyst, Mr. Balraj Puri, renowned peace activists and journalists and AVM Kapil Kak, a renowned defence analyst, presented papers.

The second session discussed 'The Valley-Centric Dimensions and Measures to Roll Back Terrorism.' This session was chaired by Prof. S.D. Muni of JNU, who had also been ambassador to Nepal. Papers were presented by Riyaz Punjabi, Dr. Mohd Wani and Dr. Rekha Chowdhary. A panel discussion followed that consisted of Mr. Nur Mohd Baba, Mr. Mirajuddin, Mr. Gohar Fazli and Choudhary Shaukat Javed. The second day session discussed 'Role of Media'. This was chaired by Mr. Shekhar Gupta. Papers were presented by Dr. Raja Mohan, Ved Bhasin and Vipul Mudgal. All of them were eminent journalists and belonged to J&K. This was followed by the valedictory session addressed by me and Mr. Farooq Abdullah, the CM. The seminar ended on a very high note. All aspects of terrorism in J&K were discussed by the stakeholders without pressure of fear or prejudice. The outcome was accepted by the public. The seminar sent a clear message to Pakistan that its interference was not welcome. Major General A.S. Bhaya, GOC, 10 Infantry Division, played a major role in the successful conduct of this seminar.

Besides a large number of visitors, the military attachés of all countries except Pakistan were hosted by us on 11 April 2001 and 26 July 2002. I had recommended their visit to show the international community Pakistan's direct involvement in terrorism and to nail all its lies on human rights violations. We allowed them a visit to the Kashmiri Pandit refugee camp where they were told horrid tales of torture, rape, destruction and murder. We also took them to the LoC where they witnessed ceasefire violations and heard firsthand accounts of harassment caused by terrorists to the local population. They also witnessed development projects. Mr. Robert D. Blackwill, the US ambassador, along with a 10-member team including Admiral Thomas Wilson visited us on 20 January 2002 after "OP Parakram" had been launched.

He was first briefed by the CM, where Mr. Ashok Jetly, the CS, Mr. C. Phunsog, the Home Secretary, Mr. A.K. Suri, the DGP, and I were in attendance. I then briefed him with Admiral Wilson and the US Military Attaché in our operations room. I told the ambassador forthrightly that Pakistan was waging relentless terrorism against us because the USA was turning a blind eye to its involvement. I also told him that we were ready for war and if it took place it would be very violent and disastrous for Pakistan. Nuclear blackmail would not work this time and unlike Kargil, India will take the war into Pakistan territory. He asked my views on the Gujarat riots and I replied that the state government actions were justified and if such incidents took place again involving the two communities the result would be catastrophic for the Muslims as other parts of India could also get involved. The Hindu pent-up anger against Pakistan would be released on Indian Muslims.

I also informed him that India could abrogate the Indus Water Treaty if Pakistan did not behave. He mentioned that the USA did not have much control on Pakistan and they could apply pressure on them only to a certain extent. He also admitted that the USA tended to ignore the errant deeds/misdemeanours of their allies like Pakistan if they were helpful to them in achieving their larger global aims. He implied this to Pakistan's clandestine nuclear activities and acts of terror for helping them defeat the USSR in Afghanistan and current operations against Al-Qaeda and the Taliban. My briefing was meant to convey that India would no longer tolerate brazen acts of terror and that the Indian Army was determined to punish Pakistan. The message was conveyed to the USA as expected by the AHQ/MOD.

Mr. George Fernandes, the RM, was a regular visitor to us. He was very informal, undemanding, a good listener and very analytical. He would order prompt action on points projected by us to him. I developed a close professional relationship with him that lasted lifelong. He visited us on 6 April 2002 when he was briefed on the overall operational situation against the background of "Operation Parakram". He interacted with the troops and had meals with them. His next visit was on 5 May 2002 when he visited Rajouri and Poonch to interact with the troops deployed on the LoC. He also witnessed cross-border firing and our troops bursting Pak army bunkers in his presence. His visit on 15 May was aimed at meeting the victims of the Kaluchak carnage by Pak terrorists. He visited the homes of all the families and the Jammu MH to assure the injured of punishment to the perpetrators. His last visit was on 21 June to take stock of the operational situation, meet people who had been displaced due to cross-border firing in the IB sector due "Op Parakram" and the state assembly elections due in October/November that year.

The parliament committee on defence also visited us in the wake of "Parakram". We took them to the border areas to apprise them of our defence preparedness and the need for more UAVs, short and medium range missiles for interdicting targets in Pakistan, modern AD systems and complete radar coverage of the area of responsibility. They also visited the camping arrangements of displaced people in the IB sector. Mr. Lyngdoh, the EC, with his team visited us and after my briefing he was convinced that elections could be held for the state assembly in October/November as planned. These were hailed as the fairest elections both by internal and international observers.

The operational tasks of 16 Corps entailed both defensive and offensive operations. We trained and exercised 29, 39 Infantry Divisions, 2 (I) and 3 (I) Armoured Brigades for offensive tasks and restoration of adverse situations. Similarly, 26 and 10 Infantry Division were practiced their operational roles. 25 Infantry Division was the largest formation deployed from Nawshera to Poonch. They were engaged in continuous border cross-firing and counter infiltration. The operational situation was managed effectively by them. Our exercises and operational rehearsals proved useful during "Operation Parakram" in December 2001.

I had inherited a very efficient Corps staff. Brigadier P.C. Dass and R.S. Jambusarwala were BGS and Brig. Administration when I took charge. Brigadier P.C. Bharadwaj and S.K. Sinha replaced them. They were outstanding in their jobs. Brig. Amresh Prasad, Commander, 16 Corps Artillery Brigade, Brig. V.K. Govil, Brig. EME, and Brig. R.P. Singh followed by Y.K. Suri as DDMS and Brig. Punita Arora, Commandant, Jammu Military Hospital, were also great assets. Col. A.K. Choudhary and Col. N.J.S. Gill of 662 Aviation Squadron and Col. Kulwant Singh, Int Corps also rendered yeoman service. My personal staff was equally good. Colonel K.V.S. Laotra, an officer of exceptional abilities managed the secretariat. He was assisted by Maj. P. Saxena, Atul Solanki and Capt. Amit Yadav, ADC.

The most important event of my tenure was "Operation Parakram". People also call it 'War Unfinished' or 'A War Gone Wrong.'[9] Twenty-seven persons were killed when terrorists attacked the J&K Assembly on 1 October 2001. The Pakistan Rangers deliberately disturbed fence construction in the IB sector. Our response was swift and furious. We blew up their civilian assets in the area opposite our posts and shelled the suburbs of Sialkot extensively on 12 and 13 October. This action was covered widely by the media as it was on a day penultimate to the visit by Gen. Collin Powell, the secretary of state for defence, USA. After the attack on the J&K Assembly, Mr. Vajpayee, the PM, had written to Mr. Bush, the President of USA, that India's patience was running out and Pakistan must be reined in. Mr. Powell's visit to Pakistan and India may have been in that context. Musharraf's statements during Powell's visit to Pakistan did not indicate that Pakistan would stop terrorism in Kashmir as the USA did not group terrorists operating in J&K with those in Afghanistan. Powell's statements in Pakistan also did not indicate that Indian concerns on terrorism were a US priority.

To them, Pakistani support for "Operation Enduring Freedom" was more important than India's security concerns. Yet, India relied on the USA. I was called up by Army HQ to say that my actions may affect the talks with Mr. Powell during his visit from 14 October 2001 and as such I was reprimanded and cautioned not to escalate the situation. I replied that my actions were in response to Pakistani terror attacks. The media had projected my actions as retaliation by India and my statement that India would not hesitate to take even stronger measures if Pakistan persisted with terrorism in future very prominently. Perhaps this message may have influenced the US visiting team as well and it appears that my military actions helped the MEA during their discussions that India's patience was indeed running out. I was informed the next day that I was free to act in the way I considered militarily correct.

However, Mr. Jaswant Singh, the Foreign Minister, announced that India would do nothing to put Pakistan under military pressure. In hindsight, Gen. Colin Powell managed to win over the Indians, lulled them with vague assurances and succeeded in his agenda to keep Musharraf on board in the war against Afghanistan and keep India engaged with various allurements. Then the attack on the Indian Parliament came on 13 December 2001 when it was in session. It was a huge embarrassment to the government. They had to do something for domestic political reasons and to send a message to Pakistan and the international community.

The Indian Army was mobilized on 18 December 2001. We were in our battle locations and ready. 1 Corps and 3 Corps were also in our area by the end of December. We were to provide them a firm base and launch subsidiary operations along with their operations. We had coordinated all our actions with Lt. Gen. J.J. Singh, GOC 1 Corps, Lt. Gen. V.K. Jetly,

GOC 3 Corps, and the IAF by the first week of January but the orders did not come. The first indication of hesitance on part of the government came on 5/6 January 2002 when 2 Corps was halted in its tracks while moving to the forward assembly area and Lt. Gen. Kapil Vig, the GOC, replaced. The next indication came on 11 January 2002 when Gen. S. Padmanabhan, the COAS, announced to the media that the Indian Army was ready but awaiting political clearance. We had thus missed a second opportunity to punish Pakistan within six months.

It transpires that on 17 December, Gen. Musharraf had held a meeting of his corps commanders and Mr. Vajpayee had called a meeting of the CCS on the same day, where the three Chiefs were present. No decision was taken then. However, on 17 and 18 December there was very heavy cross-border firing in the Naushera and Rajouri sectors from both sides and civilians had to be evacuated as a precautionary measure against Pakistan artillery fire in depth areas. This escalation seems to have prompted the PM to call the Chiefs again on 18 December and ordered mobilization. It is understood that no written or oral directive was issued or political/military aim given out. Mr. Jaswant Singh[10] was against the war and he managed to convince his political colleagues and the three Service Chiefs to exercise restraint and to control the country's mood – to contain its belligerence, and its desire for revenge and retaliation.

After the mobilization, there was no bar on us to fire on the entire front. Our focus had shifted to the IB sector where it hurt the Pakistanis the most. Our artillery fire set ablaze standing crops and some villages in the Shakargarh area. Pakistan was forced to vacate all the villages in the Shakargarh Bulge and it hurt it badly economically and the Punjabi population. We also evacuated our civilians to safe camps but our loss was not much compared to theirs. We also blew up all defence structures on the enemy's side. Our snipers were very effective both during day and night and many Pakistani soldiers were killed or wounded as a result. We were allotted UAVs that were employed very aggressively all along the front day and night. We had a complete picture of the Pakistani build-up opposite us, deployment of their guns, tanks and even missiles. Live pictures were available at the brigade command posts.

The Air Defence Centre under Brigadier Praveen Paul, Commander, 611 AD Brigade, was fully operational and integrated with the IAF. He was confident that the entire front was covered with our radars at all altitudes and it was not easy for the enemy to intrude. Many a time, our UAVs were detected and enemy fighter aircraft scrambled against them but we were able to complete our missions without any harm or the loss of a UAV. The Pakistanis also launched their fighters against my helicopter reconnaissance along the border a number of times but we managed to evade their tracking radar by Lo-Lo and nap-of-the-earth flying. Many a time we made emergency landings in fields to dodge them.

Gen. S. Padmanabhan also visited our Corps HQs. We flew over the operational area and discussed our plans. I assured him that we were capable of achieving all our objectives and would make sure both 1 and 3 Corps got our full support. He was extremely pleased when I assured him that the mistakes made by the Indian Army in 1947 and 1965 would be redeemed. He was happy to learn that our corps objectives were in conformity with those in his mind.

After our mobilization, the USA and the West were worried and a number of visits, including that of British PM, Mr. Tony Blair, on 5 January 2002 took place to cool the Indian temper. India was asked to await a speech to the nation by Gen. Musharraf on 12 January 2002. Pakistan did announce some cosmetic measures against the terrorists on that day but it fell well short of our expectations. Gen. Powell was again in India on 17 January as part of his mission on how to avoid war between the two countries. Such visits and vague promises lulled India time and again. India should have realized that it had to fight its own war and there was no escaping from it. We were naïve to believe that the USA and the West would now be on our side to fight international terrorism and share our perception of good and bad terrorists.

While India called Pakistan the epicentre of terrorism, the West considered it an ally and a victim. Musharraf had won the confidence of the US and Western alliance and so did nothing to stop the terrorists. Gen. Musharraf as a military man had a better equation with Gen. Powell than Jaswant Singh, who had also been an army major. So things went the way Pakistan and the USA wanted. Mr. Robert D. Blackwill, the US Ambassador, visited my HQ in this context on 20 January. I am sure he would have warned the USA then that Indian Army was ready for war and would cause great damage to Pakistan if it came to be.

The US game plan should have become clear to the Indian leadership when Mr. Bush, in his state of the union address to congress on 29 January, directly blamed Iraq, Iran and North Korea for international terrorism by calling them axes of evil but left out Pakistan. Even Mr. Powell did not mention Pakistan in passing when he expanded the list to include Syria, Libya, Cuba, and Sudan. India thus sacrificed its own security interests in the hope to endear itself to the USA. Therefore, the formations remained deployed on a highly volatile LoC without any directive for war. The Pakistanis damaged our transformer and planted some mines that damaged a tractor in the Chicken Neck area.[11] They also continued to disturb our fence construction with firing. We retaliated violently to these actions and the entire area opposite us was laid to waste by artillery fire.

The period up to 14 May 2002 passed off with diminishing hopes of war but the attack by LET terrorists on the army camp at Kaluchak on that day changed the scenario once again. The attack has been described by me in detail in the preceding paragraphs. It was an act that could not be ignored. General Padmanabhan, who was on a visit to Nepal, said that the time for action had come. Even Parliament allowed the government to take action as deemed fit. Mr. Vajpayee, the PM, during a visit to Kupwara on 22 May, asked the army to prepare for decisive action. We were sure that D-Day would be announced soon and we remained ready to be launched at 24 hours' notice.

Having realized the gravity of the situation, President Bush and Colin Powell were in confabulations with Musharraf and the Indian leadership. This time, India had made only one demand – that Pakistan stop infiltration. The USA was able to come to some secret understanding that if Pakistan agreed to this demand from India, then it will ask India to consider the core issue of Kashmir seriously. Some analysts had argued that India was afraid of war escalating to the nuclear level and that the Indian leadership was also afraid of annoying the USA. This created a hesitation in issuing the final order to the defence forces. Pakistan had once again played the nuclear blackmail card successfully.

On the contrary, we were prepared for this eventuality and knew the Pakistan nuclear threshold well. Our Prithvi missiles had been deployed in my corps zone and we would have retaliated if they attacked. NBC suites had been selectively distributed. Thus, an assurance from Mr. Powell to the Indian leadership that Pakistan would stop infiltration was enough to put off the war. We witnessed the Indian political mindset at a meeting with the PM on 23 May at Srinagar.[12] The PM, after his visit to Kupwara, held a meeting of the Unified HQ at the SKICC on the Dal Lake. The HM, RM, Governor and the CM, were also present. The intelligence set-up headed by IB Chief Mr. K.M. Singh, all heads of CPFO and DGP J&K and important bureaucrats headed by the CS were also in attendance. The army hierarchy consisting of the Army Commander and the three Corps Commanders completed the list.

We were told that the PM would take a decision on war with Pakistan after inputs given by all of us and as such it was a very crucial meeting. To me, it looked very unusual that a meeting of such a large number of people, some of ADG level, in a convention centre was either a deception or a method of conveying some message to the enemy and the USA. It was certainly not a place and forum to give orders for war. The proceedings started with the CM addressing the gathering and expressing his views on the internal situation. The IB Chief and ADG CID (J&K) gave their assessments of the terrorist activities. Nothing new that was already known to all of us was read out. The DG BSF and DGP J&K also talked on the same lines. The Governor, Mr. G.C. Saxena, spoke in non-specific terms about the prevailing situation and added that holding of elections in October would bring about an improvement in the security situation.

The RM wanted the SF to find an answer to the unending infiltration and some other issues unrelated to mobilization or war were raised by him. The HM asked the SF to raise the cost of terrorism for Pakistan. The PM addressed us in the end. He talked of development projects in J&K and that people had to be won over in this fight against terror as we had done in Punjab. He also praised the SF and asked them to defeat terrorism and find ways of preventing fidaydeen attacks. From his talk and the entire meeting, it was obvious that war with Pakistan was not on his mind. The Army Commander may have briefed him separately but we were not asked for our views. As soon as the PM stopped speaking, we all knew that there would be no war and that the threats of action against Pakistan by the PM were hollow and empty. We returned to our HQs disappointed.

As soon as Musharraf knew that chances of war had receded, his speech on 27 May was belligerent and once again made it clear that he was in no mood to relent. Pakistan test-fired their nuclear-capable missiles to indicate nuclear threat-nuclear blackmail as in the past. A number of visits from the USA to India and Pakistan took place in June and July to avert war. It started with Jack Straw the UK Foreign Secretary, followed by Mr. Armitage, US Deputy Secretary of State, on 16 June and Mr. Donald Rumsfeld, the US Defence Secretary, on 20 June. During this period, Mr. Jaswant Singh was replaced as the FM as he had failed to get the requisite US support against Pakistan-sponsored terrorism and had fallen prey to duplicity on their part. His policy of coercive diplomacy against Pakistan had totally failed. However, India finally got a firm assurance on 16 June from Mr. Armitage that Pakistan had agreed to stop cross-border terrorism and would close down all terrorist camps in POK. In reciprocity, India immediately recalled its naval ships and opened its airspace for Pakistani aircraft. India also seems to have agreed to demobilize after elections in J&K in October as a quid pro quo. Thus, the high drama of war with Pakistan ended with a whimper. We now settled down to counter-terrorist operations even more vigorously than before to prepare a peaceful environment for the elections.

By the middle of June 2002, it was apparent that war would not take place. I was able to get a month's leave when Kanu and Ajay were married on 4 July 2002. Dr. Ajay was pursuing his post-graduation in surgery at Maulana Azad Medical College and Kanu had finished her MBBS from Rohtak Medical College. It was a simple and austere affair keeping in view the environment of war. By August, it was realized that mobilization was giving diminishing returns. Neither Pakistan nor the USA was serious about it. Due to large-scale deployment, a number of terrorists were killed and it became a disincentive for infiltration. There was a drop in infiltration by some measures taken by Pakistan also.

After successful conduct of elections, demobilization was ordered on 16 October. Thus, a sterile mobilization ended after 10 months of deployment. It cost the nation Rs. 8,000 crore, extensive wear and tear of equipment and allied administrative and operational problems. Nearly Rs. 300 crore was paid to evacuees from border areas in compensation. The mobilization resulted in some gains for us. Our mobilization drills were practiced. Operational and administrative plans were validated. Coordination with 1 and 3 Corps and the IAF was achieved. Deficiencies in equipment were made up. India's nuclear doctrine became credible and a nuclear command post was established. New technology weapons, missiles and deep penetration bombers were acquired. Satellite, air surveillance and UAVs were given importance. AD cover was strengthened and the number of special forces units was increased.

We also achieved some advantages at the political and international levels as given out by Mr. George Fernandes in Parliament on 20 November 2002. He said that the mobilization exerted tremendous pressure on Pakistan and Gen. Musharraf was forced to call off support to terrorists. Pakistan banned some terrorist groups and closed terrorist camps in POK. The mobilization also focused attention of the international community on Pakistan as a state that was sponsoring terrorism. Elections could be held peacefully in J&K and the defence forces gained experience in war fighting.

However, "Operation Parakram" is also described as a failure and a futile exercise that exposed the weakness in decision making, political will to fight war, excessive dependence on the USA and knee-jerk action by the defence forces without obtaining a war directive from the government or political and operational aims. Mr. Vajpayee could not muster enough political courage to take mobilization to its logical conclusion. It is said he regretted later his decision not to go to war. Demobilization was ordered after a presentation made by the NSAB on 16 October 2002. It was called strategic relocation instead of demobilization. By the end of August, by which time it was amply clear that there would be no war, I received my posting orders as DCOAS at Army HQ. Elections to the state assembly were held in September-October 2002 immediately thereafter and hailed as most fair. The Peoples' Democratic Party under Mufti Mohd. Sayeed, replaced the Omar Abdullah government (1996-2002) with support of the Congress party.

NOTES

1. *Amar Ujala*, *Dainik Jagran*, 17 November 2001; *Daily Excelsior*, 28 December 2001; *Kashmir Times*, 26 February 2002.
2. *Front Line*, 4 July 2003. Operations conducted in 2003 were grossly exaggerated by GOC R Force.3. *India at Risk* by Jaswant Singh, pp. 218-219.
3. Personal notes. *Line of Fire: Ceasefire Violations and India–Pakistan Escalation Dynamics* by Honneymon Jacob.
4. *Hindustan Times*, *Tribune*, *The* Hindu, *Dainik Jagran*, and *Daily Excelsior*, 16 May 2002.
5. *Hindustan Times*, *Tribune*, *Greater Kashmir*, *Dainik Jagran* and *Excelsior*, 16 May 2002.
6. *Hindustan Times*, 17 November 2001.
7. *Daily Excelsior*, *State Times*, 15 December 2001.
8. *Kashmir Times*, *The Tribune*, *Dainik Jagran*, *Himalayan Mail*, *Daily Excelsior* of 1 November 2001.
9. '*Operation Parakram*' by Lt. Gen. V.K. Sood and Pravin Sawhney.
10. '*India At Risk*', by Jaswant Singh, p. 249. He states that the aims of Operation Parakram, according to him, were 1. To end cross-border infiltration/terrorism without conflict; 2. To contain national mood to 'teach Pakistan a lesson', and 3. In the event of war, to degrade and destroy Pakistan's war fighting capability.
11. *Daily Excelsior*, 10 May 2002.
12. The record of the meeting is from my personal notes.

Map 17: Jammu Sector (Road and Rail Links)

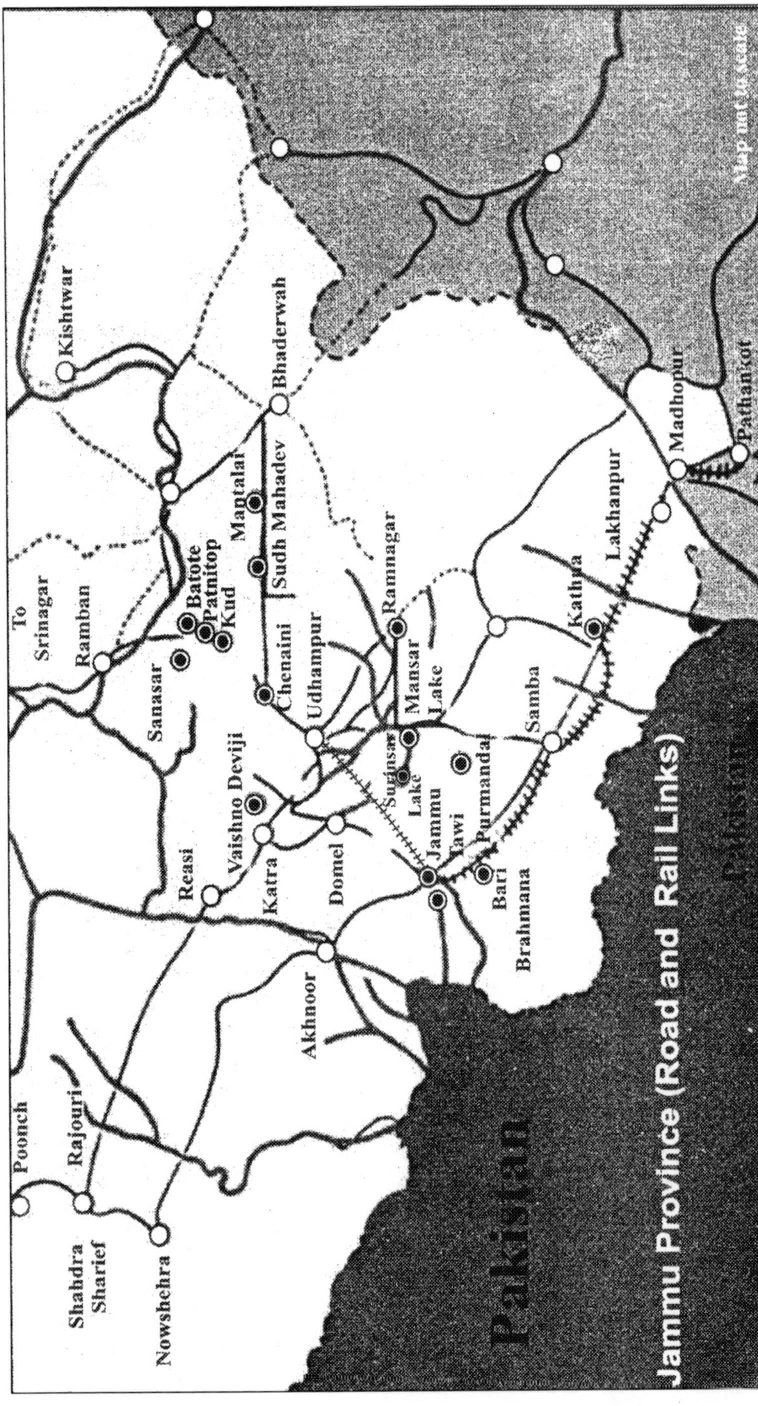

Chapter 8

Army HQ, New Delhi

Indian Army HQ is located in the majestic South Block, and Sena Bhavan, a huge modern complex but out of sync with the grand architecture of the buildings on Raisina Hill, and the hutments of Second World War vintage. To a large extent, we still followed the British methods of working and organization. The Ministry of Defence supervised our functioning and it was the final authority in most matters, even though devolution of financial and administrative powers existed to conduct business. The ministry maintained a parallel filing system and every project with major financial implications or affecting policy had to be approved by them. This effectively curbed independent functioning and initiative of staff officers and resulted in delays and inefficiency.

Over a period of time, the supremacy of the legislative over defence resulted in bureaucratic control. The defence secretary, though lower in precedence than the three service chiefs, called the shots as he was responsible for the defence of India as per the rules of business laid down by the Government. I was fully conversant with the environment having served in the AHQ twice earlier. Projects or proposals were approved only if the ministry was kept on the right side. Promotion of officers of the rank of lieutenant general was decided by the Cabinet Committee for appointments and those of brigadiers and above by the MOD.

The government had generally followed the principle of seniority in higher promotions since 1947. This system did not ensure long and stable tenures. Even less meritorious officers got promoted and that led to dismal performances during 1962 and 1965 and, in a few cases, even during the 1971 war. General Sunderji got this system changed. An officer with two years of residual service only would now be promoted to army commander and the chief. This system ensured a stable tenure but date of birth became all important and merit took a back seat again. Many meritorious and competent officers lost out and the army was deprived of the best talent. Thus, the appointment of an army commander became a weak link in the chain of operational command from which the COAS is also selected. Manipulations, favouritism, regimental loyalties, pliability, and play safe were important to reach this rank.

I was appointed DCOAS even though quite junior to all principal staff officers. The DCOAS had its origin in the chief of general staff - an all-powerful post till 1966. It was abolished and the post of VCOAS and DCOAS were created out of it. Very eminent officers had held the appointments of CGS and DCOAS before me. Military operations and military intelligence were now supervised by the VCOAS. All other general staff functions were left with the DCOAS. General Sunderji split the DCOAS in DCOAS (T&C) and DCOAS (P&S), thus diluting the appointment further.

While DCOAS (T&C) dealt with training, coordination and all other general staff functions, DCOAS (P&S) was responsible for planning and systems - basically the acquisition of weapons and equipment. In my view, this bifurcation was unnecessary. The DCOAS (T&C) still retained its superiority over the other principal staff officers and represented the COAS when required. Supervision of training, both technical and non technical, still remained my main responsibility even though the ARTRAC had been created.

All the training establishments, including the College of Combat, DSSC, IMA, OTAs, NDA, LDMC, RIMC, military schools and arms and services training establishments, PT school, Army school of education and High altitude school were under my jurisdiction. Except the E-in-C, all the arms directorates, staff duties, ASECS and admin and coordination, the TA and DSC were also my responsibility. I also supervised the training and deployment of UN contingents. Training with foreign armies was an important responsibility. After India's dismal performance at the Sydney Olympics in 2000, "Mission Olympics" was launched by the government that became a major additional responsibility of the DCOAS. Information technology, automation, communications, networking and functioning of the war deck also fell in my charter of duties.

Since training was our main charter, I visited the OTA, Madras, as my first assignment and reviewed its passing-out parade as the chief guest. The OTA has blossomed into one of the finest training institutions and cadets trained by it have done the country proud. Thereafter, I visited all the institutions within the first few weeks and asked them to formulate a vision paper to make training not only contemporary but futuristic. Automation, computerization, and simulator-based training were to be given primacy. Every institution was advised to establish links with leading civilian academic institutions in the country in their field for flow-in of knowledge. Every institution was to hold at least one national and one international seminar in their respective fields.

Exchange of faculty and students was encouraged not only within the premier institutions in the country but with institutions in the USA, Russia, UK, and France as well. Policy on training with foreign armies was liberalized after sustained efforts and we commenced participating in both bilateral and multilateral training exercises with troops. Visits by the cadets of the NDA and IMA to military academies at Sandhurst and West Point and other countries were undertaken. These measures not only helped in formulations of doctrines and concepts, learning new methods of war fighting but also in gaining knowledge about new technologies, weapon systems and promotion of defence diplomacy.

Major General Ashok Vasudeva, H.S. Panag and later Lt. Gen. Bhupinder Singh steered the MT Directorate very ably and efficiently. MT 2 under Colonel A. Ambere and MT 16 under K.A. Mutthana added value to the job. My training responsibilities took me to some very remote but excellent institutions that I had not visited during my service. The Army School of Education at Pachmarhi was one of them. Pachmarhi is located on the Satpura plateau in central India. It was under the control of Gond tribal chieftains till the Holkars became rulers of this region. The British discovered it in 1857 when their forces under Captain James Forsyth and Subedar Major Nathoo Ramji Powar were traversing this area to join the fight against the Rani of Jhansi. Nathoo Ramji later held the appointment of kotwal at Pachmari.

It is located at an altitude of 1,067 metres and had an excellent weather round the year. They established a cantonment, sanatorium and a hill station here. Pachmarhi also became the summer capital of Central Provinces. The area has pristine teak forests and abounds in wildlife. It has many waterfalls, lakes and caves. It was declared a reserve biosphere and conservation area in 1990. The town is very small with old British bungalows, an Angelic church built in 1875 and barracks as new constructions have been banned since 1990. The Army School of Education was shifted to Pachmarhi in 1939. It was designated as Army Education Corps Training College in 1961 and affiliated to Sagar University.

It recruited education havildars, and trained unit education instructors and librarians. It also conducted training in map reading and in Bachelor of Education Technology. The School of Martial Music was also located here and has done very well. It has trained outstanding music/band masters. The museum houses some rare music scores and instruments dating as far back as 1757. The library has preserved all these musical scores used by bands of the 556 state Forces, East India Company and later British India Army unit bands. I directed the ADG, Major General K.A. Bhatt and later O.P. Panwar to recruit B.Ed. qualified personnel directly from colleges to cut down training time. I also asked them to switch to smart classes, and create language, computer and math's laboratories. Every AEC officer had to be given teaching experience and appointed the principal of Sainik School to enhance their skills. All corps personnel were to be skilled to perform intelligence work.

The Defence Service Corps Training School located at Kannur in Kerala had also received scant attention even though the corps was performing vital security duties when terrorist activities were at an all-time high. The corps was required to guard defence installations, factories and depots. In the pre-independence period, these duties were performed by civilian watch and ward staff, chowkidars and garrison troops. It was reorganized as defence

Index

department constabulary with police badges in 1947 under the Ministry of defence. It was further reformed and renamed the Ministry of Defence Security Corps in 1948. Finally, it was placed under the army in 1958 with similar ranks and terms and conditions of service.

It was required to guard and defend all army, navy, air force and civil defence installations against theft, internal and external sabotage, fire, pillage or arson. The force enrolled superannuated personnel from the three services and the Territorial Army. It was thus composed of experienced and trained manpower. This also gave a second career to retired personnel. The corps training centre was located along a scenic coastal belt of Kannur town. The town had a long history of trade with the Arab peninsula and most of the people even now worked in the Gulf countries. It was dotted with affluent houses and ornate mosques.

The corps had carried out its duties very well but the security environment changed drastically after the 1990s with terrorists and anti-national elements using very sophisticated means to sabotage and destroy our vital installations. A number of fires in various depots had destroyed thousands of tons of valuable ammunition and stores. In most cases, sabotage was suspected that went undetected as the corps was not prepared for these challenges. Thus, their training had to be immediately redesigned and upgraded and new equipment provided to them. I visited the training centre frequently. We introduced new equipment for detection and surveillance by day and night. Intruder alarms, and surveillance by CCTV and metallic detectors were also introduced. The men were trained in searching, patrolling and intelligence collection besides day and night guard duties. This improved our effectiveness and efficiency in dealing with challenges and there were no incidents of sabotage thereafter.

Major General Charanjit Singh, a competent and enthusiastic ADG Aviation officer, informed me that the IAF was reluctant to allot them the required vacancies for pilot training and there was likely to be big shortfall of helicopter pilots in his corps in the immediate future. This would lead to serious implications on operational efficiency and functioning of helicopter units. This was a deliberate attempt by the IAF to compel Army Aviation to be placed under its control again.

It is then that we decided to establish an independent combat army aviation training establishment under my financial and administrative powers. The ASEC was able to find the required number of technical as well as general duties officers, JCOs and men to manage the establishment from within the army. It was decided to establish the institution at Nasik within the Artillery School and Centre that had been its parent arm. Nasik was a historic place and a seat of governance to many Hindu and later Muslim kingdoms. It was ceded by the Peshwas to the British in 1820. They created a cantonment at this place later. The School of Artillery became a lodger establishment. It had good weather all the year around for flying with surplus accommodation and land. I released funds for the training infrastructure and other expenditure.

Thus, an establishment was created without additional cost to the Government. The plan was duly approved by the COAS and the MOD as it had cost nothing to the Government. I asked Gen. Charanjit to draw up a vision plan for the corps that was to include not only basic training of pilots but conversion and advance as well. They were to teach tactics and operational doctrine in all such roles as reconnaissance and observation, troop carrying and evacuation, communications and as attack platforms including mobile air pivots. This was our singular achievement and I was able to inaugurate the Training Establishment as also preside over its maiden training-cum-operation conference.

The Aviation Corps has since grown and is capable of undertaking all types of roles and operates a variety of helicopters. We allowed officers from other arms to serve in the corps on deputation as lateral entries. This scheme proved a great success. We now had pilots from all the arms that brought a wealth of experience and talent to the corps. We also introduced training programs for our pilots with the USA, UK, France and Russia on a reciprocal basis for wider exposure as they had more experience in heli operations and had better machines.

The Territorial Army was yet another organization that received my special attention. It was headed by Maj. General Dalbir Singh, a paratrooper of great professional repute. He was an experienced soldier with ideas and indulged in his work with great enthusiasm. We both wanted the TA concept to grow and expand. It could supplement the war effort substantially at a lower cost when needed, as it was not possible to have a standing army beyond the present manpower ceiling limits. We rationalized the TA battalions as per operational necessities and relocated them. Some of them were mobilized in rotation to keep them operationally ready. Our main achievement was in raising the Home and Hearth battalions for J&K and NE. These battalions consisted of local youths who could be utilized for internal security duties, intelligence gathering and also as feeders to regular units. These battalions also generated employment as well as a sense of discipline and patriotism among the youth. This plan was approved by the MOD and implemented by us on a fast track basis.

The major arms and services like mechanized forces, artillery, signals, infantry, Rashtriya Rifles, ASC, ordnance, and army medical corps had very senior officers as their Director General. I visited all of them and held extensive discussions on modernization of training and helped them towards their planning and growth. The AD College that had moved to Gopalpur on the Odisha coast recently was given special attention and help by us. Lt. Gen. Chand, the DG, took great interest in its growth. Similarly we assisted the RR Hospital and Army Dental Corps in creating an E library and conduct of seminars by allocating large sums of training grants. My meetings with all the DGs were very fruitful on future training concepts. I remodelled their annual conferences to a platform of learning and exchange of ideas where experts discussed operational and administrative matters pertaining to the growth of their corps. Papers were presented and discussed on contemporary and futuristic topics in these conferences; everything else became secondary.

One of the important functions of the DCOAS was to select, train and position troops for UN Missions. India had a long history of participating in UN Military Missions since 1950 in Korea. Since then, we had participated in 49 missions and provided more than 200,000 troops. Between 2000 and 2005, we had fielded 7,850 troops in 10 missions. We had military observers in every UN mission. I had always been of the opinion that we should take an active part in all UN Missions offered to us. These deployments gave our troops an opportunity to function in an international environment, prepare them for inter-operability in a multi-force environment and judge their comparability.

Our troops excelled in all the missions and handled their responsibilities very efficiently. They earned immense goodwill in every country and helped in creating strong friendly relations with them. The directorate had a special section headed by a brigadier for this purpose. Units were selected as per UN mandates in consultation with the MO Directorate and then equipped and trained at Delhi Cantonment and Khanpur Camp under our supervision. We also carried out training of UN Observers from different countries at the Centre for UN Peace Keeping (CUNPK) located in the USI premises by a faculty in subjects like protecting civilians, building the rule of law, securing institutions, advising political solutions to conflict, promoting human rights, protecting women and children from abuse and exploitation, development of skills in youth and steps to bring about stability and peace in conflict-torn societies.

The Centre organized international training capsules for military contingents, officers, military observers, and staff and logistics officers. It also held seminars, joint working groups and command post exercises at national and international levels. This department was very competently handled by Major General K.S. Jamwal, Brig. V.K. Ahluwalia and later Brig. C.K.S. Sabbu. It has, since 2005, become a Secretariat of International Association of Peace Keeping Training Centres. Our attempts to create a CUNPK could not materialize due to financial reasons. I visited our missions in Lebanon and Eretria and was very happy to note their excellent work.

I also visited the UN Department of Peace Keeping Operations at New York and had a dialogue with Under Secretary General, Department of Peace Keeping, Mr. Jean Marie Guehenno, about our contributions and also about future training programs and deployment of UN advisors. I proposed that India should be given an opportunity to field an Advisor to the UN Secretary-General as the largest and oldest contributor of peace keepers to the UN. I recommended the name of Lt. Gen. R.K. Mehta after the COAS had approved him. He visited India to see our infrastructure and training modules and met a number of senior officers who had been either force commanders, commanders of Indian contingents and advisors/ observers including Lt. Gen. Satish Nambiar and others. Lt. Gen. R.K. Mehta, an outstanding officer, was selected and appointed as the Adviser to the UN General-Secretary, Mr. Kofi Anan, a second officer from India after Major General Inder Rikhe. It was a great achievement on our part.

Training with foreign countries on a bilateral and multilateral basis was also taken up with equal enthusiasm. This subject was connected with our foreign policy and relations with various countries. We were generally reluctant to engage with countries that were friendly with our adversaries. I however felt that the best way to know our adversary and neutralize his propaganda was to be associated with his friends. Our approach has paid great dividends and grown many times since then. India now trains with almost all her neighbours and important countries. This has also benefitted us in learning new concepts and gaining knowledge about new weapon platforms.

The number of officers attending important courses in foreign countries on a reciprocal basis was increased. We also provided military advisers and training teams to friendly countries in Africa. I visited our training team in Zambia that had established the Zambian staff college under Colonel Umesh Gurung and had very fruitful discussions with Lt. Gen. I.S.A. Chisuzi, their Army Chief. I had the opportunity to visit the famous Victoria Falls on the Zambezi River that is shared by both Zimbabwe and Zambia. We also visited the wildlife park that was teeming with almost all kinds of animals. Animals living in harmony with nature was a sight that cannot be described in a few words.

I also visited our military training adviser, Brig. Padam Budhwar, in Lesotho, a small and picturesque country in the heart of South Africa. Our training team in Bhutan under Major General S.S. Dhillon had made an outstanding contribution. I had an audience with HH, the King of Bhutan, who was very happy with our training team. Soon thereafter, the Royal Bhutan army carried out successful operations in coordination with the Indian Army against sanctuaries of ULFA insurgents in their country that had become a threat to peace in Bhutan and safe heavens for operations in Assam.

We had very extensive training cooperation with Nepal as well and trained their battalions in counter-insurgency role at Banbasa. I also visited the US Training and Doctrine Command and interacted with General Kevin Byrnes on mutual topics of interest. We visited their establishments including the command and general staff college and war college where I met Brig. G.M. Nair who was attending the course then. A visit to France was also very fruitful. My interaction with the Americans and French on simulator and computer-based training programs were very instructive. Both these countries extended whole-hearted support to enhance training cooperation. The military training program and exercises with troops also went a long way in promoting military diplomacy and military-to-military cooperation. In subsequent years, the scope of this training co operation increased manifold.

A department of Information and systems also functioned under me. Its task was to implement automation, computerization and develop software for various management systems. Ideally, this organization should have been under the Signal Officer-in-Chief who had the technical resources and competence to steer it but the GS branch wanted it as part of their turf and it functioned under the DCOAS. Maj. Gen. Nischal, the ADG, worked in isolation and there were hardly any meaningful requirements, directions or supervision from the GS branch or the users as they were ignorant of its potential and averse to use of information technology. They did not grasp the power and significance of this force multiplier.

Some of the projects such as artillery command, control and communication system, battle field surveillance system, air defence command and reporting system, command information and decision support system and battlefield management system had been lingering for years due to lack of expert supervision and participation by the users. Even after the post had been upgraded to the rank of a Lieut. General with S. Pattabhiraman as the first incumbent, and a state of the art campus to house them, very little progress has been made by this directorate. The Army will do well if it exploits the potential of this organization with proper command and control and staffing. Responsibility and accountability are important to produce results. The War Deck, an organization tasked to prepare software for conducting war games, was also located in the same campus. War gaming centres were created at all command HQs along with some important training institutions for this purpose. Once again due to lack of supervision and interest by the users, this organization, manned by talented officers, was underutilized in spite of my best efforts.

India's performance in Olympics 2000 was dismal. The PM, Mr. Atal Bihari Vajpayee asked Gen. Padmanabhan, the COAS, to assist in preparing our team for the next Olympics. Accordingly, the DCOAS and the Directorate of Physical Training under Brigadier S. Dangwal and later Ashok Rathore were asked to draw up a road map. Thus "Mission Olympics" was born. A study carried out by sports experts, sports medicine specialists and sports psychologists identified eight sports disciplines in which Indians could excel. It also indicated that Indians generally performed well in sports that required skills and not prolonged endurance or power games. A sum of Rs. 50 crore was allocated to create a world-class infrastructure, identify sports talent and train it for the 2004 Olympics. Wrestling, weight lifting, boxing, shooting, archery, sailing, rowing, diving, equestrian, fencing; and selected events in athletics were identified under this mission.

The initial ground work had commenced in 2001. I was able to complete all the projects in time with M/S Somi Tandon, Addl. CGDA, as co chairman of the steering committee. We created a world-class sports facility at the Army Sports Institute, Pune, for training in wrestling, weight lifting, boxing, athletics, fencing, archery and diving. It also included a sports medicine centre with specialists. Physiotherapists, Yoga, meditation and alternate medicine experts were also part of the centre. We banned the use of performance enhancing drugs and supplements peddled by various companies. Only approved supplements were permitted under the direct supervision of doctors. An international rowing channel was created at CME, Pune. The sailing node came up at Bombay and a auxiliary node was created at Hussain Sagar, Secunderabad. The Army marksmanship unit at Mhow became the centre of excellence for shooting. An equestrian node came up at Meerut.

Foreign coaches of repute were hired to train selected sportspersons. Regimental centres were identified as sub nodes and catchments for talent. Such centres were allowed to raise boys' sports companies to identify and nurture talented sportsmen. We fielded these sportsmen in various national and international events to give them wide exposure. By the 2004 Olympics, "Mission Olympics" was still in its infancy when the first success came. Major Jayavardhan Rathore won a silver medal in shooting in the Olympics and our participants in all other fields gave promising performances. By the time I retired in 2005, all the projects had been completed except for the acquisition of horses from Ireland/Germany for the equestrian node. It was a very satisfying achievement on the part of all associated with the project.

An adventure cell functioned under Brigadier A.K. Chopra in the MT Directorate. Nodes for mountaineering, hot air ballooning, para gliding, para sailing and rafting were operational in every command. An Indo-Nepal team under Colonel Ashok Abbey scaled Mount Lhotse on 13 May 2003. The same team climbed Mount Everest on 22 and 26 May 2003. Nine Indians including Capt. S.S. Shekhawat were successful in reaching the summit. An expedition to Mount Kanchenjunga in 2004 under Colonel S.C. Sharma successfully reached the summit on 10 October. A women's expedition to Mount Everest under Major S.S. Shekhawat as team leader consisting of 10 women and 18 men successfully climbed it on 2 June 2005. He, along with Captain Sipri Majumdar, Ashwani A.S. Pawar, Dechen and Tsering reached the summit from the North Col-Tibetan side which is more difficult than the climb from the South Col on the Nepal side. Hav. Topgay Bhutia of 3/11 GR was also one of the summiteers. They made us proud.

Even though some events were not my concern, but since they were in my knowledge, I feel they require commenting. The raising of 9 Corps and SW Command and realigning the boundaries and responsibilities of 9 and 16 Corps and those of Northern, Western and SW commands do have operational advantages against Pakistan but if the same effort had been allotted against China the situation would have been quite different. Our obsession with Pakistan tended to blind us against Chinese threats.

Force level was increased against Pakistan - a stagnant front, while it should have been other way round. Threat from China was totally ignored. The entire exercise resulted in creation of additional senior appointments to benefit some officers. A fence was created behind the LoC in J&K to stop infiltration at a cost of Rs. 800 crore. I thought it was waste of resources as no fence can stop infiltration unless it is guarded continuously. The initial successes as claimed were not entirely due to this fence but because Pakistan had stopped infiltration under the ceasefire agreement and troops of 3 Corps deployed for "OP Parakram" were available to hound the residual terrorists. The fence is now selectively guarded and in disrepair; it is no more effective. The Adarsh scam at Mumbai, and land scams at Jodhpur and Pune also took place at that time. These would not have happened if officers of doubtful integrity, who were responsible for them had not been promoted against the assessments of their superiors.

As DCOAS, I had a variety of responsibilities and we were able to achieve substantial results in almost all fields. My tenure came to an end on 28 February when I retired after serving with three Chiefs. I was ably assisted by Colonel Rakesh Sharma, A.L. Chavan, Mathew, Sanjay Saran and Lt. Col. Sandeep Yadav.

Chapter 9

Colonel 11 GR and President Gorkha Brigade

The institution of Colonel of the Regiment is unique and prestigious in the Indian Army. It has a hoary past and is as old as the Indian Army. I took over as the Colonel of the 11 Gorkha Rifles in September 1994. I was overwhelmed when the Regiment bestowed this honour and trust in me as a young brigadier. The appointment is ceremonial but one can contribute immensely to the operational fitness of the regiment depending on his indulgence.

After I had been briefed by Maj. Gen. S.C. Kashyap, the incumbent Colonel of the Regiment, and Colonel Samuel, the Officiating Commandant, I realized that I had a daunting and challenging task ahead of me. As a regiment, we were going through a low phase. The Centre was besieged with numerous administrative issues, including the KLP. The Central Command was not happy with the Centre and wanted it out of Lucknow. For them, it was a delinquent child who would not improve. The overall picture was dim and future prospects looked equally bleak if immediate remedial measures were not undertaken. The Regiment however reflected tremendous potential and it only needed a small course correction to unbind it. Colonel M.S. Samuel, the Commandant, Colonel P.K. Rampal, B.J. Gupta and G.M. Nair at the Army HQ, helped me rejuvenate the Regiment. We formulated a vision paper and decided to initiate the following steps immediately.

(a) Focus on the Centre to make it a nodal agency for all regimental activities and a Centre of Excellence. Get the KLP finalized at the earliest. Harmonize, synergize, and make its relationship symbiotic with the battalions. Improve standard of recruitment and training.

Take such measures that will improve its financial health and enhance the stature and image of the Regiment.

(b) Give the battalions maximum material and moral support to improve their operational functioning. Tone up the command structure by visits and guidance.

(c) Build up future leadership within the Regiment by proper career planning and training of officers.

(d) Reach out to the ex-servicemen fraternity and make them stakeholders in the wellbeing and development of the Regiment.

A "Vision Paper" clearly indicating the focus area, priorities and milestones to be achieved with timelines was formulated. Both Colonel Rampal and B.J. Gupta and later Mohan Nair were a great help in its implementation. We sent copies of the "Vision Paper" to each and every officer of the Regiment, both serving and retired. We also translated it into Nepali so that the JCOs and men were also aware of our goals and expectations from them. The Rais and Limbus are outstanding warriors and perform well under challenging and adverse situations. I thus set very high targets for them and the battalions were posted to operationally challenging areas to exploit their inherent talent.

On an average, I visited every battalion at least twice during their tenure in a station: once during their settling down period to know their problems and assist them to overcome and a second time before their departure to the next station to prepare them for their future tasks. During my visits, I spoke to all ranks collectively and after that to the JCOs and officers separately sharing with them my vision and the issues facing us at the army and regimental levels. This created a special understanding, rapport and bond between all of us. It improved the battalion's relations with its formation and the Centre; and the confidence levels between all of us also improved. We also decided to share and retain the best talent within the regiment even if it meant cross-posting of COs and other officers.

This cross-posting resulted in infusion of fresh and better ideas from one battalion to another. It also created oneness, brought the officers and ladies of the regiment closer and promoted a uniform and strong regimental culture. Officers with high potential were placed in appointments that would benefit not only them professionally but also the Regiment as a whole. Consequently, all the battalions started performing well. 1/11 performed exceeding well in the Kashmir Valley under me and thereafter it gave an outstanding performance in Siachen and during the Kargil[1] war. I allowed them to wear a special lanyard in recognition of their performance. It was declared "Bravest of the Brave" an honour shared by selected Battalions of the Army. They were first battalion from the Regiment to go on UN assignment in Lebnon. 2/11 GR performed well in all theatres and were selected to serve in Congo on UN mission as a result. 3/11 GR earned a number of awards including KC in J&K. They too were selected to serve in Lebnon on UN mission because of their good performance. 5/11 GR also did well that resulted in promotion to a number of officers to senior ranks, notably Bipin Rawat to COAS and CDS and Rakesh Sharma to AG. 6/11 GR also had an equally good run in promotions to senior ranks with Anil Chouhan as army commander and CDS. 7/11 GR outperformed every one in the Northeast and North Siachin. They were awarded two KC in a single operation in the NE. 107 Infantry Battalion TA was fully integrated in all regimental activities and has done the Regiment proud. Part of the battalion served under me in 8 Mountain Division and performed commendably well. It has looked after the ex-servicemen belonging to Sikkim, Darjeeling and Jalpaiguri with dedication.

The problems of the Centre were rather acute and it took me a while to set them right. When I visited it for the first time, I was really not happy with the state of affairs. The infrastructure was falling apart and the MES took no interest because the station had not been declared our KLP. Men were living in stables that had been modified into living barracks. All the offices and institutions also functioned in stables or dilapidated buildings. The Regiment did not take interest in development of the area and institutions because it was not sure if they would stay at Lucknow at all. The uncertainty and suspense had adversely impacted the work culture and functioning of the Centre.

There were no sources of income for the Centre as there had not been any long-term financial planning. None of the Regimental Institutions was viable financially. The training infrastructure was in a shambles and training standards poor. There was no harmony between the PAO, the Records and the units. Relations between the Centre and the battalions were indifferent. Regimental land at Dehradun was as good as lost to encroachers and we had no will to take it back. The Army Commander, Lt. Gen. A.K. Gautama, was unhappy with the Centre and he conveyed his adverse impressions to me during my courtesy call on him. His blunt remarks about the Centre upset me. I explained that the non-finalization of KLP was the main reason amongst many others for the existing state of affairs and sought his assistance to set things right.

I realized that we had to first sort out our own house before others could help us. We had to therefore find a suitable senior officer to take over its command. Fortunately Brig. S.P.S. Uppal was available to take on this job which he did enthusiastically. He started well and brought a semblance of discipline and order in the rank and file that had otherwise become slack. He improved the work culture and ethos. He also toned up the administration and cleaned up the mess to a great extent. Our relations with the Command HQ however continued to be lukewarm and the new Army Commander, Lt. Gen. Chander Sekhar, was as blunt as the previous Army Commander in his opinion of the Centre. He had recommended that we be moved out of Lucknow.

I once again explained to him that non-finalization of the KLP was the main reason for all the ills of the Centre and unless Command helped to give us a permanent home, it would be difficult for the Regiment to achieve our dreams of a model centre. I reminded him that his recommendations to shift the Centre to Varanasi had further demoralized us as it would be our fifth move in 50 years. No Regimental Centre could grow if it did not have a permanent home. I took up the KLP issue and the move of the centre with the COAS and VCOAS who knew me well. They seemed to be more understanding and sympathetic to our problems. I also requested the other Colonels of the Gorkha Regiments and the MO Directorate to stall this move and give us a permanent home at Lucknow.

Fortunately, we succeeded and finally Lucknow was declared as our KLP. However, we were in a fix to find a suitable replacement when Uppal's tenure ended in 1997. The golden jubilee was also upon us and time was running out. The only person I could think of was Colonel Vijay Lalotra who would be available after his HC course in June. Both the MS Branch and the College of Combat were against posting a high-profile officer to the Centre. However, once Vijay agreed to undertake this challenging assignment, we were able to persuade the MS branch to make the officer available for only one year. He created a fine team of officers with Lt. Col. Bipin Rawat to assist him. Vijay's achievements in one year were unparalleled and cannot be quantified. He defied all logic and calculations to give us what was considered not possible.

He created the most unique war memorial, refurbished and renovated a dilapidated Officers' Mess into a wonderful heritage building, gave the Regiment a unique postage stamp and pictorial history book, the first of its kind in the army, and, above all, showed the will and set up benchmarks that became minimum standards for the future. The KLP was progressed expeditiously with help of Command HQ. The Army Commander could not believe that 11 GR could achieve all this in six months. Gens. Chander Sekhar and Surjit Singh Sangara who followed him, realized that the neglected child of Central Command could deliver results if a level playing field was given to them. Their prejudices were replaced by confidence and patronage.

The golden jubilee was conducted in an outstanding manner. The Defence Minister, Mr. Mulayam Singh, along with Mr. Beniprasad, Minister for Communications and Post and Telegraph were our Chief Guests. We were able to get a special stamp along with a first day cover released by the Defence Minister during the golden jubilee which by itself was an achievement. When the QMG and ADG Army Postal Services expressed their inability, we took up the matter directly with the RM and Minister of Post and Telegraphs, Mr. Beniprasad, who acceded to our request. It is one of the best postage stamps designed by Vijay Lalotra and released.

Vijay finished his commitment by June and Colonel Hardev Singh took over from him. Hardev, though a reserved and reticent man, proved to be a hard task master and as result-oriented as Vijay. He was equally aggressive, competent and carried forward the processes set in motion by

Vijay with vigour and dedication. I was very heartened to see the progress made by the Centre every time I visited it. There were many mid-course corrections in the design of various buildings. We made the Command, the Area and the Sub Area our partners in development of the Centre and ensured that the projects were executed smoothly.

The QMG branch was great help in expediting the KLP. We were able to get various phases of the project to run concurrently to cut down the timeframe from 12 years to seven. Hardev also improved the training area and training standards. The institutions were revitalized and now we had good sources of income from them. By the time Hardev handed over to Brigadier Ajai Choudhary, the Centre had started taking shape as perceived by us. Ajai volunteered to return to the Regiment when I explained the need and the challenging tasks ahead of him. Like Vijay, he did not flinch even once and immediately agreed to join us. He vigorously pursued the Dehradun land case and succeeded in getting its possession. He also set about giving finishing touches to the works in progress and future planning for development of the Centre.

However, his tenure was cut short by his nomination for the NDC. We had no choice but to ask Colonel Hardev to fill the gap for a second time. He cut short his study leave to join the mission. The Centre continued to grow under his supervision. By now, we had introduced the volunteer contributory distress welfare scheme and also created the 11 GR Association. We also instituted the annual conference of the COs at the Centre so that they could come there to deliberate on regimental issues and share their views and experiences with each other. We found it a very useful forum. They became part of the inclusive growth of the Regiment. After finishing NDC, Ajai had the choice of going on a staff assignment but on my suggestion he agreed to resume command of the Centre. I admire both Hardev and Ajai for their commitment and understanding the needs of the Regiment. They worked selflessly and in the complete interest of the Regiment.

We added an Olympic-size swimming pool and an auditorium during this period. Ajai and Colonel Inder Narain gave the final shape to the

Centre that it is today. Everything about the Centre is unique. It has what others don't have and has not only become a model but the envy of others. Besides the mess and Institutional areas, we have the best sports and training infrastructure. Our mandir is yet another prominent institution. Its design is unique, based on the Pashupati Mandir at Kathmandu. We got the main doors imported from Nepal. The statues of the main deities came from Jaipur. The others came from as far as Bhubaneshwar. Every building in the Centre has a unique character of its own and represents the highest aspirations and dreams of every Kiranti.

During my tenure, we also started reaching out to our retired colleagues. We held regimental get-togethers at all the important stations where our retired fraternity was located. These get-together helped us all to remain connected with each other. The spirit of brotherhood took root within the fraternity. Consequently, Delhi, Dehradun, Lucknow, Darjeeling, Pune and Bangalore have become active and vibrant independent chapters of 11 GR Association. We also gave the Regiment a new motto **यत्राहं विजयस्तत्र** that reflects its true character and aspirations.

I have tried to reflect on a period of the one decade that I had the honour of being the Colonel of Regiment. Every one joined to make it what it is today. Undoubtedly we are the "Excellent". We have only one way to go from here, and that is to go forward; and always stand true to our motto.

President Gorkha Brigade

All the Gorkha regiments in the Indian Army are collectively known as the Gorkha Brigade. The senior Colonel of the Regiment from the seven regiments is nominated the president. Field Marshal S.H.F.J. Manekshaw and General G.G. Bewoor, the COAS, had been presidents earlier, among many other illustrious officers. I took over this prestigious appointment in December 2003. The president coordinates common aspects related to recruitment, training, administration, welfare and resettlement of retiring personnel. The Gorkha recruiting depot at Gorakhpur acts as the secretariat. Brig. Vinod M. Mani, the commandant, was one of the most effective and dedicated secretaries I have known for a long time.

The president presides over the annual conference attended by all the colonels of the regiments and centre Commandants. The AG and the military attaché at Kathmandu are special invitees. The brigade is a well-knit organization that takes pride in its history and achievements. I visited the recruiting depot at Kunraghat and Ghoom. These depots were raised in 1886 and 1890, respectively, and have done a great service in not only recruitment but also in forging strong Indo-Nepal relations and endeared the people of Nepal. I also visited all the four centres. 14 GTC at Sabatu has an iconic campus and the regimental museum is very well laid out. It is a repository of the hoary past of both the regiments. 39 GTC at Varanasi is also located in the old British lines dating back to the battle of Buxar in 1764. 58 GTC at Shillong is comparatively new but has done very well. I was pleased to see the excellent infrastructure and standards of training at all these places.

I also visited Nepal to discuss important issues with the Government of Nepal and our embassy. My meetings with General Pyar Jung Thapa, the army chief, Lt. Gen. C.B. Gurung, the CGS, and other senior officers not only reinforced our mutual friendship but enhanced the level of training. The visit was aimed to renew our relationship not only with the ex-servicemen but also with the Nepal army with whom we have historic bonds. The PPOs at Pokhra and Dharan are doing a yeoman's job for the welfare of our men. I was happy that my contribution helped in forging and cementing our long enduring relationship with Nepal.

The Gorkha Brigade has performed very well in all operations, training events, sports and adventure activities. We have dominated football, boxing, shooting and mountaineering within the services and made substantial contributions at the national level. Our men from Nepal are our greatest assets in sustaining good Indo-Nepal relations. My tenure as the president ended with my retirement on 28 February 2005 and I carry reminiscences of a golden era in the history of the Gorkha Brigade.

Chapter 10

The Twilight Years

We moved into our house in Gurgaon a month after retirement. It was small but comfortable and met our requirements. We did not feel any post-retirement blues. Neera got down to her medical practice in earnest while I joined Bharat Electronics Limited as an adviser. She travelled to Mirpur near Rewari once a week to provide anaesthesia in the Mirpur Institute of Medical Sciences. This hospital was run by Dr. S.S. Yadav, an internationally renowned orthopaedic surgeon. She also provided anaesthesia cover to other hospitals in Bilaspur, Rewari, Metro Hospital, Palam Vihar, and Government Hospital, Gurgaon, whenever needed. I was happy to work with the BEL. I was required to advise them on C4 I projects, simulators, night vision and optical devices and all communication equipment, including radars that were under development or projected by the army.

It was a great experience to work with a Navratana public sector defence unit. BEL was established in 1954 at Bangalore to meet the electronic and telecommunication needs of the defence forces. Since then, it has created nine research and manufacturing hubs and grown exponentially as a giant among defence PSUs. It played a key and very significant role in meeting our communication needs. Their corporate office is located at Bangalore in a modern campus. Mr. Gopal Rao was the CMD; Mr. V.V.R. Shastry was his deputy while S.K. Mehta was Director R&D. The Bangalore unit is the oldest and headed by Mr. Basvarajaiah.

The scientists working with them were highly devoted and competent. This unit has a good track record and provides some of the top-of-the-line radio communication equipment not only to the defence forces but also exports to other countries. They were working on a number of simulators and other software but could not make a breakthrough with our defence users. I found that all the simulators met our requirements such as motion platform, facility for training a driver, gunner, and commander as also interfaced to run tactical exercises. They were as good as those I had been shown in France during my visits. They were not able to sell their products due to a poor marketing strategy, lack of interaction with users and absence of a project officer from the user side. I opened a dialogue for them with DG Infantry, DG Mechanized Forces, and Commandant, Infantry School and other users. On my advice the BEL arranged visits by users to their production units and also gave presentations at Army HQ to showcase their products and capabilities.

Similarly the electro optics unit at Machlipattam had the capability to manufacture and upgrade almost all-day-and-night optical devices such as night vision devices, high-resolution binoculars for MFC and FOO, spotter scope with digital camera and hand held thermal image device and many more. They had the most modern R&D facilities and are capable of meeting all requirements of the army and also central police forces but had no orders. Once again, I met various senior officers of the concerned organizations and arranged visits/demonstrations of their equipment. The Hyderabad unit that produced a huge array of radar equipment and the Pune unit that dealt with X-ray tubes, various types of batteries and some electro-optical items also faced the same challenges. The Chandigarh and Ghaziabad units fared no better. Unfortunately the users were greatly influenced by foreign vendors and were obsessed with their products. They were generally sceptical of the reliability of our equipment.

They were not ready to accept indigenous products even though they are better in quality and cheaper. BEL and for that matter other defence PSUs had to follow government guidelines for marketing and could not influence the buyers through commissions, allurements and other gratification. Foreign vendors thus had an edge. Tehelka and many other scams proved this point. I found both users and the MOD were also not really serious about our products as they did not lead to foreign visits and kickbacks. On the other hand, BEL and other PSUs wanted a captive market and shied away from competition with foreign manufacturers. In many cases, they just assembled the components imported from foreign vendors and labelled them as indigenous products. Thus, in this game, the country was the loser. I firmly believe that a country that is not self-sufficient and reliant in its defence equipment needs can not aspire to be a great power.

Our defence forces that were fighting with foreign equipment and highly dependent on imports were living in an illusionary world even though they are the fourth largest in the world. We have great facilities with young qualified and capable scientists who were keen to contribute to self-reliance but most of them are disillusioned, disheartened, and de-motivated when their efforts are not recognized by users on flimsy grounds. Many of these highly qualified scientists left in disgust after some years and joined foreign manufacturers who were their rivals. I left BEL after a richly knowledgeable and useful tenure with them at the end of 2006. It is my view that all PSUs should adopt modern (transformational style) management techniques, be autonomous and should be worthy of profit making. In fact, all PSUs have become holy cows. They were bureaucratic in their functioning. They are lackadaisical with unreasonable overheads and lavish perks. Their work culture and ethics are nowhere their European counterparts. It is my view that where a PSU failed to make profit, it should be privatized. Many countries in Europe had done so.

Soon thereafter I was approached by ITC, a famous MNC, with their corporate HQ at Calcutta to join them as an adviser. Imperial Tobacco Company was established by W.D. and H.O. Wills in 1910. It primarily manufactured cigarettes and tobacco products. Later, in 1975, it entered the hospitality sector and subsequently diversified into apparel, food processing, information technology, and paper manufacturing. The "Welcome Group" under the hotel division was facing grave problems in execution of their plan to establish "Grand Bharat" a hotel in the suburbs of Gurgaon on the lines of "Camp David" in the USA. This was to come up on the Gurgaon–Nuh road. The company had already created a world-class 27-hole golf course designed by Jack Nicklaus that was functional and highly popular. The proposed hotel nestled in the Aravallis, an opulent all-suite retreat located in the heart of a triangle formed by Delhi, Agra, and Jaipur. The architecture was to represent our pan-India character. It was to provide the ultimate luxury to visitors.

The associates of ITC in this venture not only cheated them financially but created labour problems to stall the project when money laundering and frauds were detected in their dealings. It is believed that "Tarudhan Valley" with a 9-hole golf course very close to the ITC project had been created out of the siphoned money. The company could not afford to lose their investment and be held hostage to blackmail. The locals who provided the land and work force had become pawns in the hands of the former partners of ITC. In the violence that followed, they beat up the staff, smashed valuable property, and forced the management to close all activities. Land Base, a subsidiary of ITC that was in the business of land acquisition and construction, was in deep financial and labour trouble because of the forced lockout.

Maj. Rehman was head of the hotel division with Nakul Anand and S.C. Sekhar as his senior colleagues. Rehman supervised the hotel division from his office in Delhi while Anand and Sekhar were based in "ITC Green Centre" Gurgaon. Mr. Vijay Katre was CEO of the ITC "Classic Golf Course" that was to become part of "Grand Bharat". When I joined the hotel division as an Adviser for a period of two years, my main task was to start the "Grand Bharat". I was to deal with only Rehman, Anand and Sekhar. ITC is one of the best companies in the corporate sector in terms of work ethics/work culture, financial dealings and quality of work. The work force is highly qualified, dedicated, motivated and professional. There was no room for non performers. This is perhaps the only company that takes care of its employee's post–retirement, hence there are no walkouts. The work force was loyal to the company and worked for its well being.

My first task was to sort out the labour unrest and end the lockout so that the project valued at Rs. 400 crore at that time could take off. The delays had already escalated the cost. After a series of meetings with Mr. Rehman, Anand and Sekhar, it was decided to replace Mr. Katre with Ravee Puri, a dynamic man with a vision. I took Mr. Puri to all my meetings with Mr. Bhupinder Hooda, the CM, Mr. R.S. Dalal, the DGP, chairman, HSIDC, and secretary, town and country planning, and locally to Rao

Inderjit Singh, the MP, Mr. Badhana, the MLA, and Capt. Ajay Yadav, the PWD and tourism minister of Haryana and the commissioner labour. Our concerted effort with the administration succeeded in removing their prejudices and misunderstandings about the labour unrest and the machinations of the powerful people and vested interests behind the whole episode. We explained to them the advantages this project would accrue to the state in employment generation, development and financially when completed. An investment of Rs. 400 to 600 crore was not a small amount for any one single company. The state would get bad publicity if a company like ITC walked out.

We also met some important people in the local villages and were able to wean them away from the trouble makers. Thus, in a matter of four months, we were able to not only break the labour unrest but also lift the lockout. The trouble makers tried to intimidate the staff and those who joined work but this eventually failed due to a stern warning to them by the DC and SSP. This was a landmark achievement for the ITC. Col. Narender, R.K.S. Mann and Wing Comdr. Dhankkar were of great help to me during this period. Mr. Puri and I were complimented by the Board and particularly Mr. Rehman who had showed explicit trust in me. By December 2007, all activities had been resumed to make "Grand Bharat" a reality.

My tenure with ITC ended abruptly when the CM, Mr. Bhupinder Hooda, spoke to me personally on phone and asked me to join the Government of Haryana as information commissioner, a statutory post created recently. Even though I wanted to stay and see the completion of "Grand Bharat" for which I had worked so hard, the call to duty by the CM could not be ignored. The ITC was sad on my departure and I left them with a heavy heart. The "Grand Bharat" today stands proudly as the most prestigious hotels in the national capital region with unique architecture, unparalleled natural beauty and luxury.

Dr. Kanu Priya, our daughter had graduated as a specialist in Radiology from RR Hospital, and her husband, Dr. Ajay Yadav, was already a consultant in vascular surgery at Ganga Ram Hospital. Agastya , their son, born on 11 January 2011 brought great cheer to the family. Akshay, our son, in the meantime had completed his post-graduation in finance management from Stern School of Business, New York University. He was a US citizen and well settled in his job with Lloyds Bank. Unfortunately, his fairy tale wedding in India was short lived.

"The Right to Information Act," enacted by Parliament, had come into effect from 2005. The Centre and all states were to implement it by creating their own state information commission. This was a statutory appointment unfettered by interference and influence by any individual, agency or organ of the state. Only eminent persons who had achieved the highest level of expertise, knowledge, experience and excellence in their fields were eligible. They were selected by a panel headed by the CM, for a term of five years or till the candidate attained 65 years of age, whichever was earlier. They were accorded the status of a chief secretary of the state.

The aim of the Act was to promote transparency in functioning of the Government and remove corruption. In substance, it was a meant to achieve good governance. The Act covered all departments of the state and organizations that were financially aided, wholly or partially or public money was spent on them, including NGOs. This included grants or money spent by ministers and MLAs from their development funds. The Act covered all organizations and enterprises that were under the regulatory control of the government.

This was one of the best Acts passed by Parliament that was simple to understand, people-friendly and inexpensive. It empowered the ordinary citizen and held every one under its ambit accountable for acts of omission and commission. A simple application with a nominal fee to a public authority was enough to obtain information that the authorities zealously held back to deny justice/fair play to affected citizens. The entire process would end in three steps with the final hearing of appeal with the commissioner within a matter of 90 days. Empowered with the information obtained, a citizen could now obtain justice. The commissioner could summon the highest authority if necessary through a warrant. No one could deny information when ordered unless the commissioner was convinced that it was not in the public interest or prejudicial to state security.

His orders were final and could not be appealed or challenged in any court of law except through a writ petition on a point of law.

The Commissioner however had to pass detailed speaking orders after deliberations and give a fair hearing to the information seeker and the public authority. The commissioner could impose a maximum penalty of Rs. 25,000 or order departmental action against the public authority who had defaulted. This big personal financial loss and fear promoted transparency and efficiency.

I took the oath and joined my duties with effect from 1 January 2008. We were seven commissioners in all. Two of them had been chief secretaries and one a secretary. It was a great experience and a very satisfying job where we redressed the grievances of an aggrieved party without favouritism or favour. The satisfaction rate was very high. Many a time the public authority was reluctant to share information, particularly where selection for appointments and promotions or award of contracts were concerned. However, we got over them by issuing suitable warnings, departmental action and finally imposing severe penalties. A discussion with the relevant secretary or DG also helped. I met the CM once a month to apprise him of public sentiments, the functional efficiency of the departments and the level of public satisfaction. He was happy to get a feedback about the government's image. There were many rogue information seekers as well whose aim was to misuse the Act to harass, intimidate or blackmail government officers.

A commissioner could easily discern the intent of such information seekers and reject their requests. Though the commissioner did not have the power to punish such elements, a warning of legal action against them was enough as a deterrent. I gave some landmark judgments that became benchmarks in improving good governance in the state. My order to the Haryana Staff Selection Commission and Haryana Public Service Commission to show the candidates the results of both their written exam and interviews and publish the result within 30 days of final selection was challenged by the Government of Haryana. My order was upheld by the High Court.

All private construction companies, hospitals, educational institutions, NGOs and other organizations that had public dealings were also brought under the Act through respective government departments that earlier had remained opaque. Their misdeeds were now under scrutiny. I conducted seminars, meetings and lectures to promote and spread awareness of the Act among general public. I was invited by universities, private and government institutions, NGOs and the Haryana Institution of Public Administration for lectures and seminars on the subject. Special workshops were held to educate public authorities and the general public in each district. I was more than satisfied with the work that not only enriched me in dealing with the public but also in spreading happiness when my tenure ended in 2010 at the age of 65.

I joined RS India Wind Energy Ltd. soon thereafter, a company that was in renewable energy - producing electricity through wind, solar and biomass. The corporate office was in Bikaji Cama Place, New Delhi. Mr. Thakkur, an IAS officer and chairman, public finance corporation and Mr. Allahavadi, ex-chief secretary, Haryana were directors. Production facilities for windmills were at Bawal Industrial Area and projects were mostly executed in Maharashtra and Tamil Nadu. I was CEO-cum-MD and responsible for all activities from floor to board room. We managed to set up our first windmill farm near Satara with 50 windmills and sold the entire power produced to the Maharashtra Electricity Board.

There were numerous impediments and problems at the local level in executing this project. Every official involved in various clearances had to be bribed before the project reached its final stage. We were frequently shuttling between Satara, Pune and Mumbai to meet various secretaries, DCs/police/forest and revenue officers and ministers to resolve one issue after another. That is when I realized that it was not easy to do business or function in India unless we had the patronage of a senior cabinet minister at the centre and the CM at the state level. The local MP and MLA too had to be on board for smooth functioning and to manage the rogue elements, blackmailers and extortionists at project sites; and every one had a price. Our production facility at Bawal was managed by a British engineer cum manager who had vast experience in this field. We had in-house requirements of 400 machines as per our projections. Anil Yadav, an engineer, was the project manager at the site. He was very competent and energetic. While the work on wind energy was progressing satisfactorily, our efforts in solar energy did not succeed in spite of my meetings with Dr. Farooq Abdullah who was the minister for renewable energy.

Managing bank loans for expansion of the project was yet another challenging task. The banks had their own rules and practices for granting large loans. We had endless meetings at various levels and even the finance ministry to get sanctions for a loan of Rs. 400 crore. Once again, nothing happened without a price. I enjoyed my job that once again enriched my knowledge and gave me an opportunity to work in the corporate sector. However, after about two years, I resigned due to personal reasons. When I rejoined the company as a director on their board in 2015, we made good progress in solar energy in UP, while the windmill project moved slowly in spite of exports.

The welfare of ex-servicemen was another area very close to my heart. I joined the All India Ex-Servicemen League, Delhi, and Ex-Servicemen League, Haryana. I was also a member of the Ex-Servicemen Board, Haryana, for two years. Brig. K.S. Budhwar, was the president of the Haryana Rajya Sainik Board then. The CM, Mr. Bhupinder Hooda, sanctioned a number of welfare schemes at our suggestions. He and the Governor also attended ESM rallies organized by me at Rewari in 2005, Gurgaon in 2006 and Jhajjar later.

The government agreed to outsource billing by the Haryana Vidyut Nigam to the Haryana Ex-Servicemen League resulting in mass employment of retired soldiers near their homes and efficient billing that saved thousands of rupees for the Haryana Electricity Board. Unfortunately the League got aligned politically with the Congress. As soon as the government changed in 2014, the scheme was abolished and finally the government took over the management of the league as well. During this period, I was also member of the Ex-Servicemen Committee of the All India Congress Party along with Lt. Gen. Surinder Nath and Lt. Gen. R.S. Kadian. We met at the Congress HQ office on Akbar Road frequently to work out welfare schemes for ex-servicemen. We also met Mrs. Sonia Gandhi and Rahul Gandhi to discuss the One Rank One Pay issue and got Rs. 500 crore approved for the scheme but the announcement of the elections of 2014 stalled further progress on it. The Congress lost the goodwill of the ex-servicemen to the BJP with a rally by Shri Narender Modi at Rewari who pulled the carpet from under their feet by implementing it when he became the PM.

I led a Government of India-sponsored delegation of 1971 war veterans to Dacca, Bangladesh, from 14 to 19 December 2017 for the Victory Day celebrations. The Government and defence forces of Bangladesh hosted us with great warmth and respect. They were grateful to India and veterans like us who had shed blood in the war for their liberation. We were feted at their Victory Day parade and later had an audience with both the President and the PM, Mrs Sheikh Hassina. The reception by Mrs Sheikh Hassina was remarkable. She was very gracious and met every member of the delegation, chatted with us freely and attended to us personally. She narrated the turbulent events of 1970-71 and later the coup against her father and how all members of her family had been assassinated. She and her sister survived and returned to the country in 1981 after living in exile in India.

The period from 1981 to 1996 and subsequently the period up to 2006 were indeed difficult for her. She shared her vision of the country and discussed all the topics related to Indo-Bangladesh relations. Mr. A.K.M. Mozammel Haque, the Minister of Liberation War Affairs, personally conducted us during the tour, including the imposing war memorial and the Banga Bhavan where the massacre of Sheikh Mujib and his family had been perpetrated. This place is now a memorial and museum that is visited by thousands of people daily. General Abu Belal Muhammad Shafiul Huq, COAS, hosted a dinner for us where he highlighted the best of Indo-Bangladesh defence relations and how thankful they were to India for not only helping in their war of liberation but subsequent reconstruction of the country and their armed forces. There was a convergence of views on common security threats and the strategic relationship was strong.

We also interacted with Admiral Nizamuddin Ahmed, the Chief of Naval Staff, Air Chief Marshal Abu Esrar, the Chief of Air Staff, and

Lt. General Md. Mahfuzur Rahman, the principal staff officer in HQ AFD. All of them were extremely friendly and reiterated not only our good relations but a bright future in joint operations and collective security against common threats. A reception with our former colleagues—the Mukti 'Jodhas' was organized by Major Matin Choudhary who was the president of the War Course Foundation. It was very nostalgic. It brought back a flood of memories of the great sacrifice that they had made during that holocaust and the bonds of brotherhood with their Indian colleagues that had stood the test of time. Mr. Syed Shahed Reza, who was also a Mukti 'Jodha' and an ambassador later, hosted us at the historic Dacca Club as the president. The table that was used for the surrender ceremony on 16 December 1971 by Lt. Gen. J.S. Aurora and Lt. Gen. A.A.K. Niazi, is the property of the club and a proud exhibit for visitors.

The other notable personality who created a lasting impression on us was Ms. Mahajbeen Khalid, Member of Parliament, and daughter of Brig. Mussharaf Khalid who had commanded the Khalid Force in the Comilla sector with distinction during the war. He was later killed in a countercoup in support of Sheikh Mujib. Mahajbeen was hounded by the Pakistani forces during the liberation but escaped to India and survived. She completed her education in India and was provided asylum during Gen. Zia's rule as her father was opposed to Zia. She was very dynamic and a true patriot and nationalist.

We were happy to see the progress made by Bangladesh. Though still poor, the country has risen from the ravages of destruction and exploitation to a stable, economically vibrant, progressive, moderate and modern state.

I also devoted my time to development of my village where a number of government schemes were either languishing or in a state of neglect. I focused my attention on education and got funds released to repair infrastructure, class rooms and various laboratories of the girls higher secondary school. We were also able to set up a computer laboratory. The GOC 33 Armoured Division at Hissar, helped me to create playgrounds in the school and a stadium for the village. They also donated equipment for a gymnasium. We were also able to get both the girls and boys schools affiliated for NCC training with the help of Lt. Gen. Prakash Choudhary, DG NCC.

All this helped the school immensely in raising their standard of education. I also got the boys school upgraded to higher secondary and got funds released to improve its crumbling infrastructure. The village dispensary was in a pathetic condition. The building was repaired with a proper boundary wall and staff quarters to make it fully functional following my intervention with the Secretary Health, Haryana. I also got the minor water canal repaired and de-silted and installed a pump for lift scheme to ensure regular supply. Many farmers benefitted from this effort and today we have water in all corners of the village.

It was most satisfying to see girls and boys from our secondary schools qualify as doctors, engineers and army officers. My mother, Smt. Gyan Devi passed away at the age of 95 in April 2012. She was a revered person in the village who had devoted all her life to the well-being of women and children. The ladies of the village requested us to construct a hall in the premises of Dadi Shilha temple in her memory where they could meditate and pray. A redstone hall for this purpose was constructed as per their wishes.

Our life after retirement has been as satisfying as my service life. We have continued to work for the well being of our, community and country. Our strength is strong family ties, loyalty, a positive attitude, and faith in our heritage, culture, religion and God.

Index